Urban Informality

TRANSNATIONAL PERSPECTIVES ON SPACE AND PLACE

Nezar AlSayyad, Series Editor

Transnational Perspectives on Space and Place is a publication Series of Lexington books based on conferences, symposium, and projects organized by the Center for Middle Eastern Studies and The International Association for the Study of Traditional Environments at the University of California at Berkeley as part of their transnational initiative. Unlike comparative research, which focuses on similarities and differences between regions, transnational research examines the socio-spatial connections through which global cartographies are constituted and transformed. It is also an epistemological technique that pays attention to how concepts and discourses are produced within specific geopolitical regions and histories, and that allows knowledge of one region to be used to interrogate another.

Muslim Europe or Euro-Islam: Politics, Culture, and Citizenship in the Age of Globalization,
edited by Nezar AlSayyad and Manuel Castells (2002)

Urban Informality: Transnational Perspectives from the Middle East, Latin America and South Asia,
edited by Ananya Roy and Nezar AlSayyad (2003)

A Medieval City for a Modern World: Cairo in the 19th Century,
edited by Nezar AlSayyad, Irene Bierman, and Nasser Rabbat (expected 2004)

Urban Informality

Transnational Perspectives from the Middle East, Latin America, and South Asia

Edited by Ananya Roy
and Nezar AlSayyad

LEXINGTON BOOKS
Lanham • Boulder • New York • Toronto • Oxford

2 2 bolton

LEXINGTON BOOKS

Published in the United States of America
by Lexington Books
An imprint of The Rowman & Littlefield Publishing Group, Inc.
4501 Forbes Boulevard, Suite 200, Lanham, Maryland 20706

PO Box 317
Oxford
OX2 9RU, UK

British Library Cataloguing in Publication Information Available

Library of Congress Cataloging-in-Publication Data

Urban informality : transnational perspectives from the Middle East, Latin America, and
    South Asia / edited by Ananya Roy and Nezar AlSayyad.
        p. cm. — (Transnational perspectives on space and place)
    Includes bibliographical references and index.
    ISBN 0-7391-0740-2 (cloth : alk. paper)—ISBN 0-7391-0741-0 (pbk. : alk. paper)
        1. Urbanization—Economic aspects. 2. Urbanization—Middle East. 3.
    Urbanization—Latin America. 4. Urbanization—South Asia. 5. Squatter settlements.
    6. Land use, Urban—Social aspects. 7. Informal sector (Economics) I. Roy, Ananya.
    II. AlSayyad, Nezar. III. Series.

    HT361.U717 2003
    307.76—dc22

                                                                                2003054619

    Printed in the United States of America

⊖™ The paper used in this publication meets the minimum requirements of American
National Standard for Information Sciences—Permanence of Paper for Printed Library
Materials, ANSI/NISO Z39.48–1992.

CONTENTS

PREFACE

The idea behind this book goes back to Spring 2000, when we first co-taught a graduate seminar at UC Berkeley entitled "Housing and Urbanization in Developing Countries." In the process of assembling the case studies for this course we became convinced that although the analytical frameworks we often use — which evolved primarily from Latin American research — were still sound, it was time to decouple "urban informality" as a subject of study from Latin America as an area of study. We became interested in interrogating and expanding this Latin American model by developing a transnational perspective that could draw upon the urban experiences of other regions with which we were intimately familiar: the Middle East and South Asia.

To achieve this goal, we approached the Crossing Borders/New Geographies initiative of the Ford Foundation which was being administered on the Berkeley campus by the Institute of International Studies (IIS). Their generous funding of our proposal allowed us, in Spring 2001, to convene a two-day symposium and invite a distinguished group of scholars and practitioners from these three world regions. A key feature of this event was its format, which required commentary by scholars from one region on the work of scholars from others. And following what turned out to be a successful exchange, we asked some of the symposium participants to revise their papers for possible publication. We also invited or recruited additional contributors to cover themes or areas which we felt were essential for a comprehensive transnational interrogation. This book is the result of this three-year-long project.

We would like to thank the many individuals and institutions that have made this book possible. The Ford Foundation has long played a leading role in setting the agenda for urban research in different world regions. We would like to acknowledge the administrators and advisors of the foundation for innovating the Crossing Borders initiative as a means of redefining disciplines and area studies. We recognize that the foundation has been hard hit by the recent decline of the stock market and hope, for the sake of all of us in the field of urban research, that it will soon resume a pivotal role in this arena.

At UC Berkeley, we would like to thank Michael Watts, Director of the Institute of International Studies (IIS), and David Szanton, the former Executive Director of the International and Area Studies division (IAS), for articulating Berkeley's New Geographies, New Pedagogies project as part of the Crossing Borders initiative. New Geographies, New Pedagogies allowed us to develop a teaching component to our research project. Also at Berkeley, we would like to acknowledge the co-sponsorship of the Center for South Asia Studies (CSAS) and the Center for Latin American Studies (CLAS). The staff of the Center for Middle Eastern Studies (CMES), which officially hosted the symposium, deserves special recognition. In the early stages Casondra Sobieralksi was in charge of administering our grant, and Amanda Bleakley helped administer the final stages of the book project.

Many of our students also played important roles in the project. We are grateful to the students enrolled in our class, City Planning 231/Architecture 219, for their comments during the three years of the co-taught seminar. Madhuri Desai and Mrinalini Rajagopalan helped with the organization of the symposium and provided much needed administrative support. Grace Woo assisted with the logistics of the symposium. Renu Desai was our principal research assistant. She did library research, communicated with authors, and managed the papers. We greatly appreciate her efforts. Dr. Sofia Shwayri helped with various chapters of the book in the last phase of the project. David Moffat, as always, provided valuable editorial advice. Annabelle Ison and Stuart Chan of Ison Design constructed an elegant design for the book. At Lexington Books, our editor Jason Hallman competently handled the manuscript in its final stages.

We hope that our students and colleagues will find this book as engaging and useful as it was challenging and rewarding for us to put together.

ANANYA ROY AND NEZAR ALSAYYAD
Berkeley, July 2003

PROLOGUE/DIALOGUE

Urban Informality: Crossing Borders[1]

Nezar AlSayyad and Ananya Roy

The first round of path-breaking research on informal housing and land markets was conducted in Latin America in the 1970s and 1980s and involved a wonderful diversity of political scientists, anthropologists, and sociologists. These studies dismantled notions of a "culture of poverty" and of "marginality," and instead situated informality firmly within the larger politics of populist mobilizations, state power, and economic dependency.

But there were, of course, earlier rounds of discussion about the informal sector, notably the Kenya debates of the early 1970s. However, these debates were primarily about the nature of informal work and dual economies and did not directly tackle the spatial aspects of urbanization and the emerging forms of urbanism. So we can say that the analytical framework to study urban informality has evolved primarily from Latin American research, to the extent that it has become impossible to untangle urban informality as a discipline from Latin America as an area study. By urban informality I mean the manifestation of informal processes in the urban environment.

This Latin American toolkit is of great use in other regional contexts. For example, in the case of urban research in South Asia, the Latin American perspective allows us to look at the political economy of informality. This is essential because the South Asian debates around urban informality are quite limited. There are only a handful of systematic studies of informal land and housing markets, despite the widespread prevalence of these processes in South Asian cities. Many of the policy discussions are dominated by architects or architectural considerations which view informal housing solely as a type of built form. The Latin American concepts, when transported to South Asia, reveal the social structures and political struggles embodied in urban informality. I look at the Latin American legacy as tremendously useful when used not as a repository of universalized models, but rather as the source of analytical concepts, the precise meanings of which can only be fixed in historically specific settings.

In the context of the Middle East, which by no stretch of the imagination can be considered a homogeneous region, urban experience has rarely been incorporated into an analysis of the informal sector. And this is where the Latin American legacy is useful. But it is important to recognize how discussions of urban informality in different regions of the world have to be anchored in the area studies that shape research vocabularies. For example, one may ask, in talking about the Middle East, "middle" of where? And "east" of what? The Middle East is clearly one of the few world regions whose geographic territory remains open-ended, without clear borders, and this is fundamentally due to its historic evolution as part of a colonial/postcolonial paradigm. Nevertheless, the Middle East is an area study, which demarcates objects and methodologies of research. The Latin American school may also be looked upon as another area study with a unique history and geography of its own, but one that is influential beyond its immediate region. Most scholars of the urban Middle East are trained in Latin American models, and indeed we can argue that to be trained as an urbanist is to be raised on the traditions of the Latin American school.

So what we are talking about are not only different geographies of informality but also different geographies of knowledge. The point about area studies indicates that there are distinctive regional genres of research, some of which interact, but often in hierarchical ways. Our intention, with this "Crossing Borders" project, has been to redirect some of these area studies interactions. Partly, this will serve to update the Latin American toolkit. Now more than ever it is important to investigate liberalization as a process of socio-spatial restructuring, manifested in such things as informal urban development and negotiated through elaborate legal and extra-legal systems of regulation. Such an examination becomes even more imperative given the recent celebration of urban informality in a whole spectrum of policy positions. From the World Bank agenda of "enabling" informal urban development to the newfound enthusiasm for self-help strategies of the urban poor, there is a growing consensus on the benefits of harnessing the efficiencies of urban informality. This "new" moment requires a direct engagement with the nature of liberalization as a distinctive phase of development and urbanization.

In this regard, we can note that starting in the 1980s, and in much of the Third World, the illegal subdivision of agricultural land seems to have become the largest source of informal urban development. This process implies some important breaks with earlier forms of urban informality, two of which are particularly important. First, these new forms of informal urban development are taking place at the rural-urban interface, in liminal zones of middle-class suburbanization and transnational real estate investment. Second, under conditions of globalization and liberalization, we can see the rise of practices of religion and ethnicity in the shaping of the urban environment. Of course, none of this is new, as urban informality is not new. But clearly what makes this phase of globalization and liberalization different is the intensifying reality of these geographies and practices.

Let me address the first dimension –- the tremendous expansion of informal subdivisions through the illegal urbanization of agricultural land. We are seeing the rapid transformation of the *ejidos* on the outskirts of Mexico City, the incredible volatility of land transactions on Calcutta's eastern fringes, and upscale gated communities in theme-park settings on Cairo's sandy edges. These emerging patterns of informal urban development are often taking place on private or privatized, rather than public, plots of land. They often involve new and shifting configurations of actors: real estate developers, transnational investors, liberalizing government officials, bourgeois urbanites, and peasants with de facto land rights. While this is a reality present in many world regions, I would argue that the South Asian genre of research has the potential to make a significant contribution to our understandings of such processes. Its sharp focus on the agrarian question, the spatiality of rural-urban linkages, and the implications of neoliberal reforms for state power may help answer such questions as: How is the rural-urban interface determined by urban and agrarian laws and regulations? How are these being restructured in the context of liberalization? What agrarian transactions and struggles make agricultural and peripheral land available for informal urbanization?

But there is also the question of the changing nature of state and civil society — the second dimension of liberalization that I outlined. Both Latin America and South Asia offer rich traditions of theorizing about the structures and mechanisms of state power. The Middle East experience, which has rarely been incorporated into these discussions, offers an interesting variance. For example, the Egyptian case highlights how religion is increasingly invoked in urban struggles. Whether it is the sprawl of informal districts that surround Cairo or the public housing projects that have been appropriated by residents, there can be no denial of the rise of a populist fundamentalism and its challenge to the state. Urban informality in the context of wartime Lebanon points to the crucial role of ethnic politics. And this is also true in the case of Israel/Palestine, where the informal land rights of settlers have been so intensely ethnicized that they are now a major hurdle to the prospects of peace. The Israeli state, having prevented the Palestinians from building legally, has left them with no alternative but to expand informally (the Gaza Strip can be considered the largest squatter settlement in the world). That same state for a while found itself in the position of having to declare its own citizens "squatters" to justify their forced removal as a part of political compromise. Indeed, a Middle East perspective raises another set of interesting questions not fully studied in the Latin American and South Asian contexts: What role does ethnicity play in urban informality? How does the discourse on religion and ethnicity frame some of the basic rights of citizenship, e.g., access to land?

So this is what we mean by the transnational method. There are of course transnational geographies, the real crossing and drawing of borders, the landscape of global interconnections. But what we are concerned with here is transnational interrogation, which is the idea of using one context to ask questions of another. In the realm of teaching, I have encouraged students to pose Third World questions of the First World, to actively deviate from the old-style practice of evaluating underdevelopment in light of development, and to engage with "elsewhere" in order to unsettle "home" and its certainties. This is of course an explicitly political project. But this interrogation can also be extended. One can think of Latin America as the core of knowledge production, with South Asia and the Middle

East as marginalized peripheries. In this case, asking South Asian questions or Middle Eastern questions of the Latin American urban condition could generate new configurations in both disciplinary discourses and area studies conversations.

At the core of the Crossing Borders initiative is the belief that area studies scholars can indeed transcend the borders of both their disciplines and their areas. However, scholars interested in comparative and transnational work always approach such exercises with the hope of extracting lessons from other regions to apply to their own. If we are to conceptually cross borders, then this traditional strategy has to be reversed. It is our intention to get the South Asianists to contribute that unique insight which may potentially explain an issue within the rural-urban continuum in the context of the Middle East, or to get the Middle East analyst to be the translator of a condition of ethnicity in a Latin American or South Asian context. This means that Crossing Borders is not an abandonment of area studies; rather, it is a deepening of area studies knowledge — but one that attempts to ground the prevailing units of analysis, such as the nation-state or the region, in a larger context of globalization and liberalization. This also means that urban informality can ultimately only be defined in the context of specific regional experiences. This book is ultimately about these regional definitions, and I think it is important for us as editors to resist the temptation of a universal definition of the concept. Each of our authors has in fact implied a particular content to urban informality, and each of their conceptualizations is grounded in a regional genre of research.

Unlike urban informality which may remain a fluid concept, acquiring shape only in regional locations, liberalization has a global register. It is a historical marker, indicating a paradigm shift in international development. It is an ideology and practice advocating privatization and austerity. It is a redefinition of the role and scale of the state. It is also a process that has resulted in significant socioeconomic inequalities that cannot be ignored in the urban domain. Indeed, liberalization has generated an intense commodification of informal land and housing markets. If in earlier phases of development, urban informality was located primarily on public land and practiced in public space, now we can also talk about the privatization of informality.

The commodification of informal housing and land markets is, however, not a new phenomenon. What we are really looking at are new actors and new spaces, such as religious groups and fundamentalist practices in the Middle East that are consolidated through their active role in the provision of urban services. This may sound like the same old urban populism, but it is not the Latin American style of populism because most of these activities and forms of organization do not really become acts of political rebellion or political co-optation. Rather, they often remain struggles of survival, meant to evade any form of politicization. This is a rise of fundamentalism in some parts of the world like the Middle East as a structure that dominates the urban process.

But none of this can be understood outside of liberalization and the pressures it creates for land and housing markets. In South Asia we are witnessing the many ways economic struggles over tight housing markets may spawn brutal interreligious or interethnic conflict. We can understand these processes according to a post-9/11 vocabulary of terrorism — one that leaves us with the paralyz-

ing discourse of civilizational conflict, religious essentialisms, and an "axis of evil."
Or, we can understand these processes in a historicized framework of urbanization and urbanism, whereby the fascism of contemporary religious fundamen-
talisms may be related to the fascism of neoliberal free markets and the new
American imperialism. For the latter is a type of fundamentalism as well.

*More significantly, I would argue that we are looking at a new mode of urban existence or a
new way of urban life, one that pervades every aspect of the private and public spheres. While we
primarily deal with the sectors of housing and land, the implications of urban informality go beyond
these discrete sectors, and instead imply a logic that structures the very fabric of urban life.
Additionally, I have always believed, like many of my colleagues who study Latin America, that the
urban informal sector is not a new or a novel phenomenon. Rather, it became important with the
rise and maturity of a formal sector which organized and consolidated many aspects of the relationship of the state to the economy. Similarly, we are becoming increasingly aware that urban informality as a way of life is not new. Indeed, one may argue that it has existed since the Middle Ages in
different forms, and that informal economies have persisted in many rural areas, particularly in the
developing world. What may be new now is the re-emergence and retrenchment of urban informality as a way of life at this moment of globalization and liberalization. The acquiescence of the
neoliberal state in practices of informality is a key dimension of this transformation, and bears resemblance to earlier moments of informality, including similar practices during the Middle Ages.*

I would agree that urban informality, while manifested in distinct sectors, is
an organizing urban logic. It is a process of structuration that constitutes the rules
of the game, determining the nature of transactions between individuals and
institutions and within institutions. If formality operates through the fixing of
value, including the mapping of spatial value, then informality operates through
the constant negotiability of value and the unmapping of space. In this, it bears
uncanny resemblance to liberalization, which can also be understood as an organizing logic that determines interinstitutional and interurban transactions and
practices. However, the problem with the notion of urban informality as a way of
life is that it evokes Wirthian notions of an urban ecology that somehow correlates with social organization and cultural mindsets. While such a conceptualization may draw attention to important aspects of lived experience and identity, it
can obscure the political economy of cities. In particular, it implies that urban
informality is a coherent mode of life when, in fact, in an era of liberalization I
would argue the organizing divide is not so much that between formality and
informality as the differentiation that exists within informality — that which
marks off different types of informal accumulation and informal politics. The
neoliberal state, of course, deepens such forms of differentiation, fostering some
forms of informality and annihilating others. It is this uneven geography that
requires us to pay renewed attention to urban informality.

*This is the challenge of this book. And it is also the challenge of the transnational approach.
Beyond the concept of urban informality as an organizing urban logic, we can perhaps postulate that*

the idea of urban informality as a new way of life is anchored in a Middle Eastern context, as much as the articulation of urban informality as differentiated modes of urban transactions is situated in the South Asian context. The significance of this book is that it makes evident the territoriality or the geopolitical basis of our concepts, thereby presenting the hope of sometimes "crossing borders."

NOTE

1. This prologue was written as a dialogue between the editors of this volume, Ananya Roy and Nezar AlSayyad, and is meant to evoke the discussions that have helped shape the project. Ananya Roy's words are presented in regular font while Nezar AlSayyad's words are presented in italicized font.

1

Urban Informality as a "New" Way of Life

Nezar AlSayyad

Some sixty years ago Louis Wirth wrote that the urbanization of the world in the late nineteenth and early twentieth centuries was one of the "most impressive facts of modern times," bringing profound changes to the social and economic life of nations.[1] Most importantly, Wirth argued that while the city was the "locus of urbanism," the urban mode of life was no longer confined to cities. Instead, it involved a more general acceptance of social factors like density, which often accentuated friction and spatial segregation; heterogeneity, which often resulted in social instability and insecurity; and anonymity, which often led to the emergence of individualistic survival mechanisms among urban residents, who were assumed to have come from the less conflictual countryside.

Wirth suggested that "as long as we identify urbanism with the physical entity of the city, . . . and proceed as if urban attributes abruptly ceased to be manifested beyond an arbitrary boundary line, we are not likely to arrive at any adequate conception of urbanism as a mode of life."[2] He went on to articulate the view that urbanization no longer denoted merely the process by which persons are attached to a place, but the development of a larger system of social relations arising in response to the cumulative accentuation of the above-mentioned urban conditions. Wirth's urbanism should not be confused here with physical/spatial processes of urbanization, or with the locally driven culture of cities. Indeed, Wirth reasoned that the central issue in studying the city was to discover "the forms of social action and organization that emerge among individuals under these conditions of density, heterogeneity and anonymity."[3] All of this gave rise, of course, to a particular idea of city residents as (to use Georg Simmel's language) "blasé" urbanites with highly segmented roles.[4]

In a similar vein, the contributors to this book also look at forms of urban-ization and urbanism in an attempt to discover social actors and forms of social organization. However, they target their concern toward practices of urban "informality" that have emerged in recent decades in a variety of Third World contexts in response to worldwide economic liberalization. In regard to such studies, one of Wirth's seminal contributions was to emphasize that urbanism as a way of life may be approached from three interrelated perspectives: the physical structure, comprising a population base; a system of social organization, involving a characteristic social structure and related patterns of social relationships; and a set of attitudes and ideas of individuals or groups engaged in or operating under forms of collective behavior and/or social control.[5] As the contributors to this book demonstrate, all three of these aspects remain relevant in seeking to under-stand the meaning and practice of urban "informality."

Many of Wirth's ideas, and those of the Chicago School of Urban Sociology of which he was a part, gained tremendous currency in the decades around the mid-twentieth century. The Chicago School represented the first systematic effort to theorize the study of community and urbanism. In the city around them, its scholars witnessed patterns of rapid and dynamic growth driven by migration, which resulted in such recurring ecological patterns as invasion, survival, assimilation, adaptation, and cooperation. These patterns demanded three important strands of research: the first dealt with the relationship between individual and communi-ty; the second involved the nature and meaning of progress; and the third focused on the relationship between the patterns and processes of urban life.[6]

By the end of the century, however, the Los Angeles School of Urban Geography had fundamentally shifted the agenda away from Chicago School concerns. Using the suburbanizing region of postmodern Los Angeles as its urban model, it introduced a new framework for analysis driven by several key structur-al features. Among these were an emphasis on the role played by the capitalist economy rather than a concern for ecology and behavior; a focus on urbanization patterns where the form of the center was determined by the hinterland; an appreciation of decentralization as the main engine of growth in the contempo-rary city; and an awareness of the importance that cities such as L.A. play as loci in a globalizing political economy.

To date, the ideas of the Chicago School, and more recently, the Los Angeles School, have dominated discourse on cities, urbanization and urbanism, not only in the United States and Europe, but also in the countries of the developing world. It is particularly important to recognize how the notions and discourses around Third World cities were mainly generated in the crucible of the Chicago School. Charles Abrams's seminal *Man's Struggle for Shelter in an Urbanizing World*, one of the first books to deal with Third World cities, is a good example.[7] In this work, Abrams's training in Chicago School techniques caused him to assume the existence of a particular rural-urban continuum and a particular mode by which rural folks were transformed into urbanites. And according to these assumptions, he argued that the new urban migrants often failed to complete the transformative cycle, and hence, for a variety of structural reasons, became squatters.

Despite the origins of this preexisting discourse, the phenomenal growth of cities around the Third World in the last four decades indicates that the urban future does not lie in Chicago or L.A., and that it will not be shaped according to the schools of thought named after them. Rather, the future lies in cities like Cairo, Rio de Janeiro, Istanbul, and Bombay, and can best be investigated by looking at them. One important and common characteristic of these places is that older modes of urbanism are being replaced by "new" forms of urban informality that challenge the relevance of previous thinking about "blasé" urbanites. It is in this regard that urban informality, as situated in many Third World cities, may be emerging as a new paradigm for understanding urban culture.

So what is this urban informality, and who are these urban informals? Over the years a fundamental shift has taken place with respect to the idea. In talking about the new migrants to the city, Georg Simmel invoked the socio-psychological concept of the "stranger."[8] Similarly, Robert Park observed that many immigrants were "marginals" — a trait he felt was embedded in their social structure.[9] In general, Simmel believed the marginal personality to be a manifestation of cultural hybridity — of living on the margin of two cultures without being a full member of either.[10] And such notions of passivity were legitimated by the ethnographic work of Oscar Lewis in the late 1950s and early '60s. By generalizing from research among the urban poor in Puerto Rico and Mexico, Lewis was able to advance a theory about the "culture of poverty" that had much in common with Chicago School views.[11]

In the late 1960s, however, this dominant perspective was challenged by scholars working in Latin America. Among others, Janice Perlman and Manuel Castells argued respectively that marginality was a myth employed as an instrument for the social control of the poor, and a mechanism of collective consumption that determined the social order of the urban poor.[12] Such scholars stressed the view that the urban poor were not "marginal," or excluded from society. Rather, as Asef Bayat has written, such populations were fully integrated into society, but on terms that often caused them to be economically exploited, politically repressed, socially stigmatized, and culturally excluded.[13] As Castells noted, however, this did not stop the poor from aiming for "social transformation" through their everyday struggle for urban services or "collective consumption."[14]

Whether they are today called "urban marginals," "urban disenfranchised," or "urban poor" (and these terms are often used interchangeably), the current era of global restructuring has greatly increased the number of such people, and it has led to an explosion in the range of their activities. Indeed, according to Bayat, urban informals today represent an "[ever] increasing number of unemployed, partially employed, casual labor, street subsistence workers, street children and members of the underworld."[15] It is within this context that we should try to understand how the concept of urban informality has developed and taken root in contemporary urban discourse.[16]

URBAN INFORMALITY: A HISTORIOGRAPHY

Any discussion of informality inevitably must begin with the emergence of the "informal sector" as a concept in the early 1970s. The discussion was ultimately rooted in descriptions of the movement of labor to cities in the 1950s and '60s. Among the earliest to identify this trend, W. Arthur Lewis proposed a two-sector model for understanding the new migration of people and the manner of their employment.[17] Lloyd George Reynolds further identified these groups as a state sector and a "trade-service" sector. He described the latter as "the multitude of people whom one sees thronging the city streets, sidewalks and back alleys in the developing countries: the petty traders, street vendors, coolies and porters, small artisans, messengers, barbers, shoe-shine boys and personal servants."[18] Eventually, studies of the informal sector were to diverge in many different directions. And by the late 1970s Caroline Moser was to describe the informal sector as simply "the urban poor, or as the people living in slums or squatter settlements."[19] Moser did note, however, that certain activities, such as those related to the improvement of housing in squatter areas (particularly by rural migrants), could be considered typical of it.

In hindsight, it is curious to note how, even though the "informal sector" embodies a broad set of activities and people without clearly identifiable characteristics, scholars continued to represent it by means of a dualistic framework. To understand the source of this distinction, it is important to trace the term to the work of Keith Hart.[20] In the 1970s Hart first made a distinction between formal and informal sectors, basing his distinction on types of employment — whether wage-earning or self-employment — with the degree of rationalization serving as the key variable. Specifically, Hart noted that the "informal" (or traditional or underemployed) urban poor often engaged in petty capitalism as a substitute for the wage employment to which they were denied access.[21]

A few years later, Dipak Mazumdar designated as informal the unprotected urban labor market, as opposed to the "protected" one in the formal sector.[22] And a similar two-sector dichotomy came to dominate the position of the International Labor Organization (ILO). In a 1972 report, the ILO stated that the informal sector referred primarily to the activities of "petty-traders, street hawkers, shoeshine boys and other groups 'underemployed' on the streets of the big towns, and includes a range of wage-earners and self-employed persons, male as well as female."²³ The report argued that these informal activities represented a way of doing things "characterized by: a) ease of entry; b) reliance on indigenous resources; c) family ownership of enterprises; d) small scale of operation; e) labor-intensive and adapted technology; f) skills acquired outside the formal school system; and g) unregulated and competitive markets."²⁴ It is important to note how the ILO's assumptions about these immigrants — forming the majority of the urban informals — were little changed from those of the Chicago School. However, the ILO's contribution to the evolving understanding of urbanization (and the ensuing characteristics of urbanism) lay in its shift of focus from the social life of settlements to the forms of production within them.

In the years that followed, the ILO's dualistic conception of the informal sector gained widespread popularity. As Ray Bromley has argued, this was in part due to its "embodied policy implications, which were convenient for international organizations and politically middle-of-the-road governments." Specifically, support for the informal sector appeared to offer the possibility of "helping the poor without any major threat to the rich."²⁵ However, the seemingly ambiguous definition of "informals" underlying the ILO view — focused on unorganized, self-employed individuals — soon also became the subject of more serious scrutiny. In particular, the work of two groups, based principally on Latin American case studies, came to dominate urban-theory debates. One group dealt with questions relating to the internal structure and function of the informal sector, focusing on whether informality consisted of particular groups of individuals and/or specific types of enterprise. The other examined the nature of the informal sector more generally, and ultimately led to two comprehensive theories. One considered informality to be a marginalized sector, a temporary manifestation of underdevelopment characterized by survival activities of the urban poor. The other considered it to be closely connected to the formal sector — an essential, permanent component of a modern economy.²⁶

URBAN INFORMALITY: A TYPOLOGY

In 1994 Cathy Rakowski analyzed the debate on urban informality that had emerged in the 1980s according to four main approaches.²⁷ At the time her typology was primarily concerned with understanding the informal sector in Latin America; and today it cannot fully account for the development of this sector in other regions of the Third World. Nevertheless, it is convenient to adopt Rakowski's typology here, and modify it to accommodate the cases of South Asia and the Middle East. Rakowski's typology made a fundamental division between two groups — essentially the structuralists and the legalists. The former comprised the ILO and advocates of the underground economy; the latter included Hernando De Soto and the advocates of microenterprise perspectives.

According to Rakowski, the roots of the structuralist approach could be traced to ILO urban labor-market research conducted in the 1970s, and to later neo-Marxists and dependency theorists. The ILO school emphasized "cleavages in economic and social composition between formal and informal economies," and "infer[red] that the proper role of the state [was] to help equalize differences."[28] By contrast, advocates of the underground economy (also known as the black market) rejected such notions of dualism and focused on the way "forms of production, productive units, technologies, and workers" were integrated into local, regional, and international economies.[29] The latter group was particularly critical of the view that the informal sector was a small-scale, easy-entry, "way of doing things." Alternatively, they conceptualized informality as a "status of labor" (undeclared and noncontractual, lacking benefits, paid less than minimum wage, etc.); a "condition of work" (hazardous, unprotected); and "a form of management of some firms" (involving such strategies as fiscal fraud and unrecorded payments).[30]

Rakowski argued that the significance of the structuralist approach lay in its view that informality in peripheral societies was the "expression of the uneven nature of capitalist development."[31] Indeed, under certain conditions, structuralists even believed the informal economy could be considered a growth economy.[32] By contrast, proponents of the underground-economy approach considered the "informalization" concept to be little more than "a mechanism to reverse the costly process of proletarianization and weaken the rights of workers and unions with the acquiescence of the state in the interest of renewed economic growth."[33]

According to Rakowski, the other major approach to informality encompassed neoliberalist perspectives, and stressed the "legal, bureaucratic" position of the state underlying the sharp divisions between formal and informal economies.[34] This legalist approach relied heavily on economic modeling of concepts like "efficiency," and "rational process"; and social concepts like "moral" positions. It was probably best exemplified by its proponents' use of such terms as "informality," "informal sector," and "informals" interchangeably with such terms as "enterprising activities" and "entrepreneurs." But much of the discussion within this group focused on "entrepreneurs and institutional constraints that make informality a rational economic strategy."[35]

Proponents of this approach often adopted views similar to the structuralists — in particular, in terms of their notions of dualism and the marginalization of certain economic activities and actors. The legalists, however, emphasized the importance of income-generating efforts and expenditure/saving activities.[36] They also generally differed with the structuralists as to the root causes of informality and its effects, particularly its role in economic growth — although they did agree that rural-urban migration acted as a catalyst for informality.

One of the main figures within this group, Hernando De Soto, regarded informality in his early work as a "survival strategy" — "a safety valve for societal tensions."[37] He wrote that this was undertaken by the poor with "ingenuity and "entrepreneurial spirit."[38] De Soto rejected the notion of a defined informal sector; instead, he viewed the informal economy as including all extralegal activities — both market and subsistence production, as well as trade. In general, legalists like De Soto attributed the rise of the informality phenomenon to excessive state regulations, and not to the dynamics of the labor market. Consequently, they saw informal activity as a means for breaking down legal barriers. According to De Soto, informality was a natural response to real market forces, and not to the rise in unemployment and the need for jobs. For him, the informal entrepreneur was an economic hero who managed to survive and prosper despite the state's continuous controlling measures. Thus, informals served a beneficial purpose in the development of a competitive capitalist economy, both by helping reduce imports and by supplying goods and services. And, although it was officially unaccounted for, the wealth created by the informals provided a real path to development.

Despite its many weaknesses (as pointed out by scholars such as Alejandro Portes and Ray Bromley), the legalist approach had a significant impact in a number of contexts, particularly microlevel professional interventions by nongovernmental organizations, international donor agencies, and private entrepreneurs. The goal of their work was often poverty alleviation through the encouragement of small enterprises, and practitioners of such work had little interest in broad theories about the informal sector.[39] Instead, they were concerned with designing programs to address the needs of the poor, and with raising funds to implement them, primarily through credit programs.

The neoliberalist, legalist approach of De Soto and the microenterprise NGOs has garnered great political support in the last decade and a half in much of the Third World. This has occurred simultaneously with the introduction of new possibilities for development based on market mechanisms. Today such mechanisms include the proliferation of integrated international production and the growing hegemony of the International Monetary Fund and the International Bank for Reconstruction and Development. Characteristically, the latter institutions have promoted a worldwide regime of trade liberalization, reform of exchange rates, and privatization.[40] However, this global framework of restructuring and capital flows has had highly uneven spatial effects. For example, the promise of the market, as measured by the inflow of Foreign Direct Investment (FDI), has played an instrumental role in the rapid industrialization of some Asian countries. But elsewhere the internationally mandated structural-adjustment and austerity measures of the 1980s have caused economic collapse, with little evidence of subsequent recovery — particularly in sub-Saharan Africa.

OTHER INFORMALITIES

Research in Latin America throughout the 1980s not only brought to light the crucial role of informal processes in shaping cities, but also situated informality firmly within the larger politics of populist mobilizations and state power. Today, however, it may be this political orientation of the formative Latin American research that may need most to be reworked in terms of Middle Eastern and South Asian contexts.

Some years ago I argued through a comparison of the Middle East to Latin America that the process of urban informality, at least in the housing sector, seemed quite distinct in these two contexts. This was not merely due to the existence of different mechanisms of land-market operation, but also (and mainly) because the different contexts were marked by different cultural specificities.[41] Based on selected case studies of housing practices, I suggested that while urban informality in Latin America normally engaged organized political affiliation and established a reciprocal relation between squatter groups and the state, in the Middle East it was the relative depoliticization of such processes that best guaranteed the prospects of the urban poor. Thus, I concluded that if land invasions were most likely to occur, or be encouraged, in Latin America under conditions of *political* change — say, at election times — such occupations were more likely to occur in the Middle East during times of *economic* transformation. I further suggested that while political participation in some Latin American contexts often sustained important gains, in a place like Egypt the conditions were exactly the opposite: that is, a withdrawal from all formal channels and an attempt to achieve political invisibility was the best strategy for illegally subdividing agricultural land and transforming it into informal urban housing.

Asef Bayat's work has supported this point.[42] He has argued that the struggle of Middle East informals is "not a politics of protest, but of redress." As such, it has two main goals: "the redistribution of social goods and opportunities, and attainment of cultural and political autonomy."[43] Furthermore, these goals can best be achieved through relatively invisible means such as bribery and/or settlement in low-profile areas.

In 1993, when I first compared informal housing practices in Latin America and the Middle East, I was concerned with the political culture of urban space. I defined culture as a broad system of values and norms that mediated relations among the urban poor, and between them and the state. What I did not take into account were the aspects of culture that contributors to this book deal with at a variety of detailed levels: ethnicity, race, and class.

In this moment of neoliberalism, we are starting to see the reconceptualization of poverty as a form of efficiency of production. Yet while NGOs are often complicit in this neoliberal agenda, the driving paradigms in their spheres of influence are often ethnic and social difference — sometimes more gendered in the context of the Middle East, or more racialized in the context of Latin America. Thus, projects such as de-Arabization, de-indigenization, Judaization, Creolization, and Mestisozation often reveal forms of tension that go to the heart and substance of urban informality as a concept and a lived experience. For example, at the end of their chapter in this book, Oren Yiftachel and Haim Yakobi tell us that in Israel liberalization and nationalism have evolved in parallel, but with little mutual coordination. A new empirical exploration and intellectual conceptualization is urgently needed to engage such projects. Similarly, the contemporary processes of informal urban development requires us to update our analytical toolkit.

As we go about this task it is important to recognize that both Latin America and South Asia have rich traditions of theorizing about the structures and mechanisms of state power; by contrast, these views are largely absent from Middle East scholarship and experience.[44] Beyond this, the South Asian perspective raises two particular sets of issues about informal urban development under conditions of liberalization that resonate strongly with empirical evidence from Latin American and Middle Eastern contexts.[45] First, what transactions and struggles make agricultural land available for informal urbanization? And second, what are the forms of vulnerability that are being engendered by these processes of informality?

Most importantly, even though such questions emerge from specific historical and sociopolitical contexts, they enable the extension of inquiry concerning urban informality from one initially dominant and important region — namely, Latin America, with its specific political regimes — to other regions, which may be characterized by a variety of political systems ranging from military to authoritarian to Communist. It is just such a goal that provides a focus for the contributors to this book.

LIBERALIZATION, GLOBALIZATION, AND URBAN INFORMALITY

It is easy to argue that globalization and liberalization are today giving rise to new geographies. Likewise, new forms of informality are emerging in some areas, while in others old forms are reestablishing themselves. However, the relationship between globally driven liberalization and locally based informality is often ambiguous. In the first section of this book, Alan Gilbert, Arif Hasan, and Asef Bayat attempt to unravel aspects of this relationship with reference to Latin America, Southeast Asia, and the Middle East.

In his chapter "Love in the Time of Enhanced Capital Flows: Reflections on the Links between Liberalization and Informality," Alan Gilbert attempts to

define various elements of this linkage with a focus on Latin America — specifically the relationship between economic liberalization and the "informal sector."
He demonstrates that despite some success, particularly in terms of the legalization of informal housing, economic liberalization has brought a general deterioration in living conditions. However, he emphasizes that no general conclusions
can be reached as to the impact of liberalization on informality, since both phenomenon are shaped by local social and global economic processes.

Gilbert's view emerges from observation of the liberalization drives of seven
Latin American countries and subsequent impacts on employment patterns. His
comparative exercise focuses on countries once characterized by policies of
import substitution which have now passed through periods of structural adjustment and the introduction of the New Economic Model. Latin America may be
unique in this regard, he says, because liberalization often started under unpopular military regimes, sometimes succeeded by democratic governments — a
process resulting in a "potent blend of anarchic liberalization." Yet, in spite of
some variation, Gilbert argues that one common outcome has been that local
firms have been put out of businesses and forced to modify employment practices. He hypothesizes that a "new structural situation has developed whereby
economic instability produces moments of high unemployment so suddenly that
the informal sector is unable to absorb the surplus labor force." He points out
that volatility in working conditions often means that individuals must move
from one sector to the other during the course of a single day. For example, an
individual may work in the formal economy eight hours a day, but then spend the
rest of his or her time living in informal housing.

Gilbert also identifies three key issues at the heart of the ambiguity underlying economic liberalization and its workings: first, that government-advertised
liberalization varies from real-life, ground-level liberalization; second, that it is
often impossible to clearly define the informal sector and its extent; and third,
that both liberalization and informality are highly localized processes. He notes
that the link between liberalization and informality becomes particularly ambiguous with regard to housing. This is due to the long history of informal housing in
Latin American cities — what he views as a form of self-help — which manifested itself decades before the era of liberalization. Gilbert concludes by suggesting
that local-level analysis is critical to unraveling the relationship between liberalization and informality.

Arif Hasan's chapter, "The Changing Nature of the Informal Sector in
Karachi due to Global Restructuring and Liberalization and Its Repercussions,"
explores some important breaks with earlier forms of informality by examining the
effects of liberalization on the informal sector in Karachi. Hasan's observations
show that in some parts of the world, liberalization has resulted in the emergence
of a First World economy and sociology with a Third World wage and political

structure. He argues that economic liberalization and structural adjustment have increased the socioeconomic divide within the urban populations in Pakistan. For example, liberalization has led to increasing inflation, which has forced ever more people to take on more than one job — with the other job usually being in the informal sector. Simultaneously, privatization has made formerly cheap government land an important commodity that is now inaccessible to the urban poor.

Hasan contends that the communications revolution is creating new consumerist aspirations in Pakistan, as an ever greater part of the population desires to belong to the "contemporary" world portrayed by the media. He argues that in the absence of formal means to achieve these aspirations, the informal sector has stepped in to provide products and services to bridge the gap. This means that the informal sector in Karachi today mainly caters to upwardly mobile residents, since serving the needs of the poor means less profit and greater marginalization from formal-sector processes. This situation has led to increased crime, mainly in informal settlements where households do not have access to the same level of security as the upper class.

Liberalization has had political implications as well. For example, Hasan points out that most new informal settlements are located on cheap land far from the city center. As a consequence, their residents cannot dominate the politics or economy of the city in the same way residents of older informal settlements once did. As formal-sector industries have become less labor intensive, Hasan also points out that links between informal workshops and formal-sector industries are slowly eroding. And with the state sector diminishing, politicians are no longer able to hand out favors. Such a patronage system is now being replaced by cash payments to protect activities that do not comply with state regulations. In conclusion, Hasan points out that liberalization has transformed old forms of informality, and given rise to new forms that are focused mainly on the new middle class. However, many members of this class are now rejecting the global order through political and religious practices.

In his chapter "Globalization and the Politics of the Informals in the Global South," Asef Bayat looks at the politics of marginalized urban groups in Third World cities. He begins by examining the shortcomings of prevailing perspectives about such people: the essentialism inherent in notions of the "passive poor"; the reductionism of the "survival strategy"; the Latino-centrism of "urban territorial movements"; and the conceptual perplexity of "resistance literature." Instead, he argues that the politics of the urban poor can best be understood by means of a model of "the quiet encroachment of the ordinary." According to this model, ordinary people challenge structures established by the propertied and powerful through silent, largely atomized actions that allow them to survive and improve their lives.

Bayat suggests that these quiet actions contest many fundamental aspects of state prerogatives, including the meaning of order, the control of public space, and access to public and private goods. His perspective emerges out of observations of urban processes in the Middle East. Thus, he tells how postrevolutionary Iran saw a movement of quiet encroachment of street sidewalks, apartments, and public and private urban land by the poor and middle class. And in Cairo, millions of rural migrants, the urban poor, and the middle class have quietly claimed cemeteries, rooftops, and public lands on the periphery of the city. Similarly, for Bayat, the refusal by many of the urban poor to pay for public services in Alexandria and Beirut is another form of "quiet encroachment." Bayat points out that when street vendors occupy public spaces, they infringe on formal businesses; but the gains they make through such quiet encroachment come not at cost to themselves or their fellow poor, but to the state, the rich, and the powerful. Although this model of quiet encroachment is based in the Middle East, Bayat believes it has relevance for understanding the actions of marginalized groups in other Third World cities.

Bayat further argues that recent neoliberal policies have led previously privileged segments of the workforce, such as state employees and professionals, to resort to repertoires of quiet encroachment. However, such unlawful action is based on necessity, and is not carried out with deliberate political intent. Bayat insists that theirs is a politics of redress, involving the struggle for immediate outcomes through individual direct action. Yet at the same time that these groups are seeking autonomy from regulations, institutions, and discipline imposed by the modern state, they also need the security that comes from state surveillance. Thus, in their quest for security, they are engaged in a constant negotiation between autonomy and integration, carving out autonomy in any space available. While quiet encroachment is not likely to bring crucial social services such as education, health, and security within reach of urban marginal groups, Bayat believes it remains a viable enabling strategy for individuals and groups.

THE POLITICS OF URBAN INFORMALITIES

The second section of this book, containing chapters by Janice E. Perlman, Ananya Roy, Ahmed M. Soliman, and Oren Yiftachel and Haim Yakobi, takes up the politics of urban informalities and their connection to marginality and space.

In the late 1960s it was argued that squatter communities were populated by those who were doomed by their own laziness and poverty to remain on the margins of life. Through her study of *favelados*, or rural migrants to the *favelas* of Rio de Janeiro, Janice Perlman was among those who helped debunk this myth. In her seminal book *The Myth of Marginality*, Perlman examined the populations of five informal communities in Rio against a backdrop of rapid urbanization, development, and growing animosity toward their residents. These "others," as they were called, lived on the margins of society and were considered the "cancerous sores on the beautiful body of the city." However, after closely examining the lives of 750 individuals and families, both in squatter settlements and unserviced subdivisions, Perlman concluded that their social, cultural, political, and economic marginality was "empirically false, analytically misleading, and insidious in its policy implications." Perlman observed that the *favelados* did not exhibit attitudes or behaviors characteristic of marginal people; instead, they were socially well organized, culturally optimistic, and economically hard working. Further, they aspired to a better life, and they held patriotic values. She concluded that the persistence of the myth of marginality was primarily due to class bias. It also fulfilled a political function by isolating different sections of the working class, while reinforcing the idea that marginals could only be integrated by populist policies.

In her chapter in this book, "Marginality: From Myth to Reality in the *Favelas* of Rio de Janeiro, 1969–2002," Perlman revisited Rio de Janeiro to examine the present status of her 1969 study population. After an interval of three decades, her methodology consisted of locating as many of her original participants as possible and conducting a series of in-depth, open-ended interviews with them. Among other things, Perlman writes that the restoration of democracy in Brazil since her earlier study and the ensuing international investment has been a mixed blessing for these people. On the one hand, political and economic shifts have brought a general improvement of living conditions. But in other regards — such as in quality of education and access to jobs — many inhabitants of Rio's informal settlements remain "marginal."

Among other things, Perlman observes that since her earlier study inequality between the rich and the poor has increased dramatically; the number of *favelas* has doubled from the original three hundred she recorded in 1969; and *favela* populations have increased by 40 percent (at a time when Rio as a whole witnessed a population drop of around 7 percent). In addition, crime is now a significant problem for most people in informal settlements. Based on her preliminary findings, Perlman concludes that in many ways marginality has ceased to be a myth; it has now become a reality.

In the following chapter, "The Gentleman's City: Urban Informality in the Calcutta of New Communism," Ananya Roy explains how the city of Calcutta is being remade at a moment of neoliberal restructuring. She focuses on the urban revitalization efforts of the regional government, the Left Front, calling this a New Communism. A central aspect of this *perestroika* is the eviction of informal vendors and squatters. Thus, on the fringes of the city, long-standing squatter colonies have been demolished to make way for middle-class housing developments initiated through public-private partnerships. Roy points out that these displacements are couched in a rhetoric of cultural improvement, allowing the neoliberal city to be inscribed as the "gentleman's city," a genteel city of charm and grace.

While at first glance the urban remaking of Calcutta seems to be an outright annihilation of the informal sector, it turns out that behind the scenes there is a complex choreography of resettlement and rehabilitation. While all informal vendors or squatters are evicted, not all are resettled. But who will be resettled? And under what terms and conditions? The inherent uncertainty of these processes ensures the loyalty of the urban poor, despite the evictions. And it is thus that urban populism continues in the shadows of urban developmentalism. Such cycles of eviction and resettlement also extend to the urban frontier, bringing remote tracts of land into the realm of urbanization.

How is the neoliberal state able to balance these projects of populism and developmentalism? Roy argues that the power of the state is derived from certain regulatory techniques, such as "unmapping," that ensure a constant negotiability regarding land rights, property titles, and land use. This territorialized uncertainty guarantees the territorialized flexibility of the state. But Roy also argues that such forms of flexibility come at a cost, most notably in an impasse in urban development. Mimicking the techniques of the state, rival political parties have now capitalized on the unmapping of the city to constantly contest the various land uses and housing projects proposed by the state.

Is there the possibility of social transformation in such a system? Roy shows that there is a deepening vulnerability of the rural-urban poor in the context of neoliberal Calcutta. This is evident in the unceasing circulation of labor across city and countryside. However, it is precisely in this movement that she locates moments of critique, as in the rowdy narratives and everyday political action of women commuters. She argues that such forms of critique do not take hold in the lived spaces of the city. Here, structures of masculinist patronage reproduce a hegemony that includes consent to the very idea of the "gentleman's city."

Following this chapter, Ahmed Soliman examines the diversity and complexity of informal housing on the periphery of Greater Cairo and Alexandria in a contribution he calls "Tilting at Sphinxes: Locating Urban Informality in Egyptian Cities." Among other things, Soliman indicates that global restructuring and market liberalization have led to the emergence of new forms of informal development here in the last several decades that are often characterized by complex and bizarre intersections of urban and rural restructuring. As in Hasan's Karachi, informality is no longer the domain of the poor in Egypt, but has become a primary avenue to home ownership for the lower-middle and middle classes. Soliman ultimately attributes the diversity of informal housing in Egypt to the great variety of ways informal development has taken place, and to the role of various actors in sustaining it. To examine all the complexity of the situation, he creates a typology of three main informal housing types — semi-informal, squatting, and hybrid or exformal — which he further breaks down into subtypes and variants.

Soliman writes that several factors lie behind the emergence of the semi-informal and squatter types of housing in Cairo and Alexandria. Among them are land-reform regulations, unfavorable farming conditions, and increasing demand for housing — all of which encourage agricultural landowners to subdivide their land into small lots for sale. Other important factors are the unclear tenure status of desert lands, patterns of agricultural land subdivision based on Islamic inheritance laws, and the construction of mosques within informal settlements to ensure that government agencies cannot demolish illegal settlements. He also shows how fundamentalist groups in Egypt have deployed religion strategically in informal settlements through specific practices that enable them to realize their objectives. For Soliman, the third type of informal housing (hybrid or exformal) emphasizes the often fluid status of housing in Egypt. Thus, formal housing may be transformed into informal, and vice versa, in response to changing economic and social conditions.

As part of his survey, Soliman identifies various actors who influence and facilitate the emergence of informal housing development — including landowners, private developers, informal service suppliers (such as brokers and contractors), state agencies, and formal-sector institutions (such as banks). Likewise, his estimates of the quantity and asset values of various types and subtypes of informal housing in Greater Cairo and Alexandria reveal how important the informal housing sector is to both cities. In both cities agricultural land on the periphery plays an important role as a spatial reservoir for further informal development. Finally, pointing to the large informal housing sector in both cities and the associated high asset values, Soliman argues that informal ownership should be regularized, allowing housing to play a proper role in the socioeconomic development of the country. The main purpose of research into urban informality in Egypt should be to regularize these informal housing types, he claims.

The last chapter in the section, "Control, Resistance, and Informality: Urban Ethnocracy in Beer-Sheva, Israel," presents yet another face of urban informality. Its authors, Oren Yiftachel and Haim Yakobi, contend that the phenomenon of informality can be the product of a multitude of forces, including but not limited to the logic of capital. In Israel, in furtherance of the politics of an ethno-nation, planning has been used as an instrument of ethnic control. Thus, urban informality is "created" for the purpose of marginalizing, excluding, and impeding the development of an entire ethnic subpopulation.

In particular, Yiftachel and Yakobi explore state and planning policies that have given rise to practices of informality in Arab residential areas of the Beer-Sheva region. Here the "legal" expropriation of nearly all Arab land by the state has meant that, despite holding Israeli citizenship, most Arabs have lost all rights to land. And in the few cases where Israeli Arabs have documented proof of ownership, they have been given only partial holding rights. In this way Arab areas are deprived of basic development and planning authority, creating massive informality. Unlike other countries in the Middle East, informality in Israel has thus emerged mainly from a drive to maximize Jewish land control — not from the dictates of capital accumulation.

In response to these conditions in the Beer-Sheva region, Yiftachel and Yakobi explain how the Israeli state has given Bedouin Arabs the choice of subsidized relocation into specific serviced towns in exchange for formally withdrawing their outstanding land claims. Spatial segregation and isolation is thus offered as the only alternative to the insecurity and deprivation caused by the original expropriation. Yiftachel and Yakobi point out that similar policies to these in the Beer Sheva region have caused growing tensions across Israel. At the same time that globalization and liberalization of Israel's economy and culture have opened up avenues for Israeli Arabs to break out of their structural and spatial marginalization, the ethnographic politics of the Israeli state stand squarely in their path.

Yiftachel and Yakobi argue that to understand the dynamics of urban space and informality in ethnocratic cities or states, three forces have to be taken into consideration: the logic of capital accumulation, the evolution of modern governance, and the drive for ethnic and national control. The chapter makes an important argument about the contradictions embodied in the ethnocratic nation, or city. On the one hand, this contradiction emerges out of the city's globalizing culture and economy, which deems the city to be "officially" open and accessible. On the other, a city may also be the product of a nationalist logic of "purified" ethnic space, which marginalizes and excludes ethnic and national minorities. The Beer-Sheva case is also instructive in that it shows how informality may result from state practices and not from migrants settling on the urban fringes. Here, the creation of informality allows the segregation and control of a subject ethnic group. The case also makes evident how informality, as a status, may be determined by the nature of a political regime or the form of a state.

TRANSNATIONAL INTERROGATION

Third World urbanization has normally been studied either as a place-based process in an attempt to explain broader phenomena, or as measured against commensurate First World examples in a dualistic fashion. Since its early days, the study of informality has taken a similar path. Initially, the existence of First World models to be copied in the Third World triggered wide interest in comparative research. This varied from comparing particular urban processes across cities within a country, to comparing cities and approaches across countries and even regions. However, the shortcomings of this comparative method are what today necessitate a transnational approach to urban informality, one that transcends the limitations of comparisons. And by transnational here we mean the idea of using questions and answers generated at one site to more substantially interrogate other, fundamentally different sites. While such an approach underlies many of the chapters in this book, the contributors to its third section set out to actively employ it and reflect on its validity.

The section begins with Peter M. Ward's chapter "Informality of Housing Production at the Urban-Rural Interface: The 'Not So Strange Case' of the Texas *Colonías*." Ward's transnational approach involves an examination of informality in the United States along the Texas-Mexico border. He argues that the unregulated, substandard subdivisions there are similar to *colonías* in Mexico, and to informal settlements in other Third World countries. As elsewhere in the world, in Texas low incomes and socioeconomic inequality, coupled with the reluctance of the state to provide alternative forms of affordable housing, make unregulated subdivisions the only viable way for low-income families to gain a foothold in the property-owning market. Ward's discussion offers valuable insights on the mechanisms that have facilitated the emergence of the Texas *colonías*. These include the informal Contract for Deed often employed to sell *colonia* plots; the location of *colonías* on county land just outside the city's urban limit where there is little land-use planning and regulation; and the relatively little security offered by quasi-formal subdivisions.

Ward's research also attempts to show how the prevailing perspective of Texas *colonías* as crime-ridden and inhabited by illegal immigrants is as false as were perceptions of squatters in Latin America in the 1960s. Indeed, most of the inhabitants in the Texas *colonías* are legal immigrants and U.S. citizens. Ward's intent is to encourage Texas policy-makers to look at the upgrading programs for informal settlements in Latin America as a model, and to adopt a similar attitude of flexibility toward code-compliance. For example, he writes that policy-makers in Texas have much more to learn about the importance of community participation in determining reasonable standards and planning regulations. In this regard, "illegal" informality in the United States might more profitably be viewed as a transitional stage for bringing affordable housing up to higher standards over time. By focusing upon the border region and adopting a transnational approach, Ward also sheds light on the inequalities reproduced in the United States as a result of the tightening of restrictions on mobility between the United States and Mexico.

Next, in his chapter "Power, Property, and Poverty: Why De Soto's 'Mystery of Capital' Cannot Be Solved," Ray Bromley exposes the shortcomings of Hernando De Soto's recipe for altering the conditions of the poor in the Third World and former Communist countries. In a recent book entitled *The Mystery of Capital*, De Soto proposed creating "liquid capital" from "dead capital" by "legalizing" or "formalizing" "extra-legal" or "informal" assets through a system of property entitlement.[46] Such a liberalizing framework is based on what De Soto has called "deregulation, de-bureaucratization and privatization . . . [to] reduce the role of government and focus the state's energies on law and order, defense, money supply, infrastructure, and protecting private property so as to unleash the power of market forces to accelerate economic development."

Bromley bases his critique of De Soto on an examination of three main underlying metaphors: "the mushrooming extra-legal sector"; "lifting the bell jar";

and "going out into the streets to listen to the barking dogs." According to Bromley, these metaphors form a toolkit for a "why-to-do-it" book, not a "how-to-do-it" one. For example, when he talks about "listening to the barking dogs," De Soto is suggesting that courts should recognize indigenous and traditional practices in order to legalize existing property holdings. But the problem with such a metaphoric approach is that it lacks evidence and meaningful sources, Bromley writes. For example, there is no single contemporary case that illustrates that the financial costs of such legalization are worth pursuing. Bromley also claims that De Soto fails to recognize how the local actors who would be in charge of this transformation also often have vested interests in the status quo.

De Soto's views supposedly emerge from ten years of research, recently completed by his Lima-based Liberty and Democracy Institute in five cities on three continents — Lima, Manila, Port-au-Prince, Cairo, and Mexico City. Yet, despite the vagueness of the sources, Bromley reminds us that De Soto's argument is not new, and that, in fact, it dates back to early work by De Soto on Lima.[47] However, the real issue, according to Bromley, is that the views expressed in *The Mystery of Capital* both fail to anticipate cracks in the system and to accommodate change. For example, the recent scandal involving the Enron Company's collapse showed how financial and regulatory structures in the developed world (whose integrity and functioning De Soto takes for granted) may themselves have serious flaws.

The concluding chapter of the book is Ananya Roy's "Transnational Trespassings: The Geopolitics of Urban Informality." In her final essay, Roy examines how urban informality has come to be studied and even celebrated in transnational circuits of pedagogy, policy-making, and academic research. Emphasizing the double nature of representation — that it is at once a portrait and a proxy — she shows how the aesthetic framing of the informal sector silences the voices and experiences of informal dwellers and workers. Roy argues that this aestheticization of poverty is a transnational transaction, one where a First World gaze sees in Third World poverty hope, entrepreneurship, and genius. Against such forms of knowledge and representation, she calls for a critical transnationalism, "one given to learning the paradoxes and contradictions of place-based policy rather than prone to copying a litany of best practices or development miracles."

INFORMALITY: AN OLD URBAN MODE OR A "NEW" WAY OF LIFE

What is it then that makes the idea of urban informality new, relevant, or important to study at this time? The answer to this question is very complex, but it is directly or indirectly hinted at, if not answered, in the chapters of this book. At some basic level, as I have already argued, urban informality may neither be a totally new analytical concept, nor a new urban process. As the debates on the informal sector indicate, informality has been with us for a while. Perhaps it is time, then, to come to terms with the idea that formality may be the "new" mode — that it was introduced to organize urban society only in the nineteenth century. In this regard, many features of the formal/informal dichotomy may owe their origin to unresolved issues in this historical process. Indeed, these may only become evident in different countries at different times, or at different stages of development.

In *The Great Transformation*, Karl Polanyi argued that all known economic systems up to the end of the period of feudalism were based on the three principles of "reciprocity, redistribution or householding or some combination of the three."[48] These three principles were underscored by patterns of symmetry, centricity, and autarchy. Within this structure, production and distribution were motivated and disciplined informally by general rules of behavior. Economic gain was not a prominent motive in this system. However, Polanyi argued that the "new invention" of formal markets in the nineteenth century made social relations subservient to the economic system, instead of the other way around.

Around the same time, Georg Simmel has argued, the city was emerging as an environment where all human drama was conditioned by the larger social forces of capitalism. Using an agricultural migrant to illustrate the experiences of the city dweller, he noted several key characteristics of urbanism. These included the development of the "blasé" attitude I referred to earlier — what he defined as "a blurring of the senses, a filtering out of all that was loud and impinging but also irrelevant to his/her own personal needs." But successful transformation from an agricultural migrant to an urbanite also involved an ability to replace quality of work with quantity of paid labor time; to live in an impersonal environment of pure monetary exchange; to become an anonymous customer and an actor in the spectacle of mass consumption; to adopt a rational, calculating attitude fully adjusted to clock time; and to free the self from the time-bound dictates of rural society.[49]

In contrast to such notions of formal social interaction, informality should not be read as social disorganization or anarchy. As Loïc Wacquant has argued in relation to the American ghetto, disorganization itself can be an institutional form, a socio-spatial mechanism of ethno-racial closure and control.[50] Therefore, what may most be needed today in thinking about urban informality is a shift of analytical framework. Thus, the current era of liberalization and globalization should be seen as giving rise to a new form of informality — one with several key attributes. To begin, it has created a situation in which individuals may belong, at one and the same time, to both the informal and formal sector, often with more than one job in the informal sector. Next, it has allowed informal processes to spread not only among the urban poor and rural migrants, but among what were once seen as the formal lower and middle classes, including such privileged segments of the populations as state employees and professionals. Finally, informality is now manifest in new forms and new geographies, both at the rural-urban interface and in terms of developments that may serve as a principal avenue to property ownership.

Yet while I am calling for an understanding of urban informality as a "new" way of life, I also accept its limitations, and realize that critiques once targeted at Chicago School ideas may also apply here. Principally, it would be absurd to continue to believe that spatial ecology produces social processes, because we now understand the importance of the capitalist economy in defining and sustaining urban conditions. Outdated dualities, such as country/town, rural/urban, agricultural/industrial, traditional/modern, community/association, and local/cosmopolitan — together with outmoded value systems — were what fuelled Manuel Castells's critiques of the Chicago School in the first place.[51] For Castells, space has no inherent meaning, being only an expression of social forces. In other words, social relations cannot be deduced from spatial facts, and there may be only a tenuous correlation between social and spatial variables. Because there were such difficulties in uncovering any empirical criteria for the definition of the "urban," evolutionary and dualistic ideas came to dominate. However, Castells has argued that within a capitalist system (with its concomitant political base) the structuring of space always extends beyond the boundaries of the individual city, making it a dubious unit of analysis.

In this regard, we have learned many things from the contributors to this volume. We have learned that urban informality does not simply consist of the activities of the poor, or a particular status of labor, or marginality. Rather, it is an organizing logic which emerges under a paradigm of liberalization. Within this paradigm, it may only be the slogan of urban governance that is invoked by governments involved simultaneously with liberalizing and informalizing.

We have learned that the concept of the urban is highly differentiated. Thus, it may be as difficult to identify the urban through the presence of actual urban conditions as it is to identify the informal solely through the lens of liberalization. However, liberalization does offer a tool with which to understand shifts in the urban condition.

And we have learned that none of the phenomena of urban informality can be understood outside the context of globalization and liberalization. Structural adjustment once promised the utopia of the market. But, in reality, it has left entire regions of the world at the mercy of the most vicious of fears and hatreds, reinforcing rather than challenging authoritarian, fascist, and fundamentalist regimes.

Much discourse about the urban has been anchored in the discourse of modernity. Similarly, much of the discourse on urban informality must be anchored in the structure of liberalization. If informality can be seen as structured through "extra-legal" systems of regulation, then so can these new or newly noticed processes of medieval modernity be seen as modes of governance.[52] They may even involve the "quiet encroachment of the ordinary."[53] Despite the Internet and the spread of information technology, patterns of urban behavior and exchange at the beginning of the twenty-first century in many ways resemble those common during the Middle Ages. Such a mode of urbanism is made of segregated enclaves, and is dominated by militarization, religious ideologies, and the maintenance of political structures that govern through patronage, division, and economic oppression.

We have finally learned that urban informality cannot be disentangled from geography, or from certain area-studies discourses. In other words, as the examination of the three regions that dominate discussion here has illustrated, we cannot talk about urban informality without considering the more targeted concerns of area studies. Only then can we truly start to unpack urban informality not only as a political economy but also as a way of life.

NOTES

1. L. Wirth, "Urbanism as a Way of Life," *American Journal of Sociology* 44, no. 1 (July 1938), 1.

2. Ibid., 4.

3. Ibid., 10.

4. G. Simmel, "The Metropolis and Mental Life," in D. Levine, ed., *On Individuality and Social Forms* (Chicago: University of Chicago Press, 1971), 329–30.

5. Wirth, "Urbanism as a Way of Life," 18–19.

6. A. Vasishth and D. Sloane, "Returning to Ecology: An Ecosystem Approach to Understanding the City," in M. Dear, ed., *From Chicago to L.A.* (Thousand Oaks, Calif.: Sage Publications, 2002), 350.

7. Charles Abrams, *Man's Struggle for Shelter in an Urbanizing World* (Cambridge, Mass.: MIT Press, 1964).

8. Simmel, "The Metropolis and Mental Life," 324–39.

9. As referred to in M. Gottdiener, *The New Urban Sociology* (New York: McGraw-Hill, 1994).

10. Simmel, "The Metropolis and Mental Life."

11. O. Lewis, *Five Families: Mexican Case Studies in the Culture of Poverty* (New York: Basic Books, 1959); *The Children of Sanchez: Autobiography of a Mexican Family* (New York: Random House, 1961); and *La Vida: A Puerto Rican Family in the Culture of Poverty* (New York: Random House, 1966).

12. See, for example, J. Perlman, *The Myth of Marginality: Urban Poverty and Politics in Rio de Janeiro* (Berkeley: University of California Press, 1976); and M. Castells, *The City and the Grassroots: A Cross-Cultural Theory of Urban Social Movements* (Berkeley: University of California Press, 1983).

13. A. Bayat, "From 'Dangerous Classes' to 'Quiet Rebels': Politics of the Urban Subaltern in the Global South," *International Sociology* 15, no. 3 (September 2000), 539.

14. Castells, *The City and the Grassroots*.

15. Bayat, "From 'Dangerous Classes' to 'Quiet Rebels,'" 534.

16. The term "urban informality" first appeared in Spanish (*"informalidad urbana"*), specifically in Juan Pablo Pérez Sáinz's work in the late 1980s. See R. Menjivar and J.P. Pérez Sáinz, *Informalidad urbana en Centroamerica: evidencias e interrogantes* (Guatemala: FLAC-SO-Guatemala, Fundacion Fiedrich Ebert, 1989). Pérez Sáinz used the term to describe the informal economy, with particular emphasis on forms of employment. To date, however, few English-language authors have invoked the term in their discussions of the informal sector and informal settlements. Nevertheless, in the context of this project, the term "urban informality" is used to denote social and economic processes that shape, or are manifest in, the urban built environment.

17. W.A. Lewis, "Economic Development with Unlimited Supplies of Labour," *Manchester School* 22, no. 2 (May 1954), 139–91.

18. L.G. Reynolds, "Economic Development with Surplus Labor: Some Complications," *Oxford Economic Papers* 21, no. 1 (March 1969), 91.

19. C.O.N. Moser, "Informal Sector or Petty Commodity Production: Dualism or Dependence in Urban Development?" *World Development* 6 (1978), 1051.

20. K. Hart, "Informal Income Opportunities and Urban Employment in Ghana," *Modern African Studies* 11, no. 1 (March 1973), 61–89.

21. Ibid., 68.

22. D. Mazumdar, "The Urban Informal Sector," *World Development* 4, no. 8 (1976), 655–79.

23. *Employment, Incomes and Equality: A Strategy for Increasing Productive Employment in Kenya* (Geneva: International Labour Office, 1972), 5.

24. Ibid., 6.

25. R. Bromley, "Introduction — The Informal Sector: Why is it Worth Discussing?" *World Development* 6 (1978), 1036.

26. A. Portes and R. Schauffler, "The Informal Economy in Latin America: Definition, Measurement, and Policies," Working Paper #5, Program in Comparative and International Development, Johns Hopkins University, December 1992.

27. C.A. Rakowski, "The Informal Sector Debate, Part 2: 1984–1993," in Rakowski, ed., *Contrapunto: The Informal Sector Debate in Latin America* (Albany: State University of New York Press, 1994), 31–50.

28. S. Annis and J.R. Franks, "The Idea, Ideology and Economics of the Informal Sector: The Case of Peru," *Grassroots Development* 13, no. 1 (1989), 10.

29. Rakowski, "The Informal Sector Debate," 38.

30. See, for example, A. Portes and S. Sassen-Koob, "Making it Underground: Comparative Materials on the Informal Sector in Western Market Economies," *American Journal of Sociology* 93 (1987), 30–61; and M. Castells and A. Portes, "World Underneath: The Origins, Dynamics, and Effects of the Informal Economy," in Portes, Castells, and L.A. Benton, eds., *The Informal Economy: Studies in Advanced and Less Developed Countries*

(Baltimore: The Johns Hopkins University Press, 1989), 11–37.

31. In "The Informal Sector Debate," Rakowski analyzed these issues according to the work of several scholars. In addition to Portes and Sassen-Koob, "Making it Underground"; and Castells and Portes, "World Underneath"; this included L.R. Peattie, "Real-World Economics," *Hemisphere* (Fall 1990), 32–34.

32. Rakowski's specific reference was to Portes, Castells and Benton, eds., *The Informal Economy*, 302–3.

33. Rakowski's specific reference was to Bryan Roberts, "Introducción," in J.P. Pérez Sáinz and R.M. Larín, eds., *Informalidad Urbana en Centroamérica: Entre la acumulación y la subsistencia* (San José, Costa Rica: Editorial Nueva Sociedad, 1991), 13–20.

34. Annis and Franks, "The Idea, Ideology and Economics of the Informal Sector," 10.

35. Rakowski "The Informal Sector Debate," 38.

36. Ibid., 40.

37. H. De Soto, *The Other Path: The Invisible Revolution in the Third World* (New York: Harper & Row, 1989), 243.

38. R. Bromley, "A New Path to Development? The Significance and Impact of Hernando de Soto's Ideas on Underdevelopment, Production, and Reproduction," *Economic Geography* 66 (1990), 328; and J. Main, "An Interview with Hernando de Soto," and "The Informal Route to Prosperity," *International Health and Development* 1, no. 1 (1989), 10–17.

39. Rakowski, "The Informal Sector Debate," 43.

40. M. Watts, "Development II: The Privatization of Everything?" *Progress in Human Geography* 18, no. 3 (1994), 371–84.

41. N. AlSayyad, "Squatting and Culture: A Comparative Analysis of Informal Developments in Latin America and the Middle East," *Habitat International* 17, no. 1 (1993), 33–44.

42. For example, A. Bayat, *Street Politics: Poor People's Movements in Iran* (New York: Columbia University Press, 1997).

43. Bayat, "From 'Dangerous Classes' to 'Quiet Rebels'," 548.

44. A. Richards and J. Waterbury, *A Political Economy of the Middle East: State, Class, and Economic Development* (Boulder: Westview Press, 1990).

45. See, for example, A. Roy, *City Requiem, Calcutta: Gender and the Politics of Poverty* (Minneapolis: University of Minnesota Press, 2003).

46. H. De Soto, *The Mystery of Capital* (New York: Basic Books, 2000).

47. De Soto, *The Other Path*, 47–55.

48. K. Polanyi, *The Great Transformation* (Boston: Beacon Press, 1957).

49. As cited in Gottdiener, *The New Urban Sociology*, 103–5.

50. L.J.D. Wacquant, "Three Pernicious Premises in the Study of the American Ghetto," *International Journal of Urban and Regional Research* 21, no. 2 (1997), 341–53.

51. M. Castells, *The Urban Question: A Marxist Approach* (Cambridge, Mass.: MIT Press, 1977).

52. Medieval modernity is a concept we have been developing for some time. It is expounded by Ananya Roy in "Marketized? Feminized? Medieval? Urban Governance in an Era of Liberalization," in J.S. Tulchin, D.H. Varat, and B.A. Ruble, eds., *Democratic Governance and Urban Sustainability* (Washington, D.C.: Woodrow Wilson International Center for Scholars, 2002), 39.

53. Ibid, 39.

PART I

LIBERALIZATION, GLOBALIZATION, AND URBAN INFORMALITY

2

Love in the Time of Enhanced Capital Flows: Reflections on the Links between Liberalization and Informality

Alan Gilbert

My title both applauds Latin American literature and constitutes an up-front admission about my difficulty in writing this chapter.[1] There is a very good reason why "magical realism" began in Latin America. In this fascinating region it has seldom been easy to distinguish fact from fiction. If magical realism had to begin anywhere, there was nowhere more obvious than Cuba before Castro.[2] And if it had to flourish, there was nowhere more obvious than coastal Colombia.[3]

In this globalized, postmodern world — and increasingly in our meandering academic discourse — life is how it is portrayed, rather than how it is. Although I usually try to maintain the belief that it is still possible to view things objectively, I feel that I am in an increasing minority. So let me temporarily join the majority and admit freely that reality is often very difficult to comprehend. There are too many ways of viewing highly complex subject matter. Perhaps my recent sojourn in Washington, D.C., compounded this feeling. Was not the "electile dysfunction" of the U.S. election not straight out of the pages of magical realism? Surely, Gabriel García Márquez must have invented "hanging" or "pregnant" chads? Or was it that Florida has just been "polluted" by too many Latin Americans and their bad, undemocratic ways? Perhaps it just shows that the whole world is so unreal it is difficult to write objectively about anything.

WHAT IS LIBERALIZATION?

It is fairly easy to define certain elements of what is meant by liberalization. In economic terms, liberalization entails reducing controls on imports, capital, and foreign exchange to allow more goods, services, and money to flow across national borders. (Liberalization should also encourage the flow of labor, but that is a subject usually left off international negotiating tables, even if the flood of illegal migration arguably constitutes liberalization through the back door.) Liberalization also embraces political and social change, although this is altogether more complicated to define. And certainly, economic liberalization is supposed to lead to democratization — although China poses some interesting questions in that regard.[4]

In Latin America it is probably true that democracy is on the rise. Certainly, there are fewer military regimes in power, even though there are renewed signs of old-fashioned populism in Venezuela. Liberalization has certainly changed the role of the state — the drive for competitiveness having cut fiscal deficits, reduced government expenditure, decentralized authority, and "sold off the family silver" (as former British Prime Minister Harold Macmillan once so wonderfully described privatization). But few countries have fully embraced political democracy. Thus, there are still few blacks or Indians in national parliaments, rules and regulations are still far too complicated, and governments still intervene in all kinds of areas where their intervention does little good. Political liberalization means a great deal more than voting every few years. But in saying how much more is required for a country to be truly democratic, one soon gets into difficult areas.

If political liberalization is difficult to define, social liberalization is a total minefield. Presumably, liberalization makes people freer. But as experience in the former Soviet Union shows, that does not necessarily help families eat properly or find work. In Latin America there is more autonomy for civil society, and NGOs are flourishing. But some of that autonomy serves only to fill the gap left by the demise of the fledgling welfare state. Perhaps social liberalization means watching more episodes of *Friends* or more Hollywood blockbusters on imported TV sets. Perhaps it means Latin American women are freer than they once were — freer at least to go to work and then do the washing up.

Given these problems of definition and the limited space available here, I have decided to limit my efforts to the theme of economic liberalization. Unfortunately, even this narrower scope presents difficulties, because economic liberalization is not just about what happens at the international border. In order to participate fully in the new world economy, national economies have to be able to compete. They need to attract foreign capital and export new kinds of products. And in order to do this, they need to modernize their infrastructure, communications systems, and ways of conducting economic life. They certainly need to reform the way their governments operate.

In Latin America, efforts to do all this have been labeled the New Economic Model (NEM).[5] The NEM has brought a new macroeconomic approach based on greater reliance on markets. This brushed-down and freshened-up version of free-market orthodoxy has sought to homogenize economic policy across the globe. It means cutting the limbs off that old dinosaur the labor movement, pensioning off state social security systems, and privatizing health, education, and anything that moves. It means that old-fashioned advocates of "dependency theory" may become presidents of Brazil and disown the jottings of their misspent sociological youth. It means that democratic governments may take over from unpopular military regimes and continue with very similar policies. It means that Social Democratic governments today are further to the ideological right than their Conservative predecessors were two or three decades ago.

But is the New Economic Model just rhetoric? For if it is relatively easy to see in which direction the model points, it is much more difficult to observe its route on the ground. Of course, there are plenty of signs of change in Latin America, but not consistent change.[6] There is plenty of privatization in Chile and Mexico, but it is much less apparent in Colombia or Venezuela. Every government speaks responsibly about its expenditure, but many still manage to run large budget deficits. And even if governments try to apply the new orthodoxy, many are unable to do so.

Finally, even when politics does not get in the way, informal liberalization does. Thus, in Colombia, economically conservative governments have tried to pretend that the country depends little on drugs and suffers from only a limited amount of corruption. Colombian politicians have pretended that the guerrillas lack power, and that there is no link between the army and the paramilitaries. Reality has now brought all those nonexistent forces together to produce a potent blend of anarchic liberalization.

To understand economic liberalization requires much more than understanding the rhetoric of government economists, impressive though their logic often is. It is necessary to see what is happening on the ground, and whether "progress" is consistent, or whether it is constantly interrupted by reality. A Colombian writer long ago entitled his book *Colombia: país formal y país real*.[7] Anticipating magical realism, enhanced capital flows, and the drug economy by some years, he knew an appropriate title when he saw one.

WHAT IS INFORMALITY AND INFORMALIZATION?

Defining informality either precisely or meaningfully is equally difficult. No doubt, it can be accepted that large numbers of Latin Americans work, live, and play in the "informal sector," at least for a considerable part of the time. In the workplace, this means that many activities do not fit into the formal sector of government employment, most kinds of white-collar work, and much of what goes on in a decent-sized factory. Those left out of the world of formality typically lack pension rights, social security cover, work contracts, and environmental safety. Meanwhile, at home, informality manifests itself in the self-help construction that has produced most Latin American homes.[8] Informality is the process whereby people engage in painstaking efforts to construct dwellings often years before services reach them.

But if it is perfectly obvious that informality exists and dominates most people's lives in most of Latin America, that does not make it easy to pigeon-hole people into an adequate definition of the "informal sector." The following are among the obvious problems of definition.

While it is usually possible to define informal activity, it is much less easy to categorize the people involved in such activity. Many people do not work wholly in either the formal or the informal sector; rather they switch between them over time, even during the working week. Thus, the construction worker at a formal building company will do freelance work in his spare time.

Many workers employed by formal enterprises have contracts which exclude them from many of the privileges of formality. As casualization proceeds in the labor market, more and more formal workers are actually informal workers; they are subcontractors or they are subcontracted.

Many workers have never been employed by the enterprise that ultimately provides their income. Street traders and garbage pickers are independent casual workers selling and collecting items that have been produced by formal enterprises, or which will be used in the production of eminently formal goods.[9] Perhaps the ultimate manifestation of this link between the "independent" and the formal sector are the Colombian street sellers who hawk the lottery tickets that produce much of the income for the country's departmental governments.

Many formal-sector workers do not live in formal-sector housing. Indeed, self-help housing accommodates a goodly proportion of people who work in the formal sector. How can we accurately classify the woman who works in a government office by day, but who lives in an illegal subdivision — who works in the formal sector for eight hours, but lives in the informal for sixteen? And what happens when the government legalizes her home and provides it with water? Does she then get put wholly in the formal sector — assuming, of course, that she has not been laid off in the meantime due to budget cuts?

Any definition of the informal sector is further complicated by the fact that few families contain workers employed wholly by one sector or the other. Thus, how do we define the family that includes a husband who is contracted legally by a large manufacturing company, and a wife who is employed as a domestic servant? Even if it were easy to classify individuals, families and households defy categorization.

Finally, what about those people who deal with informal people in the workplace, on their way to work, or at home? How formal is the business manager who is subcontracting casual labor? How formal is the government worker traveling to work on an informal minibus? How formal is the elite household that employs domestic workers without issuing formal contracts or providing social security benefits?

In sum, defining the informal sector is extremely difficult and can only be done in terms of its contraposition with respect to the formal sector. Any final categorization will also surely be a "rag bag" grouping with little homogeneity.[10] Certainly, there is little purpose to defining the informal sector for policy reasons.[11]

Nonetheless, if we are to move beyond the obvious statement that globalization creates new forms of informality and reconstitutes old forms of formality and informality, we need a definition of informality. If we are to say whether informalization is occurring or not, we have to be able to establish how it affects people's lives and whether it affects more people now than it used to. We need some numbers if we are to compare the impact of the informal sector today with its impact ten, twenty, or thirty years ago. If we lack the numbers, we cannot say whether or not informalization is actually occurring. But without a definition of informality we cannot estimate the numbers.

Of course, even if we could calculate those numbers, we would still have difficulty making sense of the changes over time, let alone the causality. A few examples of the problems will suffice.

First, is the informality of yesteryear the same as the informality of today? An informal worker in the past was automatically excluded from any opportunity of obtaining pension rights. Today it is possible, albeit uncommon, for independent workers to open a pension plan in one of the new privatized pension funds. If the world of work is becoming less formal, are the difficulties of being informal less than they once were? In addition, technology and economic growth are creating new opportunities for informal-sector work. Thus, the invention and widespread use of the car has provided many new opportunities for informal-sector work: driving, repairing, cleaning, protecting — and, increasingly, stealing.

Second, how do we evaluate two different trends with regard to informalization? One is that a higher proportion of people live and work in the informal sector, however constituted; the other is that the same proportion of people live and work in the informal sector for more of the time. If both processes are moving in the same direction, fine. But what if they are not? The relationships may best be illustrated in the form of a table (see FIGURE 2.1).

TIME	PERCENTAGE OF PEOPLE WORKING FULL-TIME IN THE INFORMAL SECTOR AND LIVING IN THE INFORMAL SECTOR	PERCENTAGE OF PEOPLE'S TIME SPENT INVOLVED IN THE INFORMAL SECTOR
Beginning	A	X
End	B	Y

When B is larger than A, and Y is larger than X, informalization is occurring.
When B is smaller than A, and Y is larger than X, formalization is occurring.
But if B is larger than A, and Y is smaller than X, or if B is smaller than A, and Y is larger than X, both formalization and informalization are occurring.

Figure 2.1. What is informalization?

Fortunately, since I have put on temporary hold my attempt to come to an "objective" conclusion, I can duck this issue. Or perhaps in the light of the rest of this chapter, is there any point in measuring the growth or decline of informality at all?

IS LIBERALIZATION GOOD FOR YOU?

We are told that economic liberalization is a good thing because it encourages trade. More trade is good because it reduces the cost of what we consume and increases productivity. Higher productivity produces economic growth. Economic growth is good because it creates jobs and higher incomes and gives us more time to relax. Economic growth is also good because it produces healthier societies—both in the physical sense and in the sense that we live in more democratic and participative communities.

Such thinking has become conventional wisdom because some of the forecasts have come true, at least in many places. Most countries are benefiting from positive economic growth rates for much of the time. The number of dictatorships and military regimes has diminished across the globe. It is probably true that greater world trade and interdependence have increased the likelihood that world peace will hold — by which I mean that World War III is unlikely to break out. It is also likely that a majority of the world's population is better off than it was. And, absolutely critically, if that segment of the world's population that is actually taken seriously — those who live in the United States, Western Europe, and the Far East — are the ones who have benefited most from economic liberalization, it must be true, mustn't it?

But the new orthodoxy has also become so firmly established because the voices hostile to it lack a feasible alternative. Defenders of socialist alternatives are constantly reminded of the past failings, real and imagined, of communism. Advocates of welfare states are told to recall the public-sector dinosaurs that mismanaged everything from government budgets to railway companies — and that still produce schools that do not teach their students, and operate modern hospitals that infect patients with new diseases. It is the lack of defensible past alternative models, and (with the demise of communist states) the lack of any obvious alternative model, that gives greater intellectual strength to the new orthodoxy.

Belief in the benefits of free trade is also sustained by outbreaks of myopia and amnesia. Too many economists seem not to have noticed that the new orthodoxy is failing to produce the goods in vast regions of the globe. Economic instability is dismissed as a temporary inconvenience, usually caused by bad domestic policy rather than a structural problem. Rising unemployment is not a structural feature of the new model, but is caused by the failure of local governments to reform their labor legislation. Amnesia is rampant, with everyone seemingly having forgotten the horrors of the 1930s, when the state was a very insignificant little creature.

What is also worrying is that the old assumptions that underlay modernization theory no longer seem to fit the new orthodoxy. In the past, economic growth was justified because it brought benefits to everyone. Not only that, but it brought equilibrating forces that would remove sickness, illiteracy, and inequality. Simon Kuznets's Nobel Prize for Economics was his reward for showing that economic growth made a better world for everyone.

Unfortunately, the results of the new orthodoxy in practice seem to be producing the opposite of what the advocates of modernization anticipated. Let me touch on a few negative indicators.

First, modernizers have long believed that economic growth produces greater equality both because of market forces and because of increasing government intervention.[12] Surely, no one observing income trends in any country in the world today can be under any illusion that the new orthodoxy is generating equality anywhere.[13] There is certainly not much evidence from Latin America that things are getting better. According to Londoño and Székely,

> aggregate inequality reduced significantly during the 1970s, deteriorated
> sharply during the 1980s, and has remained around the level registered in
> 1990 during the present decade. The reason why there has not been signifi-
> cant improvement during the present decade is that the individuals located at
> the lower tail of the distribution do not seem to have benefited from growth
> to the same extent as other sectors of the population.[14]

This in a continent with probably the highest level of income inequality in the world! Even the World Bank and the multilateral development banks now accept that some changes have to be made in the model, and they are now heavily committed to poverty alleviation and social safety nets.[15]

Second, free trade is meant to stimulate economic growth. In practice, that idea does seem to be valid at a global scale; at the very least there is an apparently positive correlation. But free trade is not producing growth everywhere, and most of Africa is certainly not benefiting very much. Even within countries that are experiencing sustained periods of growth, particular areas seem to get left out. The lesson appears to be that free trade does stimulate economic growth, but only in those areas that are able to compete either globally or nationally. Those that are uncompetitive lose out. The problems of Chiapas, Mexico, neatly sum up the dilemma of the unsuccessful region in an era of free trade.

Third, do enhanced capital flows bring more jobs? Foreign direct investment is able to generate employment and also bring in the new technology that can cut the cost of telephones and reduce production costs. When foreign capital sets up new factories, hotels, or banks, it does generate more work. The manufacturing plants along the northern border of Mexico prove beyond doubt that FDI can generate work; increased agricultural export production in Chile has also increased employment. On the other hand, some forms of foreign investment produce few jobs because of the capital-intensive technology employed. And sometimes workers are displaced when labor-saving technologies are brought into existing workplaces.

Finally, perhaps the greatest weakness of the new model is that it seems to be increasing the risk of economic instability across the globe rather than reducing it. One of the major problems with the new world economy is the amount of highly mobile capital that is invested in local stocks or bonds. Such investments move wherever the return is highest. When it pours into a potentially profitable country it forces the exchange rate upward and makes exporting more difficult. But the real problem comes when it suddenly pours out. This can occur when countries fail the latest Standard and Poors test of economic competitiveness, or even because of events occurring outside the country. Both the Tequila Effect that spread across the rest of Latin America from Mexico in 1994 and the Asian Flu that hit Brazil in 1998 show how suddenly, and often unfairly, money managers in London, New York, and Tokyo can pull the plug on even the comparatively innocent.[16] Recent events in Argentina may or may not bring about similar effects.

The world economy has always been less than stable, but currently the sheer amount of capital that can be transferred at the flick of a switch suggests that it is becoming less stable than ever. And if that were not bad enough, the speed of technological change is much faster today. In the past, technology did not change all that much over a thirty-year period. Today, in the fields of electronics, computing, and bioengineering, it can change in five years. Thus, plants set up in one place are in constant risk of being outmoded. Enhanced capital flows based on rapidly changing technology do not guarantee stability. Keynesian thought combined with the establishment of the Bretton Woods institutions were meant to remedy economic instability at a world scale, but it is clear that they cannot cope with the increased quantities of capital moving around the globe.

In sum, economic liberalization *can* be good for you, but for far too many it may not be. Countries and regions can increase their chances of doing well in the new game. But ultimately the power of international capital and the speed of technological change mean that much depends on who you are, where you live, and whether the sun is shining today.

IS INFORMALIZATION GOOD FOR YOU?

I have already discussed the problems of defining the informal sector, but I have so far avoided the ideological overtones of the informal-sector debate.[17] Is an informal-sector worker an exploited pawn of the capitalist system, or the brave entrepreneur of the Peruvian *barriadas*?[18] If he or she is the former, then the fault lies with capitalism. If he or she is the latter, the fault lies with the mercantilist state and with the government's failure to legalize their businesses or give the poor title deeds to their homes.[19]

Most governments have been in favor of integrating the "marginal," "informal," call-it-what-you-will sector into mainstream society. Only a few on the far left have been in favor of more informalization as a way of protecting the poor from the cause of their poverty — capitalism. Thus, the ideological right praises the informal sector, but is intent on making it formal by removing most of the arbitrary state rules that have forced these brave entrepreneurs into informality. And most on the ideological left want to help informal people become more formal by giving them greater security in the workplace and at home. On this issue, the ideological divide is currently more about the role of government and the best means of including these people than about whether they should be included.

But in the real world of everyday suffering, greater informality does not always bring greater problems. Let me briefly provide three examples where informality does not necessarily make life worse.

First, for those without work, the formal response is unemployment. When the state pays unemployment benefits that formality has its compensations. But in Latin America unemployment benefits are almost never paid. As such, finding a temporary job in the informal sector represents a major improvement that millions have pursued over the years. Informal work may often be the only way to survive.

Second, during a period of rapid inflation formal-sector wages tend to fall very rapidly. By contrast, some in the informal sector can maintain the value of their incomes by raising the prices of their goods and services. For this reason, many formal-sector workers have long supplemented their incomes by taking on informal second jobs as taxi drivers or traders.

Third, the contribution that self-help housing has made to improving housing conditions in Latin America demonstrates that informalization is not always a problematic development. Millions would be living in far worse housing were it not for that informality.

Perhaps, therefore, whether Latin Americans work and live in formal or informal conditions is irrelevant in determining their standard of living. What is critical is not whether they have a work contract or a title deed to their home, but whether their living conditions are improving. Frequently, informalization is a sign that things are getting worse. And when we can demonstrate that wages are falling and housing quality is declining within the informal sector, then we should decry the processes that are producing more informality. But when conditions within the informal sector seem to be improving, then whether the sector is growing or not matters little. If de Soto's entrepreneurs are driving their taxis around, feeling free, and earning a decent living, fine. If, on the other hand, mothers and children are begging on the streets, then clearly informalization is a major cause for concern.

Experience in Britain and the United States seems to underline this point. Both economies are experiencing a strong degree of informalization through casualization of the labor force. The changing standards of corporate behavior mean that many more people work in the "informal" sector now, for at least part of the time. Specifically, subcontracting became much more commonplace, and perhaps earned its fifteen minutes of fame, when Big Blue announced it had cut its permanent staff by three-quarters in the 1980s. Today more people make some of their income in the "black" economy than in the days when most had full-time jobs in the formal sector. There are surely more domestics, au pairs, pizza delivery boys, and window cleaners employed than has been the case for one hundred years. Most are only part-time members of the black economy. But, in the basement, there are also many full-time participants, as the beggars and street-dwellers of London and Washington testify.

If in the developed world all of us are spending more of our time in the informal sector than we once did (and are certainly more dependent on informal processes to get through our lives), are we better or worse off for that development? The case can only be demonstrated by producing a balance sheet of pluses and minuses. The point is that informalization is not in itself a problem so much as what it means for our lives. The extremes are clear: it is bad if the informal sector consists of more and more street-dwellers; it is good if it consists of more and more people who are their own bosses and are making out just fine.

LINKS BETWEEN LIBERALIZATION AND THE INFORMAL SECTOR IN LATIN AMERICA

How does current economic thinking view the links between liberalization and the informal sector, and what actually happens in practice? The direction of causality is relatively unproblematic. Although some elements of informalization may influence the process of liberalization, most of the causes begin with liberalization. However, deciphering the precise effects of liberalization on informality is much less easy, and is complicated by at least three major issues.

First, liberalization on the ground is not like the liberalization advertised in the government plan. A particular country may free up its capital controls but only some of its trade controls, or it may introduce reforms to its labor regulations without establishing an effective savings system. In short, it is difficult to calculate precisely how much economic liberalization has actually occurred.

Second, because we cannot define precisely what the informal sector contains, it is difficult to calculate the extent of informalization. As such, we are trying to evaluate the effects of a highly inconsistent and difficult-to-measure process called liberalization on a second highly inconsistent and difficult-to-measure process called informalization. Even if we were certain what either term really meant, would it be possible to link the two in terms of causality? If the informal sector grew both during the days of import-substituting industrialization and enhanced capital flows, are we not going to have problems defining cause from effect?

Finally, both the process and effects of liberalization are highly localized. Liberalization within a Latin American economy will produce very different results in different cities and regions. Not only that, but the effects on different social classes and groups within cities and regions will vary greatly.[20] As such, the level of analysis is critical.

Despite these probably insurmountable problems, I will attempt in the following sections to examine first, what liberalization intends to achieve; second, whether liberalization has actually taken place; and, third, what effect it has had on the informal sector in Latin America. As I will attempt to show, it is very difficult to demonstrate clearly what is happening on the ground.

THE EFFECTS OF TRADE LIBERALIZATION ON INFORMALITY — EXPORTS

In crude terms, those who approve of liberalization argue that greater integration in the world economy has brought faster growth and major benefits in terms of employment creation in Latin America.[21] Critics of liberalization argue that greater exposure to international markets has led to higher unemployment, the casualization of labor markets, economic instability, greater inequality, and deteriorating living conditions for a large number of people.[22]

In principle, free trade increases both the volume and variety of exports. More exports increase the amount of economic activity, which in turn cuts unemployment and the amount of informal-sector work. A counter argument is that exporting helps the first two but not the last. If the process of developing competitive exports requires more subcontracting and more informal kinds of work, then more export activity may produce more kinds of informal work. What has happened in practice?

First, it is by no means certain that export production has increased significantly in most Latin American countries. If we measure the change in export production in terms of its impact on the economy — that is, the changing contribution of exports to gross domestic product (GDP) — the results for the region as a whole are not all that impressive. Thus, while the accompanying table shows that the overall contribution of exports almost doubled between 1965 and 1999, what is fascinating is that so little changed after 1980, the period of structural adjustment and introduction of the New Economic Model (see FIGURE 2.2). Most of the changes seem to have occurred during the final stages of the period of import substitution! Considering the evidence of the region's largest seven countries also shows considerable variation. Two countries, Chile and Mexico, stand out as export "success" stories; Colombia is a partial success; and Argentina, Brazil, Peru, and Venezuela might be described as failures.

Exports as a Percent of GDP					
COUNTRY	1965	1980	1983	1990	1999
Argentina	8	5	13	10	10
Brazil	8	9	8	8	10
Chile	14	23	24	35	27
Colombia	11	16	10	20	18
Mexico	8	11	20	19	31
Peru	16	22	21	12	14
Venezuela	26	29	26	39	21
Latin America	9	13	na	14	16

Figure 2.2. Latin America: export performance of selected countries, 1965–1999.
Source: World Bank, World Development Report (New York: Oxford University Press, various years).

Of course, part of the problem with measuring exports as a proportion of GDP is that a number of variables are involved. These variables can change in ways that conceal the real changes occurring in the economy. For example, the export share will rise if the national economy shrinks during a period of recession, as most Latin American economies did during the 1980s. Similarly, the share can rise if the terms of trade increase in favor of the exporter; thus, the value of exports rises even though nothing structural has happened at all. These two kinds of change appear to have dominated what has occurred in both Peru and Venezuela, and to a lesser extent Brazil and Mexico. Specifically, changes in the world price of petroleum have been very important in Mexico and Venezuela, and the price of copper in the case of Chile. Nevertheless, I would defend use of this indicator in the sense that if the New Economic Model is working as it is supposed to, then exports should rise as a proportion of GDP. The figures suggest that it seems to have worked in only a limited number of countries.

What has changed more consistently is the form of export production. Today, a smaller share of foreign earnings is generated by primary products, and much more is generated by manufactured exports — although the accompanying table exaggerates the extent of change, insofar as the terms of trade have shifted fairly consistently against primary exports and in favor of manufactures (see FIGURE 2.3). Nevertheless, Latin America has shifted from an almost total dependence on primary products to a position where most countries have become significant exporters of manufactures. For the region as a whole, the table shows how the share of manufactures in total merchandise exports increased from 20 percent in 1980 to 49 percent in 1998. Every one of the large countries shifted its export structure in a similar direction, although the extent of change varied considerably. For example, Chile and Venezuela still concentrate on primary exports, whereas Mexico and Brazil now produce large quantities of manufactured exports. The fact that the region's major success story, Chile, produces so few manufactures should be a salutary lesson for current orthodoxy. Clearly, liberalization as measured in terms of export production has had a very mixed impact in Latin America.

| Manufactures as a Percent of Total Merchandise Exports | | | |
COUNTRY	1965	1980	1990	1998
Argentina	6	23	29	35
Brazil	8	39	52	55
Chile	4	10	11	17
Colombia	7	20	25	32
Jamaica	31	63	69	70
Mexico	16	12	43	85
Peru	1	18	18	24
Venezuela	2	2	10	19
Latin America	8	20	34	49

Figure 2.3. Development of manufacturing exports, 1965–1998.
Source: World Bank, World Development Report 1982 (New York: Oxford University Press, 1982); and World Bank, World Development Report 2000 (New York: Oxford University Press, 2000).

Where export earnings have increased, the number of jobs generated directly has usually risen. The exception is when production levels remain the same (only the price has risen), or when highly intensive oil or petrochemical exports are involved and capital-intensive technology has little effect on employment. In Chile the increase in agricultural exports has certainly generated a lot of jobs, and in Mexico manufacturing has had a similar result. In the latter case the growth of jobs in the *maquila* plants in the north of the country has been impressive. In 1976 the *maquiladoras* employed 75,000 people; in 2000 more than 1.3 million (INEGI). Insofar as new jobs have been created in factories or on large farms, fewer people should be reliant on work in the informal sector (more on this below).

The example of Mexico also reveals another component of change: the location of export-generated employment. In Mexico, the growth of manufacturing exports has given a strong boost only to those urban areas located close to the U.S. border. Since most of the manufacturing growth has been confined to *maquiladoras*, the traditional manufacturing centers of inland Mexico have benefited little from the shift. Indeed, when linked to the decline in manufacturing jobs in Mexico City, brought about by domestic recession and reduced import controls, liberalization has created a profound geographical shift in the Mexican labor market. The accompanying table shows that Mexico City, so dominant during the days of import-substituting industrialization, lost much of that dominance in the 1980s and 1990s (see FIGURE 2.4). In Chile, however, the geographical impact of export production has been very different. There, the expansion of agricultural exports has given a strong stimulus to the rural areas — although it also seems to have given something of a boost to Santiago.[23] In Brazil a further pattern has emerged; most of the new manufactures have been produced in the state of São Paulo, although again not in the state's capital city.[24] Rio de Janeiro and many other Brazilian cities have benefited little.

How has greater export production, where it has occurred, affected the nature of employment? Here the evidence is contested. At one level it must have

YEAR	MEXICO (000s)	MEXICO CITY (000s)	% OF NATIONAL TOTAL
1930	285	54	19.0
1940	363	89	24.6
1950	626	157	25.0
1960	885	407	46.0
1970	1,596	658	41.2
1980	2,139	1,059	49.5
1985	2,509	845	33.6
1988	2,595	756	28.8
1994	3,341	822	24.6

Figure 2.4. Concentration of industrial employment in Mexico City, 1940–1994.
Source: G. Garza, et al., eds., Atlas de la Ciudad de México (Departamento del Distrito Federal y El Colegio de México, 1987), 100; A. Rowland and P. Gordon, "Mexico City: No Longer a Leviathan?" in A. Gilbert, ed., The Mega-city in Latin America (Tokyo: United Nations University Press, 1996), 173–202; B. Rodríguez and M. Cota Yáñez, "Evolución Interna de las Principales Zonas Metropolitanas de México," Comercio Exterior 49 (1999), 690–95; and D. Hiernaux, "Los Frutos Amargos de la Globalización: Expansion y Reestrucuración Metropolitana de la Ciudad de México," Revista EURE 25 (1999), 76, 57–78.

reduced the amount of informal work by creating new opportunities in formal enterprises. But insofar as many of the new opportunities generated have been for women, it may simply have encouraged women's labor participation to rise.[25] If that should be the case, then the number of informal-sector workers will have remained constant. In either case, the number of workers employed by formal enterprises will have risen only in the export zones.

However, the evidence is that many of the jobs created by formal enterprises are less than formal. Export production seems often to have created a large number of unskilled low-paid jobs, on short-term contracts, in nonunionized companies.[26] But although some of the new forms of employment are clearly exploitative, it is uncertain whether working conditions are worse than they were in older manifestations of the informal sector. Certainly, workers seem to have voted with their feet by taking advantage of the new opportunities. And there are those who argue that the workers benefit from the new opportunities offered by export production, even when working conditions are far from satisfactory. It is said that women gain from the independence that new work opportunities offer them by no longer being incarcerated at home.[27] Even the employment generated in the wholly informal export sector of drugs may well have raised living standards among the peasantry and among those involved in trafficking. For that reason, opposition to Plan Colombia does not come only from the guerrilla movements in Colombia. Of course, there is a Catch 22 in this particular case: if incomes have risen as a result of exporting coca and cocaine, so too has insecurity — not only of employment but also in terms of life expectancy.

THE EFFECTS OF TRADE LIBERALIZATION ON INFORMALITY — IMPORTS

Trade liberalization has been a central component of most structural adjustment programs and a key element in the New Economic Model. Latin American governments have lowered import tariffs, variably and not always enthusiastically, and imports have poured in. Indeed, one of the vital problems facing Latin American economies is imports. Latin America has long demonstrated an affection for imported consumer goods, and this affection has hardly diminished in recent years.[28] Globalization has increased the propensity to import, as tastes have been influenced by the advertising campaigns of international companies spread through the increasingly ubiquitous television set. Imported services have followed in the track of imported manufactures. The new altars of international consumer culture, such as McDonald's and shopping malls, have been spreading wildly in Latin American cities.

Although some imported goods have helped improve the productivity of Latin American industry, a considerable proportion of the new imports have substituted for what was once produced domestically. One consequence of trade liberalization, therefore, has been to put local firms out of business. There is no doubt that Latin American manufacturing has been forced to shed large numbers of jobs as a result of the combined forces of domestic recession and cheap imports. The latter has been particularly problematic when it has been associated with contraband and the laundering of drug monies. In Colombia, the impact of liberalization on formal manufacturing enterprises has been clear cut. Imported manufactures from the Far East have led to the closure of many local plants employing formal-sector blue-collar workers. This has led to higher unemployment and more people being employed in informal-sector work (see below).

But, of course, there has been an additional factor encouraging the growth of informality: the efforts of formal companies to try to compete with imports by reducing the costs of domestic production. By increasing the level of competition, liberalization has forced companies to maintain profits by modifying their employment practices. As Roberts has put it, "The large firm has become leaner, concentrating on essential and profitable functions through a core of stable workers, while less profitable or more volatile functions are subcontracted or performed by temporary workers."[29] Frequently, these strategies have led to an increase in the size of the informal labor force. From the 1970s on Latin American cities have seen an expansion in the size of the informal sector, fuelled in part by this kind of process (see below). More workers have been engaged in part-time or casual work. More firms have been subcontracting to small producers in the shantytowns.

In addition, most corporations have been trying to cut the rights of their permanent staff. In this they have been assisted by government efforts to modify labor and social security legislation, increasing the power of companies relative to unions.[30] Thus, of the six largest Latin American economies, union membership among the nonagricultural labor force is now less than 20 percent in Colombia, Chile, and Venezuela; and between 20 percent and 30 percent in Argentina, Mexico, and Brazil.[31] While there have been strikes and protests about this shift, the union movement has been strangely muted in its reaction.[32]

But again it is difficult to generalize across the whole of Latin America because the effect of increasing imports has varied from place to place. Most cities have benefited in the sense that lower prices have allowed more people to buy television sets, hi-fis, and refrigerators. But in terms of employment, the large cities, which contain most of the companies that previously satisfied domestic demand, have been badly affected by the flood of imports. It is no coincidence that unemployment rose very rapidly during the 1990s in the region's major industrial centers (see below), nor that the pace of metropolitan growth slowed markedly in the 1980s.[33]

CAPITAL FLOWS AND INFORMALITY

Liberalization is intended to increase capital flows. Indeed, Dicken has written that direct foreign investment "has become a more significant integrating force in the global economy than the traditional indicator of such integration, trade."[34] In this regard, the current literature on globalization probably exaggerates the importance of foreign capital flows because overseas investment in Third World countries today is proportionally much smaller than it once was, and is arguably much smaller than it should be. Certainly, the volume of foreign investment flowing into the economies of Argentina, Australia, and South Africa before World War I was relatively much greater than the capital flows into Latin America, or even the Far East, in the last few years. Fernández-Arias and Hausmann have made the case that Latin American countries are too dependent on internal savings, and that favorable capital-labor ratios, relative to those in developed countries, should be attracting much more investment into the region.[35]

Nevertheless, foreign currency flows into Latin America are generally rising rapidly, with net private capital flows rising from US$12.4 billion in 1990 to US$126.9 billion in 1998.[36] Foreign direct investment has been rising as a proportion of local investment and in terms of local GDP — impressively so in dynamic economies such as Chile and Colombia (see FIGURE 2.5).

Such investment has generated new manufacturing facilities in formerly far-flung parts of the globe. In Latin America, the expansion of *maquila* plants along the Mexico-U.S. border is the classic example. But increasingly such investment has focused less on manufacturing and more on services. The accompanying table shows that the proportion of U.S. direct investment going into manufacturing fell from 38 percent in 1980 to 28 percent in 1996 (see FIGURE 2.6). By contrast, investment in banking, finance, and services rose dramatically, from 32 percent in 1980 to 54 percent in 1996. The most significant branch of investment has been

COUNTRY	% OF TOTAL PRIVATE INVESTMENT		% OF GROSS DOMESTIC PRODUCT	
	1980	1998	1980	1998
Argentina	3.5	10.4	0.9	2.1
Bolivia	10.2	50.9	1.7	10.2
Brazil	3.5	19.3	0.8	4.1
Chile	3.7	22.2	0.8	5.9
Colombia	2.5	15.1	0.5	3.0
Dominican Republic	5.6	16.9	1.4	4.4
Ecuador	2.3	17.1	0.6	4.5
Guatemala	8.9	22.2	1.4	3.6
Mexico	3.6	10.7	1.0	2.6
Peru	0.4	12.7	0.1	3.1
Venezuela	0.3	23.8	0.1	4.7
Latin America and Caribbean	3.2	16.1	0.8	3.5

Figure 2.5. Foreign investment in selected Latin American countries, 1980 and 1998.
Source: World Bank, World Development Indicators, 2000 (Washington D.C.: The World Bank, 2000), Table 5.1.

in producer services, and in Latin America the expansion of major international hotel, communications, transport, accounting, and banking systems has been very obvious. No major city in Latin America lacks a Marriot, InterContinental, or Hyatt Hotel; none is without the subsidiaries of the major international banks; and all contain offices of the major accounting and consulting companies. Perhaps most significant of all has been the expansion of financial services and the development of electronic transfers and 24-hour trading.

What is the direct effect on the informal sector of foreign investment moving into less traditional areas of activity within Latin America? In terms of investment in banking and financial services, the answer is probably very little. In general, most of the jobs generated are in formal-sector businesses that employ workers in-house. The most pronounced impact on the informal sector arises from indirect effects, particularly the consumption of workers employed in the new activities. Hence, bankers will spend money on food, drink, and leisure, which will create work in the informal sector. Demand for domestic help in and around the home will rise. Overall, the employment effects will be similar to those from domestic investment, and are no more troubling.

YEAR	TOTAL	PETROLEUM	MANUFACT-URING	BANKING, FINANCE, AND SERVICES	WHOLESALE TRADE	OTHER
1980	38.9	4.3	14.6	12.5	3.9	3.7
1985	28.3	4.7	14.7	3.6	2.9	2.3
1990	70.8	4.2	23.4	37.1	2.7	3.4
1996	144.2	6.5	40.6	78.3	7.7	11.1

Figure 2.6. U.S. foreign direct investment in Latin America, 1980–1996 (US$ billion).
Source: J. Wilkie, J. Alemán, and J. Ortega, Statistical Abstract for Latin America 34 (Los Angeles: UCLA, 1998).

What is worrying about external capital flows is their volatility and the fact that Latin America has been increasingly sucked into a very unpredictable world financial system. During the 1970s the recycling of Eurodollars led to vast sums of money pouring into the region; and with the onset of the debt crisis in the 1980s, what had poured in flooded out. Between 1982 and 1989 Latin America lost the equivalent of 4 percent of its gross regional product.[37] While Latin American decision-makers bear some of the responsibility for that nightmare, it could not have occurred without the OPEC-inspired rises in world oil prices, the development of the Eurodollar currency market, and the manifest incompetence of the international banking community.[38] Financial liberalization was responsible at least for the scale of the problem.

Latin America is supposed to have changed as a result of the debt crisis, and that is supposed to have brought economic stability. Structural adjustment during the 1980s transformed its economy. Market forces were reestablished and the amount of government meddling reduced. The aim of the IMF was to make the region a safer place in which to invest, and the increasing flow of foreign direct investment into the region during the 1990s was testimony to its success.[39] Unfortunately, the new conditions seem to have produced anything but stability. Private capital flows into Latin America have ranged from a peak of US$108 billion in 1997 to a low of US$41 billion in 1995. Money now moves in and out of Latin America very quickly — something clearly demonstrated by the Mexican crisis of 1994, the Brazilian troubles of 1998, and the current problems in Argentina.

In the past, troubles tended to affect one country at a time. But since 1980 crises have seemed to spill over from one country to another. Thus, the Mexican crisis of 1994 quickly crossed the southern border, and the so-called Tequila Effect hit stock markets and foreign exchange markets throughout the region. In the three weeks after the Mexican peso crisis of December 20, the São Paulo stock market fell by 34 percent and that of Buenos Aires by 29 percent.[40] No doubt Latin America's integration into the global financial system is excellent when foreign traders have confidence in the local economies. But the Mexican crisis showed that economic and social volatility is part of the new form of liberalization. When Mexico got into trouble, Wall Street, London, and Tokyo immediately removed huge sums of portfolio investment from that country. That, at least, was understandable. But the same investors immediately began to question the safety of their investments in the rest of Latin America. Eventually, the Tequila Effect caused major problems in Argentina, Brazil, and even in Chile.

The Tequila Effect was vaguely rational: if Mexico had problems, investors might be right to worry that Argentina or Brazil would soon have similar problems. But recent international crises seem to obey an altogether more mysterious logic. Why, for example, did the Russian financial crisis affect Latin America so badly when the region has virtually no economic links with that country? The reasons behind the current volatility are so little understood that they have even caught bankers by surprise. If there was a clear relationship between international financial prices and real market conditions, the next crisis could be anticipated. But there seems to be no such link. This is truly worrying because it seems to indicate that Latin American governments may do everything to obey the rules of international lenders and yet still be hit by a financial or currency crisis originating in a region far across the globe.

Even economists seem prepared to accept that there is something wrong with the world financial system. According to Fernández-Arias and Hausmann,

> Financial liberalization and integration have not worked out as advertised. . . . Instead, emerging markets have been rattled by financial turmoil, especially during the past two to three years. Depending on one's viewpoint as optimist or pessimist, financial integration and globalization have either generated excessive volatility or run amok.[41]

What makes such volatility so dangerous today is that it occurs so suddenly. The new global financial community, with its reliance on the latest communications technology, reacts instantly to any local change in political or economic expectations. The extent of fluctuations in international exchange rates during 1999, which bore little relationship to real economic changes, suggest that the financial world is living constantly on a knife edge. In effect, the mere hint of a change in interest or exchange rates may now send billions of dollars cascading around the financial circuits. Mention of a problem in one emerging market hits every emerging market.

If the changing technology underlying the world's financial system encourages volatility, so too does the process of international competitiveness. As Quandt has put it: "Despite the high level of concentration in the leading global industries, competition appears to be increasing as the international structure of production changes. Accordingly, comparative advantages tend to be a fleeting phenomenon."[42] One day Brazil may be producing most of Latin America's cars; the next day it may have lost its comparative advantage and be struggling to sustain its competitive edge because of a shift in the external value of the real.

The impact of all this on the informal sector is difficult to decipher. Since it seems that many newly unemployed workers find it difficult to move into informal-sector employment, and that the sector does not provide a limitless supply of work for the otherwise unoccupied, the answer may be that economic volatility has most effect on the level of unemployment.[43] This would be compatible with the great fluctuations that occurred in the unemployment rate in the 1990s in countries like Colombia (see below).

GOVERNMENT ECONOMIC POLICIES AND INFORMALITY

Liberalization from the tyranny of government forms part of the new economic orthodoxy. The responsibilities of the state today are much reduced compared with those during the days of import substitution. According to the new orthodoxy, the state should no longer produce goods and services, it should no longer act as a banker, its central banking role should be delegated to an independent body, and its primary purpose should be to establish a safe environment which will encourage local and overseas businesses to invest. Its social role has also been much reduced, insofar as it should now delegate most responsibility for service provision to the private sector, and generally act only as a regulator and provider of last resort.

What makes life difficult for the analyst is that governments in Latin America have not always done what they are supposed to. Certainly, there are very clear general moves towards economic liberalization across the region. For example, there have been tendencies toward establishing realistic exchange rates, encouraging the free flow of capital, reducing trade controls, cutting the role of the state, balancing the government budget, privatizing public enterprises, restructuring labor regulations and financial markets, and modernizing the country's infrastructure. But while every government has embraced the New Economic Model to some degree, they have done so with differing levels of enthusiasm. Just as the form of structural adjustment has varied widely (for example, the heterodox models of Brazil and Peru versus the orthodox models of Mexico and latterly Argentina), so behavior under the NEM has been highly variable. Some countries have taken on the new orthodoxy enthusiastically, others more reluctantly.[44] Perhaps the extreme cases are Chile and Venezuela.

More importantly, what governments say they are doing is not the same as what they often do. For example, despite the rhetoric of good behavior, government consumption as a share of GDP remained constant at 13 percent across the region between 1990 and 1998.[45] And every government was supposed to cut its budget deficit — but as the accompanying table shows, only some governments in the larger countries managed to do this (see FIGURE 2.7). Admittedly, the tendency has been exaggerated by the current recession, but it was apparent before. Even the Colombians, long conservative economic managers and paragons of virtue, have seen their budget deficit soar from less than 1 percent of GDP in 1991 to almost 5 percent in 1999.

The record on privatization across the region is also highly variable. In Mexico and Chile, the state has sold most of its productive activities (PEMEX being a major exception in Mexico), and manufacturing, hotel, banks, and transport companies have all been privatized. But the changes have been much slower in Brazil, Colombia, and Venezuela, even if the rhetoric of privatization has been deafening.

If liberalization on the ground is so inconsistent in terms of government practice, it is also very difficult to provide a clear picture of its impact on the informal sector in Latin America. However, one thing is clear: most governments were spending less on social services as a proportion of the GDP in 1995 than they were in 1980, and in some countries the proportion spent on social services per capita has declined.[46] Despite better targeting and more efficiency in the delivery

COUNTRY	1991	1995	2000
Argentina	-1.6	-0.6	-2.4
Bolivia	-4.3	-1.8	-4.1
Brazil	-0.2	-7.2	-4.6
Chile	1.7	2.6	0.1
Colombia	0.2	-0.6	-4.1
Guatemala	-0.1	-0.5	-1.9
Mexico	3.3	-0.2	-1.1
Peru	-1.5	-3.4	-2.5
Venezuela	-2.2	-4.3	-1.7
Latin America	-0.3	-1.6	-2.7

Figure 2.7. Budget surplus/deficit in selected countries, 1991–2000.
Source: CEPAL, Balance de la Economía de América Latina y el Caribe *(2001).*

of social services, it is likely that the social safety net has been weakened — although yet again the overall effect will vary from country to country.[47] If official forms of social welfare have been weakened, the role of the informal sector has undoubtedly become more important; in other words, the family has stepped in where the state fears to tread.

ECONOMIC GROWTH AND INFORMALITY

Liberalization is supposed to have improved the economic performance of Latin America.[48] In fact, the economic record during the 1990s has not been that impressive. Even if the 1990s were far better for most Latin American economies than the 1980s, the average rate of growth was lower in most countries than it had been in the 1950s, 1960s, or 1970s (see FIGURE 2.8). Of course, some countries have gained much more under the new model than others. Since liberalization means that Latin American countries have been forced to compete more with one another and with every other country for a share of world markets, that outcome should not be surprising. For countries like Chile, which are winning, all may be well. But for those that do not liberalize properly, or that liberalize and run into trouble anyway, the advantages of the New Economic Model appear to be more questionable.

Figure 2.8 does not reveal the instability that has characterized growth during the last decade. Latin American economies have always been subject to pressure from outside, a consequence principally of their dependence on primary exports. The danger from liberalization is that despite the shift away from primary production, the NEM is making Latin America still more vulnerable to sudden fluctuations. In 1995 Argentina and Mexico both suffered from bad recessions after several years of growth, and during 1999 even successful Latin American economies like Brazil, Chile, and Colombia experienced major economic downturns. Today it is the turn of Argentina. Insofar as liberalization has occurred throughout the region, it has failed to bring economic stability.

COUNTRY	1950–59	1960–69	1970–79	1980–89	1990–98
Argentina	2.4	4.4	3.0	-0.6	5.9
Brazil	6.5	6.2	8.6	2.9	2.5
Chile	3.8	4.5	2.0	3.2	7.7
Colombia	4.7	5.0	5.7	3.7	3.9
Guatemala	4.0	5.2	5.9	0.9	4.0
Mexico	5.9	7.1	6.5	2.1	3.1
Peru	4.9	5.6	4.0	-0.2	4.9
Venezuela	8.3	5.4	3.2	-0.8	2.9
Latin America	4.9	5.7	5.6	1.7	3.1

Figure 2.8. Economic growth by decade in selected Latin American countries since 1950 (annual growth in GDP).

Source: United Nations, "Fifty years of the Economic Survey," in Economic Survey of Latin America 1997–98 *(Santiago, Chile: United Nations, 1997–98), 343–68; and Inter American Development Bank, "Facing up to Inequality, Economic, and Social Progress in Latin America," in* Inter American Development Bank Annual Report 1998–99 *(Washington, D.C.: Inter American Development Bank, 1999).*

The liberalization of trade, capital flows, and labor markets, together with its direct and indirect effects on economic growth, may well have led to the "normal" level of unemployment rising in Latin America's cities. Falling aggregate demand and the opening of previously protected domestic markets created major problems for many companies producing for Latin American markets. Private firms began to restructure themselves, and huge numbers of industrial workers were laid off in the major cities. Between 1985 and 1988 Mexico City lost around one-quarter of its manufacturing jobs. In addition, large numbers of public-sector jobs have been shed as state corporations have been privatized. In Bolivia, the huge COMIBOL mining enterprise was savagely cut, the labor force falling from 28,000 in 1985 to 5,000 in 1992. In Argentina, the number of railway workers fell from 87,000 in 1991 to 5,230 in 1995, and the state petroleum company reduced its workforce from 52,000 to 6,000 during the early 1990s.[49]

The average level of urban unemployment was generally higher in the 1990s than in the 1980s both in Argentina and Colombia, two countries that definitely liberalized their economies, and in Venezuela, which most definitely did not (see FIGURE 2.9). In Mexico and Peru, a great deal of liberalization seems not to have made much difference, while in Brazil limited liberalization has also had little effect. Only in Chile has a clear commitment to liberalization reduced unemployment, although it has to be pointed out that Chile had a very poor employment record during the 1980s. What we can say is that 1999 was a year that did not do much for the reputation of liberalization in the region. Record levels for unemployment in the 1990s were set in five of the seven countries.

But whether liberalization is really the cause of rising unemployment is an open question. Certainly, the experience of Colombia, a country that started to liberalize seriously in 1990 and seemed to be benefiting from that approach in the middle 1990s, does not help answer that question. Arguably, the boom that brought low

	Argentina	Brazil	Colombia	Chile*	Mexico	Peru	Venezuela
1970	4.9	6.5	10.6	4.1	7.0	6.9	7.8
1978	2.8	6.8	9.0	13.3	6.9	8.0	5.1
1980	2.3	6.2	9.7	11.7	4.5	7.1	6.6
1982	5.7	7.7	9.3	20.1	3.7	6.6	8.2
1984	4.6	7.1	13.4	18.5	5.7	8.9	14.3
1986	5.6	3.6	13.8	13.1	4.3	5.4	12.1
1988	6.3	3.8	11.2	10.2	3.5	7.1	7.9
1990	7.5	4.3	10.3	6.5	2.7	8.3	10.4
1992	6.9	5.9	10.5	7.0	2.8	9.4	7.8
1994	11.5	5.1	8.9	8.3	3.7	8.8	8.7
1996	17.5	5.4	11.2	7.0	5.5	8.8	11.8
1997	14.9	5.7	12.4	7.5	3.7	9.2	11.4
1998	12.9	7.6	15.3	(6.4)	3.2	8.4	11.3
1999	14.3	7.6	19.4	(9.8)	2.5	9.2	14.9
2000	15.1	7.1	17.2	(9.2)	2.2	8.5	14.0

* Bracketed figures for 1998–2000 are total national rates; the earlier figures are for metropolitan regions where unemployment is typically a little higher.

Figure 2.9. Rates of open urban unemployment, 1970–2000 (%).
Source: CEPAL, Balance de la economía de América Latina y el Caribe (2001).

unemployment had less to do with liberalization than with property speculation, high commodity prices, and the repatriation of drug monies. Similarly, the terrible recession that began to hit the country in 1998 had as much to do with internal policies as with external pressures. If liberalization opened the economy to the financial instability that was affecting the Far East and Brazil, it did not determine the U.S. decision to decertify the country, nor explain the rising expenditures of the Samper government. Arguably, internal decisions made by the central bank and by the Constitutional Court made the situation far worse than it needed to have been. Bogotá saw unemployment rise from 6 percent in 1995 to more than 20 percent in 1999. While some blame liberalization, it is difficult to blame it for everything.[50]

Even if we assume that liberalization has raised the level of unemployment, what effect has this had on the relative size of the informal employment sector? After all, conventional wisdom once held that unemployment was low in Latin America because poor people found work in the informal sector in order to keep body and soul together.[51] The luxury employment hypothesis seemed to have some credibility in a number of countries during the 1970s. But the deep crisis of the 1980s produced a phenomenon of rising unemployment and rising informal-sector employment. The accompanying table shows that informal-sector employment grew in most countries, principally because of the decline in the amount of employment provided by large private firms (see FIGURE 2.10). Only in Chile, which was in recession only for a couple of very bad years, did both informal-sector employment and unemployment decline.

The question is whether the liberalization of the 1990s, together with the partial reactivation of most Latin American economies during that decade, has reversed the general trend for informal-sector employment to rise. I suspect that it has not. Indeed, my hypothesis is that a new structural situation has developed whereby economic instability produces moments of high unemployment so suddenly that the informal sector is unable to absorb the surplus labor force. Formal-sector firms under liberal labor regimes are now able to lay off workers suddenly, something that they could not do in the past. What makes the unemployment situation far worse is that the informal sector is unable to absorb the rapid influx of potential new workers and is itself putting people out of work. The latter occurs because more work in liberalized regimes is now subcontracted to the informal sector. As a result, when an economic recession strikes, formal-sector firms cut back on the contracts they offer to people in the informal sector. This action shakes the subcontracted workers out of the informal sector into unemployment. Of course, poverty forces some back into the informal sector as household survival strategies take hold.[52] But more informal-sector workers are laid off than new workers enter. That tendency is more likely today, insofar as labor participation rates have been rising consistently since the 1970s. If a higher proportion of people want work, and a recession cuts the amount of work available, more people are likely to be unemployed. Certainly, fewer are able to enter the informal-sector workforce than is suggested by the household survival strategy. In short, we have a very different labor market in Latin America today compared to that of the 1970s. The labor market of the 1970s combined low unemployment with a large formal and a large

COUNTRY	INFORMAL SECTOR	FORMAL SECTOR			
		TOTAL	PUBLIC SECTOR	LARGE PRIVATE FIRMS	SMALL PRIVATE FIRMS
Argentina 1980	26.4	73.7	18.9	41.8	13.0
Argentina 1990	32.6	67.4	19.3	33.2	14.9
Brazil 1980	24.0	76.0	11.1	55.2	9.7
Brazil 1990	28.6	71.5	10.9	36.6	23.9
Chile 1980	36.1	63.9	11.9	37.7	14.3
Chile 1990	31.7	68.4	7.0	43.0	18.3
Colombia 1980	32.0	68.0	13.8	33.7	20.5
Colombia 1990	31.3	68.7	10.6	30.2	27.8
Mexico 1980	24.2	75.8	21.8	29.1	24.9
Mexico 1990	36.0	64.0	25.0	19.6	19.5
Venezuela 1980	25.7	74.2	25.6	39.8	8.8
Venezuela 1990	26.4	73.6	22.6	28.9	22.1
Latin America 1980	25.6	74.4	15.7	44.1	14.6
Latin America 1990	30.8	69.2	15.5	31.6	22.1

Figure 2.10. Growing informal-sector employment during the 1980s.
Source: PREALC

informal sector; the labor market of today produces higher unemployment, a comparatively smaller formal sector, and a larger informal sector.

LIBERALIZATION AND INFORMAL HOUSING

A discussion of housing reinforces the argument that the relationship between liberalization and informalization is less than clear, for while liberalization is arguably a phenomenon of the last twenty years, informal housing goes back further, and in most cities began to develop on a large scale in the 1940s and 1950s. The accompanying table shows when self-help housing began to develop for the few large Latin American cities for which approximate data are available (see FIGURE 2.11).[53]

The figures show that the most rapid period of growth of self-help housing (arguably the meaning of informalization in the housing field) occurred when urban planning regulations were strict and before trade, capital, and exchange-rate liberalization had any real constituency in Latin America. Bogotá, Caracas, Lima, and Mexico City all had at least 25 percent of their housing stock created by self-help construction by 1970. The less-than-reliable figures cited even suggest that the relative importance of self-help housing began to decline in Caracas and Bogotá after 1980.

If liberalization does explain the shift toward greater formality, it is because in the last two decades most governments have begun to realize that tight planning regulations are in many ways counterproductive, and in any case are rarely applied in low-income areas of cities anyway.[54] Indeed, few governments today remove illegal settlements, and most try to upgrade them and integrate them into the "city proper." Today the argument coming from both the political right and left is similar: poor settlements need to be left in place, serviced, and legalized.[55] And the development banks are actively pushing this line.[56]

One element of this integration process has been to provide illegal settlers with title deeds. Most governments within the region — legitimate and illegitimate, authoritarian and nonauthoritarian — have responded to, and in some places anticipated, this advice by giving out titles to large numbers of self-help settlers. The military government in Chile gave out more than 500,000 land titles between 1979 and 1989, and the two democratic governments that succeeded it distributed a further 150,000 titles by 1998.[57] In Peru, the new Commission to Formalize Informal Property (COFOPRI) managed to register some 500,000 urban land titles from 1996 to 1999.[58]

The reason for giving title deeds is to provide security for low-income people so that they will improve their homes, and so they can use their legalized homes as collateral to take out loans.[59] This is why the policy is so popular with the right. Legalized self-help housing permits people to become proper citizens; they can borrow money against their homes to build businesses and improve their lives. Ironically, you are not recognized as a full citizen in modern society until you have been in debt and have a credit rating.

CITY	YEAR	CITY POPULATION (000s)	POPULATION IN SQUATTER SETTLEMENTS (000s)	PERCENT
Mexico City	1952	2,372	330	14
	1966	3,287	1,500	46
	1970	7,314	3,438	47
	1976	11,312	5,656	50
	1990	15,783	9,470	60
Lima	1956	1,397	112	8
	1961	1,846	347	17
	1972	3,303	805	24
	1981	4,608	1,455	32
	1989	6,234	2,338	38
Caracas	1961	1,330	280	21
	1964	1,590	556	35
	1971	2,200	867	39
	1985	2,742	1,673	61
	1991	2,966	1,238	42
Bogotá	1955	917	367	40
	1965	1,782	766	43
	1975	3,069	921	30
	1985	4,123	1,278	31
	1991	4,824	1,254	26

Figure 2.11. The growth of self-help housing in selected Latin American cities.
Source: Adapted from A. Gilbert, The Mega-city in Latin America (Tokyo: United Nations University Press, 1996), 74–75.

Whether or not legalization makes any real difference to the speed of housing improvement, whether banks are actually prepared to lend to poor people when they have title deeds, and whether poor people are actually prepared to borrow money at the risk of losing their home are questions which have been investigated in other places.[60] Certainly, the real motive behind the policy has been electoral gain. People generally like to receive a formal title for their property, and governments gain kudos through the distribution of title deeds. It is also cheap, especially when the beneficiaries are charged for the service, and when they begin to pay property taxes.[61] It is certainly very much cheaper than the theoretical alternative of providing poor people either with proper homes or even with infrastructure and services.

My point here is that in the field of self-help housing, legality or illegality is not the key issue.[62] Nor does it much matter whether housing has been built through some kind of self-help construction or not. What is critical is whether the accommodation provides adequate shelter — that is to say, does it have services, is it affordable, and does it keep out the rain and the cold? In this regard, there is plenty of evidence that over the last thirty years the quality of housing has actually improved in Latin American cities, despite what Figure 2.11 suggests. But the record is spotty, and in places housing conditions have probably deteriorated. Where they have deteriorated, cities have suffered from one or more of the following problems: declining per-capita incomes, rising unemployment, a shortage of cheap urban land, ineffective servicing agencies, a repressive government, a poorly designed housing policy, and a scarcity of cheap building materials. That list of factors, of course, goes well beyond many of the processes inherent in liberalization. No doubt liberalization can affect land prices, inflows of foreign capital can induce an economic boom and raise prices, and strong outflows can have the opposite effect. But many of the processes involved are internal to the country, and arguably have little relationship with liberalization. For example, the willingness of governments to tolerate land invasions seems to be very tenuously linked with the New Economic Model and liberal economic policy. In Chile, neither Pinochet nor the subsequent democratic regimes have tolerated the wave of *tomas* that characterized the years up to 1974. In short, attempting to link housing trends to liberalization is extremely difficult.

CONCLUSION

It is less than clear what the term liberalization means. Even trying to define the narrow term economic liberalization is a complicated task. Part of the problem is that liberalization embraces so many different things that it is difficult to quantify what has actually happened. That is important because what governments do is rarely what they say they do, or even what they mean to do. Governments introduce some parts of the liberalization package but not others; they try to introduce more but political reality prevents it. If we can broadly say that Chile, Colombia, and Mexico have liberalized and Venezuela has not, it would be very difficult to actually measure the degree of liberalization that has occurred in any of them.

In principle, liberalization can improve living standards, but equally some of the processes unleashed are thoroughly undesirable. The key point about liberalization is that it is extremely dangerous to try to generalize. Sometimes liberalization is good for you, and sometimes it is bad for you. The welfare impact depends on who you happen to be and where you live. It also matters greatly whether the world or local economy happens to be in a boom or in a slump.

Similarly, it is difficult either to measure informalization or to judge whether or not the process, however defined, is good or bad. The same problems apply. Informalization occurs at different speeds and directions in different parts of the economy. Whether any society is becoming less or more formal over time is very difficult to answer. Again, the degree of informality perhaps matters little. What matters is how greater formality or informality affects living standards. It is not much help being a public-sector worker in hyper-inflationary days; no doubt there are economic benefits to be derived from being an international drug dealer.

And even if we succeed in defining liberalization and informalization, we will find it very difficult to provide satisfactory links between the two processes.

Liberalization creates new forms of legality and illegality. It destroys some forms of informality while creating new ones. Liberalization frequently produces contradictory effects, particularly when we consider its impact over space; thus, it may create formal jobs in one place and destroy them in another.

The issues involved are fundamentally important, and my attempts at humor and literary allusion are not intended to trivialize them. There is a vital debate going on about labor standards and minimum wages and the need for this kind of regulation in the new global economy. Discussions about the appropriate role of the state in proving a social safety net, or even something more substantial, are critical. There are important issues to be discussed about how best to deal with low-income housing. But perhaps the only way to deal adequately with these issues is to consider them at the local scale, and consider their impact on different social groups. We can at least make some sense of what is creating problems for particular neighborhoods.

At the same time, it is unlikely that we will be able to resolve local issues at the local level, for global forces are increasingly affecting people's lives. Everyone can succeed, providing that they compete successfully and keep on competing. As Sebastian Edwards has pointed out, the new international game is about constantly striving to keep up: "The global economy of the late twentieth century is a bit like Alice's observation in *Through the Looking Glass* that 'it takes all the running you can do to keep in the same place. If you want to go somewhere else, you must run at least twice as fast as that.'"[63] Even if his literary reference is different from mine, it is interesting that he too offers an element of magical realism.[64]

Perhaps the magical element is essential because Edwards's and official Washington's vision of the future is broadly optimistic. It is possible to succeed if you compete. And you can compete successfully because the Far East has shown that it is possible to move from poverty to development. What is essential according to the Washington mantra is that Latin American governments should "get the basics right."

Unfortunately, many would argue that development thinking has become the art of illusion. Magic is necessary to cover up the mismatch between theory and practice. In this latest version of the global economy, where life is so volatile and we lack effective mechanisms for doing what the Bretton Woods institutions were intended to do, local effectiveness can rapidly be compromised. What is the point of getting the basics right when the rules of the game keep changing? Does this not explain why much of Latin America is currently in recession after twenty years of attempting to liberalize? Perhaps it is right to blame the victims for not competing successfully; perhaps the recipe is wrong?

NOTES

1. My title is a play on the title of Gabriel García Márquez's book *Love in the Time of Cholera*.

2. Magical realism was probably invented by the Cuban writer Alejo Carpentier. It is used to describe a style that blends fact with fiction.

3. Acute observation in such a region, allied to García-Márquez's imagination and sense of humor, were almost bound to produce *One Hundred Years of Solitude* and its sequels.

4. P. Cammack, *Capitalism and Democracy in the Third World: The Doctrine for Political Development* (London: Leicester University Press, 1997); Anon., "Happy 21st Century Voters! A Survey of Democracy," *The Economist* (December 21, 1996); R. Gwynne and C. Kay, eds., *Latin America Transformed: Globalization and Modernity* (London: Arnold, 1999); S. Huntington, *The Third Wave: Democratization in the Late Twentieth Century* (Norman, Okla.: University of Oklahoma Press, 1991); and T. Skidmore and P. Smith, *Modern Latin America* (New York: Oxford University Press, 1997).

5. V. Bulmer-Thomas, ed., *The New Economic Model in Latin America* (London: Institute of Latin American Studies and Macmillan, 1996); S. Edwards, *Crisis and Reform in Latin America* (Oxford, U.K.: Oxford University Press, 1995); and B. Stallings, ed., *Global Change, Regional Response: The New International Context of Development* (Cambridge, U.K.: Cambridge University Press, 1995).

6. F. Stewart and A. Berry, "Globalization, Liberalization, and Inequality: Expectations and Experience," in A. Hurrell and N. Woods, eds., *Inequality, Globalization, and World Politics* (Oxford, U.K.: Oxford University Press, 1999), 150–86.

7. D. Montaña Cuellar, *Colombia: país formal y país real* (Buenos Aires: Editorial Platina, 1963).

8. Many academics need reminding that whatever the informal sector means, it includes much more than informal employment. Too many discussions of the informal sector omit any reference to housing whatsoever. Not only does this exclude where most informal workers live, but it also excludes many of the ways in which they generate a not-inconsiderable part of their income: running shops, small businesses, and other kinds of home enterprises, and particularly, renting rooms.

9. R. Bromley, ed., *The Urban Informal Sector: Critical Perspectives in Employment and Housing Policies* (New York: Pergamon Press, 1979); R. Bromley and C. Gerry, eds., *Casual Work and Poverty in Third World Cities* (New York: John Wiley & Sons, 1979); and M. Hays-Mitchell, "The Ties that Bind. Informal and Formal Sector Linkages in Streetvending: The Case of Peru's *Ambulantes*," *Environment and Planning A* 25, no. 8 (August 1993), 1085–102.

10. L. Peattie, "An Idea in Good Currency and How it Grew: The Informal Sector," *World Development* 15, no. 7 (July 1987), 851–60; and V. Tokman, "Policies for a Heterogeneous Informal Sector in Latin America," *World Development* 17, no. 7 (July 1989), 1067–76.

11. B. Lautier, "Wage Relationship, Formal Sector, and Employment Policy in South America," *Journal of Development Studies* 26, no. 2 (January 1990), 278–98; Tokman, "Policies for a Heterogeneous Informal Sector in Latin America"; J. Thomas, "The New

Economic Model and Labour Markets in Latin America," in Bulmer-Thomas, ed., *The New Economic Model in Latin America*, 79–102; R. Tardánico and R. Menjivar-Larín, eds., *Global Restructuring, Employment, and Social Inequality in Urban Latin America* (Boulder, Colo.: Lynne Rienner, 1997); and C. Rakowski, ed., *Contrapunto: The Informal Sector Debate in Latin America* (Albany, N.Y.: State University of New York Press, 1994).

12. A. Hirschman, *The Strategy of Economic Development* (New Haven, Conn.: Yale University Press, 1958); S. Kuznets, "Economic Growth and Income Inequality," *American Economic Review* 45, no. 1 (March 1955), 1–28; and *Modern Economic Growth: Rate, Structure, and Spread* (New Haven, Conn.: Yale University Press, 1966); but recall the warnings of G. Myrdal, *Economic Theory and Underdeveloped Regions* (London: Gerald Duckworth, 1957).

13. Stewart and Berry, "Globalization, Liberalization, and Inequality," 150–86.

14. J. Londoño and M. Székely, "Persistent Poverty and Excess Inequality: Latin America, 1970–1995," in IADB Working Paper Series, no. 357 (Washington, D.C.: Inter American Development Bank, 1997), 34.

15. World Bank, *World Development Report 2000* (New York: Oxford University Press, 2000); E. Iglesias, *Reflections on Economic Development: Toward a New Latin American Consensus* (Washington, D.C.: Inter American Development Bank, 1992); and Inter American Development Bank, "Facing up to Inequality, Economic and Social Progress in Latin America," in *Inter American Development Bank Annual Report 1998–99* (Washington, D.C.: Inter American Development Bank, 1999).

16. E. Fernandez-Arias and R. Hausmann, "What's Wrong with International Financial Markets?" in *Inter American Development Bank, Research Department Working Paper*, no. 429 (Washington, D.C.: Inter American Development Bank, 2000).

17. R. Bromley, "A New Path to Development? The Significance and Impact of Hernando De Soto's Ideas on Underdevelopment, Production, and Reproduction," *Economic Geography* 66, no. 4 (October 1990), 328–48.

18. H. De Soto, *The Other Path* (London: I.B. Taurus, 1989); and S. Annis and J. Franks, "The Idea, Ideology, and Economics of the Informal Sector: The Case of Peru," *Grassroots Development* 13, no. 1 (1989), 9–21.

19. H. De Soto, *The Mystery of Capital* (New York: Basic Books, 2000).

20. A. Gilbert, *The Latin American City* (London: Latin America Bureau, 1998).

21. World Bank, *World Development Report 1995* (New York: Oxford University Press, 1995); R. Dornbusch and S. Edwards, eds., *The Macro-economics of Populism in Latin America* (Chicago: University of Chicago Press, 1991).

22. International Labor Office, *World Employment: An ILO Report: 1995* (Geneva, Switzerland: International Labor Office, 1995); UNRISD, *States of Disarray: Social Effects of Globalization* (Geneva, Switzerland: UNRISD, 1995); and S. Sassen, *The Global City: New York, London, Tokyo* (Princeton, N.J.: Princeton University Press, 1991); D. Green, *Silent Revolution: The Rise of Market Economics in Latin America* (London: Latin America Bureau, 1995); and Iglesias, *Reflections on Economic Development*.

23. Gwynne and Kay, eds., *Latin America Transformed*; and C. de Mattos, "Santiago de

Chile, Globalización y Expansion Metropolitana: Lo que Existía sigue Existiendo," *Revista EURE* 25 (1999), 76, 29–56.

24. J. Bahr and R. Wehrhahn, "Polarization Reversal in São Paulo," in T. van Naerssen, M. Rutten, and A. Zoomers, eds., *Diversity of Development* (Assen, The Netherlands: Van Gorcum, 1997), 166–79; and C. Diniz, "Polygonized Development in Brazil: Neither Decentralization nor Continued Polarization," *International Journal of Urban and Regional Research* 18, no. 2 (June 1994), 293–314.

25. I. Arriagada, "Transformaciones del Trabajo Feminino Urbano," *Revista de la CEPAL* 53 (August 1994), 91–110; S. Chant, *Women and Survival in Mexican Cities: Perspectives on Gender, Labor Markets, and Low-income Households* (Manchester, U.K.: Manchester University Press, 1991); A. Gilbert, "Employment and Poverty during Economic Restructuring: The Case of Bogotá, Colombia," *Urban Studies* 34, no. 7 (June 1997), 1047–70; V. Lawson, "Work Force Fragmentation in Latin America and its Empirical Manifestations in Ecuador," *World Development* 18, no. 5 (May 1990), 641–58; and G. Standing, "Global Feminization through Flexible Labor," *World Development* 17, no. 7 (July 1989), 1077–96.

26. H. Browne, *For Richer, for Poorer* (London: Latin American Bureau, 1994); International Labor Office, *World Employment: An ILO Report: 1995*; Gwynne and Kay, eds., *Latin America Transformed*; A. Dwyer, *On the Line: Life on the U.S.-Mexican Border* (London: Latin America Bureau, 1994); V. Meier, "Cut-flower Production in Colombia — A Major Development Success Story for Women?" *Environment and Planning A* 31, no. 2 (February 1999), 273–89; and L. Sklair, *Assembling for Development* (Boston, Mass.: Unwin Hyman, 1989).

27. J. Momsen, ed., *Women and Change in the Caribbean* (Bloomington, Ind.: Indiana University Press, 1993).

28. D. Felix, "Income Distribution and Quality of Life in Latin America: Patterns, Trends, and Policy Implications," *Latin American Research Review* 18, no. 2 (1983), 3–34.

29. B. Roberts, "Informal Economy and Family Strategies," *International Journal of Urban and Regional Research* 18, no. 1 (March 1994), 13.

30. I. Arriagada, "Transformaciones del Trabajo Feminino Urbano," *Revista de la CEPAL* 53, 91–110.

31. *The Economist* (December 6, 1997).

32. I. Roxborough, "Organized Labor: A Major Victim of the Debt Crisis," in B. Stallings and R. Kaufman, eds., *Debt and Democracy in Latin America* (Boulder, Colo.: Westview Press, 1987), 91–108.

33. M. Villa and J. Rodríguez, "Demographic Trends in Latin America's Metropoli, 1950–1991," in A. Gilbert, ed., *The Mega-city in Latin America* (New York: United Nations University Press, 1996), 25–52; and A. Gilbert, "Third World Cities: The Changing National Settlement System," *Urban Studies* 30, no. 4–5 (May 1993), 721–40.

34. P. Dicken, "Global-Local Tensions: Firms and States in the Global Space-Economy," *Economic Geography* 70, no. 2 (April 1994), 109.

35. E. Fernández-Arias and R. Hausmann, "Is FDI a Safer Form of Financing?" in *Inter*

American Development Bank, Research Department Working Paper, no. 416 (Washington, D.C.: Inter American Development Bank, 1999), 24.

36. World Bank, *World Bank Report 2000*, Table 21.

37. O. Altimir, "Distribución del Ingreso e Incidencia de la Pobreza a lo Largo del Ajuste," *Revista de la CEPAL* 52 (April 1994), 8.

38. S. George, *A Fate Worse than Debt* (Harmondsworth, Middlesex, U.K.: Penguin Books, 1988).

39. Fernández-Arias and Hausmann, "What's Wrong with International Financial Markets?"

40. *The Economist* (January 7, 1995).

41. Fernández-Arias and Hausmann, "Is FDI a Safer Form of Financing?" 3.

42. C. Quandt, "New Opportunities in the Big Emerging Markets," *Enfoque* (Fall 1994), 3.

43. H. Hirata and J. Humphrey, "Workers' Response to Job Loss: Female and Male Industrial Workers in Brazil," *World Development* 19, no. 6 (June 1991), 671–82; and J. Humphrey, "Are the Unemployed part of the Urban Poverty Problem in Latin America?" *Journal of Latin American Studies* 26 (October 1994), 713–36.

44. Stewart and Berry, "Globalization, Liberalization, and Inequality," 150–86.

45. World Bank, *World Bank Report 2000*, Table 13.

46. R. Cominetti and G. Ruiz, "Evolución del Gasto Público Social en América Latina: 1980–1995," *Cuadernos de la CEPAL*, no. 80 (Santiago, Chile: CEPAL, 1998).

47. D. Raczynski, "The Crisis of Old Models of Social Protection in Latin America: New Alternatives for Dealing with Poverty," in V. Tokman and G. O'Donnell, eds., *Poverty and Inequality in Latin America: Issues and New Challenges* (Notre Dame, Ind.: University of Notre Dame Press, 1998), 140–68.

48. Edwards, *Crisis and Reform in Latin America*; and Bulmer-Thomas, ed., *The New Economic Model in Latin America*.

49. D. Keeling, *Contemporary Argentina: A Geographical Perspective* (Boulder, Colo.: Westview Press, 1997), 112.

50. E. Sarmiento Palacio, "Crecimiento y Distribución del Ingreso," in E. Sarmiento et al., *Cambios Estructurales y Crecimiento* (Bogotá, Colombia: Ediciones Uniandes y Tercer Mundo, 1992), 251–88.

51. R. Berry, "Open Unemployment as a Social Problem in Urban Colombia: Myth and Reality," *Economic Development and Cultural Change* 23 (1975), 276–91; and A. Portes and R. Schauffler, "Competing Perspectives on the Latin American Informal Sector," *Population and Development Review* 19, no. 1 (March 1993), 33–60.

52. Chant, *Women and Survival in Mexican Cities*; and A. Escobar and M. González de la Rocha, "Crisis, Restructuring, and Urban Poverty in Mexico," *Environment and Urbanization* 7, no. 1 (April 1995), 57–76.

53. I am using locally generated data of somewhat dubious reliability. But the figures presented in this case do match what I perceive to be real. Self-help housing — that is, shelter built and/or designed by ordinary people building in areas without formal title and almost

always preceding the delivery of services — began on a large scale during the period of rapid urban growth, when the arrival of the bus and water lines made suburban development feasible for the first time. Before then, most poor people lived in rental accommodation in the central areas of much smaller cities. See A. Gilbert, *The Latin American City*.

54. World Bank, *Housing: Enabling Markets to Work*, A World Bank Policy Paper (Washington, D.C.: The World Bank, 1993).

55. A. Gilbert, "Housing in Latin America," Inter American Development Bank, INDES-European Union Joint Program Working Paper (Washington, D.C.: Inter American Development Bank, 2001).

56. World Bank, *Cities in Transition: World Bank Urban and Local Government Strategy* (Washington, D.C.: The World Bank Infrastructure Group, 1999); and Inter American Development Bank, "Facing up to Inequality, Economic, and Social Progress."

57. A. Rugiero Pérez, "Experiencia Chilena en Vivienda Social, 1980–1995," *Boletín INVI* 13 (1998), 31 & 51; and *MINVU memorias* (Santiago, Chile: Ministerio de Vivienda y Urbanismo, various years).

58. L. Conger, "Entitled to Prosperity," *Urban Age* (Fall 1999), 8.

59. De Soto, *The Mystery of Capital*; and Conger, "Entitled to Prosperity," 7–10.

60. O. Razzaz, "Examining Property Rights and Investment in Informal Settlements: The Case of Jordan," *Land Economics* 69, no. 4 (November 1993), 341–55; A. Varley, "The Relationship between Tenure Legislation and Housing Improvement," *Development and Change* 18, no. 3 (July 1987), 463–81; G. Payne, *Informal Housing and Land Subdivisions in Third World Cities: A Review of the Literature* (Headington, Oxford, U.K.: Centre for Development and Environmental Planning, 1989); Conger, "Entitled to Prosperity," 7–10; A. Gilbert, "A Home is for Ever? Residential Mobility and Home Ownership in Self-help Settlements," *Environment and Planning A* 31, no. 6 (June 1999), 1073–91; A. Gilbert, "Financing Self-help Housing," *International Planning Studies* 5, no. 2 (June 2000), 165–90; B. Ferguson, "Microfinance of Housing: A Key to Housing the Low or Moderate-income Majority?" *Environment and Urbanization* 11, no. 1 (April 1999), 185–99; UNCHS, *An Urbanising World: Global Report on Human Settlements 1996* (Oxford, U.K.: Oxford University Press, 1996); and B. Rogaly and S. Johnson, *Microfinance and Poverty Reduction* (Oxford, U.K.: Oxfam/Action Aid, 1997).

61. P. Ward, "Land Values and Valorization Processes in Latin American Cities: A Research Agenda," *Bulletin of Latin American Research* 8, no. 1 (1989), 45–66; and E. Fernandes and A. Varley, eds., *Illegal Cities: Law and Urban Change in Developing Countries* (London: Zed Books, 1998).

62. A. Gilbert, "On the Mystery of Capital and the Myths of Hernando De Soto: What Difference does Legal Title Make?" *International Development Planning Review* 24(2002), 1–19.

63. Edwards, *Crisis and Reform in Latin America*, 303.

64. I am reluctant to leave the debate wholly in the hands of the novelist, but perhaps future articles can spend some time reflecting on appropriate titles for forthcoming literary masterpieces.

3

The Changing Nature of the Informal Sector in Karachi due to Global Restructuring and Liberalization, and Its Repercussions

Arif Hasan

This chapter is based on observation and dialogue with informal-sector operators and residents of informal settlements. Its conclusions emerge not out of rigorous research as to the effects of liberalization on the informal sector of Karachi, but out of the interaction between the actors in the informal-sector drama and myself. This interaction has been made possible by my association with the Orangi Pilot Project-Research & Training Institute (OPP-RTI), its replication in seven Pakistani cities, and the work of the Urban Resource Centre (URC) in Karachi. The OPP-RTI is a community-financed and -managed settlement-upgrading project that operates from Orangi Township in Karachi. The township has a population of 1.2 million (about 12 percent of the city) and is the largest informal settlement in Pakistan. Settlement in Orangi began in 1965. The township is also the hub of much of the informal-sector activity in the city, and was created by middlemen through the illegal subdivision and sale of state land. The URC, on the other hand, analyzes government plans from the point of view of various community organizations, informal service providers, and interest groups operating in Karachi. Its forums, supported by research, have created a space for interaction between interest lobbies and communities, on the one hand, and politicians and bureaucrats on the other. Statistics in this chapter are given as endnotes, and most of them are derived from the research work of these two organizations.

The informal sector in Karachi, as in other Pakistani cities, has served the physical and social infrastructure needs of low- and lower-middle-income communities and settlements. In the last decade new needs have surfaced, and they have been accompanied by major changes in the global, and hence, local economy. For the vast majority of Karachiites the formal sector cannot service these needs, as its products are unaffordable to them and its organizational culture is far removed from theirs. In addition, these changes have redefined the relationship between the various actors in the informal-sector drama. This chapter is an attempt to understand these changes and identify the directions they are likely to take. However, before attempting this, it is important to understand the causes for the emergence of the informal sector in Karachi and its scale and manner of operation.

THE EMERGENCE OF THE INFORMAL SECTOR IN KARACHI

The regions that constitute Pakistan today became independent in 1947 after just more than one hundred years of British rule. The elites, who took over from the British, were educated in Britain, and their view on development, as in other matters, reflected that of their colonial masters. As such, the new state adopted the British postwar "welfare state" as its model for development. According to this model, the state was responsible for providing subsidized housing, health and education, and jobs to its citizens. In addition, the state was to determine the parameters within which private enterprise could function and industrialization could take place. The model was not successful in the Pakistani context for a variety of reasons. The necessary institutional framework for its planning and implementation did not exist. Revenues to subsidize the planned social and physical infrastructure could not be generated. And the organizational culture of the postcolonial establishment was one of controlling through coercive state force, rather than dialogue, discussion, and interaction with urban interest groups. It can even be argued that such interest groups did not exist in an organized form until the late 1970s.

The failure of the state to provide was accompanied by an urban population explosion. For this there were three reasons. First, the migration from India at the time of partition of the subcontinent in 1947 more than doubled the population of a large number of towns in the Sindh and Punjab provinces.[1] Second, the eradication of malaria, small pox, and cholera and the promotion of immunization programs decreased infant and child mortality significantly. And third, green-revolution technologies and mechanization forced landless labor and small peasants to migrate to the cities. Thus, the demand-supply gap in housing, transport, health, education, and jobs increased, and with it, the state's inability to service this demand. By the late 1970s most state initiatives in these fields had declined, and those that remained operative were being run at an increasing subsidy, which the state was unable to provide. Meanwhile, the helplessness of the administration to provide, and hence administer, fuelled corruption.

Traditionally, middlemen have always existed in Pakistani society. They have provided lower-income groups, at a considerable price, with finances in difficult times, and with access to the corridors of power, and hence to patronage. Historically, their activities had been small in scale compared to the larger social and economic context. Initially, it was these middlemen who came forward to bridge the housing and employment demand-supply gap in Karachi. Since the gap was considerable, they employed apprentices from various communities, and these people, in turn, became the new informal-sector entrepreneurs. Today, it is the third generation of these entrepreneurs who are most active in informal-sector activities in Karachi. And the relationship that their predecessors established with government officials and agencies for support has long since being institutionalized. The amount of under-the-table payments to be made to different government functionaries, through whom, and at what time have also been formalized.

The vast majority of Karachiites live in informal settlements.[2] These have been developed on government land, illegally occupied by developers with the support of government servants, and protected through bribes given to the police. Almost all these settlements have residents' organizations (created by the developers), which constantly lobby government agencies for infrastructure and security of tenure. The developers also hire journalists to write about the "terrible conditions" in their settlements, and engage lawyers to help regularize tenure. Many of Karachi's important link roads and commercial areas have been developed by these informal developers. Loans, material, and advice for construction of homes are provided by small neighborhood contractors, who become the architects, housing banks, and engineers to low-income households.[3] Similarly, more than 72 percent of Karachiites travel in individually owned minibuses which have been purchased by informal loans at high interest rates from money lenders. Since these buses have no terminals, depots, or workshops, they use the roads for these purposes, and informally pay the police and the local administration for permission to do so.[4] Another important informal activity is the recycling of solid waste. Instead of taking solid waste to landfill sites, municipal waste collectors, in defiance of rules and regulations, take the solid waste to informal recycling factories spread all over the city. In the process, even organic waste, which cannot be recycled, does not reach the landfill sites. Here again large sums of money exchange hands illegally.[5]

As settlements consolidate, private schools are established in them. These far outnumber government schools, and are affordable to the residents because educated neighborhood women teach in them at low salaries.[6] Most of these schools begin as one-classroom affairs in people's homes, and some of them expand to become large institutions. They are established by entrepreneurs, public-spirited individuals, and/or community organizations, and they generally remain unregistered and unrecognized until attempts at their registration are made long after their establishment. Private medical practitioners (qualified, unqualified, and/or traditional) likewise establish health clinics in the informal settlements, and are not registered with any government agency or medical council. Entertainment and recreation also develops in informal settlements. Video machines, table football, and carom and card-game tables are set up by entrepreneurs without permission. The profits from these activities are shared between the entrepreneurs and the law-enforcing agencies.

The most important informal-sector activity, however, is related to the generation of employment. Garments, leather goods, and carpets are all produced in the informal settlements. Middlemen provide training, materials, equipment, and cash for the production of these items. The production takes place in people's homes on a contract basis. The manufactured items are then taken to a factory, where a label is placed on them before they are packed in alternative packets. In this way, exporters and industrialists are able to reduce production costs and prevent the unionization of labor and the application of labor and minimum-wage laws. Various parts for the light-engineering and the electronic industry are produced in a similar manner on lathe and rubber-molding machines in informal settlements. Spare parts for machinery, cars, tractors, and diesel engines are also manufactured in these settlements, and their price is about half that of industrially produced products. It is because of these spare parts that the transport-services and agricultural-machinery sectors are affordable to operators, and hence to primary producers.

The success of the activities of the informal sector in Karachi described above has a lot to do with the availability of cheap government land, protection of local industry through high import duties, the pioneering spirit of the first generation of migrants and entrepreneurs, and the helplessness of state institutions in the face of an increasing demand-supply gap in physical and social-sector infrastructure. However, with liberalization and other related developments, all this has started to change.

ECONOMIC LIBERALIZATION IN PAKISTAN

Economic liberalization has been accompanied by structural readjustment, a communication revolution, and major sociological changes in society. As such, its effects cannot be seen in isolation from these developments. Structural adjustment has meant reduction in import duties on all manufactured goods. By the year 2003 these duties will cease to exist. It is already becoming apparent that the Pakistani light-engineering industry cannot compete with products from Southeast Asian countries. Consequently, lathe machine operators in the informal settlements are not receiving sufficient orders, or else they are being asked by contractors to lower the quality and prices of their products.[7] Structural readjustment has also meant a huge increase in utility charges, especially electricity. As a result, carpet and textile power looms, most of which function through contractor-funded orders in informal settlements, are working on reduced profits or closing down.[8] According to a recent newspaper report, illegal electric connections to informal workshops have increased, and so has the bribe cost of acquiring these connections.[9]

One of the major objectives of the structural adjustment program is to help Pakistan service its international debts more effectively. Thus, the devaluation of the Pakistan rupee, so as to increase imports, has been an essential part of the structural adjustment plan. The rupee's constant devaluation has caused large-scale inflation and a search among marginalized and lower-income groups for additional employment. It has increased child labor and forced a larger number of women to work and have their incomes considered as more than a "bonus." Most working men now do more than one job. Teachers give private lessons in the evenings, government servants drive taxis, policemen fleece shopkeepers and motorcyclists, and white-collar workers work evening shifts as part-time employees in the service sector in addition to their full-time jobs.

Under structural adjustment, Pakistan has also undertaken to privatize profitable government institutions and utilities, and to sell state assets, mainly related to land, real estate, and industries. As a result, land that was not considered valuable has now become an important commodity. It can no longer be easily encroached upon, and where it is transferred to private ownership, it is protected. This has deprived informal-sector developers of raw land for development at places appropriate for their clients. The government has also undertaken to privatize health and higher education. All this is adversely affecting low-income groups, especially those who once had a chance for upward mobility. Many non-establishment development experts believe these factors are behind Pakistan's current double-digit inflation and recession.[10]

Privatization has also meant employment on merit rather than through political patronage or quota systems. And it has brought the sacking of a large number of government employees. With the privatization of education, merit means those who can afford education, and this marginalizes poor communities. An alternative source of education and skill acquisition from what is available thus becomes necessary for them.

This inflation and recession is taking place at a time when the older squatter colonies have been consolidating, and when such colonies constitute the majority of informal settlements. These are no longer purely working-class settlements. The younger generation in them is overwhelmingly literate.[11] Many of them have become doctors, engineers, college teachers, bank managers, and white-collar workers. Likewise, many of the small workshops and looms that were established by the first generation of entrepreneurs and artisans through the support of middlemen have now developed direct links with the formal-sector industries and exporters whom they service. Similarly, many schools (begun informally) have developed links with NGOs and government support agencies, and some health clinics have started to access government facilities in population planning and immunization. Interest groups have organized themselves to present their claims and protect their gains. As a result, there are now vocal transporters organizations, loom-operators associations, neighborhood groups, sports and cultural clubs (that manage to access government funds), and hawkers associations. Almost every sector of informal activity now has an organization registered under the Societies Act. Increasingly, these organizations are being led by second- or third-generation city dwellers who have broken with their rural culture and background. They are better educated than their parents or grandparents and more comfortable than them in dealing with those in power. Instead of seeking access through middlemen and touts of political parties, they approach the establishment through the power of their organizations, which are increasingly formalized through yearly audits and elections.

CHANGING LIFESTYLES IN AN ERA OF LIBERALIZATION

Due to the changes mentioned above, there has been a change in lifestyles, supported by the communications revolution. Nuclear families are replacing joint-family systems. Clan and tribal organizations, which the migrants brought with them, have ceased to be effective, and are being replaced by new community organizations, or by a dependence on state institutions. The communications revolution has made television and video an important entertainment tool. The television is the main source of information for the vast majority of Karachi households, more than 50 percent of whom have access to some form of cable.[12] Thus, video shops and cable operators, all too expensive in the formal sector for the lower- and lower-middle-income population, have become a necessity. *Santa Barbara*, *The Bold and the Beautiful*, MTV, and all variety of news is now available in homes in low-income settlements of Karachi, and in the tea shops and eating places located in them. Access to such programming has brought about a clash of values and cultural confusion. It has also brought about a generation gap which seems unbridgeable, and is one of the major reasons for an increase in honor killings of women in first-generation urban families. Vocabularies have also changed. Words of respect for elders or for those of a higher class have been substituted by "uncle" and "aunty," and other English-language equivalents. The whole feudal vocabulary, which the migrants had brought with them, has simply vanished with the new generation.

Liberalization and the communication revolution have also brought the corporate culture to Karachi. There is now great demand for information-technology professionals, operators, and technicians, not only for the local market but also for employment abroad. The training for these professions is provided both by government and private institutions. In the case of government institutions, this training is affordable to low-income groups, but it is on too small a scale to service the demand. As such, only exceptional students can get into government institutions. And since private institutions are far too expensive, and only the rich can afford them, a large gap has been created between demand and formal-sector supply.

The corporate culture has also introduced a measure of affluence in the city, which was unknown before. Golf clubs and various recreational and cultural facilities have been developed and are sponsored by companies for their clients and employees, and for advertisement purposes. Unlike previously, these activities are performed in new locations in elite areas, or in five-star hotels, and not in municipal or public buildings in the inner city. As a result, the inner city as a space for multiclass entertainment is dead. Such corporate-sector activities, and the glamor and pomp that surround them, provide a sharp contrast to the physical and social conditions in lower- and lower-middle-income settlements. There is an increasing feeling of insecurity among the promoters of these activities, and so they and their corporate-sector employees and clients are surrounded by security systems and armed guards. This is in sharp contrast to the Karachi of the preliberalization period.

Liberalization has also meant the introduction of fast-food chain stores and the popularization of various consumer items. McDonald's, Pizza Hut, and other chains have opened branches all over the city. Huge advertisements, colorful and well lit, dominate the urban landscape and dwarf badly constructed, poorly lit businesses and homes. New postmodern buildings of the corporate sector, with posh interiors, stand in sharp contrast to the sedate government buildings of the previous decades. Since a lot of young people from Karachi's informal settlements work in this environment, ties, white or blue shirts, and the "corporate hair cut" are becoming a common phenomena, and everyone knows what a credit card is and wishes to acquire one.

NEW INFORMALITIES IN AN ERA OF LIBERALIZATION

What has been described above is really the emergence of a First World economy and sociology with a Third World wage and political structure. It is the emergence of new aspirations related to consumerism and the desire for belonging to the "contemporary" world, as portrayed by the media, but without the means of achieving these aspirations and desires through formal institutions and processes. Thus, the most important role (and it is a new one) that the informal sector is trying to play today—and is likely to continue to play for the foreseeable future—is to help bridge this aspirations-means gap. In Karachi a whole new world has emerged to do just this.

Although the younger generation has new aspirations, state culture and family pressures prevent or hinder them from pursuing their desires. The result is conflict between the individualism of the young and the conservative social values of the older generation, who seek to protect the joint-family and clan systems. This is one of the major reasons, apart from financial aspiration, why young Pakistanis wish to migrate abroad.[13] However, getting a visa and a job, and establishing connections after you migrate to a First World country, is not easy for young Karachiites from low- or lower-middle-income settlements. Thus, middlemen have emerged to cater to this need and help in acquiring genuine and/or forged visas and arranging jobs abroad. Newspaper reports suggest that these operators have contacts in the visa sections of foreign embassies, and that large sums of money exchange hands in this trade. For acquiring an American or Japanese visa, young Pakistanis claim to have paid as much as Rs200,000 (US$3,333) to middlemen.[14] An entire street in the inner city of Karachi deals with arranging the necessary papers for migration and employment. From observation, one can see that the number of middlemen and clients there is increasing every day.

All Karachi neighborhoods, including low-income and even marginalized ones, have not one but many video shops, which rent out pirated videos. Video copies of Indian films arrive in Karachi even before the films are released in India. Similarly, videos of American films arrive well before the films are officially released in Karachi. All attempts at curbing piracy have failed. If they were to succeed, the vast majority of Karachiites would not be able to obtain video cassettes. The same holds true for the purchase of audio cassettes. More recently, cable television has also made its appearance in Karachi. Most of the cable companies are illegal and informally use the telephone network for providing home connections. They service all areas of Karachi, irrespective of class. Telephone department officials and the police are informally paid by the cable companies to let this happen. The cost of a cable connection varies from Rs450 per month for a connection from a legal company, to Rs150 from an illegal one. At a modest estimate, there are more than 150,000 people involved in the video- and cable-related trade.

All low-income settlements (formal or informal) have video halls, large asbestos-roofed shacks which show videos of all varieties. The films are advertised on the notice board outside the hall, along with the names of the stars, and are held at regular hours. In the interval, tea and chips are available. Under law, this is an illegal activity, but it provides entertainment to the male-only day-wage labor that lives around the port and wholesale markets. The video-hall operators consider their trade a "joint venture" between themseves, the police, and the excise department officials.

Meanwhile, for women, exposure through the media to a new and glamorous world has led to the opening of a number of "beauty parlors" and private tutoring centers for spoken English. Neighborhood beauty parlors are multiplying in low-income settlements, advertising various hairstyles named after Indian film stars. Being well groomed and speaking English has become an important asset for a woman in the marriage "market" in Karachi's older informal settlements. The pioneering beauticians have been trained informally through existing hair dressers in upper-middle-income beauty parlors. Now, their apprentices, who are multiplying in number, are taking over in the informal settlements. This trade has become so important that popular radio programs give regular beauty tips for women and for the trade operators.

The most important informal-sector activity today is related to information technology. Training schools, actually no more than private tutoring centers, have opened informally in all low- and lower-middle-income areas. These centers require no qualifications for admission, but offer no formal certification either. Their trainees are employed after having been tested by prospective employers. If they are well trained, employers prefer such trainees to qualified persons, since they can pay them a much lower salary for the same work. Similarly, there is a whole sector that deals with pirating computer software and marketing it to both informal and formal outlets. All attempts at curbing this activity have failed, and as a result, both international companies and the government have simply given up. The cost of such software can be as little as 5 percent of its original value. Without this sector, information technology would never be affordable to lower- or even middle-income groups in Karachi.

New lifestyles promoted by the media and the corporate sector have also had an influence on the lifestyles of the poorer sections of the population. These people wish to consume Seven-Up, Coca-Cola and beef burgers. And they are interested in designer shirts and brand-name perfumes. However, these products are all unaffordable to them. For this reason, fake Seven-Up and Coca-Cola, costing half the price, is manufactured in informal factories and marketed in the original bottles. Fake brand-name perfumes and fake designer shirts are also manufactured and marketed. A cheap alternative to the beef burger is available in every Karachi locality.

This new informal-sector activity, the result of liberalization and related changes, aims to serve the better-off and the slightly upwardly mobile residents of older consolidated or consolidating informal settlements. But it also marginalizes a large number of other people in these settlements and deprives them of employment and access to diminishing government subsidies and benefits. This division has increased the frequency of such crimes as armed robbery and car- and purse-snatching in Karachi. These "criminal" activities are not easy to carry out in Karachi's affluent areas due to the presence of the police and private-sector guards and security systems. However, they continue to happen and grow in lower-income settlements. Hence, residents of many of these settlements are organizing informal neighborhood policing systems and trying to gain approval from the government to formalize them. So far such approval has not been forthcoming, but these neighborhood policing systems continue to operate and grow in defiance of state rules and regulations.

OLD INFORMALITIES IN AN ERA OF LIBERALIZATION

Apart from the emergence of these new informal-sector activities, old ones have also undergone a change. However, informal developers are now forced to develop their settlements far from the center of the city, because land in the center has become an important asset to its owners. The diminishing purchasing power of the new migrants to the city also means smaller lots of land, narrower lanes, and less open space. Meanwhile, health and education institutions established by the informal sector in the older settlements have come of age. They are now struggling to become formal institutions, and they have tried increasingly successfully to access government poverty-alleviation funds (also a by-product of structural adjustment policies) and related programs. However, they find it difficult to establish themselves in the new settlements. This is because these settlements, unlike the older ones when they were established, do not dominate the politics or the economy of the city. They also contain a smaller percentage of the city population, and as such, politicians are less interested in them. They are also located far from the city, and can be ignored more easily by local government and entrepreneurs. Given inflation and recession, the buying power of their residents is also limited.

The future of the informal sector in Karachi is difficult to predict. However, some trends are clear. Links between informal workshops and formal-sector industry are slowly being eroded, except in the case of those industries (such as garments) where there is export potential. But it is feared that even these links will cease when formal-sector garment factories are set up through local and foreign investment. The process has begun, and since these industries have sophisticated machinery, they will be far less labor intensive. This will result in further unemployment.

The informal sector is now moving into producing cheap consumer goods for the poorer sections of the population. This means less profit and greater marginalization from formal-sector processes and economy. At the same time, the state sector is rapidly shrinking, especially in the provision of physical development and social services. This means that politicians will not be able to hand out favors and patronage. It was once through such favors and patronage that informal settlements were established and informal entrepreneurs were able to function. But favors and patronage are now being replaced by cash payments for protection of activities that are in defiance of state regulations. All this means the marginalization of all those without merit, skills, or access to expensive private-sector education.

The above trends are creating unemployment, and this will increase until such time as formal-sector private investment replaces the informal-sector job market. But this development is nowhere in sight, and as a result, the rich-poor divide is increasing, leading to violence and crime. The worst affected are those sections of the new generation of consolidated lower- and lower-middle-income settlements whose aspirations to belong to this new world cannot be fulfilled.

Also badly affected are those entrepreneurs and contractors who had established a working relationship with formal-sector businesses and industries. It is important to note that these groups are potentially the most powerful in political terms. Their marginalization creates a new situation.

A CONCLUDING NOTE

It is therefore understandable that the present situation of inflation, recession, and increasing marginalization of these groups is being blamed on liberalization, the WTO, structural adjustment, and World Bank and IMF policies. The press (especially the populist newspapers), politicians of various shades, NGOs, and now even transporters and solid waste recyclers associations, backed by academia, all participate in this debate, and issue statements against globalization. Seminars, symposiums, and workshops are held on the subject and endorse these views. It was in this context that the anti-WTO, World Bank, and IMF protests in Seattle, Melbourne, Chang Mai, and Prague electrified residents of lower-middle-income settlements in Karachi, as they did various interest groups operating in the city. The informal sector and the frustrated, potentially upwardly mobile sections of Karachi, look forward to joining this movement against "the new world order." How all this will resolve itself is important. So far, there has been no proper research into the long-term effects of liberalization on the city. There have only been observations and discussions. This chapter is yet another such attempt.

NOTES

1. Karachi's population increased from 450,000 in 1947 to 1.137 million in 1951. According to the 1951 census, 48.6 percent of Pakistan's urban population originated in India.

2. According to the Sindh Katchi Abadi (squatter settlement) Authority, more than 50 percent of Karachiites live in 716 informal settlements, which have grown at twice the annual urban growth rate of Karachi.

3. According to the 1987 "Yakoobabad Case Study" by the author, 93 percent of Yakoobabad residents had taken materials and/or cash on credit from small contractors to build their homes.

4. Of the 13,200 minibuses in Karachi, 6,000 are unregistered, since there is a ban on the registration of minibuses. In addition, the minibus operators pay Rs780 million (US$13 million) a year as bribes to the city administration to use the roads as bus terminals, depots, and workshops.

5. According to Urban Resource Centre (URC) figures, the solid waste recycling indus-

try's annual turnover is Rs1.2 billion (US$20 million). It pays about Rs220 million (US$3.6 million) informally each year to various government agencies to permit it to function.

6. In Orangi Township there are 72 government schools and 682 private schools, most of which began as informal one-class affairs (Source: OPP: 79th Quarterly Progress Report, September 1999).

7. S. Alimuddin, A. Hasan, and A. Sadiq, "The Work of the Anjuman Samaji Behbood," unpublished report, December 1999.

8. Ibid.

9. The daily *Jang,* Karachi (October 2000).

10. Akhtar Hameed Khan, "The Orangi Pilot Project Programmes," OPP, July 1998.

11. According to the 1998 census results, 74.04 percent of the Karachi age group of between 10 and 24 is literate, as compared to a total Karachi figure of 67.42 percent. In the 1981 census, 61.10 percent of the age groups of between 10 and 24 was literate.

12. According to the 1998 census, 79 percent of Karachi households said that their main source of information was the television.

13. According to a survey reported in the daily *Dawn*, Karachi (November 2000), 38 percent of Pakistanis wish to migrate. The figure for Karachi therefore must surely be higher.

14. Author's interviews with persons wishing to migrate (unpublished).

4

Globalization and the Politics of the Informals in the Global South

Asef Bayat

Notwithstanding some of the more overestimated claims of globalization theorists (such as the waning role of nation-states, the breakdown of borders, and the increased homogeneity of lifestyles, cultures, political systems, and so on[1]), it is generally agreed that the economics of globalization, comprised of a global market "discipline," flexible accumulation, and "financial deepening," have had a profound impact on postcolonial societies.[2] One major consequence of the new global restructuring in developing countries has been a double process of, on the one hand, integration, and on the other, social exclusion and informalization.

The historic shift from socialist and populist regimes to liberal economic policies, brought on by the World Bank's Structural Adjustment Program and other policies, has led to a considerable erosion of the social contract, collective responsibility, and former welfare-state structures. Thus, millions of people in the global South who once depended on the state must now survive on their own. Among other things, deregulation of prices for housing, rent, and utilities has jeopardized many people's security of tenure, subjecting them to the risk of homelessness. A reduction of spending on social programs has meant shrinking access to decent education, health care, urban development, and government housing. And the gradual removal of subsidies on bread, bus fare, and petrol have radically affected the living standard of millions of vulnerable groups. In the meantime, in a drive for privatization, public sectors have either been sold off or "reformed," which in either case has caused massive layoffs without a clear prospect of boosting the economy or creating other viable jobs. According to the World Bank, in the early 1990s, during the transition to market economies in postsocialist, adjusting Latin American and Middle Eastern countries, formal employment fell by 5 to 15 percent.[3] And in Africa the number of unemployed grew by 10 percent every year through the 1980s, while labor absorption in the formal wage sector declined.[4] By the late 1990s a staggering one billion workers, representing one-third of the world's labor force, most of them in the South, were either unemployed or underemployed.[5] Moreover, a large number of the once-educated, well-to-do middle classes (professionals, government employees, students, etc.), as well as segments of the peasantry, have been pushed into the ranks of the urban poor in labor and housing markets.

Thus, at the same time it has given rise to highly affluent groups, the new structuring has contributed to the growth of vast new populations of marginalized and deinstitutionalized people in Third World cities. These people include the unemployed, the partially employed, casual laborers, street-subsistent workers, street children, and members of the underworld — groups that have been interchangeably referred to as "urban marginals," "urban disenfranchised," and "the urban poor." Such socially excluded and informal groups are by no means new in historical terms. However, the recent global restructuring seems to have intensified and extended their operation. Thus, following the 1998 financial crisis, at least two million people lost their jobs in South Korea, three million in Thailand, and a staggering ten million in Indonesia.[6] However, what is most novel about this era is the marginalization of large segments of the middle class. Slum dwelling, casual work, under-the-table payment, and street hawking are no longer considered characteristics only of the traditional poor: such activities have now spread among educated young people with greater status, aspirations, and social skills — among them being former government employees, teachers, and professionals.

How will this growing urban grassroots population in the Third World respond to the larger social processes that affect their lives, if and when they do? Those who promote globalization suggest that the trickle-down of national economic growth will eventually compensate for the inevitable sacrifices that the poor are now making in a transitional phase. In the meantime, social funds, NGOs, and emergency aid must be encouraged to create jobs and assist in implementing social programs to alleviate hardship and avert possible social unrest. Indeed, some view the upsurge of NGOs in the South since the 1980s as one manifestation of a new form of organized activism, including the creation of new grassroots institutions for social development. However, granting that the effectiveness of development NGOs varies considerably, their potential for independent and democratic organization has generally been overestimated. As Neil Webster, reporting on India, has noted, advocates simply tend to expect too much from development NGOs.[7] And by doing so, they underestimate the structural constraints (e.g., the lack of organizational rationale, accountability, and professional middle-class leadership) that currently hinders meaningful development strategies. My own work on Middle Eastern development NGOs has supported this conclusion. Among other things, it has indicated a paradox whereby the professionalization of NGOs tends to diminish the mobilizational feature of grass-roots activism, while it establishes a new form of clientelism.[8]

Many on the left point to a number of "reactive movements" (identity politics), which they say may challenge globalization by appropriating the very technologies on which it is based. While Melluchi's "new social movements" focuses exclusively on "highly differentiated" Western societies, others like Manuel Castells and Ankie Hoogvelt, taking a Southern perspective, suggest that religious, ethnic, and feminist movements — as well as Latin American postdevelopment ideas — may serve as the backbone for anti-globalization forces. Identity movements do take up some of the challenges of globalization in postcolonial societies. However, they reflect more the sentiments of middle-class intellectuals than the everyday practices of ordinary people.

What will the grassroots think or do? What form of politics, if any, will marginalized urban groups espouse? In this chapter I attempt to address these questions. After navigating critically through the prevailing academic models, including culture of poverty, survival strategy, urban territorial movements, and everyday resistance, I suggest that the new global restructuring is reproducing subjectivities, social spaces, and a new terrain for political struggle that current theoretical perspectives cannot account for. I then propose an alternative outlook — "quiet encroachment" — that may provide a better model for the activism of marginalized groups in the cities of postcolonial societies. Quiet encroachment refers to noncollective, but prolonged, direct action by individuals and families to acquire the basic necessities of life (land for shelter, urban collective consumption, informal work, business opportunities, and public space) in a quiet and unassuming, yet illegal, fashion. This perspective has emerged out of my observation of urban processes in the Muslim Middle East, with its specific social and political structures. Nevertheless, I believe it has relevance to other Third World cities.[9]

PREVAILING PERSPECTIVES

The sociological examination of urban "marginality" dates back to nineteenth-century Europe. Problems associated with urbanization (urban crime, inner-city conditions, unemployment, migration, cultural duality, and so on) were first addressed by social scientists. Among the first ideas on the subject were those of Georg Simmel which dealt with the sociopsychological traits of new urban settlers. For his part, Durkheim was particularly keen on their "anomie." Such conceptualizations later informed the work of the Chicago School of sociology and urban study during the 1920s and 1930s, when that city acted as a laboratory in which to examine the social practices of ethnic migrants. For Everett Stonequist and Robert Park, many immigrants were "marginals" — a trait embedded in their social structure. In this view, the marginal personality was a manifestation of cultural hybridity — of living on the margin of two cultures without being a full member of either.

Unlike the Chicago School functionalists, mainstream Marxism did not take such issues seriously. Relative to the centrality of the working class as the agent of social transformation, Marxist theory either ignored the urban poor, or described them as "nonproletarian" urban groups, or "lumpenproletariat" — a term used by Marx himself. But, as Hall Draper notes, such terminology gave rise to "endless misunderstanding and mistranslation."[10] For Marx, lumpenproletariat was a category of political economy, used to refer to propertyless people who did not produce. The category included obsolete social elements such as beggars, thieves, thugs, and criminals who were in general poor but who lived on the labor of other working people. Due to their form of economic existence, such people were said to follow a politics of noncommitment which would in the end work against the interests of the producing classes.[11] It was such an uncertain politics that rendered the lumpenproletariat, for both Marx and Engels, the "social scum," "refuse of all classes," and the "dangerous classes." And although Marx would later theorize such people in terms of a "reserve army of labor" — thus, a segment of the working class — controversy continued as to the relevance of this concept to capitalist structuring, since it did not leave much chance for these people to be reemployed. Some did eventually suggest that far from being on "reserve," the urban disenfranchised were in fact already integrated into capitalist relations.[12] However, even with Franz Fanon's passionate defense of the lumpenproletariat as a revolutionary force in the colonies, the Communist Parties of the Third World never saw urban marginals as more than "toiling masses" who might have the potential for alliance with the working class.[13]

However, the continued prominence of "informals" (who came to outnumber the formal working class in many developing economies) and their assumed threat to political stability eventually brought them back to academic analysis. Thus, against the descriptive term "informals," and the derogatory term "lumpenproletariat," T.G. McGee and Robin Cohen opted for the notion of "proto-proletariat," and Peter Worsley came to describe such people simply as the "urban poor" — concepts that both accorded some degree of agency to such people.

More serious studies of the social conditions and politics of the urban subaltern in the Third World began to emerge among U.S. social scientists during the 1960s. At the time, modernization and urban migration in developing countries had caused a dramatic expansion of impoverished urban settlements. The growing urban "underclass" was thought to provide a breeding ground for radical guerrilla movements, which in the midst of the Cold War were perceived as a threat to the political interests of the United States and friendly local elites. The Chinese Revolution of 1949, the Cuban Revolution of 1959, and the expansion of guerrilla movements in the Third World were all taken as convincing evidence of this potential threat. It was in this context that Latin America became a laboratory for much-debated new theories about the social and political behavior of the urban underclass. Studies by Samuel Huntington and Joan Nelson, among others, reflected the concerns of the time.[14] In particular, scholars, mostly political scientists, were preoccupied with the question of whether the migrant poor constituted a destabilizing force. Nelson, for example, argued that there was "no evidence that the new migrants are either radical or violence-prone."[15] But such preoccupations overlooked the dynamics of the poor's everyday life. And many viewed the politics of the poor according to a binary revolutionary/passive dichotomy, which limited the possibility of looking at the matter in a more complex light. Essentialism informed both sides of the controversy. The ensuing debates were galvanized by four identifiable models: "the passive poor," "survival strategy," "the urban territorial movement," and "everyday resistance."

THE PASSIVE POOR

While some observers working in the functionalist paradigm still viewed the urban poor as essentially disruptive and imbued with the sentiments of anomie, others considered the poor a politically passive group, struggling simply to make ends meet. Oscar Lewis' theory of a "culture of poverty," based upon ethnographies among the urban poor in Puerto Rico and Mexico, offered scientific legitimacy for such a notion.[16] Highlighting certain cultural/psychological traits — fatalism, rootlessness, unadaptability, traditionality, criminality, lack of ambition, hopelessness, and so on — Lewis unintentionally extended the notion of the "passive poor." Nevertheless, with an underlying emphasis on identifying the "marginal man" as a cultural type, Lewis' theory remained a dominant perspective for many years, informing much antipoverty discourse, many of the policies of the United States, and the perception of many Third World elites.

Despite Lewis' empathy for the poor, the conceptual weaknesses of his model of a "culture of poverty" became clear before long. Simply, he essentialized the culture of the poor.[17] In other words, Lewis disregarded the varying ways in which the poor in different cultures handle poverty. And critiques, such as that by Worsley, eventually charged that Lewis, as a middle-class scholar, was blaming the poor for their own poverty and passivity.[18]

Interestingly, Lewis' conceptualization shared many traits with the work of Chicago School urban sociologists such as Stonequist and Park, and even with the work of earlier thinkers such as Simmel. However, Janice Perlman's powerful critique of this position in her *The Myth of Marginality* in 1976, together with Manuel Castells's critical contributions, undermined this outlook in academia, if not among officialdom. They demonstrated how the myth of marginality was an instrument of social control of the poor, and that the marginalized poor were, in fact, a product of capitalist social structures.[19]

SURVIVAL STRATEGY

The second conceptual model, that of "survival strategy" did not deal directly with the politics of the poor. But a relevant, implicit conceptual assumption did underlie this perspective. The survival-strategy model implies that although the poor are powerless, they do not sit around waiting for fate to determine their lives. Rather, they are active in their own way to ensure their survival. Thus, to counter unemployment or price increases, they often resort to theft, begging, prostitution, or the reorientation of consumption patterns. And to respond to famine and war, they will often leave their home places, even if emigration is discouraged by the authorities. To this way of thinking, the primary goal of the poor is simply to survive. However, their survival comes at great cost to themselves and their fellow humans.[20]

While resort to coping mechanisms in real life seems widespread among the poor in many cultures, Escobar has criticized the overemphasis on the language of survival in this model for contributing to the image of the poor as victims, denying them any agency.[21] The fact is that the poor also strive to resist and make advances in their lives when the opportunity arises. Beyond that, evidence from many parts of the world indicates they also create their own opportunities for advancement — and, in particular, they may organize and get involved in contentious politics. John Friedmann's notion of "empowerment" was one attempt to describe such an opportunity-creating tendency among the poor. He used the notion to describe how the poor self-organize for collective survival through the institution of the household; how the principle of a moral economy (trust, reciprocity, and voluntarism) emerges in many communities; and how the poor may utilize their "social power" (free time, social skill, networking, associations, and instruments of production) to improve their conditions.[22]

THE URBAN TERRITORIAL MOVEMENT

Critiques of the notions of the "passive poor" and the "culture of poverty" opened the way for the development of an outlook in which the urban subaltern emerged as a political actor — the "urban territorial movement." Perlman, Castells, and other scholars of Latin America insisted that the poor were not marginal, but integrated into urban society. Characteristically, they argued, the poor were "marginalized" — economically exploited, politically repressed, socially stigmatized, and culturally excluded from a closed social system.[23] Nevertheless, the poor did participate in party politics, elections, and mainstream economic activities. And more importantly, they established their own territorial social movements. Thus, community associations, barrios, consumer organizations, soup kitchens, squatter support groups, church activities, and the like were understood as manifestations of organized and territorially based action by the poor, who were striving for "social transformation" (according to Castells); "emancipation" (according to Schuurman and van Naerssen); or an alternative to the tyranny of modernity, in the words of John Friedmann.[24] In their immediate day-to-day activities, the poor were thus understood to struggle for a share of urban services, or "collective consumption."

In this model, the territorial character of these movements was seen to result from the mode of existence of the agents — the urban grassroots. Although quite differentiated (in terms of income, status, occupation, and production relations), the urban grassroots were thought to share a common place of residence and community. Shared space and the needs associated with common property offered these people the possibility of "spatial solidarity."[25] Attempts to highlight the contentious politics, as well as the noncontentious cooperation, of the urban poor drastically undercut both "culture of poverty" and "survivalist" arguments, granting significant agency to the urban subaltern. However, the "urban movement perspective" now appears to have been largely a Latin American model, rooted in the sociopolitical conditions of this region. Not surprisingly, therefore it was a perspective that has been offered primarily by scholars working on Latin America.[26] Local soup kitchens, neighborhood associations, church groups, or street trade unionism are hardly common phenomena in, say, the Middle East, Asia, or Africa (with the exception of countries like India and South Africa). In the Middle East, for instance, authoritarian states (of the despotic, populist, or dictatorial kind) are wary of civil associations. Together with the strength of family and kinship relations, such suspicions render primary solidarities more pertinent than secondary associations and social movements. Thus, while collective entities such as charity organizations and mosque associations do exist, they rarely lead to political mobilization of the popular classes. And although associations based upon neighborly relations, place of origin, or traditional credit systems are quite common, social networks which extend beyond kinship and ethnicity remain largely casual, unstructured, and paternalistic.[27] Some scholars have attempted to present Islamist movements as the Middle Eastern equivalent of Latin American urban social movements. Yet, a few functional resemblances notwithstanding, the fact remains that the character of Islamism does not derive from any particular concern for the urban disenfranchised. Islamism, in general, has broader aims and objectives. And unlike the Catholic church, in particular its Latin American liberation theology movement, Islamist movements aim to mobilize not so much the poor as the educated middle class, which they view as the main agent of political change.[28] Thus, it is mainly in exceptional circumstances (e.g., crises and revolutionary situations) that some degree of mobilization and contentious politics are encouraged, as in revolutionary Iran and crisis-stricken Algeria. It is true that the Islamist Rifah Party in Turkey mobilized slum dwellers, but this was so primarily because Turkey's free electoral system had granted the urban grassroots voting power (and thus bargaining leverage), which the Islamists, as a legitimate political party, could utilize.

It must also be realized that the prevalence of urban movements in Latin America varies considerably from country to country. As Leeds and Leeds have shown, due to the multiplicity of competing interest groups (government, private interests, and others), the grassroots have had more opportunity for collective action in Peru than in Brazil. In Brazil, the extremity of constraints has forced the poor to "seek their betterment through the paternalistic, individualistic channels of favors and exchange of interests."[29] Meanwhile, in Chile, in the episodes of political openness and radical groupings, the poor have been organized more extensively.

EVERYDAY RESISTANCE

The dearth of conventional collective action — in particular, contentious protest among subaltern groups (the poor, peasants, and women) in developing countries — together with a disillusionment with dominant socialist parties, has pushed many radical observers to "discover" and highlight different types of activism, however small-scale, local, or even individualistic. Such a quest both contributed to and benefited from the upsurge of theoretical paradigms during the 1980s associated with poststructuralism, which rendered micropolitics and "everyday resistance" a popular perspective. This shift of paradigm was greatly assisted by James Scott's departure from the structuralist position in his studies during the 1980s of Asian peasants. Scott used this view to explain the reciprocal relationship between subsistence peasants and landlords — what he called the moral economy. Scott developed a more ethnographic method than his predecessors, one that focussed on individual reactions.[30] In the meantime, Foucault's "decentered" notion of power, together with a revival of a neo-Gramscian politics of culture (hegemony), provided key theoretical backing for micropolitics, and thus the "resistance" paradigm.

The notion of "resistance" now stresses the view that power and counterpower are not in binary opposition, but in a decoupled, complex, ambivalent, and perpetual "dance of control."[31] The idea is based on the view that wherever there is power there is resistance, even though the latter may consist largely of small-scale, everyday activities which the agents can afford to articulate given their political constraints. Such a perception of resistance has now penetrated not only peasant studies, which had remained largely atheoretical, but a variety of other fields, including labor studies, identity politics, ethnicity, women's studies, education, and studies of the urban subaltern.

Research related to the resistance approach has discussed how relating stories about miracles "gives voice to popular resistance"[32]; how disenfranchised women resist patriarchy by relating folk tales, singing, or pretending to be possessed or crazy[33]; and how the extension of familyhood among the urban popular classes represents an "avenue of political participation."[34] Likewise, the relationships between Filipino bar girls and Western men have been discussed not simply in terms of total domination, but in complex and contingent fashion.[35] The veiling of Muslim working women has even been seen not in the simple terms of submission, but in ambivalent terms of protest and co-optation — hence, an "accommodating protest."[36] Indeed, on occasions, both veiling and unveiling have been simultaneously considered as symbols of resistance!

Undoubtedly, such attempts to grant agency to subjects who had until then been depicted as "passive poor," "submissive women," "apolitical peasants," and "oppressed workers" has been a positive development. Among other things, the resistance paradigm has helped uncover the complexity of power relations in society, in general, and the politics of the subaltern, in particular. It tells us that we may not expect a universalized form of struggle; that totalizing pictures often distort variations in peoples' perceptions about change; that the local should be recognized as a significant site of struggle as well as a unit of analysis; that organized collective action may not be possible everywhere, and thus alternative forms of struggle must be discovered and acknowledged; and that organized protest as such may not necessarily be the best strategy in situations where suppression rules. The value of a more flexible, small-scale, and unbureaucratic activism should, therefore, be acknowledged.[37] These are some of the issues that critiques of the everyday resistance model ignore.[38]

Yet a number of conceptual and political problems have also emerged from this paradigm. The immediate trouble is how to conceptualize resistance and its relation to power, domination, and submission. James Scott seems to be clear as to what he means by the term:

> Class resistance includes *any* act(s) by member(s) of a subordinate class that is or are *intended* either to mitigate or deny claims (for example, rents, taxes, prestige) made on that class by superordinate classes (for example, landlords, large farmers, the state) or to advance its own claims (for example, work, land, charity, respect) vis-à-vis these superordinate classes [emphasis added].[39]

However, the phrase "any act" blocks a clear delineation between the qualitatively diverse forms of activities Scott lists. Are we not to distinguish between large-scale collective action and individual acts, say, of tax dodging? Do reciting poetry in private, however subversive the message, and armed struggle have identical value? Should we not expect unequal effectivity and implications from such different acts? Scott was aware of this, and so agreed with those who had made distinctions between different types of resistance — for example, "real resistance," referring to organized, systematic, preplanned, or selfless practices with revolutionary consequences; and "token resistance," pointing to unorganized incidental acts without any revolutionary consequences, and which are accommodated in the power structure.[40] Yet he also insisted that "token resistance" is no less real than "real resistance." Scott's followers, however, continued to make further distinctions. Nathan Brown, in studying peasant politics in Egypt, for instance, identified three forms of politics: atomistic (politics of individuals and small groups with obscure content); communal (a group effort to disrupt the system, like slowing down production and so on); and revolt (just short of revolution to negate the system).[41]

Beyond this, however, many resistance writers tend to confuse an *awareness* of oppression with *acts* of resistance against it. The fact that poor women sing songs about their plight, or ridicule men in their private gatherings, indicates their understanding of gender dynamics. This, however, does not mean that they are involved in acts of resistance. Nor do the miracle stories of poor urbanites, who imagine the saints coming to punish the strong, rise to such a standard. Such an understanding of resistance fails to capture the extremely complex interplay of conflict and consent, and of ideas and actions operating within systems of power. Indeed, the link between consciousness and action remains a major sociological dilemma.[42]

Scott makes it clear that resistance is an intentional act. In Weberian tradition, he takes the meaning of action as a crucial element. This intentionality, while significant in itself, obviously leaves out many types of individual and collective practices whose intended and unintended consequences do not correspond. In Cairo or Tehran, for example, many poor families tap electricity and running water illegally from the municipality despite their awareness of their illegal behavior. Yet they do not steal urban services in order to express their defiance vis-à-vis the authorities. They do it because they feel they need these services for a decent life, and because they find no other way to acquire them. But these very mundane acts, when continued over a long period, may create significant changes in urban structure, social policy, and in the actors' own lives. Hence, the significance of the unintended consequences of individual agent's daily activities. In fact, many authors in the resistance paradigm have simply abandoned the search for intent and meaning, focusing instead eclectically on both intended and unintended practices as manifestations of resistance.

There is still a further question. Does resistance mean *defending* an already-achieved gain (in Scott's terms, denying claims made by dominant groups over the subordinate ones)? Or does it mean making fresh demands (to "*advance* its own claims"), what I like to call "encroachment?" In much of the resistance literature this distinction is missing. Although one might imagine moments of overlap, the two strategies follow different political consequences. And this is particularly the case when we view them in relation to the strategies of dominant power. In fact, the issue was so crucial that Lenin spent his entire *What is to Be Done* discussing the implications of these two strategies, albeit in the different terms of "economism/trade unionism" vs. "social democratic/or party politics."

Whatever one may think about the Leninist/vanguardist paradigm, it was one that corresponded to a particular theory of the state and power (a capitalist state to be seized by a mass movement led by the working-class party); and, in addition, it was clear where this strategy wanted to take the working class (to establish a socialist state). What is the perception of the state in the "resistance" paradigm? What is the strategic aim in this perspective? Where does the resist-ance paradigm want to take its agents/subjects, beyond "prevent[ing] the worst and promis[ing] something better?"[43]

Much of the literature of resistance is based on a notion of power that Foucault has articulated: that power is everywhere, that it "circulates," and is never "localized here and there, never in anybody's hands."[44] Such a formulation is surely instructive in transcending the myth of powerlessness of the ordinary people, and in recogniz-ing their agency. However, this decentered notion of power, shared by many post-structuralist resistance writers, underestimates state power, notably its class dimen-sion, since it fails to see that although power circulates, it does so unevenly. Thus, in some places power is far weightier, more concentrated, and "thicker," so to speak, than in others. In other words, like it or not, the state does matter, and one needs to take the state into account when discussing the potential for urban subaltern activism. Thus, while Foucault insists that resistance is real when it occurs outside of and independent from systems of power, the perception of power which informs resistance literature leaves little room for proper analysis of state systems. It is, there-fore, not accidental that a theory of the state — and, therefore, an analysis of the pos-sibility of co-optation — is absent in almost all accounts of "resistance." Instead, acts of resistance, cherished so dearly, float around aimlessly in an unknown, uncertain, and ambivalent universe of power relations, with the end result usually being an unsettled and tense accommodation with existing power arrangements.

Lack of a clear concept of resistance, moreover, often leads writers in this genre to overestimate and read too much into the acts of the agents. The result is that almost any act potentially becomes one of "resistance." Determined to dis-cover the "inevitable" acts of resistance, poststructuralist writers often come to "replace their subject."[45] While they attempt to challenge the essentialism of such perspectives as "the passive poor," "submissive Muslim women," and "inactive masses," they tend to fall into the trap of essentialism in reverse — by reading too much into ordinary behavior, interpreting it as involving necessarily conscious, or contentious, acts of defiance. This is so because they overlook the crucial fact that these practices occur mostly within prevailing systems of power.

For example, some of the lower class's activities in the Middle East — which some authors read as "resistance," the "intimate politics" of defiance, or "avenues of participation" — may actually contribute to the stability and legitimacy of the state.[46] The fact that people are able to help themselves and extend their net-works surely shows their daily activism. However, such struggles rarely win any new space from the state (or from other sources of power, like capital and patri-archy), and they are by no means "necessarily" challenges to domination. In fact, governments often encourage self-help and local initiatives so long as they do not turn oppositional. They do so in order to shift some of the burden of social-welfare provision and responsibility to individual citizens. The proliferation of NGOs in the global South represents a good indicator of this type of situation. In short, much resistance literature confuses what one might consider coping strategies (when the survival of the agents are secured at the cost of themselves or their fellow humans) with effective participation or subversion of domination.

There is a last question. If the poor have many ways to resist systems of domination (by discourse or action, individual or collective, overt or covert), then what is the need to assist them? If they are already politically able citizens, why should we expect the state or any other agency to empower them? Misreading the behavior of the poor may, in fact, frustrate any sense of moral responsibility toward the vulnerable. As Michael Brown rightly notes, when you "elevate the small injuries of childhood to the same moral status as suffering of truly oppressed," you are committing "a savage leveling that diminishes rather than intensifies our sensitivities to injustice."[47]

THE QUIET ENCROACHMENT OF THE ORDINARY

Given the shortcomings of these prevailing perspectives — that is, the essentialism of the "passive poor," the reductionism of the "survival strategy," the Latino-centrism of "urban territorial movements," and the conceptual perplexity of "resistance literature" — I like to assess the politics of the urban marginals in the developing world from a different angle — in terms of "the quiet encroachment of the ordinary." I believe that this notion might be able to overcome some of the above described inadequacies and better capture the essence of urban-subaltern politics in the conditions of globalization.[48]

The notion of "quiet encroachment" describes the silent, protracted, but pervasive advancement of ordinary people in relation to the propertied and powerful in order to survive and improve their lives. It is marked by a quiet, largely atomized, and prolonged mobilization with episodic collective action — open and fleeting struggles without clear leadership, ideology, or structured organization. While such quiet encroachment cannot be considered a "social movement" as such, it is also distinct from the survival strategy model and "everyday resistance" in several regards. First, the struggles and gains of the agents do not come at the cost of themselves or the fellow poor, but of the state, the rich, and the powerful. Thus, in order to light their shelters the urban poor tap electricity not from their neighbors, but from municipality power poles; and to raise their living standard they do not prevent their children from attending school in order to work, but rather squeeze time from their formal jobs in order to carry out secondary activities in the informal sector.

In addition, these struggles are seen not necessarily as defensive merely in the realm of resistance, but cumulatively encroaching, meaning that the actors tend to expand their space by winning new positions to move on. This type of quiet and gradual grassroots activism tends to contest many fundamental aspects of state prerogatives, including the meaning of order, the control of public space, access to public and private goods, and the relevance of modernity.

I am referring to the lifelong struggles of floating social clusters — migrants, refugees, the unemployed, the underemployed, squatters, street vendors, street children, and other marginalized groups — whose growth has been accelerated by the process of economic globalization. I have in mind the long processes by which millions of men and women embark on long migratory journeys, scattering to remote and often alien environs, acquiring work, shelter, land, and living amenities. The rural migrants encroach on the cities and their collective consumption; the refugees and international migrants on host states and their provisions; the squatters on public and private lands or readymade homes; and the unemployed, as street-subsistent workers, on the public space and on the established businesses of shopkeepers. And all of them tend to challenge the notions of order, the modern city, and urban governance espoused by Third World political elites.

Concrete forms of encroachment may vary considerably. For example, postrevolution Iran saw an unprecedented colonization, mostly by the poor, of public and private urban land, apartments, hotels, street sidewalks, and public utilities. Between 1980 and 1992, despite the government's opposition, the land area of Greater Tehran expanded from 200 to 600 square kilometers, and well more than one hundred mostly informal communities were created in and around the city.[49] Activity in a massive informal economy extended beyond the typical marginal poor to include a new "lumpen middle class," largely composed of educated salary-earners whose public-sector position rapidly declined during the 1980s. In a more dramatic case, in Cairo millions of rural migrants, the urban poor, and even the middle-class poor have now quietly claimed cemeteries, rooftops, and state/public lands on the outskirts of the city, creating more than one hundred spontaneous communities which house more than five million people. Once settled, such encroachments spread in many directions. Against formal terms and conditions, residents may add rooms, balconies, and extra space in and on buildings. And even those who have formally been given housing in public projects built by the state, illegally redesign and rearrange their space to suit their needs by erecting partitions and by adding and inventing new space.[50] Often whole communities emerge as a result of intense struggles and negotiations between the poor and the authorities and elites in their daily lives.[51]

At the same time, the encroachers have forced the authorities to extend urban services to their neighborhoods by otherwise tapping into them illegally. However, once utilities are installed, many simply refuse to pay for their use.

Some 40 percent of poor residents of Hayy al-Saloum, a south Beirut informal community, refuse to pay their electricity bills. The cost of unpaid water charges in the Egyptian city of Alexandria amounts to US$3 million a year. Similar stories are reported in urban Chile and South Africa, where the poor have periodically refused to pay for urban public services after struggling to acquire them, often against the will of the authorities. Likewise, hundreds of thousands of street vendors in Cairo, Istanbul, and Tehran have occupied the streets in the main commercial centers, infringing on the businesses of formal shopkeepers. Thousands of inhabitants in these cities also subsist on tips from parking cars in streets which they control and organize in elaborate ways to create maximum parking space. Finally, as in many Third World cities, such as those in South Korea, the encroachment of street vendors on copyrights of labels and trademarks has invariably caused protests by multinational companies.[52]

As state employees and professionals, previously privileged segments of the workforce, feel the crunch of neoliberal policies, they too resort to repertoires of quiet encroachment. To compensate for the meager US$40 monthly salary, the school teachers in Egypt turn to private paid tutoring of their own pupils. By doing so, they have created a massive sector of illegal private teaching which generates some EL 12 billion (US$3 billion) a year, costing "at least 25 percent of the annual earning of Egyptian families."[53] Similarly, "street lawyers" or "unregistered practitioners" encroach on the legal profession. These "street lawyers" do not hold law degrees, but have acquired some legal knowledge by working as employees in law offices. They then share their legal experience with new law-school graduates (who cannot afford the high cost of establishing their own law offices) to offer competitive services.[54]

These actors carry out their activities not as a deliberate political act; rather, they are driven by the force of necessity — the necessity to survive and improve a dignified life. Necessity is the notion that justifies their often unlawful acts as moral, and even "natural" ways to maintain a life with dignity. Yet such simple and seemingly mundane practices also tend to shift them into the realm of contentious politics. Thus, contenders become engaged in collective action and come to see their actions as political when their gains are threatened. Hence, a key attribute of quiet encroachment is that while advances are made quietly, individually, and gradually, defense of these gains is often (although not always) collective and audible.

Driven by the force of necessity (effects of economic restructuring, agricultural failure, physical hardship, war, and displacement), people set about such ventures individually, often organized only around kinship and friendship ties, and without much clamor. They deliberately avoid collective effort, large-scale operation, commotion, and publicity. At times, squatters, for instance, may even seek to prevent others from joining them in specific areas; and vendors may discourage their counterparts from operating in the same vicinity. Many also hesitate to share information about their strategies for acquiring urban services. Yet, as these seemingly disparate individuals and families pursue a similar path, their sheer cumulative effort will transform them into a social force.

But why individual and quiet direct action, instead of collective demand-making? Unlike factory workers, students, or professionals, these people represent groups in flux, and so they operate largely outside institutional mechanisms through which they might express grievances and/or enforce demands. They also lack an organizational power of disruption — the possibility of going on strike, for example. Although they may participate in street demonstrations or riots as part of a general expression of popular discontent, they do so only when these methods enjoy a reasonable currency and legitimacy (as in immediate postrevolutionary Iran, Beirut during the civil war, or after the fall of Suharto in Indonesia in 1998) and when they are mobilized by outside leaders. Thus, urban land takeovers may be led by left-wing activists, and the unemployed and street vendors may be invited to form unions (as in Iran after the revolution, in Lima, or in India). This, however, represents an uncommon phenomenon since more often than not mobilization for collective demand-making is prevented by political repression. Consequently, in place of protest or publicity, these groups move directly to fulfill their needs by themselves, albeit individually and discretely. In short, theirs is *not* a politics of protest, but of redress, the struggle for an immediate outcome through individual direct action.

What do these men and women aim for? They seem to pursue two major goals. The first is the redistribution of social goods and opportunities. This may take the form of the (unlawful and direct) acquisition of collective consumption (land, shelter, piped water, electricity, roads); public space (street pavements, intersections, street parking places); opportunities (favorable business conditions, locations, labels, licenses); and other life chances essential for survival and acceptable standards.

The other goal is attaining autonomy, both cultural and political, from the regulations, institutions, and discipline imposed by the state and by modern institutions. In the quest for an informal life, the marginals tend to function as much as possible outside the boundaries of the state and modern bureaucratic institutions, basing their relationships on reciprocity, trust, and negotiation, rather than on the modern notions of individual self-interest, fixed rules, and contract. Thus, they may opt for jobs in self-employed activities rather than working within the disciplining structure of a modern workplace; they may resort to informal dispute resolution rather than reporting to police; they may get married through local informal procedures (in the Muslim Middle East under local sheikhs) rather than by governmental offices; and they may borrow money from informal credit associations rather than modern banks. This is so not because these people are essentially non- or anti-modern, but because the conditions of their existence compel them to seek an informal mode of life. Because modernity is a costly existence, not everyone can afford to be modern. Since modernity requires the capacity to conform to types of behavior and modes of life (adherence to strict disciplines of time, space, contract, and so on), the most vulnerable people simply cannot afford it. Thus, while the disenfranchised wish to watch color TV, enjoy clean tap water, and possess the security of tenure, they are weary of paying their taxes and bills, or reporting to work at specified times.

But how far can the urban subaltern exercise autonomy in the conditions of globalization, amid the expanding integration? The fact is that not only do the poor seek autonomy, they also need the security that comes from state surveillance, since an informal life in the conditions of modernity is also an insecure life. To illustrate, street vendors may feel free from the discipline of modern working institutions, but they suffer from police harassment for lacking business permits. Likewise, the struggle of the poor to consolidate their communities and attain schools, clinics, or sewerage will inevitably integrate them into the prevailing systems of power (i.e., the state and modern bureaucratic institutions), which they might otherwise wish to avoid. In their quest for security, the urban marginals, then, are in constant negotiation and vacillation between autonomy and integration. Yet they continue to pursue autonomy in any possible space available within the integrating structures and processes.

BECOMING POLITICAL

If the encroachment begins with little political meaning attached to it, if illegal acts are often justified on moral grounds, then how does it turn into a collective/political struggle? So long as the actors carry on with their everyday advances without being confronted seriously by any authority, they are likely to treat their advance as an ordinary, everyday exercise. However, once their gains are threatened, they tend to become conscious of their doings and the value of their gains, defending them often in collective and audible fashion. Some examples are the mobilization of the squatters in Tehran in 1976, street vendors in the 1980s, and the street riots involving squatters in several cities in the early 1990s. Alternatively, the actors may retain their gains through quiet noncompliance without necessarily engaging in collective resistance. Thus, instead of collectively standing by their businesses, the mobile street vendors in Cairo or Istanbul simply retreat into the back streets once the municipal police arrive, but immediately resume their work as soon as they are gone. At any rate, the struggle of the actors against the authorities is not about winning a gain, but primarily about defending and furthering what has already been won.

The state's position vis-à-vis this type of activism is affected, first, by the extent of its capacity to exercise surveillance, and, second, by the dual nature of quiet encroachment (infringing on property, power, and privilege, and, at the same time, being a self-help activity). Thus, Third World governments seem to be more tolerant of quiet encroachment than those in the industrialized countries such as the United States, where similar activities, albeit very limited, also take place. One reason is that the industrial states are far better equipped with ideological, technological, and institutional tools to maintain surveillance over their populations. In other words, people have more room for autonomy in the vulnerable "soft states" of the South than in advanced industrialized countries, where tax evasion, infringement of private property, and encroachment on state domains are considered serious offences.

On the other hand, quiet encroachment, although an infringement on public property and power, may in many ways benefit Third World governments, for it is a mechanism through which the poor come to help themselves. It is no surprise then that these governments often express a contradictory position toward these kinds of activities. And "soft" and vulnerable states, especially at times of crises, tend to tacitly allow such encroachments. For their part, encroachers will also attempt constantly to appear limited and tolerable, while in fact expanding until resistance against them becomes formidable. They do so by resorting to tactical retreats, going invisible, bribing officials, or concentrating on less strategic spaces (for instance, squatting in remote areas or vending in less visible locations).

However, once their real expansion and impact is revealed, when the cumulative growth of the actors and their doings pass beyond a tolerable point, the state may be expected to crack down. Yet in most cases such crackdowns fail to yield much result since they are usually too late, occurring only after the encroachers have already become visible and passed the point of no return. Indeed, the description by officials of encroachment processes as "cancerous" brings home the dynamics of such movements.

The sources of conflict between the actors and the state are not difficult to determine. First, the often "informal" and free-of-charge distribution of public goods exerts a heavy pressure on the resources which the state controls. Besides, the rich — the real estate owners, merchants, and shopkeepers — also lose properties, brands, and business opportunities. The alliance of the state and the propertied groups adds a class dimension to the conflict. On the other hand, the actors' drive for autonomy in everyday life seriously undermines the domination of the modern state. Autonomous life renders modern states, in particular the populist version, rather irrelevant. Moreover, autonomy and informality (of agents, activities, and spaces) deprive states of the necessary knowledge to exert surveillance. Unregulated jobs, unregistered peoples and places, nameless streets and alleyways, and policeless neighborhoods mean that these entities remain hidden from the governments' books. To be able to exert its control, a state needs to make such entities visible. Indeed, programs of squatter upgrading may be seen in terms of opening up the unknown to be able to control it. Conflict between these encroachers and the state, therefore, is inevitable.

Nowhere is this conflict more evident than on the "streets." This public space par excellence serves as the only locus of collective expression for those who lack institutional settings to express discontent. Such groups may include squatters, the unemployed, street-subsistence workers, street children, members of the underworld, and housewives. Whereas factory workers or college students, for instance, may cause disruption by going on strike, the unemployed or street vendors can voice grievances only in public spaces. Indeed, for many of these disenfranchised, the streets are the main, perhaps the only, place where they can perform their daily functions — to assemble, make friends, earn a living, spend their leisure time, and express discontent. In addition, streets are also the public places where the state has the most evident presence, as expressed in terms of police patrols, traffic regulations, and spatial divisions — in short, in public ordering. The dynamics of the power relationship between the encroachers and the authorities is what I have elsewhere termed "street politics."[55] By this I mean a set of conflicts and the attendant implications between a collective populace and the authorities, shaped and expressed episodically in physical and social spaces — from alleyways to more visible locations such as sidewalks, public parks, and public sport places. Street politics signifies an articulation of discontent by clusters of social agents largely outside modern institutions, without a coherent ideology or evident leadership.

Two key factors render the street an arena of politics. First is the use of public space as a site of contestation between the actors and the authorities. In this sense, what makes the street a political site is the active or participative (as opposed to passive) use of public space. This is so because these sites (sidewalks, public parks, intersections, etc.) are increasingly becoming a domain of the state, which attempts to regulate their use, making them "orderly." The state expects that users will occupy such spaces passively. By contrast, active use challenges the authority of the state and those social groups that benefit from such order.

The second element shaping street politics is the operation of what I have called a "passive network" among people who use and operate in the public space. By passive network I mean instantaneous communication among atomized individuals, which is established by a tacit recognition of common identity, and which is mediated through space. When a woman enters a party full of male guests, she would instantaneously notice another woman in that party. Vendors on a street are similarly likely to recognize one another, even if they never meet or talk. When a threat occurs to the women at the party, or the vendors in the street, they are likely to get together even if they do not know each other or have not planned to do so in advance. The significance of this concept lies in the possibility of imagining a mobilization of atomized individuals, such as the quiet encroachers, who are largely deprived of organizations and deliberate networking. A passive network implies that individuals may be mobilized to act collectively without the active or deliberate intention. The space of the street seems to intrinsically make it possible for people to get mobilized through such passive networks. And once the individual actors, the encroachers, are confronted by a threat, their passive network is likely to turn into an active communication and cooperation. That is how an eviction threat or police raid may immediately bring together squatters, or street vendors, who may not even know one another. Of course, the shift from a passive network to collective resistance is never a given. Actors might feel that tactical retreat would yield a better result than confrontation, a tendency common in the streets of Cairo today, but uncommon in revolutionary Iran, where on-the-spot collective resistance prevailed.[56]

CONCLUSIONS

I suggested at the outset that a major consequence of the new global restructuring has been a double process of integration on the one hand, and social exclusion and informalization on the other. Both processes tend to generate discontent on the part of many urban grassroots in the Third World.

First, there are many among the urban grassroots who find it difficult to function, live, and work within the modernizing economic and cultural systems characterized by market discipline, contract, exchange value, speed, and bureaucracy, including the state organizations. These people attempt to exit from such social and economic arrangements, seeking alternative and more familiar, or informal, institutions and relations. Second, globalization has also a tendency to informalize through the programs of structural adjustment, rendering many people unemployed, or pushing them to seek refuge in the informal production, trade, housing, and transportation. Transnational street vendors (circulating, for instance, between the new Central Asian Republics and Istanbul, or between Jamaica and Miami) are the latest product of this age. In short, the new global restructuring tends to intensify the growth of subjectivities, social space, and terrain of political struggles that are coming to characterize the cities of the developing world.

Although the prevailing perspectives today provide useful angles to view the activism of the urban subaltern, they suffer from major drawbacks. These latter are reflected in the essentialism of the "passive poor," the reductionism of the "surviving poor," the Latino-centrism of the "political poor," and the conceptual perplexity of "resistance literature." I have suggested that the quiet-encroachment perspective might offer a way out of these conceptual problems. From this vantage point, the poor struggle not only for survival, but also to engage in a lifelong process to improve their lot often through individualistic and quiet encroachment on public goods and the power and property of elite groups. In this process, the grassroots do not directly challenge the effect of globalization. Rather, in their quest for security, they become involved in constant negotiations with globalization to maintain or seek autonomy in any space remaining unaffected. At the same time, the unintended consequences of their daily encroachments and negotiations beget significant social changes in urban structure and processes, in demography, and in public policy. I discussed earlier how crucial such a strategy is in the lives of the urban grassroots. Yet the question remains: how far can this quiet encroachment take these actors?

Given their existential constraints (limited skills and education, meager incomes, poor connections, and lack of organization) quiet encroachment serves as a viable strategy for enabling marginalized groups to survive and better their lot. However, this nonmovement is neither able to cause broader political transformation, nor does it aim for this. Only larger national movements have the capacity to create such a transformation. Yet, compared to global/national mobilization, such localized struggles are both *meaningful* and *manageable* for the actors — meaningful in that they provide a sense of purpose and produce tangible consequences, and manageable in that individual actors rather than remote national leaders, set the agenda, project the aims, and control the outcome. In this sense, for the poor, the local is privileged over the global/national.

Despite the ability of the disenfranchised to extend their life-chances through a lifetime of struggle on the local level, crucial social spaces remain out of their control. Thus, the marginals may be able to take over a plot of land to build shelters; they may tap running water or electricity illegally from the main street or their neighbors; they may secure a job on the street corner by selling things; and they may be able to bribe or dodge the police every now and then. But they cannot get schools, health services, public parks, paved roads, and security — the social goods which are tied to larger structures and processes, to national states and the global economy. In other words, the largely atomistic and localist strategies of the disenfranchised, despite their own advantages, do not answer the need for a search for social justice in a broader, national sense. This is why the urban grassroots are unlikely to become truly effective in a larger sense unless they become mobilized on a collective basis and their struggles become linked to broader social movements and civil organizations.[57] Yet it is crucial to remember that until this happens, quiet encroachment remains a viable enabling strategy, which the urban grassroots may pursue irrespective of what we, as social scientists, think of it.

NOTES

This is a slightly revised version of Asef Bayat, "From 'Dangerous Classes' to 'Quiet Rebels,'" *International Sociology* 15, no. 3, September 2000.

1. For critiques of the exaggerated globalization thesis, see C. Harman, "Globalization: A Critique of a New Orthodoxy," *International Socialism* 73 (Winter 1996), 3–20; *Marxism Today* (special issue, November–December 1998); and D. Gordon, "The Global Economy," *New Left Review* 168 (March–April 1988).

2. See A. Hoogvelt, *Globalization and the Postcolonial World* (Baltimore, Md.: The Johns Hopkins University Press, 1997), 121–31.

3. World Bank, *World Development Report 1995* (Oxford: Oxford University Press, 1995), 108.

4. J. Vandemoortele, "The African Employment Crisis of the 1990s," in C. Grey-Johnson, ed., *The Employment Crisis in Africa* (Harare, Zimbabwe: African Association for Public Administration and Management, 1990), 34–36.

5. See CIA, *The World Fact Book 1992* (Washington, D.C.: CIA, 1992).

6. For the figures see ILO, *World Employment Report, 1998–99* (Geneva, Switzerland: ILO, 1999); and D. McNally, "Globalization on Trial: Crisis and Class Struggle in East Asia," *Monthly Review* 50, no. 4 (September 1998), 7.

7. N. Webster, "The Role of NGOs in Indian Development: Some lessons from West Bengal and Karnataka," *The European Journal of Development Research* 7, no. 2 (December 1995).

8. See A. Bayat, "Activism and Social Development in the Middle East," *International Journal of Middle East Studies* 34, no. 1 (February 2002).

9. My study of the Middle East focusing in Iran and Egypt has appeared in A. Bayat, *Street Politics: Poor People's Movements in Iran* (New York: Columbia University Press, 1997). For a survey of various forms of struggles for social development in the Muslim Middle East including urban riots, organized labor, community activism, "social Islamism," NGOs, and "quiet encroachment," see Bayat, "Activism and Social Development in the Middle East."

10. H. Draper, *Karl Marx's Theory of Revolution*, Vol. 2 (New York: Monthly Review Press, 1978), 453.

11. Draper, *Karl Marx's Theory of Revolution*, Chapter 15.

12. P. Worsley, *The Three Worlds* (London: Weidenfeld and Nicholson, 1984).

13. F. Fanon, *The Wretched of the Earth* (London: Penguin, 1967).

14. S. Huntington, *Political Order in Changing Society* (New Haven, Conn.: Yale University Press, 1968); J. Nelson, "The Urban Poor: Disruption or Political Integration in Third World Cities," *World Politics* 22 (April 1970), 393–414; and S. Huntington and J. Nelson, *No Easy Choice: Political Participation in Developing Countries* (Cambridge, Mass.: Harvard University Press, 1976).

15. J. Nelson, "Urban Poor: Disruption or Political Integration in Third World Cities?"

16. See O. Lewis, *Five Families: Mexican Case Studies in the Culture of Poverty* (New York: Basic Books, 1959); *The Children of Zanchez: Autobiography of a Mexican Family* (New York: Random

House, 1961); and *La Vida: A Puerto Rican Family in the Culture of Poverty* (New York: Random House, 1966).

17. P. Worsley, *The Three Worlds: Culture and World Development* (London: Weodenfeld & Nicolson, 1984), 190–94.

18. See A. Leeds, "The Concept of the 'Culture of Poverty': Conceptual, Logical, and Empirical Problems with Perspectives from Brazil and Peru," in E. Leacock, ed., *The Culture of Poverty: A Critique* (New York: Simon and Shuster, 1971); and Charles Valentine, *Culture and Poverty: Critique and Counter Proposals* (Chicago: University of Chicago Press, 1968).

19. J. Perlman, *The Myth of Marginality* (Berkeley, Calif.: University of California Press, 1976); and M. Castells, *The City and the Grassroots* (Berkeley, Calif.: University of California Press, 1983).

20. My understanding of the notion of survival strategy is based upon J. Scott, "Everyday Form of Peasant Resistance," *The Journal of Peasant Studies* 13, no. 2 (January 1986).

21. E. Escobar, *Encountering Development* (Princeton, N.J.: Princeton University Press, 1995).

22. See J. Friedmann, *Empowerment: The Politics of Alternative Development* (London: Blackwell, 1992); J. Friedmann, "Rethinking Poverty: Empowerment and Citizen Rights," *International Social Science Journal* 48, no. 2 (June 1996).

23. Perlman, *The Myth of Marginality*; and Castells, *The City and the Grassroots*.

24. Castells, *The City and the Grassroots*; F. Schuurman and T. Van Naerssen, *Urban Social Movements in the Third World* (London: Croom Helm, 1989); and J. Friedmann, "The Dialectic of Reason," *International Journal of Urban and Regional Research* 13, no. 2 (September 1989).

25. The term comes from Bernard Hourcade, "Conseillisme, Classe Sociale et Space Urbain: Les Squatters du sud de Tehran, 1978–1981," in K. Brown et al., eds., *Urban Crisis and Social Movements in the Middle East* (Paris: Editions L'Harmattan, 1989).

26. See, for instance, M. Stiefel and M. Wolfe, *A Voice for the Excluded: Popular Participation in Development* (London: Zed Books, 1994). The book, which is commissioned by the United Nations Research Institute for Social Development, carries a section on urban social movements which covers exclusively the Latin American countries.

27. For details, see Bayat, "Activism and Social Development in the Middle East."

28. A. Bayat, "Globalizing Social Movements? Comparing Middle Eastern Islamist Movements and Latin American Liberation Theology," unpublished paper, the American University in Cairo, 1998.

29. A. Leeds and E. Leeds, "Accounting for Behavioral Differences: Three Political Systems and the Responses of Squatters in Brazil, Peru, and Chile," in J. Walton and L. Magotti, eds., *The City in Comparative Perspective* (London/New York: John Willey, 1976), 211.

30. J. Scott, *Weapons of the Weak: Everyday Forms of Peasant Resistance* (New Haven, Conn.: Yale University Press, 1985).

31. See S. Pile, "Opposition, Political Identities, and Spaces of Resistance," in S. Pile and M. Keith, eds., *Geographies of Resistance* (London: Routledge, 1997), 2.

32. See E. Reeves, "Power, Resistance, and the Cult of Muslim Saints in a Northern Egyptian Town," *American Ethnologist* 22, no. 2 (May 1995), 306–22.

33. See L. Abu-Lughod, "The Romance of Resistance: Tracing Transformations of Power through Bedouin Women," *American Ethnologist* 17, no. 1 (February 1990).

34. D. Singerman, *Avenues of Participation: Family, Politics, and Networks in Urban Quarters of Cairo* (Princeton, N.J.: Princeton University Press, 1995).

35. Pile, "Opposition, Political Identities, and Spaces of Resistance."

36. See A. MacLoad, *Accommodating Protest: Working Women, the New Veiling, and Change in Cairo* (New York: Columbia University Press, 1991).

37. Something that Frances Fox Piven and Richard Cloward wished poor people's movements in America had. See F. Piven and R. Cloward, *Poor People's Movements: Why They Succeed, How They Fail* (New York: Vintage, 1979).

38. See, for instance, M. Cole and D. Hill, "Games of Despair and Rhetorics of Resistance: Postmodernism, Education, and Reaction," *British Journal of Sociology of Education* 16, no. 2 (June 1995).

39. Scott, *Weapons of the Weak*, 290.

40. Ibid., 292.

41. N. Brown, *Peasant Politics in Modern Egypt: The Struggles vs. The State* (New Haven, Conn.: Yale University Press, 1990).

42. See A. Giddens, *Sociology* (Oxford, U.K.: Polity Press, 2000).

43. Scott, *Weapons of the Weak*, 350.

44. M. Foucault, *Knowledge/Power* (New York: Pantheon, 1972).

45. In the words of MacAdam, Tarrow, and Tilly, "Towards an Integrated Perspective on Social Movements and Revolution," in M. Linchbach and A. Zuckerman, eds., *Comparative Politics: Rationality, Culture, and Structure* (Cambridge, U.K.: Cambridge University Press, 1997), 150–51.

46. See Singerman, *Avenues of Participation*; H. Hoodfar, *Between Marriage and the Market: Intimate Politics and Survival in Cairo* (Berkeley, Calif.: University of California Press, 1997). In an interesting study of the political behavior of lower-class families in Cairo, Diane Singerman aims to show the particular ways in which the ordinary people in Egypt participate in the political processes and even change the outcome of national policies. To this end, she shows how Cairean poor families strive to extend their familial relations through intermarriage within the communities where they can stretch their security buffer. They also set up networks of mutual help and credit associations, and devise diverse strategies to go around the government requirements for subsidies, pension, and so on. The result, Singerman suggests, is not passivity and fatalism, but active participation in public life and a challenge to the state.

47. M. Brown, "On Resisting Resistance," *American Anthropologist* 98, no. 4 (December 1996), 730.

48. I have elaborated on this perspective in more detail elsewhere. See Bayat, *Street Politics*. Here, I only briefly outline some of the major points.

49. Reported in the Persian newspaper *Hamshahri*, and cited in Bayat, *Street Politics*, 79.

50. See, A. Bayat, "Cairo's Poor: Dilemmas of Survival and Solidarity," in *Middle East Report*, no. 202, special issue on "Cairo: Power, Poverty, and Urban Survival" (Winter

1997). On internal encroachments, see F. Ghannam, "Relocation and Use of Urban Space," *Middle East Report*, no. 202, special issue (Winter 1997).

51. Particularly, see, P. Kuppinger, "Giza Spaces," in *Middle East Report*, no. 202, special issue (Winter 1997).

52. See Bayat, *Street Politics*.

53. Reported by Education Committee of the Majlis al-Sha'b, and cited in *Al-Wafd* (January 21, 2002), 6.

54. See report in *The Egyptian Gazette* (January 29, 2002), 7.

55. For more details on the concept of "street politics," see Bayat, *Street Politics*, Chapter 1.

56. For many examples, see Bayat, *Street Politics*.

57. For an example of such a broader alliance in Peru, see P. Arevalo, "Huaycan Self-Managing Urban Community: May Hope be Realized," in *Environment and Urbanization* 9, no. 1 (April 1997).

PART II

THE POLITICS OF
URBAN INFORMALITIES

5

Marginality: From Myth to Reality in the *Favelas* of Rio de Janeiro, 1969–2002

Janice E. Perlman

In 1968–69 I lived in three low-income communities in Rio de Janeiro. I had become interested in cityward migration as an undergraduate anthropology student doing fieldwork in Brazil's northeast. Over the years I had followed the trajectories of families and individuals from fishing and agricultural villages to the squatter settlements and unserviced *loteamentos* (subdivisions) in Rio de Janeiro. The three communities I selected to study represented the various parts of the city where poor people could then live. They were Catacumba, a *favela* (squatter settlement) in the wealthy South Zone (which has since been removed and its residents relocated to more distant public housing); Nova Brasilia, a *favela* in the industrial North Zone (now a battleground between police and drug traffickers); and eight low-income communities in Duque de Caxias, a peripheral municipality in the Fluminense Lowlands (Baixada Fluminense).[1] In each place I interviewed two hundred men and women (sixteen to sixty-five years old) selected at random, and fifty community leaders chosen by position and/or reputation. The locations of the three communities and the two housing project sites (Conjuntos de Quitungo, Guapore, and Cidade de Deus — City of God) are shown on the accompanying map (see FIGURE 5.1).

The data on these 750 people and their communities provided the basis for my doctoral dissertation on the impact of urban experience; and after follow-up work in 1973, the research was also incorporated into my book, *The Myth of Marginality: Urban Poverty and Politics in Rio de Janeiro.* The book argued that the prevailing "myths" about social, cultural, political, and economic marginality were "empirically false, analytically misleading, and insidious in their policy implications."[2]

Ten years later, in 1979, I returned to Rio with hopes of following up on the lives of the individuals I had interviewed, and began the process of relocating

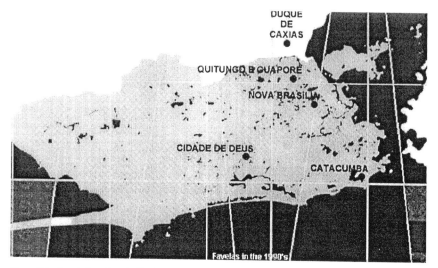

Figure 5.1. *Favela* locations in Rio de Janeiro city.
Source: Prourb – Programa de Pos-Graduacao em Urbanismo da Faculdade de Arquitetura e Urbanismo da Universidade Federal do Rio de Janeiro. Available online at www.fau.ufrj.br/prourb/index2.htm.

them, but funding fell through and the project was dropped. When I returned to the idea again in 1989, I discovered the "funding climate" was not receptive to public-policy issues or theoretical insights involving poverty, inequality, or social mobility. It was not until 1998, thirty years after the original study, that several foundations and international aid agencies expressed interest in funding a restudy of the people I had worked with and the communities in which I had lived.[3] By then, poverty, and the vast gap between the world's rich and poor, had again surfaced as an important issue — this time in relation to sustainable communities, peaceful societies, and public policy. And the question of how to break the inter-generational cycle of poverty and reverse the trend toward increased inequality had likewise regained relevance.

This chapter is based on the preliminary findings of this new longitudinal panel study. As in the original work, it draws on both qualitative and quantitative methods. Conceptually, the research follows individual lives and policy impacts in the context of macro-level political and economic transformation at both the national and city levels (see FIGURE 5.2). Phase I involved a feasibility study to determine the possibility of finding the original participants after thirty years, and then the conduct of in-depth interviews with thirty-six individuals.[4] Phase II involved the creation of a survey instrument adapted from the one used in the original research, the pretest and modification of this questionnaire, and its application to the original participants (or their spouses or eldest children in cases where the original interviewee was no longer living).[5] It also included interviews

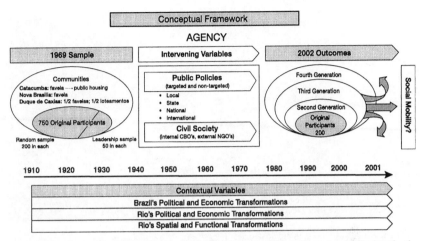

Figure 5.2. The dynamics of urban poverty and implications for public policy: a longitudinal study of Rio de Janeiro's poor (1968–2001).
Source: Prourb — Programa de Pos-Graduacao em Urbanismo da Faculdade de Arquitetura e Urbanismo da Universidade Federal do Rio de Janeiro. Available online at www.fau.ufrj.br/prourb/index2.htm.

with a random sample of the original participants' children; the completion of a series of contextual interviews about the communities themselves, leading to a "collective" reconstruction of each community's history; and a collection of year-by-year life histories, documenting all changes in residential, occupational, educational, and family conditions.

FAVELA GROWTH IN RIO DE JANEIRO

Despite three decades of public-policy efforts in Brazil — first to eradicate *favelas*, then to upgrade and integrate them into the city — both their number and the number of people living in them have continued to grow. There were approximately three hundred *favelas* in Rio at the time of my original study; there are now at least twice as many.

Furthermore, as the accompanying maps show, not only have *favelas* increased in number and size, they have merged to form vast contiguous agglomerations, "complexes" of communities across adjacent hillsides (see FIGURE 5.3). Each of these is the size of a large Brazilian city, and the largest — Rocinha, Jacarezinho, Complexo de Alemao, and Complexo de Mare — have a combined population of more than half a million. Between 1950 and 2000 Rio's *favela* population grew much more rapidly than the city as a whole (see FIGURE 5.4). The fastest growth rates were in the 1950s and the 1960s; but the growth of Rio's *favelas* has greatly exceeded that for the entire city in every decade except the 1970s, when a policy

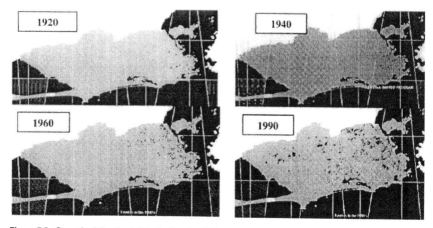

Figure 5.3. Growth of *favelas* in Rio de Janeiro (1920–1990).

Source: Prourb — Programa de Pos-Graduacao em Urbanismo da Faculdade de Arquitetura e Urbanismo da Universidade Federal do Rio de Janeiro. Available online at www.fau.ufrj.br/prourb/index2.htm.

of massive *favela* removal dislocated approximately 17,000 families, or about 100,000 individuals.[6]

Most striking perhaps is that during the period 1980–90, when the overall city growth rate dropped precipitously to 7.6 percent, *favela* populations surged by 40.5 percent. Then, from 1990 to 2000, when the city's growth rate leveled off at just less than 7 percent, *favela* populations continued to grow by 24 percent. One might add that these figures certainly underestimate real conditions, since

YEAR	FAVELA POP. (a)	CITY POP. RIO (b)	a/b (%)	FAVELA GROWTH RATE BY DECADE	RIO GROWTH RATE BY DECADE
1950	169,305	2,337,451	7.24%	—	—
1960	337,412	3,307,163	10.20%	99.3%	41.5%
1970	563,970	4,251,918	13.26%	67.1%	28.6%
1980	628,170	5,093,232	12.33%	11.4%	19.8%
1990	882,483	5,480,778	16.10%	40.5%	7.6%
2000	1,092,958	5,857,879	18.66%	23.9%	6.9%

* Includes some 144 cases, most of which fall into the "small" category, comprising colonias registered as having less than 10 lots.

Figure 5.4. Growth rates of *favelas* and Rio de Janeiro city population by decade.

Source: author with Instituto Brasileiro de Geografia e Estatistica, 2000 Census. Available online at www.ibge.gov.br/home/estatistica/populacao/censo2000).

they fail to include the numerous illegal subdivisions that have arisen recently, as areas for possible invasion and squatting have been consolidated and marketized.

By most every measure, then, the percentage of Rio's population living in *favelas* is now at an all-time high. But the figures also indicate that *favela* growth has not been spread evenly over the metropolitan region. In the twelve years from 1980 to 1992, for example, the *favela* growth rate in the South and North Zones was 21 and 15 percent, respectively. Meanwhile, in the West Zone, where the new urban elite has been moving (Barra de Tijuca), the number of *favelas* grew by 127 percent during the same period, while the *favela* population grew by 108 percent.[7] The pattern would seem to indicate that new *favela* locations continue an older pattern of residence in proximity to the service and construction jobs in more affluent areas.

THREE LIVES: FOUR GENERATIONS

The first challenge was to relocate original study participants after thirty years. To protect anonymity in 1968–69, at the height of the dictatorship, interviewees' last names were never recorded. Nevertheless, by creating teams of community residents we were able to find some information on 487 of the 750 original participants, to locate 242 of them, and to interview 227 — about one-third.

Due to the varying nature of the three communities that were part of the original work, I had expected our success rates to differ markedly. I had thought we would find the fewest number of the original interviewees from Catacumba, since families there had been forcibly evicted in 1970 and scattered among distant public housing projects.[8] Surprisingly, however, it was among the Catacumba group that we had the highest relocation success rate. This may be explained by the strong sense of solidarity created through years of struggle for collective urban services, culminating in the long battle against eviction. By contrast, the lowest relocation success rate was in Duque de Caxias — not so much in the *favelas*, but in the privately owned lots. Contrary to popular wisdom, there has been a much higher turnover rate among owners of the *loteamentos* than in *favelas*, and social ties were much weaker.

I might add that the re-encounter with the original interviewees and their families was a powerful emotional experience on both sides. It was joyful and poignant. We laughed and cried. People had gone through a lot in these thirty years and were eager to tell their stories. They wanted to bear witness, to give testimony, to be heard. They were also excited to see me again, the young "hippie-looking," "hard-working" American who had lived among them and shared their daily lives at a time when even bus and taxi drivers were afraid to stop too near their communities. They were eager to learn my life story as well. Was I married? Did

I have children? Where was I living? What was I doing? Had I been in New York on 9/11? Thus, what I am reporting on here is not only based on official questionnaire and life-history data, but on in-depth open-ended interviews involving the mutual reconstruction of lives, often lasting several afternoons and evenings. I will begin with three vignettes, one from each of the communities.

"TWICE DISPLACED": THE STORY OF MARGARIDA

When I first met Margarida (Marga) she was a twenty-five-year-old single mother living with her two young children in a small wooden shack in the *favela* of Catacumba. To get to her house you had to climb an almost vertical path around and beneath dozens of other shacks. It took about twenty minutes to wind one's way up from the street in front of the Rodrigo de Freitas Lagoon — much more if it were raining and the path had turned into a slippery slide of mud and sewage (see FIGURE 5.5).

Marga was born and raised in Catacumba. Both her parents were illiterate. Her mother was from Niteroi and had worked as a maid all of her life; her father was an unskilled manual laborer from Saquarema. Margarida was the second of four children, all of whom still live not far from one another. In 1968–69 she "came along" as the maid for a small apartment I had temporarily sublet in Apoador (a middle-class neighborhood between Ipanema and Copacabana). She had completed four

Figure 5.5. View of Catacumba from the Lagoa Rodrigo Freitas in 1969.
The location in the midst of the upscale residential South Zone gave residents abundant access to service and construction jobs as well as to the good schools and clinics in the area. Despite their removal in 1970 to disparate housing projects, their common struggles created strong communal ties which persist to this day.
Photo by author.

years of primary school, and had been working as a domestic ever since. Her daughter Beti was then eight, and her son Gilberto was seven. Their father had gone to the pharmacy one evening to get some aspirin and never returned.

The family lived in the *favela* on weekends, and in the small maid's quarters of the apartment during the week. The children went to a good school (using the apartment address for registration), and they had good health care nearby and lots of family and friends within the *favela*. Their lives were full of activities: picnics to Paqueta Island on the weekends, soccer games at the Youth Athletic Club, dances, and lots of sharing of good times and bad.

Two years later that lifestyle was eradicated forever. Marga and her family (along with 2,074 other families in Catacumba) were forcibly removed by helmeted police, put in garbage trucks with whatever possessions they could salvage, and taken to a distant public housing project called the Conjunto de Quitungo. This was at the height of the dictatorship, when 100,000 *favelados* were evicted from their homes within a period of two to three years. They were devastated. Friends and relatives were relocated to other projects, some separated by four hours of travel, and most of the community leaders disappeared.

Marga's lucky break was that she had just met Geraldo, a bright man seven years her junior who had a relatively stable job as a checkout clerk in a nearby supermarket (and is now a *gerente*, manager). Eventually, she had four more children with him (three girls and a boy) and was able to stop working outside the house (see FIGURE 5.6). Over time Marga and Geraldo made new friends and established new ways of coping with life in the housing project. I stayed in touch with them over the years and visited every time I was in Rio for conferences, meetings, or other work.

By the time I returned in 1999 to resume my research, Marga had been living in the same apartment for almost thirty years, and Beti and Gilberto had purchased their own apartments in the same housing project and were raising their own children. But one day after my return, a group from one of the *commandos* (drug gangs)

Figure 5.6. Margarida, her new husband Geraldo ("Pingo"), and myself in 1973.
The photo was taken the first time I visited Marga in her apartment in the Quitungo housing project. Like many others, she suffered severe depression and disorientation after being relocated. Today she still misses her life in Catacumba, despite having adapted over the years to apartment living.
Photo by author.

came to Marga's apartment looking for her youngest son, Wagner. Apparently, he had made friends with members of a rival gang. They said if she didn't turn him over, they would kill her and the entire family. Luckily, Wagner wasn't home, and over the weekend Marga's daughters mobilized to scan the newspapers for low-income rentals everywhere within a one-hour bus ride. By Monday they had moved to a two-bedroom apartment in Irajá. Marga now feels safer and can sleep at night. But she cries every day from loneliness and isolation, and admits they will soon have to move again, even further away, since this apartment is too expensive.

Of Marga's children, Beti is the eldest. She considers herself a seamstress, but was unemployed for a long time before finally finding temporary work as a babysitter (*baba*). Unfortunately, the job is at the extreme other end of the city, and she now only comes home once every two weeks. She has heard of another job, every other day, assisting an elderly woman in Ipanema, and she intends to interview for it. But she fears her dark skin color may reduce her chances.[9] Her only son is eighteen and an unemployed school dropout.

Marga's son Gilberto is a specialist in air conditioner and refrigerator repairs, a skill he learned working in a factory. He has worked in many types of jobs on and off and can do most anything, but has been unable to find steady work since the factory closed almost eight years ago. Recently, he was forced to sell his apartment, and he now alternates staying at Beti's or at Regina's (his mother's former neighbor). His wife supposedly "went crazy" and walked out on him and their fifteen-year-old son, Elbert, who is still in school but now lives with Margarida.

All four of Margarida and Geraldo's children — Eliana (thirty-one), Elisangela (twenty-eight), Viviane (twenty-four), and Wagner (twenty-one) — still live at home. Eliana completed high school, and has just been promoted from sales clerk to manager at a stationery store. Viviane, who never finished high school, used to work as a computer assistant, but was fired, and now works as a cashier in the same store as her sister. Wagner dropped out after the fourth year of primary school and has worked intermittently as a *marceneiro*, making wood furniture. His mother claims he does not sell or use drugs, that he just got in with the wrong crowd.

Elisangela, the most sophisticated member of the family, brings in a steady income from her job as a cleaning girl for TV Globo. Despite never having completed high school, she is intelligent, well-spoken, and well-connected. When a TV program requires someone to stand in as a maid, they often shoot her in the role. She thinks the family should combine its resources to construct a house along the north coast of the city. She says the prices for small lots there are good, and that she has friends who could help them.

"LEFT BEHIND": THE STORY OF ZÉ CABO

José Manuel da Silva (known as Zé Cabo) was one of the most respected and established leaders in Nova Brasília when I first met him in 1968. He was forty years old then, and President of the Residents Association. He had moved to Rio de Janeiro when he was sixteen from a small city in the interior of Rio Grande do Norte. Neither of his parents had attended school, and he was the fifth of nineteen children. He moved to Nova Brasília at the age of twenty-nine, after working in the Marines.

Although José did finish elementary school, he learned much of what he knows traveling across Brazil and being exposed to many ideas and people. This is why he was more politically savvy than others in the community. It was he who led the collective struggles in Nova Brasilia through the 1960s and 1970s for water, electricity, drainage, sewer connections, and street paving. And it was he who fought for land titles and negotiated with the candidates and government officials on behalf of the community. He also played a critical role in acquiring the land on which the Residents Association was constructed.

At the time of the original study, José and his wife, Adelina, had three boys and a girl. José was working for the military police — which is where he acquired the nickname Zé Cabo (*cabo* indicating the rank of captain within the military police). The family lived on the main street, Avenida Nova Brasilia (see FIGURE 5.7). There was always something good cooking on the stove, and their home was a place where others could come for help and advice. The community, being in the

Figure 5.7. Nova Brasilia's main street from the terrace of Jose Cabo's house in 1973.
Commercial uses, here visible at the street level only, have now taken over most former second- and third-floor residential space as well. People come from around the region to do their shopping here.
Photo by author.

North Zone amid factories and working-class neighborhoods, was not threatened with removal, but it was generally ignored by politicians after each election.

Over the years, I stayed in touch with José and his family. In the early 1990s his wife died of a heart attack. Then, due to medical bills, debts, and the increasing danger of drug-related violence on the street where he lived, he decided to sell his home. With the proceeds, he bought a tiny piece of land in a more remote area of the *favela*, built a new house, and financed the construction of houses elsewhere for his daughter and one of his grandsons.

In this expanded new house he supports the mother of his two "other" daughters (ages twenty-three and twenty-four), their young children, and an elderly aunt. He is discouraged that Nova Brasilia still does not have full urban services, was overlooked by the widespread Favela-Bairro program, and is totally permeated by drug dealers — including the Residents Association, the school, and the so-called nonprofits. It is part of the Complexo de Alemão, one of the most dangerous *favelas* in the city.[10] It was in this area that on June 3, 2002, the journalist Tim Lopes was tortured and murdered while working on a story about drugs and youth sex at funk dances. Police are afraid to go there except in organized raids, and even then they are often out-armed by the locals.[11]

None of José's children from his first marriage live in the *favela* anymore. José's brother and wife have since moved to Natal, capital of Rio Grande do Norte, where they were born. They have a nice house there with an upstairs apartment for José, but he only comes to visit. He tells them Nova Brasilia "is my community, and I wouldn't know what to do with myself anywhere else." But he confides that he is tired of the gunshots every night, the constant fear, and the bullet holes in his walls. He might consider selling his house if he could get a reasonable price.

"My greatest achievement in life is that none of my kids are on drugs, in jail, or murdered," he says. This initially made me suspect that his children were having great difficulties in life. In fact, all of José's four children from his first marriage are doing quite well.

Of these children, Wanderley, the eldest (now fifty-two), never finished high school but has a job with the *Caixa Econômica Federal*. He lives in Japeri (a municipality outside Rio de Janeiro). All three of his children are working in the computer field.

José's second oldest child, Waney, is forty-eight. Currently out of work, he lives on his pension from years in the civil police. He says he would be getting a higher retirement benefit if he had stayed a full term, but he left early when he was offered a good job as a deliveryman for a South Zone company. The company was owned by a woman who liked his work, but she took on two male associates, and as Waney explained it, "She was assassinated by one of them, and they took all her money and closed the business."

Waney has three children. The eldest, Wagner, used some of the money from José's house sale to build a simple, attractive wood-frame house in a nice gated community in the interior of Niteroi. He earns a decent living fixing car air conditioners, and his wife works in a boutique in a nearby shopping mall. Patricia, his younger sister (twenty-one), is known as the "smart one" in the family, and attended law school for one year. But instead of completing her degree, she dropped out to go to Candido Mendes University in Niteroi to study fashion design, and then started her own clothing line. Waney's youngest daughter, Cynthia, is fifteen years old and is still attending school.

The third of José's children from his first marriage, Wandelina (known as a "live wire" in her youth) dropped out of school after five years. She is now forty-eight and lives in Santa Cruz. This is a safe area, but more than two hours by car from the center of Rio — much longer by bus. Wandelina is retired from her job in an elementary school cafeteria, and now works in the library of a newly reno-vated cultural center. She is separated and has a fifteen-year-old son, who she is struggling to keep out of trouble. Fortunately, the son is a soccer star and can stay on the team only if he stays in school. Currently, he has a scholarship from Zico's soccer school (a well-known former player), and he has already traveled to Switzerland and the United States to participate in international competitions.

José's youngest son, Wandeney, is now forty-five. He attended a university for a few years, but never finished. He lives in Santa Cruz and works for the state Motor Vehicle Bureau. He is very involved in local politics. Although he does not have any children, he has been with the same girlfriend for two years, and his father and older brothers hope he will marry her.

Both José's daughters from his second marriage are having their difficulties. The oldest, Sandra (twenty-four), managed to finish high school, but she is unemployed and still lives with José. She is a single mother of Caroline (six) and Catarina (three months). Sandra's sister, Solange (twenty-three), never finished junior high school. She lives next door and is supported by her father, as she has been unable to find work.

It is Zé Cabo's dream to move out of the *favela*, but not to Natal or even Niteroi or Santa Cruz, where his children live. Instead, he wants to live in an apart-ment in Gloria, a wonderful neighborhood close to the center of downtown Rio.

"NO MORE FRUIT ON THE TABLE": THE STORY OF DJANIRA

In 1968, when I first met Djanira, she was an activist in Vila Operaria, a planned invasion in the municipality of Caxias (see FIGURE 5.8). Beautiful, ener-getic, and articulate, she had helped in planning the invasion and organizing the community. As part of the invasion, lands were set aside for schools, churches, sports facilities, and other public uses. No one with a police record was allowed to squat there, and all had to sign the local statute, which, among other things, protected women's rights to their homes.[12]

Djanira was born in 1936 in Recife (the capital of Pernambuco), one of twenty-five children, twenty-one of whom survived. Of her three siblings who

Figure 5.8 The Municipal Building and Plaza in the center of Caxias in 1969.
This is about a fifteen-minute bus ride from Djanira's neighborhood, Vila Operária. Today the buildings around the plaza are more sleek and sophisticated. The plaza itself has been taken over by vehicles, reflecting the explosive growth of the municipality.
Photo by author.

are still alive today, her brother is a clerk in Campo Grande, one sister is a widow living in Olaria, and another sister lives in Caxias. Djanira's parents were both illiterate, and neither attended school. Growing up, her family was extremely poor and often hungry. Her mother, who took in laundry to supplement her husband's earnings as a traveling salesman, died of tuberculosis when Djanira was seven. Afterwards, Djanira went to a Catholic school for two years, but was forced to leave when she was nine, the year her father died from a brain hemorrhage. Together with her older brothers and sisters, she made her way to Irajá, a neighborhood in Rio's North Zone, where she continued for two more years of school. She then worked as a babysitter and maid, living in the homes where she worked, often being badly treated, even beaten.

When Djanira was twenty-one, she married and moved to Niteroi, where her husband's family had a plot of land. Then, at the age of twenty-seven, she moved to Vila Operária, where she could finally have a house of her own. Today, Djanira lives in that same house, which her family built. The street outside is now paved with cobblestones, and the house is hidden behind iron gates. But inside it is the same. Her small courtyard is filled with flowering plants and songbirds in cages, and the front door is always open, leading directly to her living room and large kitchen. From the courtyard you can ascend to the second floor where the rest of the family lives — varying in size depending on the fortunes of her extended clan.

I remember Djanira fighting for land tenure, urban services, and the local school. Early on, the Residents Association set up an amusement park to generate income so they could pay for more qualified teachers (see FIGURE 5.9). Djanira was rounded up after one of the demonstrations for property titles, and was with the others at the police station when she went into labor and almost delivered her daughter. On the spot she says she named the little girl "Janiss" in my honor. Djanira eventually had ten children by two husbands, and raised them by working as the *merendeira* (lunch preparer) for the school next door. Then, when she was thirty-three years old, she went back to finish high school, qualifying to become a social worker in the Municipal Hospital Duque de Caxias, where she worked for the next twenty-nine years.

When I revisited Djanira she was still slender and beautiful, but she was nearly destitute, and suffering from health problems. Her only income was a small pension of about US$70 per month, a sum that only covered her electricity and phone bills. Her food is now being paid for by her daughter, Celia Regina, who lives with her and works at the same hospital where she once worked.

Djanira's life is today consumed by a fight for the pension of her common-law husband of forty years. They were together until his death three years ago, but he never registered any of their four children, and so all his assets have gone to his two children from his first wife. Before he died, he and Djanira led a relatively comfortable life. He had many assets: two homes, a *sítio* in the country, and stocks (including Petrobras, Banco do Brasil, Light, and Correios). But today all Djanira is legally entitled to is his pension, and she not even been able to get this because she cannot afford a lawyer.

"When you were here before, I always had a bowl full of fruit on my table," she told me. "Now it is empty. I can barely afford rice and beans."

One morning our team came to a meeting of old-timers at Djanira's house, but we could hardly get past the police cars. A dead body had been dumped near-

Figure 5.9. Djanira (left) with one of the teachers from the Vila Operária Municipal School in 1969. As part of their fight for the school, the Residents Association set up an amusement park, and used the proceeds to help construct the building and hire qualified teachers. *Photo by author.*

by at dawn, and the police were just taking it away. Fear is pervasive in her neighborhood, and Djanira is afraid to visit the public areas she fought so hard to create. Even the Residents Association has been taken over by drug dealers.

> Back then I participated in everything. . . . Now I can't participate in anything. . . . I see things going wrong and cannot do anything about it. It's too dangerous. The violence is so bad here that no one will deliver anything to my house. They are afraid of being robbed. If you interview for a job and they see your address, they say the job has been filled. In our time, we at least had respect and each other's solidarity; now everyone keeps to themselves.

The life stories of Djanira's children and grandchildren vary considerably. Her eldest child, Marco Antonio (forty-five), never finished high school, but now works as an administrative assistant in the Community Health Office. He is married, has three children, and lives in Vila São Luiz, a neighborhood of Caxias. His eldest son, Marcio (twenty-two) is married, and his wife is expecting a baby, but because the young couple has no money, they are living with his parents. Marco Antonio's other son, Sandro (nineteen), was accepted to a prestigious preparatory course for university (*pré-vestibular*) with a full scholarship, and wants to be a doctor. His daughter, Bruna (fifteen), is in her first year of high school.

Two of Djanira's ten children have university degrees. Marta Janete (forty) has a degree in pedagogy and has worked in the housing department of the Caxias city government for twenty-three years. She lives in Vila Operária but is searching for a house in Santa Cruz. Marta Janete's two children and one granddaughter live with Djanira in the upstairs apartment. Paulo (eighteen) is finishing junior high school, wants to work, but cannot find a job. Kelly (twenty-two) wanted to be a model, but last year got pregnant, and is now attending the second year of high school. Her one-year-old daughter is named Milena.

Jorge Luis (thirty-nine) is Djanira's other child with a university degree. He studied law and accounting, and today practices law from his office near the Caxias city center. He lost his first wife to cancer at a very young age. His daughter Joicy is seven years old and attending elementary school.

Roberto (twenty-seven), another of Djanira's children, never completed high school but has a decent job as a sanitary worker at SUCAN (the Federal Public Health Agency). He lives half the time with Djanira, and half the time with Djanira's niece (who helped raise him, and now lives in Jacarepaguá, in Rio's West Zone). Janiss (thirty-two), my namesake, lives with her adopted daughter in a planned invasion in Santa Lucia, a rural part of Caxias. For ten years she also worked with SUCAN. Her job was to go around with tanks of DDT on her back spraying against dengue and malaria. During that time she inhaled a good deal of toxic spray and now has chronic bronchitis. But because she was never formally hired, she is not entitled to health benefits.

Of Djanira's other children, Jane Marcia (forty-one) completed only three years of schooling and is a poor, unemployed housewife. Raldo (thirty-three) finished junior high school and works as a transportation inspector. He lives in Santa Cruz with his wife and three kids: Luciano (sixteen), Juliete (twelve), and Felipe (six) — all of whom are attending school. Raquel (twenty-four) completed junior high school, and is a housewife with a seven-year-old daughter, Stefani, who is attending elementary school.

Finally, two of Djanira's children still live with her. One is Celia Regina (thirty-eight). She never finished high school, but she works as a clerk in the same hospital where Djanira once worked. Celia-Regina's son, Rafael (fifteen), a junior high school student, also lives with her and Djanira. Celia-Regina is also raising Mathew, a one-year-old. The last of Djanira's children, Almir (thirty-five), only studied for three years. For a time he worked as a *trocador de onibus* (bus-fare collector), and was once assaulted in an armed robbery. He now has a defective arm and sells sweets across the street from her house. He lives in the small apartment on top of Djanira's house with his wife (who supports the family selling *quentinhas*, cooked lunch, for the school and workers) and daughter Diana (eleven).

A COMPLEX PICTURE

The above stories are messy and contradictory, revealing a mixture of despair and hope. Overall, they reveal several general changes since 1969 in the world of Rio's *favelas*. For example, there is a sense of isolation in comparison to earlier times, and a fear that pervades all aspects of life. Principally, this may be traced to the violence between drug dealers and the police, and among various gangs. A part of everyday life now, this was barely present in 1968–69.

At the same time, there has been a clear upgrading of infrastructure in the communities and an overall increase in household goods and appliances. But the simultaneous increase in the gap between rich and poor is vividly reflected in the sense that these individuals feel more distant from the world of *asfalto* (the formal life of pavement) than they did thirty years ago.

The respondents to our new survey also do not feel like full-fledged citizens. And, ironically, they are less empowered within their communities than they were during the military dictatorship. Nevertheless, their children and grandchildren — to varying degrees — have more education and higher incomes (if they are working) than they did. And many among this new generation have moved out of the original "irregular" communities, into low-income neighborhoods (some quite peripheral), where they participate in the legitimate world of rental or ownership.

Considered as a whole, the above stories help illustrate five major themes I have noticed since 1969. I have termed these the metamorphosis of marginality; the sphere of fear; mobility with inequality; disillusionment with democracy; and optimism for the future.

THE METAMORPHOSIS OF MARGINALITY

I researched and wrote *The Myth of Marginality* during a specific historical moment, in the context of fundamental disagreements over the nature and consequences of rapid urbanization and dependent development. My work was part of a profound critique of then-prevailing paradigms used to explain the urban poor and the irregular settlements in which they lived.

In the modernization literature, migrants from the countryside to the city were seen as maladapted to city life, and thereby responsible for their own poverty and failure to enter formal job and housing markets.[13] Squatter settlements were seen as "cancerous sores on the beautiful body of the city," dens of crime, violence, prostitution, and social breakdown. It was widely assumed that the dwellers in the precarious shacks were precarious themselves, and that comparing their condition with the surrounding opulence would turn them into angry revolutionaries. Such was the nightmare/fear of the Right and the daydream/hope of the Left.[14] However, on both sides the sense that squatters were "other" and not part of the "normal" city was pervasive. This seemingly common-sense view was legitimized by social scientists and used to justify public policies of removal.

Starting in the mid-1960s several seminal writers challenged this conventional/academic "wisdom." These included Alejandro Portes, Jose Nun, Anibal Quijano, Manuel Castells, Florestan Fernandes, and Fernando Henrique Cardoso.[15] Empirical studies in Latin American cities including Rio de Janeiro, Salvador, São Paulo, Santiago, Buenos Aires, Lima, Bogota, Mexico City, and Monterrey served to discredit the propositions of marginality and the erroneous stereotypes surrounding the urban poor.[16] Lastly, Morse and Mangin wrote excellent review articles on the subject, which appeared in the 1970s.[17]

These works, along with my own, showed how the concept of marginality had been used to "blame the victim" in academic and public-policy discourse.[18] We demonstrated that there was a logic and rationality to the attitudes and behaviors in slums, and that there were strengths and assets in the squatter settlements of Latin America that belied the stereotypes of deficits, deficiencies, disorganization, and pathologies of all types.

THE MYTH OF MARGINALITY

One of my first objectives in *The Myth of Marginality* was to synthesize the collected body of literature regarding the social, cultural, economic, and political dimensions of marginality into a series of propositions and concepts that could be empirically tested.[19] For Rio de Janeiro, I found that despite their wide acceptance at all levels of society, these "myths" were "empirically false, analytically misleading, and insidious in their policy implications." As I wrote then:

The evidence strongly indicates that the *favelados* are not *marginal*, but in fact integrated into the society, albeit in a manner detrimental to their own interests. They are not separate from, or on the margins of the system, but are tightly bound into it in a severely asymmetrical form. They contribute their hard work, their high hopes, and their loyalties, but do not benefit from the goods and services of the system. *It is my contention that the* favela *residents are not economically and politically marginal, but are excluded and repressed; that they are not socially and culturally marginal, but stigmatized and excluded from a closed class system.*[20]

I went on to show how the marginality ideology was so strong in Brazil in the 1970s that it created a self-fulfilling prophecy. In particular, the *favela*-removal policy it justified perversely created the conditions it was designed to eliminate. In fact, the *favela* was an extremely functional solution to many of the problems faced by its residents. It provided access to jobs and services, a tightly knit community in which reciprocal favors mitigated hardship, and above all, free housing. This was clearly not the case in the housing projects (*conjuntos*) to which *favela* residents were consigned by the government. In the government projects, they were separated from kin and friendship networks; located far from jobs, schools and clinics; and charged monthly payments beyond their means.[21] Relocation also diminished family earnings by eliminating many of the services and odd jobs family members could perform after school, while caring for children, or when filling in time between other tasks.

Javier Auyero aptly summarized the idea of the "marginal mass" as a permanent structural feature of late capitalism as follows:

In contrast with the behaviorist and value-centered approach, the structural-historical perspective on marginality focused on the process of import substitution industrialization and its intrinsic inability to absorb the growing mass of the labor force . . . the functioning of the "dependent labor market" was generating an excessive amount of unemployment. This "surplus population" transcended the logic of the Marxist concept of "industrial reserve army" and led authors to coin the term "marginal mass." The "marginal mass" was neither superfluous nor useless; it was "marginal" because it was rejected by the same system that had created it. Thus the "marginal mass" was a "permanent structural feature" never to be absorbed by the "hegemonic capitalist sector" of the economy, not even during its expansionist cyclical phases.[22]

In my concluding discussion of "Marginality and Urban Poverty," I explored this in greater depth, contesting the validity of the assumptions underpinning the behaviorist approach, and showing the structural, functional, and political utility of the myths and their relation to the objective conditions of poverty and dependent development.[23] I also concluded that *favela* residents:

do not have the attitudes or behaviors supposedly associated with marginal groups. Socially, they are well organized and cohesive and make wide use of the urban milieu and its institutions. Culturally, they contribute (their music, slang, soccer, and samba) to the "mainstream," are highly optimistic, and aspire to better education for their children and improved homes and living conditions. Economically, they do the worst jobs for the lowest pay, under the most arduous conditions, with the least security. Politically, they are neither apathetic nor radical. They are aware of and keenly involved in those aspects of politics that affect their lives, both within and outside the *favela* . . . [but] they are politically intimidated and manipulated in order to maintain the status quo.[24]

And I asserted that:

they have the aspirations of the bourgeoisie, the perseverance of pioneers, and the values of patriots . . . what they do not have is the opportunity to fulfill their aspirations. The closed nature of the class structure makes it extremely difficult to achieve the hoped-for social mobility.[25]

In deconstructing the erroneous assumptions underpinning the marginality framework, I challenged the presumed co-variation (rather than independence) of dimensions; the idea that poverty is a consequence of characteristics of the poor (rather than a condition of society itself); and the use of a consensus rather than conflict model of society. Furthermore, I noted how the persistence of the myths, despite their lack of correspondence with reality, could be explained not only by the ethnocentric snobbery and prudish moralizing of class bias, but by "the ideological-political function of preserving the social order which generated them."[26] To wit:

The marginality myths justify the existence of extreme inequality and the inability of the system to provide even minimal standards of living for vast portions of its population. By blaming these conditions on the lack of certain attributes of the squatter population, the myths preserve the legitimacy and credibility of the structural rules of the game.[27]

As Jose Artur Rio confirmed:

The *favela* is a necessity of the Brazilian social structure. It demands relations of economic dependence, which result in temporary or permanent misery of the dependent element for the benefits of society.[28]

This dependency-school critique proposed that the traits which defined marginality were only the external symptoms of a form of society rooted in the historical process of industrialization and economic growth in Latin America. In fact, the symptoms of marginality resulted from a model of development (or underdevelopment[29]) defined by the exclusion of vast sectors of the population from society's main productive apparatus.[30]

Yet, as the dependency school pointed out, even if this population segment was excluded from the *benefits* of the new dominant sector, it was *included* in processes of capital accumulation, both through a chain of exploitation linking their labor to productive processes, and through lowering the reproduction cost of labor.[31] From this perspective, I wrote that marginality could be seen as "the inevitable reverse side of new capital accumulation, insofar as new multinational monopoly investment was increasingly separating the places where the surplus value is produced and the markets where people have sufficient income to consume the products."[32]

I also wrote that the myths of marginality persisted because they played useful psychosocial functions. In particular, they provided a scapegoat for a wide array of societal problems, thus legitimating dominant norms. Marginality was considered the source of all forms of deviance, perversity, and criminality, thus "purifying" the self-image of the rest of society (what I called a "specular relationship").[33] Even more insidiously, the myths shaped the self-image of those labeled marginal in a way that was useful for society, as *favelados* internalized the negative definition ascribed to them, and blamed their own ignorance, laziness, or worthlessness for their lack of "success."[34]

Finally, the issue of marginality also had powerful political implications which supported the populist politicians, and then military dictatorship, of the period. According to Manuel Castells, "marginality became a political issue not because some people are 'outside the system,' but because the ruling classes were trying to use the absence of organization and consciousness of a particular sector in order to obtain political support for their own objectives, offering in exchange a clientelistic or patronage relationship."[35] The underlying dynamic of populist politicians consisted of playing off the masses' desire for mobility against the oligarchy's fear of revolution. To the oligarchy, they could promise to keep the masses in check; to the masses, they could claim the ability to win concessions from the elite.[36]

NEW MEANINGS OF MARGINALITY

Brazil has changed dramatically over the past thirty years. A gradual political *abertura* (opening), starting in the late 1970s, led through a series of incremental steps to the end of the dictatorship in 1984–85 and the redemocratization of the country. However, the "economic miracle" of the 1970s also gave way to triple-digit inflation during the 1980s, then stagnation and a series of devaluations of the currency. Efforts to curb inflation culminated in the Real Plan (Plano Real) of 1993, but this did not solve the problem of economic growth, which remained low during the 1990s. Continued financial instability has also contributed to growing unemployment and inequality over the past decade. Thus, while the discourse on poverty may have changed in Brazil, the reality of poverty remains, with the top 10 percent of the population earning 50 percent of the national income, while about 34 percent live below the poverty line.[37]

The term "marginality" was not widely used in academic or activist circles after the 1970s. The 1970s were characterized by deconstructing the "theories of marginality" from the "phenomenon of marginality."[38] And then, with the democratic opening of the 1980s, new voices of opposition emerged, and the discourse turned toward concepts of social exclusion, inequality, injustice, and spatial segregation. These issues were also linked to issues of transparency, participatory democracy, and citizenship. In particular, the concept of exclusion was seen to extend beyond economic dualism and underemployment, to a question of rights and opportunities of full citizenship. In policy terms, the most recent response has been the Favela-Bairro program, which has focused on upgrading the physical infrastructure in *favelas* as a means of integrating them into surrounding neighborhoods. However, this massive program has not addressed issues of insertion in the labor market, or provided an inclusive model of development.

Ironically, however, the word "marginal" is now appearing with more frequency in the press, popular music, and common parlance than at any time since the publication of my book in the mid-1970s. The principal reason is that it has been invested with new connotations, specifically as a reference to drug and arms dealers and "outlaws" (*bandidos*). Daily headlines in the newspapers scream about the violence between the *bandidos* and/or *marginais* and the police. Likewise, rap songs and funk music talk about being "marginal" as a bad/good/tough thing — almost a black-pride spin-off, a call to rise up in revolt. In response, the middle class is again fearful of *favelas*. As police and gangs confront each other, everyone else worries about being caught in the crossfire. Meanwhile, discussion has emerged in the press of having the government declare a state of emergency and send in the federal police or the army.[39]

Today, therefore, even if *favelados* are no longer considered marginal, the *favelas*, as territories controlled by drug dealers, are seen as harboring "marginals," "the marginality," or "the movement" (i.e., drug dealers). As a result, the *favelados*, whose space has been occupied by drug traffickers (because it was unprotected and easier to hide in) are now associated with the dealers themselves. Inside the *favela* a distinction is made — we are "the workers" (*trabalhadores*), they are "the movement." But outside, a sense that the *favelas* are the source of the problem, rather than the home of its most obvious victims, has once again arisen. Today, for example, the rates of violent death inside *favelas* are much higher than in the rest of the city. Considering that half of all deaths among Rio de Janeiro youth are caused by homicide, it is clear that many young *favelados* (especially men) are being murdered every day, both by the dealers and the police.[40]

As Loïc Wacquant has written, "the strong trope of disorganization reinforces the logic of making a few 'worst cases' stand for the whole."[41] This is
nowhere more evident than in Rio, where the press alternatively presents *favelados*
as hostages of the *bandidos* and as their accomplices. Both stereotypes are daily
renewed by stories of *favelados* being killed by police, dealers expelling residents
from their homes (with police protection), and mass riots and the burning of
public buses in protest against police killings.

Meanwhile, in academic circles, such terms as "the underclass," the "new
poverty," "the new marginality," or "advanced marginality" have (re)emerged in
the analyses of excluded populations in advanced capitalist countries, particularly
the black ghettos of the United States and the stigmatized slums of Europe. Most
pointedly, Wacquant has documented the contiguous configuration of color, class,
and place in the Chicago ghetto, the French *banlieue*, and the British and Dutch
"inner cities," out of which emerges a "distinctive regime of urban marginality."[42]

The argument is that in addition to the effects of "industrial marginality," in
which massive unemployment leads to low incomes, deteriorated working conditions, and weakened labor guarantees (for those lucky enough to have jobs), a
"postindustrial" marginality has also arisen, with properties all its own. Thus,
thirty years later, we are witnessing a resurgence of the term in relation to new
constraints, stigmas, territorial separations, and dependencies (on the welfare
state). And it has emerged in relation to institutions within "territories of urban
relegation" which serve functions parallel to those of the state.[43]

Indeed, Wacquant has posited four structural dynamics ("logics") that are
jointly reshaping the nature of urban poverty in rich societies. These can be par-
aphrased as follows: 1) the resurgence of social inequality in the context of overall prosperity and the elimination of jobs for unskilled workers; 2) an "absolute
surplus population" that will never work again, as well as a form of poverty that is
becoming more persistent for those who do have jobs, as a result of low rates of
pay and the exploitation of temporary workers; 3) the retrenchment of the welfare state, as programs for the poor are cut and turned into instruments of surveillance and control; and 4) spatial concentration and stigmatization and a
diminishing sense of community life.[44]

In general, the first two of these dynamics apply to Rio's *favelas*. In fact, they
were part of the "old marginality" — although they have intensified over the
decades. However, the second two do not fit the realities of Rio's poor, partly
because Brazil has never fully developed a welfare state, and partly because poverty is more spatially dispersed in Rio. Recent research in Buenos Aires and
Guadalajara has enriched this discussion.[45]

Today, with regard to the *favela* communities I studied thirty years ago, I want
to know to what extent propositions of "advanced marginality" hold in relation to
Rio de Janeiro. Is there a marked difference in the life trajectories of the original

participants compared with those of their children? And how do the fluctuations in people's lives vary (or not) with fluctuations in their community, and in the macro-political economy of their city and their country?

NEW RESPONSES TO MARGINALITY

Despite the importance of the new manifestations of informality described above, Wacquant's definition of the ghetto as a segregated space organized in response to certain constraints only partially applies to *favelas*.[46] Yes, they arose and persist due to economic necessity and material deprivation, physical and social insecurity, racial and class prejudice, and territorial stigma. But increased inequality, deindustrialization, erosion of worker protections, and growth in the informal sector are equally powerful contextual factors.

Likewise, bureaucratic apathy and administrative ineptness do not precisely capture the reality of present state-*favela* relationships (and never did, as populist politics is so very different). Yes, bureaucrats can be apathetic and administrators can be inept. But there are larger issues of political corruption; of links between *bicheiros* (gambling rings), drug and arms dealers, and the police; and of electoral favors and patronage politics. Similarly, Wacquant's notion of "parallel institutions that serve as functional substitutes for and a protective buffer against the dominant institutions of the encompassing society, duplicating the latter only at an incomplete and inferior level" does not apply well to *favelas*—although some believe the drug lords have established a "parallel power" (*poder paralello*).[47]

Nor do various aspects of the supposed "retrenchment of the welfare state" apply in the case of Rio. In Brazil, the welfare state is still under construction. Many of the most important existing guarantees were put into place by Getulio Vargas as part of the Estado Novo (1937–45).[48] More than half (55 percent) of our original random sample, and 84 percent of the leadership sample, defined state-supported retirement payments (*aposentadoria*) as their main source of current income (often supporting children and grandchildren). Between the Estado Novo and the 1964 military coup, and during the twenty years of military dictatorship that ensued, Brazil's welfare state did not expand significantly. Throughout this period there was little concern for a "social safety net." This may explain why, when asked "Who is the politician who has done the most to help you and people like you?" the answer most often given by those in our sample was not any recent mayor or governor, but Getulio Vargas. Since the mid-1980s, however, and particularly in the last five years, the welfare state has been expanding, with new programs and benefits for the poor.

The notion of "parallel power" or "a parallel state" to depict authority and benefit structures in the *favelas* is facile. It is true that in many *favelas* drug traffickers are better armed and more evident than the police, but this often comes with the complicity of the police. The police may even confiscate arms and drugs in one community and sell them in another, and they certainly supplement their meager wages with the payoffs they receive to turn a blind eye to drug sales. It is no wonder they will not risk answering calls for help at night.

Similarly, the concept of parallel power might imply that dealers run schools, day-care centers, health clinics, job-training centers, and soup kitchens — as well as control *favela* community organizations, sports groups, and religious associations. But the reality is that the state, though inadequate to the task, is very much in evidence. It runs the day-care centers (insufficient and inferior as they may be); the schools (although drug lords have the power to close them during periods of high conflict); the clinics and hospitals (understaffed and underequipped as they are); and the "popular restaurants" and skills-training programs. Certain favors may be conferred by the drug lords: for example, they may arrange to drive people to the doctor, or get school fellowships. But this is more akin to old-school "boss"/patronage politics than the "new marginality."

Meanwhile, religious associations have largely maintained their independence. In fact, some who have left the drug world have only done so with support from the rapidly growing evangelical movement.[49] In fact, it is where the state is most absent — in Residents Associations, local sports clubs, and funk dances — that the tension is greatest between *favela* residents and traffickers. Generally, there is peace as long as space is not contested by rival gangs. But when turf wars heat up, the loss of lives equals that of countries engaged in civil war.

All these conditions exist simultaneously with the expansion of the Brazilian welfare state and the persistence of patronage, clientelism, and corruption. And in this regard, the real policy challenge may be to move away from paternalism and toward universalistic rights, entitlements, and guarantees. This is beginning to happen — slowly. One example is the "citizen check" (*cheque cidadão*), a social program started by former state governor Antony Garotinho (1998–2002). It provides a monthly stipend to poor families, which must be spent on food and personal hygiene items.[50] The state government has also gained popularity by setting up "popular restaurants" (equivalent to soup kitchens), which offer subsidized meals for one real (approximately US$0.30).[51] A further example of the electoral power of Rio's poor is a city-run social program, the "guaranteed minimum income" (*programa de renda mínima*), which complements the earnings of poor families with average payments of approximately R$120 (US$40) per month.[52]

At the national level, the two most important new initiatives are the Bolsa Alimentação (Food Grant) and Bolsa Escola (School Grant). The Food Grant was started in 2001 to fight malnutrition and child mortality; by the end of the year it had reached 1.6 million people.[53] The School Grant is supposed to compensate families for what a child could earn working on the streets (begging, parking/watching cars, doing circus tricks at traffic lights, etc).[54] Although certainly no match for what a child could earn as an *avião* (delivery boy) or *olheiro* (police lookout) in the drug trade, it does represent a step forward.

While clearly representing an advance over the period of military rule, all these programs are still based on state handouts. The only program which really aims to change the structural logic of the system may be Comunidade Solidária (Community Solidarity). Created in 1995 by Ruth Cardoso, wife of President F.H. Cardoso, its goal is to raise US$2 billion a year to strengthen civil society; create social programs for literacy, job-training, and income-generation; and motivate college students to perform volunteer work in low-income areas.[55]

Returning to Waquant's final point, that concerning spatial and racial concentration, there are other disconnects between social reality in Rio's *favelas* and the "new marginality." Specifically, not all of Rio's poor live in *favelas*, and not all *favelados* are poor. Indeed, rental and sales prices in some *favelas* are higher than in some areas of Copacabana or Botafogo.[56] Furthermore, Rio's *favelas* are not ethnically, socially, culturally, nor economically homogeneous. People of many types live there for many reasons. In contrast to the almost total racial segregation described by authors of the new marginality, Rio's *favelas* have always been racially mixed.

At the time of my original study, the random sample showed 21 percent of *favelados* were black, 30 percent mulatto, and 49 percent white. I wrote,

> This approximate racial balance is typical of Rio's *favelas*, but should not be taken to reflect racial equality in the society as a whole. The third who are black represent nearly all of Rio's blacks, while those who were white are but a fraction of all whites living in the city.[57]

In the 2002 restudy the percentages of each racial group were almost identical. Interestingly, among those we were able to relocate, we found little correlation between race and social mobility, educational level, occupational status, political attitudes, or perception of prejudice. However, after these thirty years there was a clear tendency for blacks to remain concentrated in *favelas*, and for whites to move to residential neighborhoods. Half of the blacks but only one-third of the whites from the original study still lived in *favelas*, compared to one-seventh of blacks and one-third of whites who had moved to residential neighborhoods. While this does reflect a certain level of racial discrimination in the housing market, it does not support the more comprehensive notion of "bounded territories of urban relegation." Furthermore, we found that both the perception of racial prejudice and the sense of "black pride" had increased over the years.[58]

THE FRAMING OF FEAR

To live in a place where daily you do not have the liberty to act freely, to come and go, to leave your house whenever you want to, to live as any other person that is not in jail. It is prison to

think: "can I leave now or is it too dangerous?" Why do I have to call someone and say [that they shouldn't come here]? It is terrible, it is oppressing. Nobody wants to live like this.
(Quitungo resident, sixty years old)

I now turn to the second of the five themes that have emerged from our restudy. The single biggest difference in the *favelas* today as compared with thirty years ago is a pervasive atmosphere of fear. In the late 1960s people were afraid of being forcibly relocated by the housing authorities of the dictatorship. Today they are afraid of dying in the crossfire between police and dealers, or between opposing gangs.

> *Sixteen Favelas in Rio De Janeiro To Be Raided by Police* (O Globo, May 30, 2002)
> Schools and business closed, and people fled the streets as several squads of police searched for marginals in *favelas*. The day after the confrontation between police and criminals in the *morros* of Coroa and da Mineira, which left four injured and stopped traffic in the Santa Barbara tunnel, the atmosphere was tense in Catumbi. On order from the general commander of the Military Police, . . . the Special Operation Squad will raid 16 *favelas* in Rio.

> *Six Buses Set on Fire in Protest* (O Globo, June 20, 2002)
> Violence and acts of vandalism broke out on the streets of Rio de Janeiro. The population was rioting against the police . . . accusing them of killing two young (19 and 25) residents of Favela Vila Cruzeiro where the journalist Tim Lopes was murdered on June 2. According to the police, the two victims were dealers who fired first against the police.

> *Innocence in the Territory of Fear* (Jornal Do Brasil, March 4, 2002)
> Mothers in the Morro of São Carlos raise their children in the crossfire and lose hope of seeing them grow up removed from drug dealers.

These three newspaper accounts highlight the different ways the media portrays the relationship between *favelas* and violence. In the first, *favelas* are portrayed as the locus of violence, instigating a coordinated police action to retake control for the state. The second reports on the reaction of *favelados* to perceived police injustice in the murder of two youngsters who were taken to be armed drug dealers, thereby justifying their deaths. The third depicts the *favelados* as innocent victims. In all three, violence is integral to daily life in the *favelas*.

The people we interviewed are afraid of dying every time they step out their front doors, and they fear their children will not come home from school alive. Even inside their homes they do not feel safe. At any moment they fear the police may kick in their doors on the pretense — or reality — of tracking down a dealer.

Alternatively, they fear someone fleeing the police might put a gun to their heads and insist on being hidden, fed, and housed. Such violence is the major motive cited by those who have moved out of *favela* communities.

In the 1960s there was serious drinking and some drug use, mostly marijuana; but cocaine changed everything. Cocaine first appeared in *favelas* in the late 1970s, where it would be divided up and repackaged for local sale. First the rich of the city, then the middle and popular classes, became buyers, and eventually the dealers became better organized — and armed. In the 1960s a few outlaws in Rio had handguns, but now all dealers carry automatic weapons. There is complicity between narcotraffickers and the police, and certain government officials, including candidates for city council and state assembly. With such potential wealth at stake, there is limited interest in stopping the inflow of drugs from Colombia and Bolivia or curtailing the outflow to the United States and Europe.

The new reality is reflected in the lives of *favelados* in multiple and pernicious ways. Most importantly, the very communities in which they are trying to lead normal lives have become "contested spaces," increasingly occupied by mid-level dealers and their legions. Meanwhile, the kingpins are said to live in luxury in South Zone penthouses, or in the United States and Europe. Almost one out of every five of our respondents had a family member who had been a victim of homicide. When asked in 1969, "What do you most like and dislike about living in Rio?" 16 percent said that crime and violence were their main complaints. Today, on informal inquiry, 60 percent gave this response.

As discussed above, we found little evidence that drug dealers had set up a "parallel state" of paternalistic benefits for the poor. There is a lot of talk about the new *caciquismo*, wherein the drug lords provide schooling, health care, food, and protection to residents in exchange for loyalty. But this was not the case in the communities we studied. While it is undoubtedly true that some people come to the dealers in cases of emergency — needing a ride to the hospital for an ailing relative, money for food if they are hungry, or perhaps access to a place in the local school — this is the exception rather than the rule. Only 10 percent said that the drug dealers had ever helped them in any way (3 percent said the police had helped); and 13 percent said the dealers had harmed them (10 percent said the police had harmed them). The majority of respondents were afraid to even answer the question. What seems to describe the situation best is not the loyalty of residents to the dealers, but a de facto state of domination by violence. Several people explained they needed to stay on good terms with the dealers, because "the police go home at night and leave them and their families at the mercy of those with the weapons."

The pervasive presence of the dealers has had devastating effects on community life. Compared with thirty years ago there is considerably less "hanging out" in public space, less participation in community associations, and (especially when there is a war between *commandos*) less visiting among friends and relatives. Membership in every kind of organization, with the exception of evangelical churches, has declined drastically. The internal space of the community is no longer the locus for leisure or recreation. These were the things that formerly united and bound the community together.

In 1969 more than half (54 percent) of the original interviewees felt their communities were "very united," and another 24 percent said "united"; only 21 percent said there was a "total" or "partial lack" of unity. Today the numbers are reversed: 58 percent claim there is a "lack of unity," while less than 6 percent feel the community is "very united."

LEVEL OF LIVING, MOBILITY, AND THE INCREASE IN INEQUALITY

Another major finding that is emerging is that although collective consumption of urban services and individual consumption of household goods has increased notably over the last three decades, the gap between rich and poor has increased even more. This is reflected in an ever-receding sense of becoming *gente*, the Brazilian word for "person" or "human being." One of the most successful of the original interviewees (one who gave his daughter a computer for her fifteenth birthday) was full of hope when I first met him. At the time, he was in his late twenties, had graduated from an excellent Jesuit high school, and thought that if he worked hard enough and long enough he could achieve the dignity and status of a person from the South Zone. Now, after having worked for thirty years in the military police and continuing after retirement as a private security guard (his wife having held a job in a sewing factory and continuing to sew after her retirement), he said he still feels "light years away" from being *gente*.

No doubt, there have been significant improvements in the quality of life of those I interviewed. For the vast majority, living standards have improved. This is readily apparent with regard to access to collective urban services such as water, sewerage, and electricity, which are now virtually universal. Homebuilding materials have also gone from stucco or wood for at least half of the population, to brick and mortar for nearly everyone.

Of these improvements, perhaps the most dramatic has been piped water. In 1969 only one-third of the households had running water. I distinctly remember the long lines of girls and women waiting to fill their square five-gallon metal cans at the slow-running water spigot and then walking long distances up steep hills with the cans balanced on their heads. For large families, getting enough water for cooking, cleaning, and washing could take the better part of a day, and lines formed before dawn. One date everyone remembers is the arrival of running water. In the communities we studied, although not in all of Rio de Janeiro's *favelas*, access to running water is now virtually universal.

The second biggest transformation has been the advent of electricity — i.e., access to a "legal" power connection. Traditionally, illegal connections were run from the city's electric lines into *cabines* controlled by one (or a small group) of residents. Since electric meters were unavailable, a flat monthly rate was charged based on the number of outlets in a home. This meant that poor families frequently paid more than the wealthy in the surrounding neighborhoods for considerably more precarious service. Failure to pay meant immediate cutoff and a return to kerosene lanterns for light and ember-filled irons for pressing clothes. In 1969 less than half of all *favela* households had any electricity at all; today it is close to 100 percent. The advent of electricity preceded that of running water in almost every case, as it was a private, not a public service.[59]

In terms of individual consumption of household appliances, the pattern is equally impressive (see FIGURE 5.10). In 1969 only 64 percent of families owned TVs, 58 percent refrigerators, and 25 percent stereos. The most striking lifestyle change involves having a refrigerator. This has meant freedom for women from daily shopping — and from spoiled foods, especially milk for infants and young children.

For anyone who recalls the level of living in Rio de Janeiro's *favelas* thirty years ago, or is familiar with squatter settlements in Africa or pavement dwellers in India, the *favelados* and ex-*favelados* of Rio seem to live in relative luxury. They might not have savings accounts, but their purchasing power provides impressive proof that not all people living in *favelas, conjuntos,* or low-income neighborhoods are poor.

Still, the reality is considerably more complex than the percentages suggest. For example, 86 percent of interviewees said they owned their own homes, but almost none had legal title to either property or dwelling. Many had built their own homes or expanded the homes their parents had built earlier. Others had purchased their homes, but in the informal market (i.e., without legal title). Even then, the prices they paid were shockingly high. In fact, in some of the more desirable *favelas* real estate prices are higher than in Botafogo, or certain parts of Copacabana (see FIGURE 5.11).

While there have been major upgrading projects over the past decade — bringing water, closed sewers, electricity, and paved access roads into the *favelas* (most recently, and on the largest scale, through the Favela-Bairro program) — the issue of land ownership remains unresolved. The de facto use of land through "squatters rights" (*usucapião*) and the informal titles of sale exchanged upon purchase would not hold up in court if land or home ownership came into dispute. Still, since it is no longer politically feasible for the government to engage in massive eradication on the scale of the late 1960s and 1970s, people feel they own their homes if they are not paying rent.[60] Most importantly, they have the right to pass them on to their children. In addition, of the original sample, only 30 per-

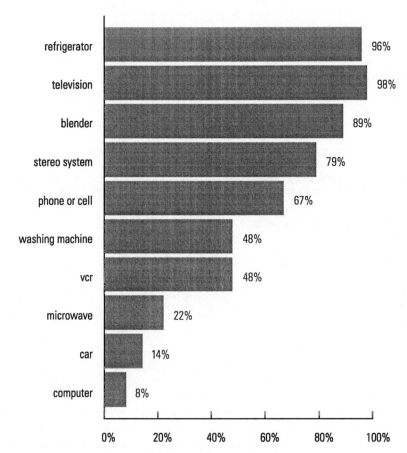

Figure 5.10 Ownership of consumer goods by *favela* family in 2002.
Source: author.

cent still live in *favelas*. Another 37 percent live in housing projects (*conjuntos*) in which their rent has gone toward ownership, and the rest live in peripheral neighborhoods, where they are often owners of small land plots.

It is noteworthy that 67 percent of the original sample now have either a regular or a cellular telephone. When I did my original study, only a handful of families, mostly merchants, had private phones, and public phones were scarce in or near the *favelas*. Generally, there was only a phone in the Residents Association, which took messages as a service to members. This was a great hardship in terms of being available on the odd-job market, and especially in times of health crises. One of the classical samba songs of the 1960s talked of the disillusionment of those on the hillsides (*favelados, morros*), where people die needlessly because there were no telephones to call the doctor or cars to fetch him.[61]

MINIMUM SALARIES (%)		
YEAR	1969	2001
1 MS or less	11	15
1 MS to 2 MS	38	29
2 MS to 3 MS	29	11
3 MS to 4 MS	12	14
4 MS to 5 MS	3	11
More than 5 MS	6	20
Total	100%	100%

Note: MS stands for *salario minimo* or minimum wage. In 1969 it was approximately US$36 per month; in 2001 it was about US$77 per month. Although the dollar amount was higher, the actual value of the minimum salary decreased. The economists believe that the purchasing power of the 1969 minimum salary would be equal to only US$67 today, but in 2001 the purchasing power of the MS was US$60. I believe the increase in the number of people earning one minimum salary or less is due to age factors, with many people living on retirement pensions.

Figure 5.11. Family incomes 1969 and 2001.

Washing machines were also virtually nonexistent in the *favelas* thirty years ago. People washed their laundry in the lagoon or in rivers, and laid it out on the grass to dry. I was surprised to see that more than half of the restudy group now have washing machines. This is a luxury item — as are video players, which again are owned by almost half the families.

The family income of these original respondents has also increased, even controlling for the decreased purchasing power of the minimum wage. Forty-seven percent now have higher family incomes, while 32 percent of incomes were lower and 21 percent have remained the same. During the last thirty years income inequality in Brazil has increased significantly. In Rio, the richest 1 percent hold 11.8 percent of total income, while the poorest 58 percent hold only 13.1 percent. This means that every person in the highest strata has the income of forty-eight people in the lowest strata.[62]

One effect of this disparity is that the very people who possess all the new consumer goods just referred to still consider themselves "poor," and overwhelmingly feel they do not earn enough for a "dignified life." For example, 48 percent have a monthly family income of about R$500 (US$244) or less, but only 18 percent of the group feels this is sufficient for a "decent life." When asked, most said R$1,000 per month was the minimum for a decent life, but only 18 percent were in that bracket.[63] Only one-fifth of these original interviewees are now earning enough to live decently according to their own standards.

Despite the modest gains in family income, people feel they have lost ground, that the gap between them and the rest of society has widened. They are right. While the poor have improved their standing in absolute terms, they have lost ground relative to the rest of the population.

Such conditions may increase awareness of discrimination of all types. In 1969, 64 percent of those interviewed said that racial discrimination existed; today, 85 percent say so. It is no surprise then that of all the many stigmas faced by Rio de Janeiro's urban poor, skin color is the most widely perceived (88 percent). But racial discrimination is only one factor dividing "us" and "them." Simply living in a *favela* may be equally stigmatizing, and many people told of being afraid to give correct addresses on job interviews, knowing that eyebrows would be raised and the interview terminated if this were known. Thus, an unanticipated benefit of being removed from Catacumba to public housing in 1970 was sometimes that people were able to land jobs they had been rejected for in the past.

A further three-quarters of those interviewed reported being discriminated against for their style of dress. Regardless of skin color or place of residence, there is a strong bias against those who do not dress in the accepted style of the South Zone (i.e., of the upper-middle class). This has a lot to do with pervasive television marketing of brand-name clothing, especially jeans, sneakers, shirts, etc. On one occasion I listened to young people assessing job prospects by their earning power in terms of acquiring "status-bearing apparel." A man in his twenties explained that he had investigated the possibility of working as a bus-fare collector, but had calculated that after paying for his transportation, buying his lunch "on the street," and purchasing his uniform, his take-home would be so little that he could not buy a brand-name shirt or Nike running shoes for the foreseeable future. This was enough to discourage him from working at all (and certainly makes entering the drug traffic much more appealing).

No such reasoning was in evidence thirty years ago, perhaps because worldwide consumer standards were not as prevalent. At that time only 48 percent reported watching television every day, as opposed to 90 percent today. However, the status images in the minds of *favela* and *conjunto* residents today are not those of the Carioca or the Brazilian elite, but those of a global culture, and most of the prestige items are foreign made (or rip-offs of such). Yet when asked what impact globalization had on their lives, 88 percent said it had no impact at all. Among the rest, 10 percent said it had a negative impact (citing job loss as the main concern). Thus, there would seem to be little awareness about the effect of "created needs" on self-esteem.

When I interviewed Rita in her clothing store in Nova Brasilia, she seemed to be one of the "success stories." She had always sewn and designed clothing, and had worked in a factory while her husband was alive. After he died, she had opened up her own store on Avenida Nova Brasilia, the main commercial street in the *favela*. She was doing very well now, going in her truck monthly to Sao Paulo to purchase clothing, and then selling it at a mark-up — in addition to selling what she designed and made herself. In fact, she had moved out of the *favela* into a nearby apartment building, and owned a house on the beach. When her son got his girlfriend pregnant and had to support her, she even bought him a shoe store across the street. Nevertheless, she told me of her recent humiliation when she had gone to an upscale downtown Rio store to buy a pair of eyeglasses. At first they ignored her, but then they were openly rude when she insisted on seeing the pair she liked. As she is light-skinned, I pressed her to tell me what it was that made them treat her badly, and she explained it was because she was dressed like someone from the North Zone.[64]

What about gender bias? Fifty-six percent said there was discrimination against women. This plays itself out within the household as well as in the work world. As in Mexico, there is a high incidence of verbal and physical abuse in the home.[65] But this is not openly discussed, and the few *delegacias da mulher* (women's police stations) are not sufficient. Nevertheless, women are becoming bolder, and many told me they were fighting back.

Most of the income that women generated when I was living in Rio in 1968–69 came through domestic work. The women typically lived in the houses of their "patrons" during the week, often with their children, which gave them the opportunity to eat well, send their children to good schools, and have access to excellent health care. They returned to the *favelas* over the weekend with spending money for their households.

Today, with the decline in purchasing power of the middle class, the rising costs of housing in Rio de Janeiro (leading to a tendency to live in smaller apartments), the institution of minimum-wage and benefit requirements for domestic help, and the convenience of laundromats, food-delivery, frozen foods, and new domestic appliances, many families have cut their domestic help to one or two days a week. Much unemployment among women has ensued, especially since it has been difficult for women to break into other areas of work. This certainly deserves further study. In the city of Rio de Janeiro the mean income for men is nearly R$587; for women it is just less than R$382.

The increase in part-time work for women in their own homes does allow them to combine domestic activities with paid employment, but it also means that earnings are more erratic. As a consequence, more women are insecure about their working conditions today than they were decades ago. And although many have gone to work in stores where there is greater prestige, they work more hours and earn less. The incidence of female-headed households has also increased from 18.1 percent in 1991 to 24.9 percent in 2000.[66]

DISILLUSIONMENT WITH DEMOCRACY

There was great hope that the *abertura* (gradual reintroduction of democratic rights and principles) and the end of the dictatorship in 1984 would bring new opportunities for the underclass. It seemed reasonable that regaining the direct vote for mayor, governor, and president, along with freedom of speech, assembly, and the press (curtailed following the military coup in 1964), would lead to improvements for the urban poor. During the dictatorship strict censorship had prevented the free flow of ideas, people had been tortured and killed for opposition beliefs and activities, and the presence of military police had severely constrained civilian activity.

I had anticipated that the end of the dictatorship would bring a flourishing of democratic participation, community organizations, and civil associations of all kinds, which could engage in bargaining and negotiating with the state for increased investment in community upgrading. I imagined that the disenfranchised would have a greater "voice," demanding their fair share of urban services, good schools, local clinics, and improved public transportation. It also stood to reason this would bring improvements to the community as a whole, and to the life chances of the *favelados* and their families.

Indeed, in the years immediately following the dictatorship there was a burgeoning of participatory activity, with many grassroots organizations springing up in the *favelas*, and a plethora of nonprofits taking an active role in the cause of justice and equity for the *favela* population. However, another picture has also emerged since then. Internal community organizations have become fragmented and fragile because of a lack of resources; nonprofits have turned their attention to broad campaigns against hunger and violence; drug dealers have appeared on the scene; and party politics has shown its fickle face. With too many candidates courting the *favela* vote, and too many promises that go unfulfilled, political corruption has become too visible, and cynicism has set in.

In 1969, 36 percent of those interviewed said "the Brazilian people do not have the capacity to choose their candidates." This figure should have decreased over the last thirty years; instead, it has risen to 51 percent. The increase reflects deep and widespread frustration, which is greatest among those who believed in 1969 that Brazilians were able to choose their candidates wisely. Of the 38 percent of people who believed in the wisdom of the popular vote in 1969, 57 percent have now changed their opinion in a negative direction. This shows that those with the highest hopes for democracy were the first to notice that gaining the direct vote was not sufficient to achieve power, or even honest representation.

In our new survey, a follow-up question asked whether an individual had ever been helped or harmed by various levels of government. Less than half said government had helped them. By contrast, 52 percent said the national government of President Cardoso had harmed them. While it is true that many national initiatives are implemented through state or local governments, which claim all the credit, this was a devastating critique for a president who is a world-renowned urban sociologist, committed to social justice, and it may help explain the recent landslide election of the Labor Party candidate, Luis Ignácio Lula da Silva.

Among all levels, state government was seen as the most helpful, with 37 percent responding positively. City government was a close second, with 25 percent responding favorably. However, in both cases 16 percent of respondents said they had been harmed, while the rest were neutral.

International agencies, such as the World Bank, the IMF, and the Inter-American Development Bank received the lowest rating of all, with only 3 percent saying they had been helped by these organizations, and 25 percent saying they had been harmed by them (although about 35 percent did not know what they were). Such a high level of ignorance is interesting in light of the enormous investment in the Favela-Bairro program by the Inter-American Development Bank, along with CEF (Caixa Econômica Federal), the European Union, and the City of Rio de Janeiro. Favela-Bairro was started in 1994 (during Mayor Cesar Maia's first mandate), and since then has benefited 158 communities (4 big, 119 medium, 35 small) and more than 600,000 people. None of the *favela* communities in our study have been beneficiaries yet, although there are plans to bring the program to Nova Brasilia in 2003.

The people we interviewed said there have been improvements since the end of the dictatorship in the areas of housing, sanitation, transportation, and access to (but not quality of) education; but that health services, security, exclusion, and the economic situation had gotten worse. Indeed, Rio lost thousands of jobs in manufacturing over the past fifteen years. This makes it difficult to know whether the nostalgia for the period of the dictatorship is really a longing for better economic times and for more personal safety. One thing often mentioned in open-ended interviews is that during the dictatorship there was much less crime and violence, no gang and drug wars to worry about, and less police abuse. *Favelados* didn't have many rights (in fact, they confused rights and duties); but more of them had jobs, and while they may have worried about removal, they didn't fear for their lives.

AGENCY AND OPTIMISM

The final set of findings I will mention adds a ray of hope to the rather bleak picture I have described thus far. On the positive side, the attitudes, beliefs, and values of community members reflect much less passivity and paternalism than three decades ago. There is a much stronger belief that political participation can make a difference, especially at the local level — and that organizing and mobilizing are necessary to bring the demands of the poor to the attention of the government.

Several comparisons between current responses and those from 1969 are illuminating in this regard. For example, today 66 percent (compared with only 33 percent in 1969) said that "all Brazilians should participate in political life," rather than "politics should remain in the hands of the politicians." Furthermore, 30 percent (compared with 11 percent in 1969) thought that their participation can influence government decisions. And 67 percent (compared with 30 percent in 1969) had actually sought the help of a government agency.

During the dictatorship, many organizations emerged in *favelas* to demand water, electricity, sewage, pavement, etc., but their scope of action was limited to the community level. Today the people we interviewed felt committed to playing a role in the larger political life of their city and country. Their general cynicism about influencing government decisions may be a realistic response to what they have learned over time. But it is still encouraging that twice as many as before think they can make a difference. One-third of a population willing to act on their beliefs can indeed change the discourse, if not actually change public policy. And the population has become more sophisticated in knowing how to seek redress of grievances or assistance from public institutions. Not that they are well treated when they make such appeals. But they have learned that when they go as a group, well dressed, well spoken, and persistent, they cannot be ignored.

This issue about the importance of mobilizing to demand respect is fundamental, and is one of the most positive developments since my earlier study. For example, in our restudy, 60 percent (as compared with 40 percent in 1969) said "government acts only when the people organize." And 67 percent (as compared with 26 percent in 1969) contended that "government leaders do not try to understand the problems of the poor." But underlying these numbers is a new awareness that remaining passive and "waiting one's turn" is not the answer. The idea I heard repeatedly in the late 1960s was that "we are humble people, we do not ask for much, and if we are patient our problems will be taken care of once the more important public concerns have been handled." I did not hear anything of the kind in any conversation or interview this time, and I take that as a positive paradigm shift. Here are people ready and willing to be proactive in attaining their goals for a better life.

This raises the question of how people define a "better life." By far the most important concern was for "a good job with a good salary." Altogether, 67 percent gave this answer on an open-ended question. The next most frequent response, "health," received less than half that level (30 percent), while "education" received only 23 percent (see FIGURE 5.12).

This is the same dilemma faced by poor people in cities throughout the world. What kind of jobs can they find today when unskilled and semi-skilled employment is growing ever more scarce, and when the qualifications for good jobs are becoming ever more elevated? One person said to me that in her day, parents told their children, "If you don't stay in school and study, you'll end up being a garbage collector." Now, to even apply for the job of a garbage collector, you need a high school diploma, and even then thousands of applicants compete for the same positions.

In response to a standard set of questions about whether conditions had gotten better or worse in the past five years (and whether they could be expected to improve or deteriorate in the next five years), we found that the "closer to home" the frame of reference was set, the more optimistic the assessments were. Thus,

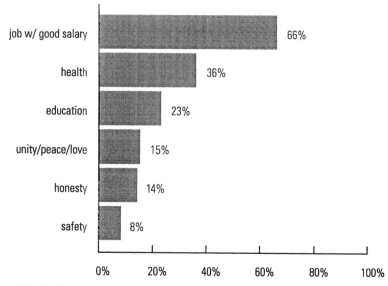

Figure 5.12. Most important factor for a "successful life."
Source: author

44 percent said conditions had become worse or much worse in Brazil in the past five years, and 38 percent thought they would get worse or much worse in the next five years. (The distribution was rather bifurcated, with 36 percent saying conditions had gotten better, and 30 percent thinking they would get better). They were more optimistic about Rio de Janeiro, with 49 percent saying conditions had improved, and 48 percent saying they would improve (33 percent said they had gotten worse, and 27 percent thought they would get worse). In terms of their own communities, optimism was still higher, with 51 percent saying conditions had improved, and 48 percent saying they would improve (versus 26 percent saying they had gotten worse, and 16 percent thinking they would get worse).

The sample was most optimistic about their own lives — perhaps because they feel they have more control and are willing to struggle hard to improve their conditions. A total of 53 percent thought their lives had improved over the past five years (versus 29 percent who thought they had gotten worse). Meanwhile, 58 percent thought their lives would improve over the next five years (compared with only 15 percent who thought they would get worse). When asked to compare their current lives with their expectations and aspirations for themselves, more than half (55 percent) said their lives were better or much better than they had expected or hoped; a fifth (22 percent) said their lives were about the same; and another fifth (21 percent) said they were worse off or much worse off. Further analysis of these groups may reveal what factors led to each outcome.

FURTHER RESEARCH QUESTIONS

The preliminary findings presented here are part of a broader research endeavor. The idea is to trace the life histories of the people interviewed in 1968–69 across time, looking for patterns about intra- and intergenerational mobility. Among the main goals will be to understand the dynamics of urban poverty, exclusion, and socioeconomic mobility; to investigate the meaning and reality of marginality, and how both have been transformed; to trace patterns of life history in relation to macro political and economic transformations at both the national and city levels (and in the context of the spatial evolution of the city fabric); to investigate the impact of public-policy interventions at the local, state, national, and international levels (not only those targeted to *favelas* and poverty, but also nontargeted initiatives that may have had an even greater impact on the lives of Rio's poor); and to explore the mediating effects of the civil society and social networks in helping cope with hard times and take advantage of opportunities in good times.

The interviews with original study participants and their children, grandchildren, and great grandchildren will provide rich insights into how life has evolved over time against the backdrop of continually transforming external conditions. Most longitudinal studies are based on interviewing a set of randomly selected people in the same community, making it impossible to discern whether apparent upward mobility is due to the improvement of life conditions for the same people, or their displacement by people of better means. This is the problem with using aggregate data such as the household census. By following the same people and their descendants over time and gathering year-by-year life histories, we will be breaking new ground. As the Director of IPEA (Brazil's National Institute of Economic Research) said, their agency's information provides only "still photos" at different points in time. Our hope is to develop information with the fluidity of a video.

NOTES

1. Of these eight communities in Caxias, three are *favelas* (Vila Operaria, Favela do Mangue, and Favela Central), and five are legal neighborhoods of unserviced lots called *loteamentos nao-urbanizados* (Centenário, São Sebastiao, Sarapui, Olavo Bilac, and Leopoldina). Half of the sample were squatters from the three *favelas*; half were homeowners from the subdivisions.

2. J. Perlman, *The Myth of Marginality: Urban Poverty and Politics in Rio de Janeiro* (Berkeley, Calif.: University of California Press, 1976).

3. Among the funders for this research have been the World Bank, the Tinker Foundation, the Fulbright Commission, DFID/DPU, the Dutch Trust Fund, and the

Starwood Foundation. In-kind support has been received from the Mega-Cities Project and Trinity College.

4. I would like to acknowledge Profs. Carlos Vaiuer and Pedro Abramo at IPPUR/UFRJ, and their graduate students Flavia Braga, Teresa Farinha, and Andrea Cunha, for their help in Phase I.

5. This chapter owes a debt of gratitude to the Phase II research team in Rio de Janeiro, composed of Graziella Moraes, Sonia Kalil, Lia Rocha, and Josinaldo Aleixo, with help from Edmiere Exaltação, and methodological guidance from Prof. Ignacio Cano.

6. Official information from Secretaria de Planejamento e Coordenação Geral do Estado da Guanabara (1973).

7. Information from IPLAN/Rio. Available online at www.armazemdedados.rio.rj.gov.br/index.htm. Also see the current study by Pedro Abramo of IPPUR/UFRJ for the Instituto Pereira Passos on the detection of irregular settlements in the 1990s.

8. Most were assigned to units in five-story walk-up housing blocks, known as *conjuntos*, principally the *conjuntos* of Guapore and Quitungo in the Vila de Penha. Others were placed in Cidade de Deus or Nova Holanda. A 2002 film on Cidade de Deus galvanized attention to the plight of those living there.

9. Beti eventually got this job, but after several months the woman died, and as this chapter was going to press she was again unemployed.

10. The Complexo de Alemão has nearly 57,000 inhabitants; Nova Brasilia, with more than 15,000, is the largest of the eleven *favelas* that comprise it. Data from "Estado Vai Disputar Jovens com o Tráfico," *O Globo* (July 14, 2002), 20.

11. When I tried to take new photos of the streets and open spaces shown in my book, I was suddenly surrounded by a group of young men who took away my camera and ripped out the film. My equipment was only returned when I was able to convince them to accompany me to the Residents Association, where the president had agreed to hold a meeting of old-timers to reconstruct the community's history for our study.

12. Among other provisions, it stipulated that if a husband and wife fought, it was the husband who would have to leave. The wife and children were entitled to stay in the house.

13. A. Inkeles, "The Modernization of Man," in M. Weiner, ed., *Modernization: The Dynamics of Growth* (New York: Basic Books, 1966); D. Lerner, *The Passing of Traditional Society* (Glencoe, Ill.: The Free Press, 1964); E. Hagen, *On the Theory of Social Change* (Homewood, Ill.: Dorsey Press, 1962); L. Pye, *Aspects of Political Development* (Boston: Little, Brown and Co., 1966); D. McClelland, *The Achievement Motive* (New York: Appleton-Century-Crofts, 1953); and M. Millikan and D. Blackmer, *The Emerging Nations* (Boston: Little, Brown and Co., 1961).

14. Even Franz Fanon, in *The Wretched of the Earth*, speaks of uprooted peasants circling aimlessly around the city as a natural source of revolutionary activity.

15. A. Portes, "The Urban Slum in Chile: Types and Correlates," *Ekistics* 202 (September 1972); A. Portes, "Rationality in the Slum: An Essay in Interpretative Sociology," *Comparative Studies in Society and History* 14, no. 3 (1972), 268–86; J. Nun, "Superpoblación Relativa, Ejército

Industral de Reserva y Masa Marginal," *Revista Latinoamericana de Sociología* 69, no. 2 (1969); J. Nun, "Marginalidad y Otras Cuestiones," *Revista Latinoamericana de Ciencia Sociales* (1972), 97–129; A. Quijano, *Notas Sobre el Concepto da Marginalidad Social* (Santiago, Chile: Economic Commission for Latin America Report, División de Asuntos Sociales, October 1966); A. Quijano, *Dependencia, Cambio Social y Urbanización en Latinoamerica* (Santiago, Chile: Economic Commission for Latin America Report, Social Affairs Division, 1967); A. Quijano, "La Formación de un Universo Marginal en las Ciudades de America Latina," in M. Castells, ed., *Imperialismo y Urbanización en America Latina* (Barcelona: Gustavo Gili, 1973); M. Castells, "La Nueva Estructura de la Dependencia y los Procesos Políticos de Cambio Social en America Latina," paper presented to X Congreso Interamericano de Planificación, Panamá, September 1974; M. Castells, "Clase, Estado y Marginalidad Urbana," in *Estructura de Clase y Política Urbana en América Latina* (Buenos Aires: Ediciones SIAP, 1974); F. Fernandes, *Sociedade de Classes e Subdesenvolvimento* (Rio de Janeiro: Zahar, 1968); and F. Cardoso, "The Brazilian Political Model," paper prepared for a workshop on Brazilian development, Yale University, April 1971.

16. For studies on Rio de Janeiro, see A. Leeds and E. Leeds, "Brazil and the Myth of Urban Rurality: Urban Experience, Work, and Values in 'Squatments' of Rio de Janeiro and Lima," paper presented at St. Thomas Conference, November 1967. For studies on Salvador and São Paulo, see M. Berlinck, "Relações de Classe Numa Sociedade Neocapitalista Dependente: Marginalidade e Poder em São Paulo" (São Paulo: mimeograph). For studies on Santiago, see Castells, "Clase, Estado y Marginalidad Urbana"; CIDU Report by the team on population studies (Equipo de Estudios Poblacionales), "Reindicación Urbana y Lucha Política: Los Campamentos de Pobladores in Santiago de Chile," *EURE* 2, no. 6 (November 1972); and F. Kuznetzoff, "Housing Policies or Housing Politics: An Evaluation of the Chilean Experience" (Berkeley, Calif.: Department of City and Regional Planning, University of California, 1974). For studies on Buenos Aires, see M. Marculis, "Migración y Marginalidad en la Sociedad Argentina," *Série SIAP* 10 (Buenos Aires: Paidos, 1968). For studies on Lima, see J. Turner, "Four Autonomous Settlements in Lima, Peru," paper presented at Latin American Colloquium, Department of Sociology, Brandeis University, May 1967. For studies on Bogata, see R. Cardona, "Los Asentiamentos Espontaneos de Vivienda," in R. Cordona, ed., *Las Migraciones Internas* (Bogotá, Columbia: ACOFAME, 1973). For studies on Mexico City, see H. Munoz Garcia, O. Oliveira, and C. Stein, "Categorías de Migrantes y Nativos y Algunas de sus Características Socio-económicas" (México: Universidad Nacional, February 1971, mimeograph); and S. Eckstein, *The Poverty of Revolution: The State and the Urban Poor in Mexico* (Princeton, N.J.: Princeton University Press, 1977). For studies on Monterrey, see Balan, Browning, and Jelin, "A Computerized Approach to the Processing and Analysis of Life Stories Obtained in Sample Surveys," *Behavioral Science* 14, no. 2 (1969), 105–20.

17. Richard Morse, "Trends and Issues in Latin American Urban Research, 1965–1970," *Latin American Research Review* 6, no. 1 (1971); and William P. Mangin, "Latin American Squatter Settlements: A Problem and a Solution," *Latin American Research Review* 2, no. 3 (1976)

18. W. Ryan, *Blaming the Victim* (New York: Pantheon Books, 1971).

19. The eight propositions and the corresponding concepts of this "ideal type" are presented in figure form on pp. 130–31 of Perlman, *Myth of Marginality*.

20. Perlman, *Myth of Marginality*, 195.

21. People were charged monthly payments of 25 percent of their former family incomes. However, the cost of bus transportation to and from the *conjuntos* was so high that in general only one person in each family (the highest earner) could afford the trip, leading to a precipitous drop in household earnings. Families who fell badly behind in their payments were relegated to "triage housing" even further from the city, in a place ironically called *paciencia* (patience).

22. J. Auyero, "Wacquant in the Argentine Slums: Comment on Loïc Wacquant's 'Three Pernicious Premises in the Study of the American Ghetto,'" *International Journal of Urban and Regional Research* 21, no. 3 (September 1997), 508–12.

23. Perlman, *Myth of Marginality*, 242–62.

24. Ibid., 243.

25. Ibid., 243.

26. Ibid., 246.

27. Ibid., 248.

28. Ibid., 245, footnote 4.

29. A.G. Frank, "The Development of Underdevelopment in Brazil," in *Capitalism and Underdevelopment in Latin America* (New York Monthly Review Press, 1967), 50–62.

30. Perlman, *Myth of Marginality*, 251.

31. Ibid., 258.

32. Ibid., 257.

33. Ibid., 259.

34. Ibid., 250.

35. Castells, cited in Perlman, *Myth of Marginality*, 258, footnote 24.

36. I pointed out that the *favelados* also provided symbolic constituencies for other political actors, from conservatives who needed them to blame for social ills, to radicals who claimed to speak on their behalf and needed them to justify their actions. See Perlman, *Myth of Marginality*, 260.

37. R. Paes e Barros, R. Henriques, and R. Mendonca, "A Estabilidade Inaceitavel: Desigualdade e Pobreza no Brasil," in *Desigualdade e Pobreza no Brasil* (Rio de Janeiro: IPEA, 2000).

38. C. Silveira, "Contribuições para a Agenda Social," in *Agenda de Desenvolvimento Humano e Sustentável para o Brasil do Século XXII* (Brasilia: Forum XXI/PNUD, 2000).

39. In 1992, during the world meeting on environment "Rio 92," the army actually occupied the *favelas* for one week, "to guarantee the security in town."

40. See, for example, I. Cano, "The Use of Lethal Force by Police in Rio de Janeiro," *Boletim do ISER* (Rio de Janeiro, April 1998), in which the author claims that the number of violent deaths caused by the police in Rio de Janeiro is the same as all police-related deaths in the entire United States. See also L. Soares, *Violência e Criminalidade no Estado do Rio de Janeiro* (Rio de Janeiro: Editora Hama, 1998).

41. L. Wacquant, "Three Pernicious Premises in the Study of the American Ghetto," *International Journal of Urban and Regional Research* 21, no. 2 (June 1997), 341–54.

42. L. Wacquant, "The Rise of Advanced Marginality: Notes on its Nature and Implications," *Acta Sociológica* 39 (1996).

43. Wacquant, "The Rise of Advanced Marginality"; Wacquant, "Three Pernicious Premises"; and L. Wacquant, "Urban Marginality in the Coming Millennium," *Urban Studies* 36 (September 1999).

44. Wacquant, "Three Pernicious Premises."

45. In testing these formulations against conditions in Buenos Aires, Javier Auyero focused on "structural joblessness, massification of unemployment and increasingly insecure wage-labor relations; the functional disconnect from macroeconomic changes; and a particular combination of malign and benign state neglect/abandonment." Meanwhile, in relation to Guadalajara, Mercedes de la Rocha has discussed a change in perspective from the "resources of poverty" in the 1960s and 1970s (which showed the ingenuous coping mechanisms and survival strategies of the poor), to the "poverty of resources" in the 1990s (in which the limits of coping are surpassed and the capacity of survival is threatened). She found that the "deep restructuring and resulting persistent economic and social hardship that have characterized much of the Americas for the past two decades" (1980s and 1990s) had eroded the poor's capacity for action, social mobility, and even reproduction. M. Rocha, "From the Resources of Poverty to the Poverty of Resources? The Erosion of a Survival Model," in *Latin American Perspectives* 119, no. 4 (July 2001), 72–100.

46. Wacquant, "Three Pernicious Premises."

47. Ibid., 341.

48. These included retirement pensions, worker identification (*carteira de trabalho*), minimum wage (*salário mínimo*), labor unions, and limited social rights such as state-subsidized health care, low-income housing programs, etc.

49. The evangelical churches have increasingly replaced the Afro-Brazilian espiritist centers (*terreiros*) of candumble, macumba, and unibanda that were so prevalent in the *favelas* thirty years ago.

50. According to Garotinho's web site, this program assists 37,000 families in the state of Rio de Janeiro. However, since this money is only distributed through religious institutions, there is no state administrative supervision, and distribution may in fact occur according to the rules of patronage rather than universalism.

51. The state pays R$1.60 (US$0.50) toward the cost of the meal.

52. São Paulo's program is even bigger. It provides an income supplement of up to R$180 (US$60) for families with children younger than fifteen (who must be attending school if they are older than seven).

53. It pays R$15 (US$5) to R$45 (US$15) per family for up to six months. However, families must achieve goals in terms of child health and weight minimums; there must be proof of child vaccinations; and prenatal exams are required for pregnant women.

54. This federal program, which (since 2000) provides families a small stipend for each

child who remains in school, is administered through the city government. It pays R$30 (US$10) per month per child for as many as three children. Altogether, it assists 4.9 million families and 8.5 million children, ages seven to fourteen.

55. Its main funding comes from private-sector and foundation partners, and its board includes public figures from every sector of society. During the two mandates of the present administration it has reached more than 53 million people. Again, this does not fit with the notion of state apathy. And, as far as we know, bureaucratic ineptitude is much greater in long-stalled programs to regularize land tenure.

56. P. Abramo, "Notas sobre a Teoria Econômica da Favela: Mobilidade Residencial e Mercado Informal," in *Anais do IX Congresso Nacional da ANPPUR*, Rio de Janeiro, May 2001.

57. Perlman, *Myth of Marginality*, 58.

58. An interesting phenomenon is the "darkening" of the original interviewees, according to their own self-definition. When asked about race today, they defined themselves much more frequently as black or mulatto than in 1968 — as if having African roots had become a source of pride rather than stigma.

59. After the Light Company was privatized in 1996, it realized it could expand markets and reduce losses considerably if it treated the *favela* population as clients/customers rather than outlaws.

60. The *favela*-removal policies prevailed from 1962 until the second half of the 1970s. Although in the first Cesar Maia government there were some removals of *favelas* in areas of "high risk" (usually in rich neighborhoods like Barra da Tijuca and Recreio), this cannot be considered a policy, especially since Maia also implemented the Favela-Bairro program.

61. "Acender as Velas," composed in 1965 by Ze Keti.

62. As documented using the THEIL-L rate, which varies from 0 to 1 — with 1 representing the highest degree of income inequality. According to this measure, the inequality rate in 1970 in Rio was 0.36. This increased to 0.59 in the 1980s, and to 0.61 in 1990. In Duque de Caxias the inequality rate was 0.19 in 1970, 0.30 in 1980, and 0.39 in 1990. See *Atlas do Desenvolvimento Humano* — IPEA, Fundação João Pinheiro and IBGE/PNUD, Rio de Janeiro, 1998.

63. The exchange rate between Brazilian *reais* and U.S. dollars used here is the mean of the 2000/2001 rates.

64. It was this anecdote, related in an open-ended interview, that led me to refine the questionnaire to include mention of both the North Zone and manner of dressing in queries about discrimination.

65. Rocha, "From the Resources of Poverty to the Poverty of Resources?"

66. 2000 IBGE Census. Available at www.ibge.gov.br/home/estatistica/populacao/censo2000.

6

The Gentleman's City:
Urban Informality in the Calcutta
of New Communism

Ananya Roy

Site One, Moment Two. In the winter of 1996 the city of Calcutta was remade. In the watery light of winter, the city's caretakers launched Operation Sunshine. Officers of the Calcutta Municipal Corporation and cadres of the dominant local Communist Party of India Marxist (CPM), along with police battalions, demolished the sidewalk stalls of thousands of petty traders, commonly known in the city as "hawkers." These stalls had lined the city's major thoroughfares for almost three decades. Operation Sunshine evictions continued through 1997. As they progressed, hawkers staged daily protests, stopping traffic at key intersections. Mobilized by opposition leaders like the fiery Mamata Banerjee, they also tried to return to the sidewalks with baskets of goods.[1] But the CPM, as leader of the region's ruling coalition, the Left Front, remained firm in its opposition, and eventually, *Newsweek* magazine hailed Operation Sunshine as a resounding success, headlining how "the world's worst city" was cleaning up its act.[2]

Moment One. The Calcutta Municipal Corporation and Calcutta Metropolitan Development Authority launch Operation Hawker, a demolition drive meant to eradicate the hawker problem. The hawkers, however, are organized in active protest by the CPM — then an opposition party. This, and other mobilizations, ensure the CPM's electoral victories against the Congress Party a few years later, and as the Left Front consolidates power, hawkers continue to be an important source of political support, while party coffers fill with revenue extracted from them through a complex web of police, unions, and cadres.[3]

Moment Two. The CPM commemorates Operation Sunshine with a bipartisan picture book, stylish in its layout, glossy in its representation. The publication coincides with celebrations marking twenty years of uninterrupted Left Front rule in West Bengal. In the text, party leaders explain the evictions, inscribing the hawkers as bourgeois shopkeepers:

The word "hawking" does not exist in Bengali. It is an English word that refers to itinerant traders. We did not evict hawkers. We evicted illegal shopkeepers who had invaded public space.[4]

The voice of the opposition concurs:

I disagree with the government in the suddenness of the evictions. But I agree that it was absolutely necessary. These were no longer poor, needy traders. They had become commercialized — they were renting out space, they owned multiple stalls, and they had ties with large merchants.[5]

Moment Three. As the city is reclaimed deliberately and surely, a mid-level CPM leader, Kanti Ganguly, known for decades of activism on behalf of the informal sector, enters a plea for the city's *sadharan manush*, the common public:

They have a right to these roads and pavements, you know. I once helped hawkers invade the sidewalks. I was wrong. They were helpless refugees then. Now, they do not need this kind of help. We must end the politics of patronage that has kept them here for so long.[6]

Moment Zero. As the success of Operation Sunshine becomes evident, the city's spokespersons hail the return of the city of their childhood, the original city. A middle-class resident of one of the liberated neighborhoods writes in a Bengali daily:

The stalls had mushroomed, crowded against each other. It was like hell, dirty, smelly, dark, and dingy. In the evenings, the smoke from the diesel generators would sting our eyes and suffocate our lungs. Suddenly, as if in a miracle, all of this is gone. I am enjoying my walk on these empty sidewalks so much that I feel as if I have been suddenly transported to a foreign land, to the city of my childhood.[7]

So it came to be that in Calcutta the city of the future was in fact the city of the past — a timeless entity, standing outside of history. And so it came to be that the bourgeois city was reclaimed through the rhetoric of leftist radicalism.

In official and popular discourses, Operation Sunshine is today most commonly cast as a return to a *bhadralok* Calcutta.[8] *Bhadralok* is an appropriately polyvalent word. Literally, it means "gentlemanly." But it also refers to a distinctive urban intelligentsia who emerged in the crucible of colonialism: a genteel elite who, as Chatterjee notes, are the very heart and soul of Bengali leftism.[9]

It is thus that we must understand the left's yearning for the gentlemanly city, for the lost city of charm and grace.

Site Two, Moment One. The southeastern fringes of Calcutta fade into a verdant landscape of paddy fields and grazing meadows. Occasionally there is a settlement of huts, nestled in a shady grove of trees. But such settlements are not rural villages; they are resettlement colonies, where urban squatters have been relocated.

Mukundapur is one such site. Unlike the squatter settlements in the heart of the city, it is clean, with wide brick roads, well-spaced huts, and a decent infrastructure of electric lines, water taps, and freestanding toilets. Its residents refer to it as *desh,* a word meaning both country and countryside, signifying a sense of belonging through a bond with the land.[10] They also refer to Mukundapur as a "colony," an English word that has become part of the Bengali vocabulary, both in official and popular usage. The use of the term is ironic, however, for the colonies are not only settlements but also spaces of systematic political control.

Colonies like Mukundapur are the territory of the CPM. Here, the party office reigns supreme, overseeing every detail of daily life from clogged toilets to domestic disputes. This is the machinery of political patronage in its most efficient form, guaranteeing votes in election after election. In India, of course, such mechanisms are not new or unique to the CPM. Chatterjee has detailed the wide range of organizations through which the Congress Party mobilized popular support in the pre- and post-Independence periods. But what is specific to the Left Front is a campaign machinery that is effective because it works in tandem with a regime of development.

According to Chatterjee: "Party politics in the West Bengal countryside is not something which arrives along the campaign trail once every five years; it is everyday business and goes hand in hand with government work."[11] He is talking mainly about rural West Bengal, where the everyday politics of village-level councils, the *panchayats,* provide the essential link between party and state. But on the urban fringe of Calcutta places like Mukundapur provide a similar institutional space for the Left Front. The Congress threat, especially dire on the fringes of the city, necessitates that the CPM engage in a constant search for new voters and new territories of support. Such a pattern implies a constant recharging of patronage, and not surprisingly, before each major election, the colonies are treated to infrastructural improvements. On some occasions this may entail the one-time provision of quasi-legal electricity; on others the paving of roads, and so forth. It is a regime created through the coupling of party and state, the combining of informal party tactics of mobilization with the formal state apparatus of infrastructure provision; it is a regime reproduced through uncertainty.

Moment Zero. The residents of Mukundapur tell detailed stories of the founding of the colony:

> We were brought here by Kantibabu. But the area was jungle. It was crawling with snakes. And it was all wetland. We had to dig for months, filling the marshes with earth, before we could even begin to build our huts. All of this

time, we slept in tents. This infrastructure that we now have — these roads, corporation taps, tubewells, electricity — none of this was there. All of this was only provided to us last year.[12]

Such stories identify an original moment, one in which urban squatters, once rural migrants, were relocated to the semi-urban periphery of the city. Each squatter family was granted a small plot of land, between 2 and 2.5 *kathas*, to build a hut.[13] These stories of origin are also frontier stories, narrating the ways in which a wild and remote land was tamed and settled. In this, the storytellings are also claims to land, and such claims are particularly important because colony residents do not have regularized land titles. As one young man from Mukundapur observed, "They will never give us *pattas*. If they did, we would no longer have to depend on them for everything, every single day. If they gave us *pattas*, the game would be over."[14] Indeed, the absence of land titles ensures the CPM's role as the ultimate proprietor of the colonies.

At one level, such tactics can be related to Herring's view of the central dilemma of parliamentary communism: the importance of tactical mobilizations in the name of land, but the conservatizing influences of actually distributing ownership of land.[15] In Calcutta the solution to this ideological dilemma involves a poor electorate which is continuously mobilized because land is always promised, but never secured. In this way, the territorialized uncertainty of informality guarantees political obedience. And in the frontier stories, this uncertainty is negotiated by claiming an original right to the land, established through settlement. It is thus that the colonies are imagined as *desh*.

Moment Two. In 1997, as I arrive in Mukundapur, it is surrounded by a growth of new houses. So are the other colonies. The Calcutta Metropolitan Development Authority is also engaged in a frenzy of infrastructural improvements in the area. The developments worry one old, wizened member of the residents' committee:

I can feel it in the air. We pay corporation taxes but we do not have any *dalils*. Last year, the party built new roads, put in new water taps, all before the elections. But these developments cannot be for us. I think that we will be evicted.[16]

All through 1997 CPM leaders assuage these fears by promising colony residents that they will never face eviction. Then, in December 1997, Mukundapur is demolished. While local party leaders assert that the colony is a peasant cooperative, state and high-ranking party leaders say the residents are squatters, occupying the land in flagrant defiance of the law. Kanti Ganguly, founder of Mukundapur, is prominently among the latter.[17]

Moment Three. The Mukundapur colony is replaced by a medical facility, a Rs.40 *crore* development initiated by the Manipal Group, which has ties to key CPM lead-

Figure 6.1. Chief Minister Basu inspecting Udayan models and plans.
Photo by author, 1997.

ers, including Chief Minister Jyoti Basu. The medical facility is billed as a "charitable institution."[18] But a few hundred yards away is another development that can make no such claim. It is a "condoville" housing development, called Udayan:

> More than fine homes and lifestyle, Udayan promises you Life. A life outside
> of your home — serene greenery, walkways and jogging tracks, parks for kids
> to play, a uniquely self-sufficient commercial centre, a club of your dreams.[19]

At Rs.135 *crore*, the Udayan project is owned by Bengal Ambuja Housing Development Limited, a joint enterprise of the West Bengal Housing Board and Gujarat Ambuja Cements. It was inaugurated in November 1997 by Chief Minister Basu, who praised it as a public-private venture into "mass housing" (see FIGURE 6.1).[20]

Thus it is that the gentleman's city finds its domestic space.

URBAN DEVELOPMENTALISM

The remaking of Calcutta looks ahead to the city of the future, the *bhadralok* city. This is the gentleman's city — gentlemanly in its sensibilities, and housing the gentleman and his family. But this moment also gestures to the past, as in the content of developmental projects, in the attempt to recover a lost city of grace and charm. *This is an original moment, a moment zero.* As Smith notes, "retaking the city for the middle classes involves a lot more than simply providing gentrified housing; it means transforming whole areas into new landscape complexes that pioneer a comprehensive class-inflected urban remake."[21]

The evictions triggered by urban remaking refer to the past in a second way, for the displacements, as in the case of Mukundapur, can only be understood in light of a previous moment of placement. This is the strategic founding of the colonies by *bhadralok* Marxists, now displaced by the *bhadralok* city. *This, too, is a moment of origin, a moment zero.*

While my interest is primarily in moment two, in the remaking of the city, I am acutely aware of the relationship between moments. For it is in such gestures of looking forward and backward that *the* city is remade, the city as de Certeau would say, remade as a universal and anonymous subject: the "city" as a proper name to which it becomes possible to attribute all the functions and predicates that were previously scattered and assigned to many different real subjects.[22] Such is the moment of urban developmentalism.

The state of West Bengal is home to the world's longest-serving democratically elected communist government, the Left Front. Indeed, the Left's stability is anomalous in a country that entered a new millennium not under the grand mantle of an enduring Congress dynasty, but marked by shifting and fragile coalitions. The Left Front has also engaged in a series of agrarian and institutional reforms, from land ceilings to a strengthening of the *panchayats*. Yet there is little consensus on the matter of West Bengal or the Left Front. Some insist that the state "has vastly improved its relative position on a broad range of economic, social, and rural indicators."[23] Others counter that "the Left Front is a dismal failure."[24]

The Left Front has long been known for its agrarian reformism. But more recently it has engaged in a strategy of urban developmentalism. In the 1990s, in keeping with India's liberalization drive, it launched a New Economic Policy, partly in order to adapt to the electoral challenges of the new millennium.[25] The policy envisaged a broad range of public-private partnerships in the provision of housing and infrastructure, thus marking a shift from prior policies of slum improvement to investments in the upper end of the housing market. Shaw sees the changes thus:

> The imperatives of economic liberalization and globalization have brought to the forefront a city management model that serves the interests of economic growth. Active supporters and beneficiaries are business and industry and the upper and middle class income groups. If successfully implemented, it will lead to an extension and an improvement of the quality of the formal city.[26]

The New Economic Policy of the Left Front has taken hold most vigorously on the eastern fringes of Calcutta. To the north here there are plans for a massive state-sponsored development project called "New Calcutta."[27] To the south, public-private ventures such as Udayan are flourishing. The New Economic Policy is thus also a territorial rewriting of the city's edges, displacing and evicting squatter settlements, resettlement colonies, sharecroppers, and informal fisheries. It is here, in the vast tracts of agricultural land poised to enter the city's tight housing market, that the previous moment of rural-urban migration and the present moment of suburban growth literally intersect.

New Communism manifests key elements of liberalization. First, the shift from agrarian reformism to urban developmentalism has involved a "productivist reordering of social policy," such that the state itself has become a site of market activity.[28] At the level of the urban, the Left has taken on the mantle of what Harvey calls "entrepreneuralism," leaving behind earlier attempts to manage the city.[29] Thus, according to Smith, real estate development has become a "centerpiece of the city's productive economy."[30] But such developments have capitalized on state assets such as public land, a peculiar characteristic of the marketization of post-socialist regimes.[31] Second, New Communism has a distinctive geography. Its prime territory is the metropolitan region rather than the core city. As state capacity is reorganized, so are new geographies created — in this case through a remaking of the land and housing markets of the city's semi-urban periphery. Here, it is not only the "urbanization of neoliberalism" that is evident.[32] As Smith argues, there is also a recasting of the scale of the urban itself.[33]

It is also interesting to note that such forms of developmentalism are being promoted through old-style populist vocabularies learned at prior moments of urban transformation. This is most apparent in the case of informal subdivisions that are appearing all across the eastern fringes. These middle-class housing developments are built informally on agricultural land, and often involve a tripartite transaction between housing consumers, peasants with de facto rights to agricultural land, and private developers. In such a scenario, the peasants sell the land to the developer, signing a "no-claims" document; the developer then sells plots or homes to middle-class consumers. These subdivisions have become an increasingly important mechanism for quickly introducing agricultural land to the urban real estate market. The continued cultivation of the plot acts as a shield from scrutiny, while sudden and rapid construction establishes claims, albeit quasi-legal, to the land. This developmental process is made possible through the populist apparatus of patronage, with CPM cadres overseeing the transactions.[34] On the one hand, this enables the electoral agenda of populism; on the other, it promotes the land-use agenda of developmentalism. By acting through the informal tactics of party populism, the developmental state is thus able to bypass its own regulations, most notably restrictions on the urbanization of agricultural land.[35] If bourgeois suburbanites, liberalizing communists, and private speculators seem to make strange bedfellows, such is the vision of communism for the new millennium.

But there is more to New Communism than simply urban developmentalism. The use of old-style populist techniques to implement development projects can

be interpreted as a moment of what Brenner and Theodore describe as the "politically contested interaction between inherited institutional forms and policy
frameworks and emergent strategies of state spatial regulation," the attempt to
"open up a space" for a new mode of accumulation.[36] But the Calcutta of New
Communism is not about the replacement of an "old" populism by a "new" developmentalism. Rather, it is about a complex choreography of developmentalism
and populism. This is not a question of balancing state functions of accumulation
and legitimation, with developmentalism embodying the logic of accumulation
and populism the logic of legitimation.[37] Rather, developmentalism involves its
own mode of accumulation (investment in property development), and its own
mode of legitimation (bourgeois nostalgia). Meanwhile, populism involves its own
mode of accumulation (informal sector), and its own mode of legitimation
(patronage). Each can operate independently of the other, but in the context of
New Communism they do not. As the moments of urban developmentalism
unfold, so emerge sites of populism, barely visible, but nevertheless present.

Moment Two, Beyond Site One. While Operation Sunshine is being implemented, CPM cadres and leaders are simultaneously engaged in establishing rehabilitation locations for evicted hawkers.[38] Many of these relocation sites are taken over
through processes of illegal occupation — a new round of squatting, if you will —
and by the very same party operatives who are supervising the demolitions.[39]

Operation Sunshine, then, cannot be read as the neoliberal annihilation of the
informal sector; rather, it is a territorial reinscription of informality in the city. This
logic, the logic of New Communism, is not simply about evicting hawkers and
squatters; it is instead about the evictions and resettlement of *select* hawkers and
squatters. Which hawkers will be rehabilitated? Which squatters will be the chosen few? The selection of a small group of hawkers and squatters, the indeterminacies of exclusion and inclusion, ensures political support, consolidating informalization as a mode of accumulation, and patronage as a mode of legitimation.

There are two aspects to how New Communism stabilizes through such
uneven geographies. First, Peck and Tickell argue that neoliberalism must be
understood not only as deregulation and destruction, but also as "purposeful construction and consolidation."[40] The choreography of developmentalism and populism may be seen in much the same way: as both a construction of the bourgeois
city, and of a territorialized uncertainty that deepens state control over the informal city. Second, it is in and through this choreographed unevenness that the
business of New Communism proceeds. Smith provocatively argues that the
urbanization of neoliberalism is a process of gentrification, a revalorization of
devalorized spaces.[41] From Operation Sunshine to Udayan such a revalorization
is evident. But gentrification is predicated on geographic differentiation and on
available techniques to revalorize devalued spaces. The spatial choreography of
New Communism provides both ingredients: a patchwork of metropolitan

spaces of varied value, and a constant relocation of the informal sector to recover new frontiers. In the words of one evicted colony resident:

> We will be given a place to stay, but it will be even more remote than this place, further from our livelihoods, isolated from all services. You see, there is an unwritten law here — that the poor like us develop areas, fill in marshes, build homes, struggle to get infrastructure, and are then evicted to make way for the rich who move into a now desirable area.[42]

THE UNMAPPING OF CALCUTTA

New Communism is a moment of great spatial creativity, with the regime moving the poor around, forging developmental alliances, and in many ways replicating capitalism's own breathless imperative for greenfield sites. Such processes play out with great intensity on the ruralized eastern fringes. In Calcutta the moment of liberalization has not only manifested itself at the level of the urban — in the city as spectacle; but it has also taken hold in particular, historicized interstices within the urban. What accounts for the territorialized flexibility of New Communism? How and why is this flexibility particularly apparent in the distinctive spaces of the rural-urban interface?

The answer to such questions lies in the regulatory context of land, specifically in the regulatory ambiguities that mark Calcutta's fringes. Over and over again I asked a simple question: *Who owns this land?* And for each settlement or colony or development I was presented with multiple and contending stories. For example, in Mukundapur, residents said that the colony's land was once *benami* property owned by a large landlord in the name of his employee, Bihari Mondol.[43] About 25 years ago, the land was taken over by quasi-legal sharecroppers mobilized by the CPM. When the CPM later sought to build a resettlement colony on this land, the sharecroppers were informally compensated in calculations that approximated 5 *kathas* for 2 *bighas*. Unable to continue agriculture on these small plots of land, the sharecroppers have been selling them off to developers, thereby fueling middle-class housing developments.

By contrast, Kanti Ganguly, the CPM leader, presented the history with greater formality, insisting that all of the colonies were situated on a stretch of 8,000 *bighas* of "vested" land (i.e., privately owned land appropriated and held by the state). "Large, rich landlords owned this land as *benami*. We confiscated this land during the agrarian revolution. This is now prime urban land."[44] He too told the story of Bihari Mondol, but not the story of the sharecroppers.

Such accounts were contradicted by the land bureaucracy. While officials at the West Bengal Land Revenue Office generally agreed that many of these areas were completely vested, officials at the Land Acquisition Cell of the Calcutta Metropolitan Development Authority disagreed, saying that the land was a complex mixture of vested and private land. And in both bureaucracies, officials laughed off the party story about Bihari Mondol and other robber barons, emphasizing that these were mainly nineteenth-century figures kept alive in the legends of the party. Further, neither bureaucracy could or wanted to explain the jurisdiction and management of vested land.[45]

To understand the significance of these multiple stories it is necessary to turn to a meta-story, one told to me by a powerful Marwari real estate developer (who I will call Anil Shah). I have tentatively titled the story "Dreaming of Tombstones."

"I dream of a landscape of tombstones," Shah said, leaning back into his leather chair, pushing away from the wide expanse of his meticulously tidy glass-topped desk.

> You want me to tell you who owns these vast expanses of land on the eastern fringes? Well, I can't tell you that. I can tell you that here there are squatters and colonies, illegal housing developments and legal housing developments; land held hostage and land for which blood is being shed. It is all tied to the politics of electoral support, every inch of it. And it is possible because there is no sure knowledge of who owns which piece of land, and so it is territory up for grabs. To get rid of this dirty politics we need to mark each piece of land with a tombstone, clearly identifying its ownership and status.

When he continued his explanation, he used a gendered metaphor:

> Think of it as *sindur*. You modern women don't wear such markings, so how can anyone tell if you are married or not. It creates a great deal of confusion for us men. So is it with land.[46]

My search for an answer to the question of ownership on Calcutta's eastern fringes had brought me to Shah's office on a monsoon afternoon in 1997. I had first met him at the offices of the Calcutta Metropolitan District Authority. It was my seventh visit to the Land Acquisition Cell, and I was frustrated at not being able to locate land records for the southeastern periphery of the city, where I had been conducting fieldwork for many months. I had also been repeatedly told that aerial maps of the eastern fringes were classified information. A city of secret maps? Why? Was it simply a question of the CMDA's institutional power and authority, its ability to shield itself from public scrutiny, as argued by Chakravorty and Gupta?[47]

On my seventh visit, however, I had received an answer — but it was not quite what I had expected: I was told there was no established system of maintaining records of land ownership and acquisition for the fringes.[48] The senior land officer admitted that this had created tremendous ambiguity regarding vesting, and that the problem was particularly acute in the open tracts of the eastern periphery:

Yes, no one really knows which part of which plot is vested. Not even I.
There are no maps or boundaries. We deal with it on a case-by-case basis.[49]

A city without maps? Was that possible? The British had systematically surveyed Calcutta, carefully detailing European areas and inhabitants. A few Bengali maps had also been drawn up in the late nineteenth century.[50] But cartography as an instrument of developmentalism, a tool by which modern states supervise and articulate their territories — this is what seemed to be missing.

As I investigated further, I realized how hard it is to trace the genealogy of such an unmapping. But this logic had clearly been present in the region's institutions for a while. For example, Bagchi's evaluation of the Ford Foundation's 1966 *Basic Development Plan* revealed certain ambiguities about the nature of land use and economic data that seemed integral to the formulation of the plan.[51] And in analyzing the legal disputes over the East Calcutta wetlands, Dembowski's diagnosis of a "problem of governance" also had a great deal to do with the absence of master plans, outline development plans, and maps — a regulatory context that seems to have consolidated the CMDA's unchecked powers.[52]

Such trends were further amply evident in a 1997 High Court case, which brought to light the lack of land records, maps, and a master plan:

Unbelievable but true: Calcutta is the only city in the country without a master plan. The absence of the master plan supposedly came to light during a court case filed by a NGO in the public interest. When the CMC failed to present the court with a master plan, the Chief Justice of Calcutta High Court directed all chief engineers of all major city agencies to appear before him. The only plan they could produce was the CMDA's Land Use and Development Control Plan for the CMC. The CMDA said that it had been unable to prepare a master plan because of the lack of reliable data. All that the agencies have in their possession is a 75-year old survey map prepared by a British expert.[53]

And so I set aside my initial questions: How can I find the appropriate map? Who owns this piece of land? How did the government vest this other piece of land? What uses are planned for it? And in their place, I formulated new ones: What does it mean to have fluid and contested land boundaries? How does this ambiguity regarding status and use shape processes of urban development? How does this establish the possibilities and limits of participating in such land games? These new questions indicated a concern with the "unmapping" of the city, the ways in which the absence of core bureaucratic and public knowledge about land makes possible the territorialized flexibility of New Communism. Appadurai writes about how colonial techniques of mapping once "recuperated the unruly body of the colonial subject through the language of numbers."[54] But in present-day Calcutta, a new spatial vocabulary of control has been created through an "unmapping."

The implications of unmapping are most clearly evident in the vesting of land. In the case of Calcutta's fringes, there are three ways land can come to be vested: through the confiscation of agricultural land in excess of the land ceilings set by agrarian reforms; through the confiscation of nonagricultural land in excess of urban land ceilings[55]; and through the acquisition of land in the "public interest" by "requiring" public agencies. In effect, vesting provides a powerful basis for multiple forms of state intervention in the ownership and use of metropolitan land. The unmapping of the city has created great ambiguity regarding vesting — a process that can be thought of as an informalization of vesting.

At first glance, "informal vesting" might seem an oxymoron. On the one hand, vesting would seem to indicate the legal expropriation of land by the state; on the other, informality would seem to signify unregulated, and possibly illegal, mechanisms. But what makes vesting such a powerful instrument in Calcutta is precisely this flexible deployment of informal party mechanisms and the official authority of the state. And, indeed, such is the case of the colonies. Here, land was informally vested through the mobilization of sharecroppers by the party. It was then informally transformed into a resettlement colony by the party, and recognized by the state through service provision. The informal nature of each vesting allows the party and the state unmatched flexibility in the acquisition of land — first for the agenda of agrarian radicalism, then for the creation of an urban electorate, and finally for a project of urban development. To put it bluntly, the colonies represent a distinctive form of informal subdivision, founded on the basis of quasi-legal land rights, where the party itself acts as developer, with unique negotiability vis-à-vis the state for infrastructure. The process allows both party and state to capitalize on the upgraded settlement through evictions of the poor.[56]

Such forms of territorialized flexibility are most evident on the eastern fringes of the city, which are not only unmapped, but also marked by an unmappable history of territorial populism. It is here that the Congress Party settled Bangladeshi "refugees" in the post-Independence period, charging its machinery of popular support.[57] And it is here that in the late 1960s the United Front, a precursor to today's Left Front, instigated widespread peasant radicalism, urging sharecroppers to directly implement agrarian reforms by grabbing *benami* agricultural land. These cycles of land grabbing and settlement eventually became crucial mechanisms for enlarging party membership.[58] The context of political instability both allowed such forms of vesting to occur, and allowed them to remain informal, never codified in legal records.[59] Such a heritage of informality has simply been maintained through the long, stable political tenure of the Left Front.

By enabling techniques such as informal vesting, the structure of unmapping makes possible an informalization of the state. Here, informality is not simply a sphere of unregulated activities, but a realm of regulation where ownership and user rights are established, maintained, and overturned through elaborate "extralegal systems."[60] Although my terminology bears resemblance to De Soto's discussion of informality, there are some important differences. While De Soto intends the idea of extra legality to stand in for a Smithian invisible hand of sorts, creating equilibrium in informal markets, I mean it as technique of discipline and power. While De Soto sees extralegality as a people's response to the bureaucratic state, I see it as inhering in the state, a structural informalization that comes to be systematized and institutionalized.[61] The informalized state is thus an entity of great power, allowing the unceasing negotiation of land claims, but never the full resolution of such claims.

This informalization also has a geographic scope. If liberalization involves the recasting of the urban, then informal vesting has taken hold in the rural-urban interface, amid rapidly urbanizing agricultural land. Such transactions — of informal subdivisions or resettlement colonies — are blatantly illegal, violating the state's declared zoning codes and plans for the rural-urban fringes. Yet they are in keeping with the imperatives of urban developmentalism. In a context of unmapping, the state can deploy the party apparatus with great flexibility and little accountability toward ends that it itself has outlawed but that it wishes to achieve. A senior officer of the CMDA Land Acquisition Cell said of the rapid increase in informal subdivisions:

> It does not really matter. There are laws against the conversion of agricultural land, the filling up of marshes, but all of this is urbanizable land. Urbanization is inevitable here.[62]

New Communism, however, generates its own contradictions. First, it is marked by a deepening of rural-urban poverty, which only renders the project of urban populism ever more desperate, ever more hard to manage. As the interface between city and countryside has come to be formed through an unceasing circulation of labor — working daughters, daily commuters on overflowing local trains, the deeply impoverished rural landless — so the territorial frontier of the Calcutta region has come to be marked by unrelenting cycles of settlement, eviction, and resettlement. Second, the very regulatory ambiguities that have allowed the regime such territorial flexibility have also created the basis for great political challenges — both from opposition parties and commercialized factions within the Left Front itself. Specifically, as the Calcutta Municipal Corporation has sought to retrieve land once informally vested by the CPM, selling off plots to large development projects, so the displaced have been mobilized by the Congress

Party. And as CPM cadres have brokered informal middle-class subdivisions, so competing factions have led squatter invasions of such territory. Urban developmentalism, then, remains damned by the very regulatory ambiguity that makes possible its existence in the first place. And the Left remains unable to capitalize on the very tracts of urbanizable land that it has so brutally carved out for itself.

THE DAILY RENEWAL OF LEGITIMACY

The city of New Communism is not a complete or stable project. It is contested by those excluded and displaced; it is a city that must be serviced by those who must be excluded and displaced. Its logic is further contradictory in that its techniques of informalization simultaneously enable and stall projects of populism and developmentalism. It is then a city of crisis, of crisis that must be managed and regulated. Indeed, its sequence of moments indicate what Harvey has termed the rescheduling of the crisis.[63] But how precisely is the crisis postponed? If, as Chatterjee has argued, the Left Front is capable of ensuring "the daily renewal of the legitimacy of power" through "the coupling of a developmental regime with the organized mobilization and reproduction of political support," what is the content of such legitimacy?[64] To borrow a turn of phrase from Jessop, what is its "ethico-political" content?[65] I have already signaled that such a content is procured by inscribing the city of New Communism as the gentleman's city. Now, I would like to take this argument a step further by showing how consent to the gentleman's city is secured and maintained.

Life in *bhadralok* Calcutta is engendered on an everyday basis by feminized labor. As the rural-urban interface is reconstituted through the growing circulation of the rural-urban poor — daily commuters, permanent migrants — so the informal sector is recalibrated through processes of feminization. The emerging structures involve a number of trends: high rates of male unemployment; the growing role of women as primary earners of rural-urban households and as primary workers in many informal occupations; and a casualization and downgrading of informal work. This feminization of livelihood has gone hand in hand with a masculinization of politics. By this I mean that the political domain of urban informality has come to be dominated by men and by a masculinist idiom of politics. This is not to say that women are not politically mobilized; indeed, they are continually mobilized, but only as mothers and wives — a practice that reinforces gender hierarchies. The issue then is not so much the fact of participation, as the terms of participation. As squatter women are mobilized through their traditional gender roles, so is their wage-earning work devalorized, and so are they supervised and regulated in keeping with models of domesticity. In the context of intense labor-force participation by poor women, the rendering invisible of women's work means that the issue of informal work is ultimately nudged off the political agenda. The irony in Calcutta is that this inattention to informal-wage work unfolds through the techniques of a socialist government committed to labor organizing and unionization.

There is also a particular class logic to such practices of populist mobilization. The discourse of motherhood creates what Fernandes, in the context of factory work and housing, has described as a "bourgeois public sphere," shaped by distinctive notions of social order and morality.[66] A historicized interpretation of the tropes of this bourgeois order indicates that there are other cultural dimensions to this hegemonic project. The *bhadralok* ideal, as Chatterjee reminds us, has roots in the nationalist imaginary of motherland.[67] It is in the gendered project of motherhood that another project is inaugurated: that of a bourgeois, Hindu nation. Here, regimes of the state and regimes of gender coincide.[68]

The masculinization of politics not only devalorizes women's wage-earning work, but it valorizes male unemployment. In a region marked by widespread male unemployment, political mobilization inscribes this unemployment as masculinist power. Thus, squatter men present their political participation as acts of resistance, an exercise of choice where menial wage-earning work is rejected in favor of party work. When asked to clarify this concept of "work," men like Sudarshan respond thus:

> The party does not pay me. But I mobilize people. During rallies and brigades, I gather them up and ensure high attendance. When the leaders come to the settlement, I organize meetings. And I maintain the club. Do you think that this is any easy task? Running the club is like running a *panchayat*. . . . We keep the neighborhood peace. We maintain unity.[69]

The sense of self-importance that poor men feel in the sphere of urban informality has to do with their constant negotiation of the state apparatus. The negotiability inherent in the informalized state perpetuates their need to be thus engaged. But the nature of their participation is very much also a negotiation of the gentleman's city, a content that exceeds the informal city. Following Connell, this negotiation can be seen as "marginalized masculinity," an ensemble of practices and discourses through which poor men locate themselves in class and gender hierarchies.[70] It is also a masculinity that takes hold in distinctive spaces.

Squatter men like Sudarshan who occupy the differentiated sites of urban informality have roots in an agrarian hierarchy. Their rural landlessness is not incidental, but rather fundamental. For it is this that denied them access to local political institutions in the villages, that made the *panchayats* impenetrable. In the city, these political boundaries, mediated through class differences, become permeable, as migrants gain access to party patronage and young men are initiated

into parties. What is negotiated then in informal settlements, in the party offices
and the political clubs, is not only electoral loyalty, but also a set of class and gender subject-positions.

But this negotiation of the gentleman's city is an illusion, poignantly evident
in the sharp disjuncture between male narratives about clubs, political work, and
leadership on the one hand, and the reality of the settlements themselves on the
other. Sudarshan, for example, lived in a wretched squatter settlement called
Chetla, where the locus of political power rested not in his club but rather
beyond, in the CPM party office. While he insisted on having garnered great
political concessions from powerful men, his wife quietly complained about the
back-breaking work generated by the absolute lack of everything in the settlement: lack of water, lack of toilets, lack of livelihood. The club itself, unlike
Sudarshan's breathless accounts of its activities, had a lethargic pace. One day,
after one of Sudarshan's long monologues on his hard work at the club, his three-
year-old daughter, Jamuna, turned to him and said: "*Baba tumi to okhane khali tash
khelo* [But father, you only play cards there all day long]."[71]

I stand here at the top of a slippery slide into "culture of poverty" arguments,
facing the dark prospect of talking about lazy men and virtuous women. That is
not my intention. Rather, I am explaining the persistence of the regime, by showing how regimes of accumulation are also regimes of the family. In Calcutta's
squatter settlements, masculinist patronage seals the deal. It can be interpreted
in Mouffe's sense of a "contradictory interpellation": a provisionally fixed ensemble of subordinate and dominant subject-positions that indicates the multiplicity
of social relations through which social agents are constituted.[72] Squatter men
participate in club politics, transforming their once subordinate role as landless
peasants into the possibilities of being an urban voter. And yet it is clear that this
newfound power rests not in urban citizenship — a status that continues to elude
them — but instead in a sense of manhood. They participate in patronage politics as men, as patriarchal heads of households. It is through the paradoxes of this
contradictory interpellation that squatter men frame their political participation
as an act of resistance. But, as Willis has so perceptively noted in his work on
hegemony, these seeming acts of resistance constitute the basis of self-damnation:

> There is a moment — and it only needs to be this for the gates to shut on the
> future — in working class culture when the manual giving of labor power rep-
> resents both a freedom, election, and transcendence, and a precise insertion
> into a system of exploitation and oppression for working class people.[73]

It is thus that Calcutta's squatters "freely" participate in the conditions of
their own oppression, ascribing resistance and choice to the very moment of their
oppression. This participation in patronage allows for the simultaneous stabi-

lization of regime and family, sealing the dependence of squatters on fickle-minded political parties. It is effective because it masks the realities of the informal city through the promise of participation in the gentleman's city.

The regime of gender is, however, subject to disruption and contestation. In the squatter settlements, one word dominates the narratives of poor men: *bekar*. It is a word that means unemployed, possibly even useless. Through their participation in masculinist patronage, squatter men have recoded the word as signifying the rejection of menial labor and the adoption of meaningful work, worthy of heads of households. Thus, Sudarshan boldly stated:

> You are categorizing me as *bekar*, unemployed, huh? Well I am *bekar*, and proud of it. All of the men who work and earn a few pennies, they would not be able to live here without men like me.[74]

This precarious construction of masculinity persists unchallenged in the squatter settlements. However, on the commuter trains, as rural women make an everyday journey to work in the informal spaces of the city, they advance a fundamentally different understanding of *bekar*. They use the term to explicitly or implicitly refer to sexual impotency, presenting male unemployment as an undermining of sexual capability and power. Another popular symbol in their idioms of critique is the figure of the *babu*, the lazy, pleasure-loving, middle-class Bengali urbanite. Domestic servants refer to their employers as *babus*, but commuter women go a step further, reinscribing their husbands as *babus*:

> We work all day long and they stay at home. They have become just like the *babus* we work for.[75]

This process of signification is a crucial struggle over meanings. The concept of *babu*, a construct with deep roots in the cultural politics of the region, is double-loaded in its gendered meanings. On the one hand, it refers to the middle-class as male, situating class oppressions within a larger structure of patriarchy and thereby merging hegemonic and marginalized masculinities. On the other hand, it constitutes elite and poor men as effeminate and weak, incapable of being manly, thereby unsettling both sets of masculinities. The gentleman's city is thus dismantled. In contrast, commuter women define themselves as androgynous, simultaneously participating in male and female realms. At the end of an afternoon in Jadavpur station, twenty different commuter women said almost in unison:

> *Amra purush ebong meye* [we are simultaneously men and women], earning for the household like a man and taking care of the house like a woman.[76]

Figure 6.2. "Men Not Allowed." Rural-urban commuting in the Calcutta region.
Photo by author, 1997.

What is striking about commuter women is not only their discursive critiques, but also their daily engagement in political action. Every day thousands of poor women travel ticketless on the trains to and from Calcutta, and are militant in their refusal to buy tickets. While male ticketless commuters are at times arrested by checkers, female commuters are aware that they can use gendered techniques to ward off harassment by ticket checkers. They therefore crowd into the "Men Not Allowed" compartments of local trains, taking over spaces reserved for genteel femininity, the wives of the gentleman's city (see FIGURE 6.2). Here are some of their responses to ticket checkers:

Let them arrest us all. There isn't enough space in the hold for all of us.

When she came to fine me I said, "take off your coat and give it to me so that I'll have your job. Then only will I be able to afford the fine."

You want to arrest me? First get my children from the village. We'll all stay in your jail and you can feed us.

Most striking is the ability of commuter women to articulate and press claims vis-à-vis the state, defining ticketless travel as an entitlement of citizenship. Their most common statement is this:

We vote, and therefore why should we have to pay for what we cannot afford?[77]

Within the heterogeneity of Calcutta's rural-urban interface, among the multiple strands of commuting that link city and countryside, ticketless travel remains a distinctive practice of poor women.

There are, of course, severe limits to the commuter critiques. Unfolding in a context of deepening casualization and immiserization, these narratives of contestation are ultimately unable to transform the structural realities of the rural-urban interface. And yet they deserve careful consideration, for they stand in contrast to the daily renewal of legitimacy that takes place in the informal settlements of Calcutta. I am convinced that the ability of commuter women to resist, critique, and challenge has to do with the experience of commuting, of being together with women who are strangers from strange villages, but who are intimate in that the conditions of their lives are agonizingly similar. Commuter women form a collectivity in sites where they gather, such as waiting points on platforms and on the trains. Commuting then creates a specific embodied subjectivity with its own set of discursive critiques and political practices. The experience can be understood in terms of Young's "politics of difference," an environment of physical inexhaustibility where difference, the presence of strangers, is unavoidable.[78] The tangible experience of traveling on the overflowing trains has a distinct texture — a sense not only of one's own body, but also of other bodies, jostling against one's own, usurping space. While such journeys create a sense of self as different from others, the boundaries of distinction are constantly violated and refashioned. It is in this dialectic of self and otherness that commuter women articulate a collective identity. The space they occupy — a liminal zone between city and countryside — seems at first glance to be a brutal and claustrophobic site, and yet it turns out to show signs of life and living. It is one necessitated by the gentleman's city and yet not fully regulated by it. As Pile notes, it demonstrates that "resistance might have its own distinct spatialities," that are not simply mirror images of geographies of domination.[79]

Why is it that such disruptions are not evident in the informal settlements of Calcutta? Why is it that family and regime come to be sutured? I use the term "suturing" to indicate a wound, a raw scar, that requires a process of what Williams calls "lived hegemony."[80] But why is it that this wound does not tear apart and bleed? The commuter critiques make evident how there are spaces of the rural-urban interface where masculinist patronage is not fully able to take hold. Here, the suturing comes undone. In the squatter settlements and colonies, by contrast, masculinist patronage comes to form the social basis of informality. And there is more: at the moment of New Communism, this masculinist patronage takes hold in and through volatile geographies, through an unmapping. Such spatial techniques ensure both the territorialized flexibility of the regime and an unceasing uncertainty that secures the political consent of the poor. In this sense, the regime of accumulation is not only a regime of gender, but also what Linda

McDowell would call a "regime of place."[81]   It is thus that urban politics in a liberalizing Calcutta produces deep antagonisms, but not transformative struggles.

The city of New Communism is a city of movement. But it is also a city of stasis. Amid the cycles of land invasion and eviction, the endless transactions on the edges of the city, the countless reformisms of this party and that, the hurrying to work of the daily poor, the street-blocking rallies, the fist-shaking wrath of squatter leaders, and the sickly sweet celebrations of last-bastion communism, there is a chilling stillness at the heart of Calcutta. The stasis cannot be read as gentlemanly stability; nor can the movements and transactions be read as grassroots resistance. What is at work is a regime seeking to reinvent its forms of hegemony at the margins of global change.

NOTES

This chapter draws upon research presented in my book, *City Requiem, Calcutta: Gender and the Politics of Poverty* (Minneapolis: University of Minnesota Press, 2002).

1. *Telegraph*, September 29, 1997; and *Asian Age*, December 16, 1997.

2. *Newsweek*, "Kolkata's Glow," March 31, 1997.

3. N. Dasgupta, *Petty Trading in the Third World: The Case of Calcutta* (Avebury: Brookfield, 1992), 260–61; and *Anandabazar Patrika*, December 22, 1996.

4. S. Chakravorty, "Operation Sunshine," in S. Lahiri, ed., *Operation Sunshine* (Calcutta: Bishwakosh Parishad, 1997), 5–6.

5. S. Mitra, "Footpath-Rasta Parishkar Kore Darkar Chilo (It was Necessary to Clean Up the Sidewalks and Roads)," in Lahiri, ed., *Operation Sunshine*, 11.

6. K. Ganguly, "Sunshine-er Pore Abong Age (Before and After Sunshine)" in Lahiri, ed., *Operation Sunshine*, 12.

7. *Anandabazar Patrika*, November 28, 1996.

8. Mitra, "It was Necessary to Clean Up the Sidewalks and Roads."

9. P. Chatterjee, *The Present History of West Bengal* (Delhi: Oxford University Press, 1997), 4.

10. The word *desh* parallels the English word "country," which can mean both nation and countryside, thereby linking national identity to a particular ruralized identity. See R. Williams, *The Country and the City* (New York: Oxford University Press, 1973).

11. Chatterjee, *The Present History of West Bengal*, 160.

12. Interview of colony resident by author, 1997. Kantibabu refers to the CPM leader, Kanti Ganguly.

13. One *bigha* is equivalent to one-third of an acre; 20 *kathas* constitute a *bigha*; 1 *katha* equals 720 square feet.

14. Interview of colony resident by author, 1997. *Pattas* are property titles.

15. R. Herring, "The Dilemmas of Agrarian Communism," *Third World Quarterly* 11, no.1 (1989), 89.

16. Interview of colony resident by author, 1997. *Dalils* are property deeds.

17. *Bartaman*, December 21, 1997.

18. Ibid.

19. Udayan advertisement in *Anandabazar Patrika*, March 8, 1997.

20. *Asian Age*, November 17, 1997.

21. N. Smith, "New Globalism, New Urbanism: Gentrification as Global Urban Strategy," *Antipode* 34, no. 3 (2002), 443.

22. M. De Certeau, *The Practice of Everyday Life* (Berkeley: University of California Press, 1984), 94.

23. B. Dasgupta, "Institutional Reforms and Poverty Alleviation in West Bengal," *Economic and Political Weekly* 30, no. 41 (1995), 2691.

24. R. Mallick, *Development Policy of a Communist Government: West Bengal Since 1977* (New Delhi: Cambridge University Press, 1993), 212–13.

25. P. Sengupta, "The 1995 Municipal Election in West Bengal: The Left Front is Down," *Asian Survey* 37, no. 10 (1997), 905–17.

26. A. Shaw, "Heart of the City," *Telegraph*, June 24, 1997.

27. S. Chakravorty and G. Gupta, "Let a Hundred Projects Bloom: Structural Reform and Urban Development in Calcutta," *Third World Planning Review* 18, no. 4 (1996), 415–31.

28. B. Jessop, "Post-Fordism and the State," in A. Amin, ed., *Post-Fordism: A Reader* (Cambridge: Blackwell, 1994), 263–64.

29. D. Harvey, "Flexible Accumulation through Urbanization: Reflections on 'Post-Modernism' in the American City," in Amin, ed., *Post-Fordism: A Reader*.

30. Smith, "New Globalism, New Urbanism," 443.

31. J. Zhu, "Local Growth Coalitions: The Context and Implications of China's Gradualist Urban Land Reforms," *International Journal of Urban and Regional Research* 23, no. 3 (1999), 534–48.

32. N. Brenner and N. Theodore, "Cities and the Geographies of 'Actually Existing Neoliberalism,'" *Antipode* 34, no. 3 (2002), 375.

33. Smith, "New Globalism, New Urbanism," 427.

34. *Bartaman*, March 12, 1997.

35. For a discussion of how, in Alexandria, government bodies encouraged the development of "semi-formal housing areas," and thereby the urbanization of agricultural land through private subdivisions, see A. Soliman, "Legitimizing Informal Housing: Accommodating Low-Income Groups in Alexandria, Egypt," *Environment and Urbanization* 8, no. 1 (1996), 183–94.

36. Brenner and Theodore, "Cities and the Geographies of 'Actually Existing Neoliberalism,'" 356.

37. My terminology of accumulation and legitimation, of course, comes from J. O'Connor's work on the state. See J. O'Connor, *Accumulation Crisis* (New York: Blackwell, 1984).

38. *Anandabazar Patrika*, January 23, 1997.

39. *Asian Age*, July 15, 1997; and *Anandabazar Patrika*, December 27, 1996.

40. J. Peck and A. Tickell, "Neoliberalizing Space," *Antipode* 34, no. 3 (2002), 384.

41. Smith, "New Globalism, New Urbanism." For a theoretical analysis of gentrification, see N. Smith, "Gentrification, the Frontier, and the Restructuring of Urban Space," in N. Smith and P. Williams, eds., *Gentrification and the City* (Boston: Allen and Unwin, 1986).

42. Interview of colony resident by author, 1997.

43. Interviews of colony residents by author, 1997. The term *benami* literally means "false name." In West Bengal, the term has come to be irrevocably tied to land reforms and the attempt on the part of landowners to conceal ownership by listing land in the name of fictitious relatives.

44. Interview of Kanti Ganguly by author, 1997.

45. Interviews of officials in state and city-level land offices by author, 1996–1997.

46. Interview of Anil Shah, a pseudonym for a well-known real estate developer, by author, 1997. *Sindur* is the red powder used by married Hindu women on their forehead and in the parting of their hair to indicate their married status.

47. Chakravorty and Gupta, "Let a Hundred Projects Bloom," 425.

48. Based on various interviews, and interpreted in the context of my ethnographic presence in the land bureaucracies, I see this to signal the absence of a centralized, knowable set of land records for the southeastern fringes.

49. Interview of land officer by author, 1997.

50. K. Dasgupta, "A City Away From Home: The Mapping of Calcutta," in P. Chatterjee, ed., *Texts of Power: Emerging Disciplines in Colonial Bengal* (Minneapolis: University of Minnesota Press, 1995).

51. A. Bagchi writes: "If the basic data was not available, one wonders how could the transport planning group obtain land use and economic data which the other groups did not use or were not aware of?" See Bagchi, "Planning for Metropolitan Development: Calcutta's Basic Development Plan, 1966–86 — A Post-Mortem," *Economic and Political Weekly* 22 no. 14 (1987), 599.

52. See H. Dembowski, "Courts, Civil Society and Public Sphere: Environmental Litigation in Calcutta," *Economic and Political Weekly* January 9, 1999, 49–56. Among other things, Dembowski shows how the Master Plan for the CMD area is still not charted even though the CMDA was statutorily established 27 years ago to do so; how the Outline Development Plans required by the West Bengal Town and Country Planning Act of 1979 have never been formulated; how Geographical Survey of India maps of the area have been unavailable throughout the 1990s; and how the various maps used in High Court and Supreme Court decisions are of varying and inadequate scale and tucked away in unpublished court files.

53. *Telegraph*, December 2, 1997.

54. A. Appadurai, *Modernity at Large: Cultural Dimensions of Globalization* (Minneapolis: University of Minnesota Press, 1996), 132.

55. The urban land ceiling act was recently repealed. The repercussions thereof are still not known.

56. As outlined in G. Bhargava, *Socio-Economic and Legal Implications of the Urban Land Ceiling and Regulation Act, 1976* (New Delhi: Abhinav, 1983), some of the regulatory indeterminacies are common to all Indian cities, with complex land use jurisdictions and multiple ceilings governing various forms of land. But the issue is of quite a different nature in Calcutta where the regulatory mechanisms for resolving these conflicts — survey maps, master plans, and land records — are all absent.

57. Chatterjee, "The Present History of West Bengal," 186–87; and A. Ghosh, *Peaceful Transition to Power: A Study of Marxist Political Strategies in West Bengal, 1967–77* (Calcutta: Firma KLM, 1981).

58. S. Basu, *Politics of Violence: A Case Study of West Bengal* (Calcutta: Minerva, 1982), 58.

59. D. Bandyopadhyay, "Not a Gramscian Pantomime," *Economic and Political Weekly* 32, no. 12 (1997), 581.

60. H. De Soto, *The Other Path* (New York: Harper & Row, 1989), 66.

61. My terminology of informalization comes from K. Meagher, "Crisis, Informalization and the Urban Informal Sector in Sub-Saharan Africa," *Development and Change* 26 (1995), 259–84.

62. Interview of CMDA officer by author, 1997.

63. Harvey, "Flexible Accumulation through Urbanization."

64. Chatterjee, "The Present History of West Bengal," 154, 160.

65. B. Jessop, "A Neo-Gramscian Approach to the Regulation of Urban Regimes: Accumulation Strategies, Hegemonic Projects, and Governance," in M. Lauria, ed., *Reconstructing Urban Regime Theory: Regulating Urban Politics in a Global Economy* (Thousand Oaks: Sage Publications, 1997), 72.

66. L. Fernandes, *Producing Workers: The Politics of Gender, Class, and Culture in the Calcutta Jute Mills* (Philadelphia: University of Pennsylvania Press, 1997), 124–25.

67. P. Chatterjee, "The Nationalist Resolution of the Women's Question," in K. Sangari and S. Vaid, eds., *Recasting Women: Essays in Indian Colonial History* (New Brunswick: Rutgers University Press, 1990).

68. For a discussion of such issues, see S. Radcliffe, "People Have to Rise Up — Like the Great Women Fighters: The State and Peasant Women in Peru," in S. Radcliffe and S. Westwood, eds., *Viva: Women and Popular Protest in Latin America* (New York: Routledge, 1993). Radcliffe brilliantly shows how peasant and squatter women can deploy such hegemonic femininities back against the state.

69. Interview with Sudarshan, a pseudonym for a squatter leader, by author, 1997.

70. R.W. Connell, *Masculinities* (Berkeley: University of California Press, 1995).

71. Statement by Jamuna during interview with her father, Sudarshan, 1997.

72. C. Mouffe, "Hegemony and New Political Subjects: Toward a New Concept of Democracy," in C. Nelson and L. Grossberg, eds., *Marxism and the Interpretation of Culture* (Chicago: University of Illinois Press, 1988), 95.

73. P. Willis, *Learning to Labor: How Working Class Kids Get Working Class Jobs* (New York: Columbia University Press, 1977), 120.

74. Interview with Sudarshan by author, 1997.

75. Interviews with commuters by author, 1996–1997.

76. Ibid.

77. Ibid.

78. I. Young, "The Ideal of Community and the Politics of Difference," in L. Nicholson, ed., *Feminism/ Postmodernism* (New York: Routledge, 1990).

79. S. Pile, "Opposition, Political Identities, and Spaces of Resistance," in S. Pile and M. Keith, eds., *Geographies of Resistance* (New York: Routledge, 1997), 2.

80. R. Williams, *Marxism and Literature* (New York: Oxford University Press, 1977), 112.

81. L. McDowell, *Gender, Identity, and Place: Understanding Feminist Geographies* (Minneapolis: University of Minnesota Press, 1999).

7

Tilting at Sphinxes: Locating Urban Informality in Egyptian Cities

Ahmed M. Soliman

In the majority of developing countries the low incomes of many urban house-holds, combined with the high costs of urban land, conspire to make access to affordable, appropriate, and legal housing extremely difficult. In Egypt, the result is that about twenty million people live today in houses that are detrimental to their health and safety. Yet as Egyptian urban centers continue to expand, these problems become daily more urgent. In Egypt housing is essentially an urban problem, one closely linked with development processes, socioeconomic change, and political milieu. Its main features are overcrowding, a shortage of affordable housing for those most in need, the continued emergence of informal housing areas, and a general deterioration of the built environment.[1]

Informal housing development is not a new phenomenon in Egypt. In fact, it is as old as modern urbanization and development, which have existed in the country for more than five decades. Indeed, Egyptian cities, particularly Cairo and Alexandria, have played a decisive role in the country's socioeconomic development. The key to this role has been the complementary development of industrial technology and sprawl growth. In Egypt, the twin phenomena of industrialization and urbanization, formally or informally, have been virtually inseparable, and have directly affected housing delivery systems.

Acting as a partner in housing production, the Egyptian government has sought to protect public health and provide safety in overcrowded cities, and recently it began to seriously tackle the problem of informal housing areas. As a result, policies and programs are now being devised to address such important concerns as the continuing deterioration of housing conditions, the low level of formal housing production, the spread of informal housing areas, and the restricted nature of building regulation.

This chapter aims to show that there are diverse mechanisms behind the complexity of informal housing in Egyptian cities. Toward this end, it develops a typology of informal housing and estimates quantities and values of different types of informal property. Its research includes case studies of Greater Cairo and of Alexandria, Egypt's second largest city and main port. In both urban areas, informal settlements satisfy the basic needs of many people. In addition, the chapter seeks to question the roles of various actors and of local political and economic structures in the development of Egypt's informal housing areas. Finally, it examines the prospects for further informal residential development in the present socioeconomic and political milieu. In this chapter, all housing that is not in compliance with building and zoning laws will be termed "informal," rather than "illegal." All illegal housing in Egypt is deemed informal, and as will be shown, formalization occurs only through the process of legalization.

The diversity, complexity, and widespread nature of informal housing development in Egypt has resulted in a situation where various types of housing have been created to suit various strata of society. The quality of information on such informal housing and its typologies is one of the most important factors influencing the success of international development assistance. Yet in Egypt little is known about this subject from the perspective of local intermediaries and residents. A central purpose of this chapter, therefore, is to introduce a typology of informal housing which reflects accurate information, and which may facilitate the process of developing a proper policy of government intervention. In particular, the quality of information presented here may assist decision-makers in arriving at a conceptual framework for legalizing much of this sector. This would allow housing to play a proper role in the socioeconomic development of the country.

Research for this chapter was conducted in three phases. First, a preliminary study was carried out to examine informal housing and land-use patterns within the two cities. Second, an intermediate study was formulated to examine the causes of informality and housing mechanisms. Third, fieldwork was conducted within the study areas to investigate how informal housing developed according to certain characteristic typologies. The preliminary study was carried out in 1996 by two local consultants and a team from the Institute of Liberty and Democracy (ILD). It involved the observation of random samples of informal areas.[2] The ILD team, the two local consultants, and expert teams then carried out the second and third phases of the study from August 1999 to July 2000.

A related task involved mapping informal areas in the two cities by typology and subtypology. This first involved reviewing other attempts to map informal areas. Topographic maps from different periods were also examined. Finally, numerous field checks were carried out in different parts of the two cities.

The analysis proposes three main informal housing types: semi-informal, squatting, and hybrid or exformal. Within these types, twelve subtypes were identified, and within several of the subtypes an additional thirteen minor variants were distinguished. In order to estimate the quantity of property associated with each informal housing type in Greater Cairo and Alexandria, analysis was carried out at the lowest census enumeration level — that of the *shiakha* (part of a district) and village (*qaria*).[3]

Using the most detailed local maps, the analysis then moved on to estimating asset value. This first involved calculating the extent of built-up area for each informal subtype in each *shiakha* or *qaria*. This gave the percentage of each enumeration district that could be attributed to each. To estimate the total asset value of these dwellings, it was then necessary to ascribe average physical characteristics and assign monetary values by dwelling type.[4] This was done for each of the informal types to reflect generalized differences between informal residences on agricultural and desert land. Throughout this process, conservative estimates were used — in other words, average physical attributes and values were held at the lower end of possible ranges.

The chapter is organized into seven parts: first, an overview of the Egyptian urbanization process; second, a discussion of the problems posed by the emergence of urban informality in Egypt; third, a description of some important general characteristics of Egyptian informal housing development; fourth, a categorization of important actors, organizations, and institutional mechanisms; fifth, a description of informal/exformal housing types; sixth, a quantification and valuation of informal/exformal units; and last, a concluding section offering recommendations for future government action.

THE EGYPTIAN URBANIZATION PROCESS

In Egypt, the urban population has grown steadily through the twentieth century, tripling from 1947 to 1976 while the overall population doubled. According to the 1996 census, the national population was about 59.272 million, with an annual projected increase of 1.25 million, or 2.1 percent. Some 48 percent of this population lived in urban areas, principally in Cairo, Alexandria, and the Suez Canal cities, with the rest scattered throughout 157 medium-size towns.[5]

At the beginning of the twenty-first century, the total population of the country is now approaching 68 million. Natural increase has been responsible for two-thirds of Egyptian urban growth between 1966 and 1996, and migration for one-third.

The rapid increase of the urban population in Egypt has combined with a continuously changing socioeconomic situation and a shortage of formal affordable housing to intensify housing pressures. Formal urbanization has generally involved only the development of main roads and the construction of public buildings on former agricultural lands. Meanwhile, much more far-ranging informal urbanization has taken the form of illegal/informal residential development (*el manatiqe el ashwaíyya*) on the periphery of the major urban centers.[6] The introduction of the Infitha System (Open Door Policy) in the mid-1970s, followed by the adoption of free-market economics, the growth of financial investment companies, and a capital-oriented privatization program, have helped accelerate the level of urbanization, and have put further pressure on housing resources in Cairo and Alexandria, where demand is greatest.[7]

These changes have now led to the spread of urban centers and the development of continuous, informally built-up areas between medium-size and small cities. The haphazard form of new informal residential areas has also weakened planning controls over urban development, raised the cost of providing services and roads, added to the financial burden on government, and increased the physical diversity and legal complexity of urban areas.

Informal housing areas (*ashwaíyyat*) today constitute a considerable proportion of many Egyptian cities (see FIGURES 7.1–7.5). According to official estimates, the total number of people living in such areas is about 8.1 million.[8] But there is considerable doubt about this figure, since a single informal settlement in Greater Cairo, Ezbet El Haganah, today accommodates at least one million people.[9] In fact, El Akhbar has estimated that the total population of Egypt's informal areas today exceeds 15 million people, or more than 50 percent of the total urban population.[10] Recently, a study carried out by Hernando De Soto's Institute of Liberty and Democracy (ILD) in Cairo showed that 52.7 percent of Greater Cairo's residential areas, 50 percent of Alexandria's, and 25 percent of Tanta's are informal. This represented a net surface area of 129.2, 49.38, and 10.5 square kilometers per city, respectively.[11]

7.1

7.2

7.3

7.4

7.5

Figure 7.1. (bottom, previous page) **Privately owned semi-informal housing on agricultural land.**
Figure 7.2. Exformal settlement (public housing).
Figure 7.3. Squatter housing on municipal desert land.
Figure 7.4. Semi-informal housing on lakeside land.
Figure 7.5. Semi-informal housing on core village agricultural land.
Source for Figs. 7.1–7.5 : author.

Such a situation may partly be due to the considerable increase in informal construction activities in the last three decades, mainly using savings accumulated by migrant workers in the Gulf and dividends from financial investment companies. The ownership of land and housing are also culturally valued as an important form of social prestige and security. In response to these conditions, small and medium-sized contractors have developed a variety of cheaper "model houses" for informal areas by adjusting formal standards to local needs. Construction costs are thus far lower than in formal areas, and owner-builders also avoid paying fees for architectural services and official approvals. However, most informal settlements suffer from a serious lack of both basic and public and social services, and serious environmental problems further undermine living conditions.

THE EMERGENCE OF URBAN INFORMALITY

The total population of Egypt is today approaching 68 million, and this figure is expected to reach 80 million by the end of this decade. The rapid increase of population has combined with continuously changing socioeconomic and political conditions to create an excess of housing demand over supply. In an attempt to understand how this situation developed, the following subsections briefly examine the issues of political strain, the general concept of informality, and the specific causes of informality in Egypt.

POLITICAL STRAIN

Political decisions depend on the nature and interests of a state and its social and economic objectives. In this way, they reflect the distribution of power within a society.[12] In Egypt, state intervention in the housing field has followed the powerful interests of both the affluent class and the poor, depending on the development process within a given area. However, social investments have generally only been made in Egypt after the needs of industrial enterprises for direct aid have been satisfied. And there has also been a tendency to ensure that publicly subsidized projects are profitable, so they can eventually be transferred to private-sector interests. In this sense, state interventions in housing have privileged the interests of private capital over the local working class (the lowest strata of the society). An early example of this was state intervention in housing supply during the New Era movement of the mid-1950s and early 1960s.

There are various reasons why a government should become involved in housing. The most common involve humanitarian reasons, functionalism, social control, and human-rights considerations.[13] In relation to housing, human-rights considerations have recently become one of the Egyptian government's main concerns. Today, government debate centers on who is in need of housing, what constitutes adequate housing, how the government may ensure that those in need obtain housing, and how government resources may best be spent to fulfil housing needs. However, these policy orientations have not always been paramount. Indeed, Egyptian housing policy has passed through various eras. Among these were Nasserism (1952 to 1970), a period of extensive intervention; Sadatism (1970–1981), a period of active but ad-hoc intervention; and the period of the early 1980s, when the state backed off from interventionist policies and housing markets fluctuated constantly. It is important to point out that before 1952 there was no housing policy in the country. The only publicly constructed housing project before then was Workers' City in Imbabah, with about 1,000 dwelling units.[14]

In Egypt, dominant political groups have influenced the housing process and the formulation of housing policies. As a result, in certain circumstances the state may take steps in favor of the poor, while in others it may act against the poor in favor of dominant political/capitalist groups.[15] Political support, in this sense, may be crucial. Thus, in the mid-1970s, within the framework of the Open Door Policy, Egypt was forced to balance the imperatives of capital accumulation against the needs of those with few personal resources. This policy led directly to changes in housing policy, leaving the supply of luxury housing to the market, while reserving a role for the state in the provision of housing for the lower classes. Since then, for many reasons, the state has intervened more widely to increase housing production across social strata. One reason has been to maintain control over the urban poor. Another has been to use housing policy to enhance economic development in order to cope with the increasing needs of the population and match the goals of international development assistance. A third reason has been to overcome the problem of the international debt (this was around US$45 billion in 1976, and is currently nearly US$28 billion).

In 1989 former Prime Minister Attaf Sadekey interpreted informal housing areas to be like cancers, belonging neither to the city nor the village. To address this problem, in 1991 the Egyptian government established a wide range of Economic Reform Structure Programs, according to which the private sector was engaged in a policy of market-based remedies.[16]

At the beginning of 1990s, the terrorist movement in Egypt further encouraged politicians to address the problem of informal housing areas, where much of the unrest was concentrated. Thus, in May 1993, after the terrorism of Imbabah, President Hosni Mubarak announced a national program to upgrade informal housing in Egypt, to which 106 million Egyptian pounds were allocated. This program also brought increased official presence in such areas. Thus, the state assumed a new double role — widening its control over society, and providing money to improve informal settlements.

Between the years 1995 and 2000, the government also initiated a new economic policy through its privatization program. This program took three forms. First was outright privatization, where the government sold certain assets, franchised other operations, and contracted for other services. Second was the introduction of certain free-market mechanisms, including a new rent law that allowed the private sector to put housing units on the market without restriction and according to supply and demand. Third was a program of pragmatic privatization, according to which initial agreements with private management agents might eventually lead to more extensive commitments. As part of the latter process, the government allowed private enterprises to become involved in land development within Egyptian new towns, frequently through partnerships with local governments. This kind of partnership allowed private enterprises to construct huge housing projects in newly developed satellite towns. As such, it was in line with the direction of World Bank policy.[17] Today one might ask several questions about this policy, however. Have such private/public partnerships offered a suitable environment for housing development? Can this approach accelerate housing production? And what type of partnership best serves middle- and low-income groups?

Today the track record of such public/private partnerships has not been outstanding. Many of their schemes did not develop further than designs. Others changed their objective mid-stream, often ending up as typical government-constructed housing. Such failed partnerships have resulted in a situation of confrontation rather than collaboration. In addition, construction standards, which assumed the existence of predetermined socioeconomic groups, have resulted in mismatches and conflicts that have had a direct and negative effect on environmental quality. Two main groups have benefited from the partnership policy: holders of commercial and industrial capital, and the bureaucratic and technocratic leadership within both the private and government sectors. The poor and those who live on fixed incomes — i.e., middle-income groups — have been hardest hit.

EVOLVING CONCEPTS OF INFORMALITY

In 1954 W. Arthur Lewis identified informality as presenting a dualistic model of interaction between the modern and traditional sectors in underdeveloped countries.[18] In 1971, in his study of urban migrants to Accra, Ghana, Keith Hart then proposed dividing the economy of developing counties into two sectors, formal and informal.[19] However, in recreating and renaming Lewis's categories, Hart spoke of income opportunities rather than sectors, and he defined informality simply as "self-employment." His distinctions were subsequently defined more precisely by the International Labor Office (ILO).[20] A key assumption underlying the work of all those who advocate a reconsideration of the meaning of informality has been that poor countries must diversify their economic base away from dependence on primary production through manufacturing. In this regard, they claim that small enterprises generate more jobs and require less capital investment per job than larger enterprises.[21]

Even neo-Marxist literature on petty commodity production from the early 1980s often seemed to adopt a dualist form of analysis.[22] Many observers, therefore, have concluded that debates about the utility of the concept of the informal sector are largely semantic. Recently, however, a few authors have begun to question the notion more closely, especially in the collection *The Informal Economy*, edited by Portes, Castells, and Benton.[23] This book argued that informal activities involve "the unregulated production of otherwise licit goods and services." They thus represent a "novel economic trend." The book also noted the resilience of informal arrangements in contexts in which they were believed to be extinct, or in which they were expected to disappear with the advance of industrialization. In this regard, Lisa Peattie has argued that, according to purpose and context, it would be better to substitute phrases such as "family firm," "self-employment," "small enterprise," and "working poor" for the term "informal sector."[24]

De Soto has defined informality as the refuge of individuals who find that the costs of abiding by existing laws in the pursuit of legitimate economic objectives exceed the benefits.[25] Aside from encompassing activities undertaken just outside the law, informality thus also encompasses activities for which the state has created a system of exemptions but has not provided the full benefits and protections of the law. In this regard, Arif Hasan has defined the informal housing sector as all activity, or those parts of it, related to land development (or which affects land use and land values) which does not have de jure recognition.[26] And more recently, in *The Mystery of Capital: Why Capitalism Triumphs in the West and Fails Everywhere Else*, De Soto has argued that the poor inhabitants of Third World nations — five-sixths of humanity — do have things, but they lack the process to represent their property and create capital.[27] Thus, they have houses but not titles, crops but not deeds, businesses but not statutes of incorporation. It is the unavailability of these essential representations that explains why people who have adapted every other Western invention, from the paper clip to the nuclear reactor, have not been able to produce sufficient capital to make their domestic economies work.

Why then are these countries so underdeveloped? Why can't they turn these assets into liquid capital — the kind of capital that generates new wealth? For De Soto, this is the "mystery of capital." And in his book he explains how this unwitting process, hidden deep in thousands of pieces of property law throughout the West, came to be, how it works, and how today it can be deliberately set up in developing and former communist nations.

The importance of such a program to Egypt is clear if one considers how the informal economy now represents a "dominant sector" of the national economy. For example, a full 40 percent of the national economy is now involved in informal housing development. De Soto estimates that informal housing development in Egypt represents an investment of US$225 billion.[28]

As the above discussion would seem to indicate, urban informality also represents a failure of official socioeconomic and political programs to meet the basic needs and requirements of the majority of people. When such programs fail to meet the requirements of society, informality takes place. Similarly, people may choose ad-hoc ways of obtaining goods and services to avoid complicated, time-consuming official procedures. Urban informality in this sense simply involves a form of highly rational economic behavior, allowing people to obtain what they need at lower cost.

For all these reasons, it is important to understand why the urban poor are not interested in obeying the law. Enhanced information on informal residential activities may also lead to policies that will enhance national economic development by changing the status of informal housing from covert to overt wealth.

CAUSES OF INFORMALITY IN EGYPT

Several factors have historically been associated with informal residential development on agricultural and desert lands in Egypt. The government, either directly or indirectly, has played a major role in all cases.

First, changes in official economic policy have taken economic power away from the traditional landholders and spread ownership across a wider section of society. This trend first appeared in the land-reform measures and revolutionary land-ownership strategies of the early 1960s. But it continued under the Open Door Policy of Sadat and the privatization policies of Mubarak.

Second, the announcement of official planning schemes has normally led the urban poor to occupy land close by, in order to pursue the job opportunities created by such government work. Thus, informal housing areas emerged during the construction of Nasr City (a dormitory satellite town to Cairo) and construction of the ring roads around Cairo and Alexandria. In the case of Nasr City, the government allowed those engaged in the construction process to settle temporarily on a public site near the project, eventually creating the Manshiet Nasser squatter settlement. In the latter cases, private developers purchased large areas of agricultural land in the vicinity of the proposed ring roads, and subdivided them illegally, thus creating both the Ain Shams area of Cairo and Ezbet Mohesan in Alexandria.

Third, rapid urban development has stimulated greater inequality in land holdings. In Egypt, land is seen as a far safer investment in uncertain times than industrial production or cash; meanwhile, during booms, land ownership permits lucrative profits. It is estimated that the annual total of agricultural land converted to urban use in Egypt is 20,000–30,000 hectares.[29]

Finally, Egyptian land-tenure laws have created unstable patterns of ownership. In particular, Egyptian inheritance laws dictate that children should inherit equal shares of property. But this often results in parcels being abandoned when multiple progeny cannot agree over subdivision or sale. Alternatively, if a landlord dies without children, his property is transferred to the Ministry of Awqaf. In both cases, land may change from private freehold to public title. Further instability was created by the Agrarian Land Reform of 1961, which redistributed fertile land from traditional owners to small landowners. This was confirmed in 1963, when the land tenure of large areas changed from private to public. In all cases, such movement of land from public to private ownership, and vice-versa, has had a major impact on the building patterns.

In addition to these broad underlying conditions, the main premises for the acceleration of illegal housing development in Egypt may be summarized as follows: a desire among owners of agricultural/desert lands to subdivide their land into small plots for sale, and the increasing demand for such plots; the subdivision of inherited agricultural land, causing farm plots to become too small to be cultivated economically; the desire of owners of large plots who are employed in sectors other than agriculture to avoid the difficulty of finding suitable farming tenants, and who sell their land for development instead; and unfavorable farming conditions, such as when crops on lands close to urbanizing areas are damaged by children and domestic animals from neighboring dwellings or are overshadowed by adjacent dwellings.

CHARACTERISTICS OF INFORMAL HOUSING IN EGYPT

According to Ward and Gilbert, informal housing development in Third World countries increases close to election times.[30] In Egypt, informal housing development also appears whenever land tenure is in doubt, during the transaction of land and property between various government offices, or during economic transformation.[31] The following subsections will examine several other important dynamics specific to the Egyptian case: the underlying pattern of agricultural land subdivision; the social structures governing the invasion of desert areas near cities; and the importance of mosques in informal residential development.

AGRICULTURAL LAND SUBDIVISION

In Egypt, agricultural land subdivision is a product of inheritance. According to Islamic law, all heirs obtain a share of the heritage, but a son inherits a share double that of a daughter. Such a process of subdivision is dynamic and occurs piecemeal over a locality, increasing disparities in parcel size. However, since each new plot must have access to an irrigation canal and a public road, the result is generally one of linear plots (*ahwad*) up to 400 meters long and 120 meters wide. Generation after generation, such plots have been further subdivided into narrower strips separated by small irrigation channels (*missqa*). Some today are as narrow as 15 meters.

As localities become increasingly urbanized, some canals dry up and are added to the width of contiguous roads. Furthermore, as disputes arise among heirs, courts have often transferred judgement to engineers with expertise in subdividing land according to Islamic law. Such subdivisions usually occur according to a measurement of *faddan*, which constitutes 24 *qirat* (175 square meters). Since each *qirat* contains 24 *saáhim* (7.29 square meters), the characteristic width of many plots is 7.29 meters or some multiple thereof. Large agricultural parcels (*ahwad*) are usually subdivided within the pattern of large irrigation canals and drains, and each *hoáad* (large parcel) must have side reservations for paths and canal cleaning. The pattern of the old irrigation system thus usually defines the main and secondary streets in an informal housing settlement on formerly agricultural land.

CLAIMING LAND IN DESERT AREAS

Desert land in Egypt is by default state land. But there is a long and complicated history of legal and extralegal mechanisms to exploit this land for the benefit of private and institutional interests. The process of residential occupation of
such land in Egypt has also had many typical features.

The collective invasion of fringe desert areas around big urban centers began in
Egypt in the 1920s when settlers moved onto land along Alexandria's North Coast,
in the area between Abu-Kir and Sidi Beshir, and around Lake Maryout. The
parcels settled here were mainly controlled by Bedouin. Around Cairo, collective
invasion by workers from Upper Egypt began in the 1930s in Ezbet El Haganah and
expanded to other desert areas in the 1960s, most notably Manshiet Nasser.

Following these invasions, the claims of settlers living on their plots were
rarely disputed. Only in rare situations when a claimant did not show up for a
long time might somebody else claim his plot. However, even in such cases,
should the first claimant reappear, he was usually offered compensation. Most
settlers claimed more land than they needed for themselves, selling adjacent areas
to kin or friends in order to create a pattern of familiar neighbors.

Over time, neighbors usually helped each other in construction and site
development, and they rarely interfered in subdivision activity and sales decisions.
Nevertheless, at a certain stage the oldest settlers usually developed criteria to regulate access to land by newcomers. Collective arrangements were also made for
public space.

Because the value of such desert land was low, it was generally claimed, subdivided, and sold informally. But by the 1970s the improved accessibility of desert
land and the increased demand for land plots due to the general boom in informal housing not only attracted more settlers but drew the attention of government bodies. Specifically, after decree No. 506/1984, municipalities tried to clear
some areas, beginning with vacant land claimed by the oldest settlers. However,
the latter organized themselves as community associations (for example, Abna'
Ezbet El Haganah) and filed lawsuits against municipalities, which were eventually dismissed by the courts.

For most desert areas, land tenure remains confusing, although some municipalities have recently attempted to regularize the situation by sanctioning trilateral negotiations between residents and claimants, municipalities, and the military. Nevertheless, there have been numerous conflicts and disputes concerning
formal as well as informal property rights and ownership, particularly in the Ezbet
El Haganah area of Greater Cairo and the El Dekhlia area in Alexandria. In some
cases these have involved settlers who built on land previously claimed by others.
One of these disputes reportedly resulted in the death of two people who tried to
settle on land that had already been claimed. In other cases, land — or even buildings — have been sold several times by the same owner.

THE IMPORTANCE OF MOSQUES IN INFORMAL DEVELOPMENT

Mosques are religious establishments that serve as community centers. They are usually built through mutual aid on vacant land, and members of the community organize various mutual-help projects through them. Occasionally, they are located on the ground floor of multipurpose buildings.

A fundamental aspect in facilitating informal development in both Cairo and Alexandria has been the construction of mosques (*msgahd*) or *zouhia* (small mosques) either by the community or by private developers. Mosques ensure the installation of basic services within informal sites and facilitate residential development. They also give a sense of security to settlers since municipalities do not have the authority to demolish places for prayers.

A small mosque is thus often constructed illegally by private landowners or developers and donated to the *waqf*, in full knowledge that the municipalities will not dare demolish it. This enables private developers to subdivide the remaining area and expand a settlement.

The practice of accepting a mosque as a gift and taking responsibility for it gives settlers some expectation that a municipality will ultimately accept their site's residential status. All actors benefit from this development: the municipality is released from having to provide social amenities to a growing population; private developers gain a good return for their money; and settlers find reasonable sites for housing development. Subsequently, various services are installed to serve the mosque, and citizens may resort to the power of religion to achieve their goals.[12] In this way, the settlers enhance their social environment, while the government may support this improvement for the benefit of the locality.

LAND MECHANISMS AND ACTORS

Considering the increasing demand for urban housing by low-income groups and the difficulty of obtaining economical shelter within urban centers, informality has become the principal means of urban development in Egypt. The discussion below gives insights into some of the protagonists in the development of informal housing. It also identifies some of the key organizations involved in land transactions, and explains some of the convoluted institutional mechanisms by which landowners currently attempt to formalize their holdings.

ACTORS IN INFORMAL HOUSING DEVELOPMENT

Various groups have been associated with facilitating access to informal housing in Egypt (see FIGURE 7.6). These include owners of agricultural areas (providers); private enterprises that serve as illegal land developers (operators); those who provide informal services to the operators (suppliers); government agencies (regulators) and

ACTORS	HOUSING TYPES		
	Semi-informal	Squatting	Hybrid
Providers (landowners)	Generally active	Reactive Status quo, specific	Proactive over specific issues
Operators/Speculators (private developers)	Supportive	Opportunity for development	Critical in some ways
Informal service suppliers (landlords, brokers, contractors)			
Facilitators/Regulators (public/private groups and state agencies)	Active	Lacked vision	Concerned with a wide range of issues affecting residential development
Customers (urban poor)	Increasingly active	Active/coordination	Image of future vision
Formal-sector institutions (merchants, banks, professionals, etc.)	Active	Initially opposed, later supportive and contributory	Inward investment

Figure 7.6. Actors and their roles in land provision.
Source: author.

public/private interest groups (facilitators); people who need housing (customers); and, finally, formal-sector institutions (merchants, banks, professionals, etc.). All these groups have participated or cooperated in one way or another in accelerating, formulating, or encouraging the mechanisms of this market.[33]

The main groups participating in informal housing development may be described as follows.

Providers (landowners). Such individuals may own land on the periphery of the city and may be motivated by profit to sell their plots to newcomers who are seeking affordable housing sites.

Private developers (operators/speculators). Such larger private concerns may buy large plots of desert/agricultural land in key locations. In general, they benefit from understanding the important dynamics of informal urbanization, and they see illegal subdivision as a good opportunity for profit. However, contrary to owner-subdividers, these "professional subdividers" do not often settle in an area. They are most likely to find a role when personal relations and trust are weak in an area. This may be the case when residents have little in common with each other and come to an area individually.

Suppliers of informal services. Three groups deserve mention here. First are small landlords, who may have parcels close to or adjacent to the city. Second are middlemen or local brokers (*simsar*). In the early phase of settlement activity, new-

comers usually hear about the possibility of settling in a certain area through relatives, friends, or colleagues. But later, some residents may assume a more established role in relation to the sale of both land and houses. With time and an
increase of tenant residents, they may also act as middlemen between landlords
and tenants. Such brokers normally work out of coffee shops (*qhwyya*), groceries,
or shops, and both buyers and sellers pay them a fixed amount or a percentage of
a contract's value. The third important group in this category are small and illegal contractors. Such people accelerate housing production on agricultural areas,
encouraging further invasion of agricultural land.

Public/private bodies (facilitators) and governmental agencies (regulators). Whatever
their form and organization, these agencies often support the invasion of agricultural areas on the periphery of cities by erecting religious centers (usually
mosques), public-housing complexes, administrative buildings, and/or educational complexes. Because these buildings are public or religious, they establish
new land-use patterns that replace the area's former agricultural use. In addition,
the government has taken the initiative in developing new economic activities on
virgin desert land or using such land as a location for military activities.

Prospective customers. These people may be acutely in need of housing sites.
They may generally be considered low-income.

Formal-sector institutions (merchants, banks, professionals, etc.). Whether such bodies are
private or public, they participate by providing cash and services needed to purchase
agricultural land within a city's periphery. The provision of cash must be accompanied by collateral. It is very rare that such institutions will finance informal housing
development directly, but they may play an important role behind the scenes.

THE ROLE OF ORGANIZATIONS IN DESERT LAND SETTLEMENT

Land subdivision and informal development of desert areas follow different
procedures than those which pertain on agricultural land. Here the most characteristic processes have involved collective invasion by people from Upper Egypt
or Bedouin. Therefore, kin groups, friendship networks, and popular organizations have played a major role in informal development on desert land.

During the early years of informal settlement activity in Egypt, traditional
community leaders like *sheikhs*, *'umdas*, and neighborhood and family elders played
an important role. They represented the settlers in negotiations with the local
administration and often arranged for the installation of public water taps along
main streets. Gradually, they also negotiated the extension of infrastructure
(water, electricity, and also sewerage in some areas) through self-help. However,
among younger Egyptians today, the patriarchal values underlying these traditions
have lost much of their value. As a result, the traditional role of the *sheikh al-hara*
(neighborhood leader), or the *kibir al-'a'ila* (extended family elder with ultimate
decision-making power), is rarely filled. Newer conditions of enhanced person-

al freedom and increased anonymity are instead reflected in less organized and coherent local communities.

In many cases, however, traditional leaders from particular areas of origin in Upper Egypt have organized small community organizations called *rabta* (pl. *rawabit*). These are an exclusively Upper Egyptian type of popular organization, to which membership is restricted by place of family origin — with the name of the origin place serving also as the name of the association. *Rawabit* normally collect money and build premises consisting of a mosque or a church, with an annexed multipurpose room, and in some cases additional rooms. *Rawabit* offer support on special occasions like funerals and pilgrimage, and their multipurpose rooms are sometimes used for wedding parties and festivities during religious feasts. Some of the more active *rawabit* organize additional activities like literacy classes and support for widows and orphans. A few are registered with the Ministry of Social Affairs under the NGO law (law No. 32/1964, amended by law No. 153/1999), but most operate informally.

Another informal organization that has played a role in informal settlement areas such as the El Dekhlia and Ezbet Allam areas of Alexandria is the Arab Council (Maglis Al-Arab). The council drew on traditions introduced centuries ago by Bedouin immigrants to Upper Egypt from the Arabian Peninsula. The head of the Arab Council was traditionally a charismatic figure, and like other council members, he derived his authority mainly from his socioeconomic status and his communication and negotiation skills. Over the years, the council managed to obtain some public services and have some utilities extended to desert squatter areas. It was also able to organize support for individual community members in cases of personal crisis, and it settled disputes of all kinds among residents of informal areas. However, after the head of the Arab Council died in 1989, the council ceased to exist.

Popular organizations have also played a role in both Ezbet El Haganah and El Dekhlia, as well as in other squatter settlements. While the structure of these organizations and their roles in community development have been similar, their degree of influence has varied. Generally, the more homogeneous the residents of an area are in terms of regional origin, the stronger their popular organizations will be. This has been particularly true of settlements where most residents come from Upper Egyptian villages.

LAND TRANSACTIONS

Whatever the mechanisms that determined original access to land for informal housing, planners have lacked the power, resources, and information to control, or even monitor, subsequent processes of growth. This has created problems for those who wish to formalize their ownership rights.

On agricultural land, some form of legal documentation normally exists for land claims. But in desert areas, where such documentation is generally lacking, considerable efforts have been required as settlements have matured to acquire a similar level of legitimacy for individual plots. These have involved various paper chases, including obtaining electricity connections or paying property taxes (*awayyid*) or land rents.

At the root of the problem is the fact that many sites never possessed a complete land registry. Thus, in the Ezbet El Haganah and El Dekhlia areas (and others in Cairo and Alexandria), many transactions have simply never been formally recorded. In other areas, while records have been kept by lawyers and landowners, they have been kept in ways that conceal identities so as to evade property taxes. And nearly always land transactions have been conducted in private, with the prices quoted rarely being those actually paid. While Egyptian legislation nominally regulates such private development, it has been powerless to influence events.

A further problem is that formal land transactions, when they do occur within informal areas, can only take place according to extremely complicated procedures. There are various ways to formalize a land transaction in an informal area, but the first step is usually to obtain official land title. One method of formally registering a property is through *seiht twequeh*, by which an applicant can receive court approval for a preliminary land sale contract. This does not, however, provide legal grounds for a final transaction. It only gives enough security for the purchaser and seller to place their signatures on a preliminary contract (*orfi* sales contract or *aqad abiad*).

Another method of registering land is *seiht wa nafaz*. This first involves applying to the Sahar el Aquary (the Property Declaration Department), and presenting official documents stating the size and location of land plots, and the name of their original owner (register documents). A declaration from the property-tax department must also be presented showing the details of the plots and the amount of property tax owed. After several months, an applicant may then obtain approval to register the land from the Property Declaration Department without investigating the details of previous land transactions. The applicant may then present this notice to an Egyptian court to obtain a sentence (*hokem*). This step may take between three and six months, after which the applicant may return to the Property Declaration Department, present the court order, and pay a fee. In the case of *seiht wa nafaz*, this fee is calculated at 25 percent of the total property tax required for registration.

Full property registration requires a procedure similar to the one just described, except that it does not require review by a court. However, a landowner following this course must pay the full amount of property tax owed. In addition, the Property Declaration Department must examine every previous land transaction involving the land, and document the complete history of its subdivision (either formal or informal), with the goal of recording the shares of each landholder now occupying a piece of the original parcel. Such a process may take several years, and at its completion, three outcomes are possible. If the survey of land transactions is found to be correct, the applicant may obtain the department's approval. However, if the survey is found to be incorrect, the applicant may not obtain approval, and will be denied registry. A third outcome is possible if a piece of land from the original parcel is found to be missing. If all landowners subsequently agree that the missing piece may be subtracted from the original parcel, this may be declared officially in front of the Property Declaration Department. In this case, the applicant may still receive approval of his registration request. But such an outcome may take several years to be finalized, and during this time some landholders may die, and the whole process may need to be started again from the beginning.

INFORMAL HOUSING TYPES

Typologies of informal housing have been studied in several Third World countries, with emphasis on local circumstances.[34] In Egypt, a similar housing typology was formulated in 1996 that classified informal housing according to three main categories.[35] That typology divided informal residential settlements into development on privately owned formerly agricultural land, on formerly state-owned desert land, and on land whose ownership was in doubt, or where the construction process has been illegal (see FIGURE 7.7). The first type is sometimes known in the literature as semi-informal settlement, or illegal agricultural subdivision.[36] The second type is often known as squatter housing. The third type involves housing built on public or private land which may have originated as formal housing, but which has been transformed and is now informal. This latter type is known as exformal housing. Indeed, some properties currently in this third category may have passed back and forth between formal and informal status several times. The research here further identified twelve subtypes within the three main types, and a total of thirteen minor variants were also identified within some of the more complex subtypes.

The following subsections and accompanying tables discuss the various subtypes and variants. A total of 57 settlements were examined in Greater Cairo and 51 in Alexandria. The locations of examples of the housing subtypes and variants are provided on the accompanying maps (see FIGURES 7.8 and 7.9)

SEMI-INFORMAL SETTLEMENTS (TYPE A)

Semi-informal housing is not developed through established or state-regulated procedures, and does not utilize the recognized institutions of housing and housing finance. Nevertheless, such housing is developed on land for which the owner has legal tenure and a formal occupation permit.

Semi-informal settlements are generally found in areas of essentially rural character located on the urban fringe that are interspersed with, surrounded by, or adjacent to undeveloped sites or sites that remain in agricultural use. These settlements often develop in advance of the principal lines of urban growth. Their construction is most noticeable during periods of rapid urban expansion,

	TYPE A On agricultural land (semi-informal)		TYPE B On desert land (squatting)			TYPE C On public or private land (hybrid or exformal)
SUBTYPES	A1 On privately owned land		B1 On municipal land			C1A By municipalities
	A2 On core village land		B2 On reclaimed land			C1B By cooperatives
	A3 On government land	A3A Agrarian reform land	B3 On decree land	B3A By assignment to development company	C1 Public housing	C1C By public-sector companies
		A3B Awqaf land		B3B By assignment to public-sector company		C1D By development companies
		A3C Decree land		B3C By assignment to cooperative		C1E By armed forces/ police
		A3D Nile/lake-edge land		B3D On antiquities land		C2 Dwelling units under rent control
				B4 On armed forces land		C3 Dwelling units in ex-permit buildings
				B5 On land in public domain		C4 Dwelling units in historic city with confused status

Figure 7.7. Matrix of informal areas by types and subtypes.
Source: author.

and they generally appear along major urban roads. These settlements may be classified into three subtypes (see FIGURE 7.10).

On privately owned land (A1). Such housing is generally constructed on illegal subdivisions of agricultural land. Building activity of this nature increases considerably when agricultural areas are incorporated into the municipal boundaries, or as soon as municipalities install basic services to an outlying area.

On core village land (A2). Housing may be constructed on traditional, noncadastre village land already built on before 1950. Peasants in such cases may have

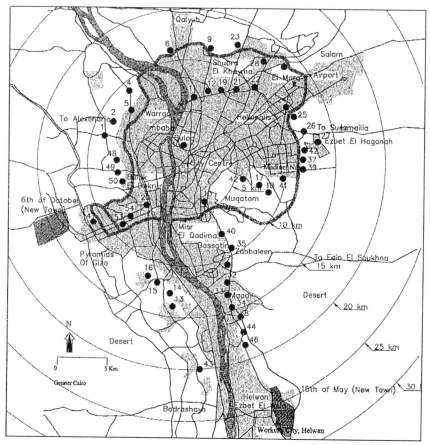

Figure 7.8. Location of informal housing types in greater Cairo region.
Source: drawn by author based on map from the General Organisation for Physical Planning (GOPP), Cairo.

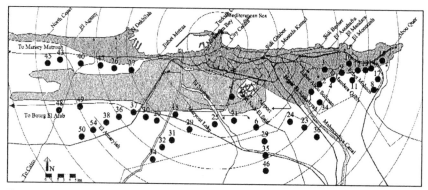

Figure 7.9. Location of informal housing types in Alexandria City.
Source: drawn by author based on map from the General Organisation for Physical Planning (GOPP), Cairo.

SUBTYPE		DEFINITION	EXAMPLES	
			Cairo	Alexandria
A1 On privately owned land		On cadastred agricultural land which was originally registered freehold (up to 1950), but which was then informally subdivided and sold to individuals.	Target areas 1, 2, 5, 6, 9, 10, 23, 28, 30, 48, 49, 50, 52, 53, 54, 56, and 57.	Target areas 1, 2, 9, 10, 11, 12, 13, 15, 16, 7, 18, 24, 33, and 34.
A2 On core village land		On traditional, noncadastred village land already built on before 1950.	Target areas 4, 31, 47, and 55. Also Mit Oqba.	Target areas 2, 3, 4, 6, 21, 25, 29, 31, and 32.
A3 On government agricultural land	A3A Agrarian reform land	On agricultural land which was confiscated and redistributed to peasants after 1953, but which has since been informally subdivided and sold to individuals.	Various small areas in Maasara and Helwan (Ezbet el Walda, Arab Ghoneim, and Arab Rashid).	Target areas 7, 10, 13, 15, 16, 17, 19, 20, 23, 30, 31 and 34.
	A3B Awqaf land	On agricultural land administered by the Awqaf Authority and rented to farmers, which has since been subdivided and sold to individuals.	Part of target area 36. Also very small parcels near city center and in Ghamra.	Target areas 2, 3, 4, 6, 11, 15, 16, 17, 21, 30, 34, and 37.
	A3c Decree land	On agricultural land assigned to various state authorities, but farmed by tenants, who have since subdivided it and sold it to individuals.	Target area 7 (El Basatiin, on Maadi Company concession).	Target areas 2, 3, 4, 5, 6, 7, 14, 18, 22, 23, 24, 25, 30, and 38.
	A3D Nile/lake edge land	On land "thrown up" by changes in the Nile's riverbed or Lake Maryout, which was farmed by peasants under nominal rents or by private developers, who then subdivided and sold it to individuals.	Target area 3 (Dar El Salaam).	Target areas 8 and 36. Ezbet El Matar and Mahwah El Siadeen.

Figure 7.10. Informal residential subtype definitions and examples: Type A — on agricultural land (semi-informal areas)
Source: author.

replaced their old houses with new ones that occupy a larger area without obtaining building permission.

On government agricultural land (A3). Housing here occupies areas that were once legally subdivided by public agencies and that were then sold to private developers for agricultural purposes. Later, the private developers subdivided this land illegally into small plots and sold it to people looking for house plots. Such activity may be divided into four minor variants.

Agrarian reform land (A3a). This is land confiscated and redistributed to peasants after 1953, which has been informally subdivided and sold to individuals.

Awqaf land (A3b). This is land administered by the Awqaf Authority and rented to farmers, which has subsequently been subdivided and sold to individuals. Such areas have usually been sold by religious institutions through auction and converted by private developers into housing sites.[37]

Decree land (A3c). This is land assigned by decree to various state authorities, but farmed by tenants, who have since subdivided and sold it to individuals.

Nile/lake-edge land (A3d). This is land "thrown up" by changes in the Nile's riverbed or Lake Maryout, which was farmed or used as storage by private developers, who have subsequently subdivided and sold it to individuals.

SQUATTER SETTLEMENTS (TYPE B)

Squatters are persons who settle on public land without title, or who take unauthorized possession of unoccupied premises.[38] Squatting has meant and continues to mean different things in different cultures and at different times in each culture's existence. In other words, it is a concept that is neither absolute nor static, but which evolves over time.[39] Squatting is thus a cultural construct; more specifically, it is a political construct.[40]

In Egypt, squatter settlements, known as *wada'yad*, have generally developed on state desert lands and have often been established outside the formal legal and economic structure of the city.[41] Such settlements can be divided into five subtypes (see FIGURE 7.11).

On municipal land (B1). Housing here occupies state desert land controlled (owned) by governorates and their local units. This land is usually located where the governorate has no interest in it, or where it is too expensive to be publicly developed. Such areas are usually located within municipality boundaries, and land ownership may be in doubt.

On reclaimed land (B2). Housing here occupies state desert land that was either sold to investors for reclamation, or was reclaimed by farmers under *wada'yad*, and was subsequently informally subdivided and built upon.

On decree land (B3). Housing may appear in such areas when ownership of land is in doubt, or when land changes ownership. This type of housing on public-owned land has four minor variants.

On development-company concessions (B3a). These areas may once have been public-sector concessions, or may have been assigned (*mukhasas*) to different government bodies. These areas usually have some sort of land-holding rights in the form of the *el heker* system (*de jure* recognition). Nevertheless, all housing on them has been illegally constructed.

On public-sector company land (B3b). Such settlements are often constructed illegally on desert or vacant public land on the fringe of urban centers. The initial invasion of these areas may have been permitted by a municipality, which later further encouraged settlement indirectly.

On cooperative land (B3c). Housing here occupies state desert land which was originally assigned to housing cooperatives, but which was then either squatted on directly by individuals, or was later deemed by the cooperative to have no value.

SUBTYPE	DEFINITION	EXAMPLES	
		Cairo	Alexandria
B1 On municipal land	On state desert land controlled (owned) by governorates and their local units, which was squatted on by individuals.	Target areas 32, 33, 34, and 35. Also Zabaaleen Settlement east of Maadi and parts of Maasara.	Target areas 26, 27, 43, 45, 46, 47, 48, 49, 50, and 51.
B2 On reclaimed land	On state desert land which was either sold to investors for reclamation or was reclaimed by farmers under *wada'yad*, but which was subsequently subdivided and built upon.	Target areas 13, 14, 15, and 16.	Target areas 29, 35, 46, 49, 50, and 51.
B3A Development-Company concession	On state desert land which was given as a concession to state development companies, but which was squatted on by individuals.	Target areas 24, 25, 26, and 27 (Ezbet El Haganah).	Target areas 44 and 47.
B3B Public-sector Company assignment	On state desert land which was assigned to public-sector companies, but which was squatted on by individuals.	Parts of El Toura.	Target area 44.
B3c Cooperative assignment	On state desert land assigned to housing cooperatives, but which was either squatted on by individuals or was developed in contravention of cooperative bylaws.	Target areas 17 and 18.	Target area 48.
B3D Antiquities land	On (mostly state desert) land designated as antiquities zones, but which was squatted on by individuals.	Target area 8 El Fustat.	Parts of Old Turkish City.
B4 Armed-forces land	On state desert land occupied or controlled by the armed forces.	Parts of target areas 24 and 25 (Ezbet El Haganah).	Target areas 43,45 and 51, and El Dekhlia and El Ameryiah.
B5 Public-domain land	On land considered in the public domain (such as right-of-ways for railways, canals, and roads), but which was squatted on by individuals.	Along Teraa El Gebel El Gedida (El Tawariq) in El Salaam and along Teraa El Towfiqia (Ezbet El Nakhal).	Along El Hadrhia and El Mahmoudyia canal.

(The B3 rows are grouped under the vertical label "B3 On government decree land".)

Figure 7.11. Informal residential subtype definitions and examples: Type B — on desert land (squatter areas)

Source: author.

Antiquities and cemetery land (B3d). Such land was originally public but was distributed to individuals for burial purposes. In such cases, people may also have built houses on vacant courts or adjacent parcels.

On armed-forces land (B4). Housing here may occupy state desert land or land controlled by the armed forces. Most of this land is on the periphery of big urban centers and had been neglected for a long time.

On public-domain land (B5). These lands were once considered in the public domain for security purposes and were occupied by the military, or else they were considered important as rights-of-way for railways, canals, and roads. These settlements are usually located on Egypt's North Coast, where municipalities had no interest in development. The Bedouin who squatted here are now confident that the government will pay them compensation before any formal urban development takes place. Their confidence derives from their attitude toward the state, and from their role as guardians of Egypt's borders. Generally, they are the ones who most resist eviction, and who help the authorities confront the leaders of protest groups.

EXFORMAL (HYBRID) SETTLEMENTS (TYPE C)

This third type of settlement includes residential units in formal areas which have temporarily or permanently acquired degrees of informality. Unlike residential units in informal areas, this type of informality relates to individual dwelling units on a case-by-case basis. In many cases some units in a formal neighborhood, or even an individual building, may be "formal" but others have either been added illegally or been modified over time into illegal configurations. Such transformations are most common in the major metropolitan areas, and are of four subtypes (see FIGURE 7.12).

Public housing (C1). Public housing in Egypt was initiated around 1950 with the Medinet el Umaal (Workers' City) project in the Imbabah District of Greater Cairo. Since the early 1960s the Egyptian government, through a variety of programs, has produced a further supply of between 40,000 and 80,000 housing units per year. There are a number of different types of public housing. While most date from Egypt's socialist days (1961–1970), others (which sometimes carry equally confusing tenancy) are of more recent origin.

It is possible to identify five minor variants of public housing controlled by a variety of local public agencies. These include *local administrations (C1a), cooperative/professional syndicates (C1b), public-sector companies (C1c), public/private development companies (C1d),* and the *armed forces and police (C1e).* Yet whether such housing is built directly by the government or by cooperatives, public-sector companies, or state housing and land companies, it is financed and subsidized in one way or another by the government. The relative weights of these different forms of public housing are hard to estimate, as there are no known overall statistics on the public housing stock in Egypt.

Various systems have been set in place to allocate public housing to beneficiaries. However, these have inevitably all been open to abuse, and political patronage has often figured prominently. As a subsidized good, there is a nearly inexhaustible demand for public housing — as much from those who have no housing problems

SUBTYPE		DEFINITION	EXAMPLES	
			Cairo	Alexandria
C1 Public housing	C1A By local municipality	Housing blocks built by governorates, with units distributed by them. Usually on municipal land.	Target areas 11, 12, 19, 21, 22, and 38.	Sidi Beshir and Moharam Bey areas.
	C1B By coopera- tives	Housing blocks built by cooperatives, usually financed through the Cooperative Housing Federation. Units distributed either by gover- norates. Usually on municipal land.	Target area 42. Also Qatamia project, masakin el zilzal partly, Saqr Quraish Cooperative east of Maadi.	Most of the North coast and New Bourg El Arab City.
	C1C By public- sector companies	Housing blocks built by public-sector compa- nies, with units distributed to company employees. Either on municipal or develop- ment company land.	Target areas 37, 39, 41, and 45.	El Hadriha and some parts in Sidi Beshir areas.
	C1D By develop- ment compa- nies	Housing blocks built by state housing and land development companies, with units distributed by them. On development-company land.	Target area 40.	El Ameryiah areas.
	C1E By armed forces/police	Housing blocks built by the armed forces or the Ministry of Interior, with units distributed by them to officers. Either on state desert land or development-company land.	Target areas 44 and 46. Also Medina Heikastep east of Airport, and Medina el Zubaat (start of Fayoum Rd).	Mostafa Kamel and Sidi Beshir areas.
C2 Dwelling units with rent control		Housing blocks built by professional syndi- cates, with units distributed to members. Usually on development-company land/private land and rent-controlled units.	Target area 43.	Parts of North Coast.
C3 Dwelling units in ex-permit build- ings		Floors added to existing buildings without building licenses. These units are difficult to sell since they are illegal.	Target area 20. Also scattered blocks in El Mohandesseen.	Sidi Beshir and El Mandriha areas.
C4 Historic city units with confused status		Housing blocks built by various public authorities, always in the historic city, distrib- uted and administered by the Awqaf Authority. Always on awqaf land.	Target area 10. Also scattered blocks in Old Islamic Cairo.	El Manshieha and Morsy Abou El Abas area in Old Turkish City.

Figure 7.12. Informal residential subtype definitions and examples: Type C — on public/private land (hybrid or exformal areas)

Source: author.

as from those who do. And despite regulations intended to prevent transfer of tenancy, many transfers are made. Public housing units are readily exchanged through
a number of informal shadow markets (which discount the risk of discovery and for-

feiture). One fact remains consistent for all public housing, however. This is that with few exceptions, title to the land upon which it sits remains in the hands of the original funder/builder, or with the local administration — even when units have been sold outright in private condominium arrangements.

Dwelling units under rent control (C2). Vast numbers of residential units in Cairo and Alexandria (as well as in other urban areas in Egypt) are rented, and remain under rental contracts which give the tenant near perpetual rights of occupation at fixed or nominal rents.

Rent control was first applied during World War II as a measure to combat wartime inflation, and it froze rents at 1941 rates. Such a situation was codified in Law 121 of 1947 (applying to properties built before 1943). Then, after the Revolution in 1952, a series of laws reduced rentals on new construction and also rents on existing units. Finally, Laws 49 and 106 of 1976 and 1977 incorporated previous legislation, codified existing rent levels, and established a system for calculating rent levels in new buildings in ways that greatly favored tenants. In addition, rental contracts were deemed inheritable as long as an original tenant's children lived on the premises.

Subsequently, several small amendments were made to restore landlord interests. For example, Law 136 of 1981 allowed one-third, instead of 10 percent, of units in a building to be sold (*tamlik*) rather than rented. However, it was not until Law 4 of 1996 that provision for an unrestricted, market-oriented kind of contract for rentals was promulgated.

However, even with this attempt to rationalize the system, a very large number of units in formal areas of Egypt remain rented at extremely low rates, with no relation to the market. In effect, tenants are sitting on significant assets, and besides waiting for the death of the lessee and his children, the only way a building owner can reclaim the unit is to offer a sizable cash incentive (sometimes approaching the real market value of the unit) for the tenant to renounce his contract and leave. (A semi-legal system does operate by which a third party may purchase the rental contract from the tenant, endorsed by the owner, but this only perpetuates the condition of informality.)

Dwelling units in ex-permit buildings (C3). Starting in the 1970s, due to the Open Door Policy, the practice of adding floors to existing buildings in formal areas became widespread. At the time, real estate investment, building licensing, and control of construction became quite lax. As a result, there are today a number of dwelling units which, although located in formal areas, are irregular in terms of building licenses and may be subject to outstanding fines and/or demolition orders. Most of the dwelling units in these buildings are owned under simple condominium arrangements (*tamlik*). And in most cases, the owners of these units hold assets that are difficult, if not impossible, to transfer/convert — except to a gullible buyer, who then is in a similar irregular situation.

In the 1990s control of construction became much more strict in Greater Cairo and Alexandria, partly as a consequence of the widespread damage caused by the 1992 earthquake. In particular, an effort was made to restrict building heights, and some scattered demolition of offending (ex-permit) structures and floors even took place. Thus, it can be said that the phenomenon was mainly a product of the years 1974–1992.

Units in the historic city with confused tenure status (C4). The historic cores of both Cairo and Alexandria were surveyed and cadastred in the 1900–1920 period, and were thus included as part of the two cities' "formal" areas. However, many of the dwelling units in these areas are subject to rent control, and a few are "ex-permit." Also, many huts have been illegally erected on top of these buildings. Such "roof-toppers" are estimated to number 500,000 and 200,000, respectively, in Greater Cairo and Alexandria. In addition, many residential buildings in Cairo and Alexandria have disputed ownership due to inheritance problems and/or religious trust (*awqaf*) involvement that sometimes extends back for centuries. Many of these buildings have partially or fully fallen in ruin, and although they represent prime real estate, they cannot be transferred or otherwise exploited. Occupation of these areas mostly takes the form of renting or occupying public land for a certain period of time (*el hekr*) and paying a symbolic rent to government agencies.

QUANTIFICATION OF RESIDENTIAL PROPERTIES IN INFORMAL/EXFORMAL AREAS

This section presents an estimate of the number and value of informal housing units in Cairo and Alexandria in the year 2000. It is based on the author's collaborative research with Hernando De Soto's ILD. Summary versions of this information are included in de Soto's (1997, 2000) estimates.[42]

The accompanying table presents a quantification of informal and exformal dwelling units in Cairo and Alexandria by subtype of dwelling unit (see FIGURE 7.13). A total of 2.63 and 0.486 million dwelling units were estimated in the informal areas of Greater Cairo and Alexandria, respectively (a figure combining all type A and type B units described above). An additional 4 million informal units were estimated in other Egyptian urban areas. The estimated number of informal units in all Egypt, therefore, is around 7.116 million (48.6 percent), compared to an estimated total of 7.524 million formal units (51.4 percent).

As expected, the greatest number of units in informal areas of Cairo and Alexandria were associated with Type A1, "on private agricultural land" — representing 48.6 percent and 22.1 percent of the total of informal units in the two cities, respectively. Second most significant in Alexandria was type B1, "on local administration land" — representing 9.83 percent of the total. However, the

number of units recorded here was much higher than the type's share of informal surface area, reflecting the two very mature and dense areas made up mostly of this category.

There are many reasons why semi-informal housing on agricultural areas is
the most popular and common type of housing in both cities. First, the inhabitants
of semi-informal housing have the advantage of legal land tenure. Second, such
housing is not only relatively cheap, but it generally retains its value. Third, the
inhabitants within such areas may acquire their land by means of incremental payments. Fourth, such housing has been provided by private developers who have
flourished using informal processes of subdivision and land commercialization.
Fifth, such settlements offer greater security of tenure than other types. Finally,
land subdivision in such areas follows the geometry of former agricultural use,
resulting in a pattern of mostly straight roads — although they may be narrow
(4–6 meters) and longer than standard requirements. This pattern has allowed
the state to install basic services (even if private developers did originally establish
the actual street network, thus allowing municipalities to avoid such expenses).

Generally, because of the differences in the size of the two cities, the average size of semi-informal housing areas in Greater Cairo is larger than in
Alexandria. Otherwise, the physical characteristics of informal areas in the two
cities are the same, except that housing blocks in Cairo are generally one floor
taller than in Alexandria.

By contrast to the semi-informal type, the second type of housing studied,
squatter settlement, is usually established on desert sites relatively far from the
city center. The major disadvantage here is that the cost of access to job opportunities is greater. The major advantage, however, is that land may be obtained
cheaply, or at no cost at all. Such settlements are usually located beside a main
road which acts as a strong edge limiting future expansion, and their streets are
narrow and mainly used by pedestrians. Such settlements generally offer only
limited basic services, and they may lack all social and public services. They were
generally established by collective invasions of people from Upper Egypt or from
Bedouin regions. Hence, popular organizations are very important within them
and, indeed, often played a major role in the original land-invasion process.

As mentioned previously, land tenure in most of such desert areas remains
confusing, although the municipalities have recently attempted to regularize the
situation by sanctioning trilateral negotiations between residents/land claimants,
the municipalities, and the military. Nevertheless, numerous conflicts and disputes have emerged concerning formal as well as informal property rights and
ownership, particularly in the Ezbet El Haganah area of Greater Cairo and the El
Dekhlia area in Alexandria.

The total number of dwelling units of the third, hybrid or exformal, type was
estimated to be around 1.827 and 0.329 million in Greater Cairo and Alexandria,

TYPE/SUBTYPE	GREATER CAIRO					
	Net surface area in km²	%	Number of dwelling units	%	Current value in LE million	Population
A1 On private agricultural land	105.5	43.0	2,207,239	48.6	109,488	5,839,362
A2 On core village land	3.5	1.4	60,584	1.3	2,816	164,824
A3 On government agricultural land	4.2	1.7	127,871	2.8	5,212	431,240
B1 On local-administered (desert) land	4.3	1.8	79,416	1.7	2,755	216,793
B2 On reclaimed (desert) land	3.9	1.6	74,657	1.7	3,139	212,284
B3 On decree (desert) land	3.2	1.3	34,402	0.8	1,373	83,270
B4 On armed forces land	1.6	0.7	17,201	0.4	686	41,635
B5 On public domain— wada'yad	3.1	1.2	33,327	0.7	1,333	80,667
TOTAL TYPES A AND B	129.3	52.7	2,634,697	58.0	126,802	7,070,075
C1 Public	31.4	12.8	635,841	14.0	119,488	1,505,939
C2 Under rent control	45.4	18.5	624,049	13.7	50,324	1,366,528
C3 Dwelling units ex-permit	27.8	11.4	327,966	7.3	18,483	754,312
C4 Core historic/confused	9.1	3.7	239,582	5.3	10,608	497,035
TOTAL TYPE C	113.7	46.4	1,827,438	40.3	198,903	4,123,814
Nonclassified	2.0	0.9	77,889	1.7		201,446
TOTAL ALL TYPES	245.0		4,540,023		325,705	11,395,335

TYPE/SUBTYPE	ALEXANDRIA					
	Net surface area in km²	%	Number of dwelling units	%	Current value in LE million	Population
A1 On private agricultural land	23.8	24.4	184,500	22.1	62,119	922,500
A2 On core village land	1.5	1.5	61,470	7.4	18,265	307,350
A3 On government agricultural land	2.2	2.2	62,350	7.5	2,076	311,750
B1 On local-administered (desert) land	9.8	10.0	82,000	9.8	2,448	410,000
B2 On reclaimed (desert) land	4.5	4.6	47,850	5.7	1,428	239,250
B3 On decree (desert) land	3.0	3.1	19,140	2.3	571	95,470
B4 On armed forces land	1.3	1.3	8,294	1.0	247	41,470
B5 On public domain— wada'yad	3.2	3.3	20,416	2.5	609	102,310
TOTAL TYPES A AND B	49.3	50.4	486,020	58.3	87,763	2,430,100
C1 Public	14.8	15.1	114,451	13.7	20,601	501,379
C2 Under rent control	15.8	16.1	112,328	13.5	8,986	456,850
C3 Dwelling units ex-permit	12.2	12.4	59,033	7.1	3,305	240,425
C4 Core historic/confused	3.8	3.9	43,124	5.2	1,910	160,900
TOTAL TYPE C	46.6	47.5	328,936	39.5	34,802	1,359,554
Nonclassified	2.0	2.1	18,500	2.2		60,850
TOTAL ALL TYPES	98.0		833,456		122,565	3,850,504

Figure 7.13. Extent of informal housing in greater Cairo and Alexandria, year 2000*.
*The author calculated the figures for Alexandria, while David Sims calculated the Greater Cairo figures.

respectively. In both cities, public housing type C1 represents the greatest percentage in this category, representing 14 percent of all informal units. The share of the rent-control type is only slightly lower in both cities. It should, however, be pointed out that Greater Cairo contains the oldest and largest, and also most deteriorated public housing projects in Egypt. Exformal housing areas in the historic core of Cairo also have serious problems of registration, as a high percentage of this type has changed ownership several times or occupies land whose tenure is in doubt.

Field investigations and work by ILD teams have shown that in a small number of cases properties in exformal areas have become more-or-less formal, in the sense that buildings and land have been registered and titled. This formalization has mainly been due to the Herculean efforts of individual owners and their lawyers.

Employing the same analytical framework used to estimate informal dwelling units, it was possible to estimate the population residing in informal areas. Using census figures as a base, the total 1996 population of all informal areas was estimated at 4.5 and 1.07 million inhabitants in Greater Cairo and Alexandria, respectively. However, the field survey estimated that the total population in semi-informal and squatter areas of the two cities in 2000 was 7.07 and 2.43 million. The field survey estimated an additional population in hybrid/exformal housing typologies of 4.12 and 1.36 million in Greater Cairo and Alexandria. Therefore, the total population in all informal housing types was found to be 11.40 and 3.85 million people in the two cities. This represented 85.9 percent and 78.7 percent of the total population of the two cities.

It should be noted that these figures are higher than official estimates. The official estimate of the population in informal areas in Alexandria is 72.7 percent of the total 1996 population. However, the informal share of total built-up residential areas was 50 percent, indicating that informal areas are considerably denser than formal areas—even though informal areas are newer and mostly located at the urban fringe. The official estimate of population in informal areas in Greater Cairo represents 62 percent of the total 1996 population (10.256 million inhabitants). Compared with the informal share of total built-up residential areas, 52.7 percent, this too indicates that informal areas are considerably denser than formal areas.

Finally, the study estimated a total of 2.74 persons per dwelling unit in informal areas, whereas the estimate for the Cairo Governorate as a whole was 2.40 persons per dwelling unit. The figure reflected both slightly greater household size and a greater degree of utilization (fewer vacancies) in informal areas than the average. The proportion was slightly higher in Alexandria, where the number of people per dwelling unit was 2.85.

Figure 5.13 also presents the estimated aggregate current values of informal properties in the two cities. The estimated value of residential assets in the informal areas of Greater Cairo and Alexandria (types A and B) was estimated at

LE 126.80 billion and LE 18.7 billion, respectively.[43] Of this amount, building assets were estimated to account for 52 and 69.1 percent, with land assets estimated at 48 and 30.1 percent, respectively. A full 86 percent and 70 percent of this total value — LE 109 billion and LE 62 billion — was accounted for by one informal type — A1, "on private agricultural land." The estimated value of hybrid/exformal housing in Greater Cairo and Alexandria (type C) was LE 198.90 billion and LE 34.80 billion, respectively.

RETROSPECT AND PROSPECT

In the last few decades Egypt has passed through economic and political difficulties that have led to the creation of urban informality on the periphery of both Greater Cairo and Alexandria. The result is an unprecedented diversity and complexity of informal housing development. This chapter has identified three main types — semi-informal, squatting, and exformal housing. Both state agencies and various private actors have been involved in these development processes.

The development of the informal sector in Egypt has largely resulted from the failure of the government to deal with the housing needs of low-income groups. However, understanding the built environment of informal housing development may assist both government officials and private professionals today to properly value this sector so that these assets may be harnessed to promote development and alleviate poverty.

The great increase in informal housing in Greater Cairo and Alexandria was originally caused by the acceleration of industrialization and urbanization in Egypt during the 1950s. However, plans for the two cities never included areas where low-income migrant groups could be housed. As a result, today more than 62 percent and 72 percent of the two cities' populations, respectively, live in areas that were developed informally. Interventions in these areas of the two cities are extremely complex, in part due to their location and the complexity and diversity of housing types described above.

Informality is no longer simply the domain of the poor; in fact, it has become a major condition of land ownership and housing for the urban lower-middle and middle classes. This has meant that the urban poor may now have little choice in housing short of obtaining rented units within that sector. This chapter has tried to identify the mechanisms of informal housing development and indicate that their complexity is a result of a diversity of socioeconomic and political situations within the country.

Informal areas are now dominant features of the urban fabric of Egyptian cities. However, as their built environment continues to deteriorate, many questions arise. Should the government allow continued growth of this sector? How should the government control further development of this type of housing? If controls are instituted, what will be the impact on the urban poor? What consequences would housing controls have for socioeconomic development within the country? How should the government house the urban poor? And, finally, as a matter of practical concern, how much can the state do? If this chapter has shown anything, it is that the government alone cannot hope to house the nation's increasing urban population.

The previous discussion has defined the mechanisms by which informal settlements arise and grow; it has established a typology of informal housing; and it has estimated the total value of informal housing in Egypt, which constitutes around 48.6 percent of the nation's total housing stock. Particular emphasis has been given to the fact that informal and formal housing are fluid categories. Thus, informal housing can be formalized — but formal housing can also be informalized, creating a type of exformal housing. The transformation of housing from formal into informal, and vice-versa, is a process of continuous adjustment to changing economic and social conditions.

It is clear that semi-informal housing on formerly agricultural land at the edges of both cities is the most widespread of the types investigated. The many reasons for this were discussed in the preceding sections. However, the value of all informal and exformal housing types constitutes a considerable investment that should be used to promote economic development and reduce poverty. The estimated value of this sector in Greater Cairo and Alexandria in the year 2000 was LE 448.27 billion (equivalent to US$131.84 billion).

A major problem today is that the success or failure of efforts to formalize informal properties depends on the tenure status of the land invaded, the presence or absence of pressure from landlords, and the strength of groups backing such actions. Public authorities might help the formalization process by facilitating access to official channels for property registration and the installation of services.

In hindsight, it is possible to see how the government created the situation by which informal urbanization has flourished. Urbanization in Egypt was neither planned nor integrated with established processes of land regularization. Neither have government practices contributed much to the effective improvement of dwellings in informal areas. Public investment has been largely wasted, and the population of informal areas has become accustomed to inadequate patterns of improvement. Even today, many families have no documentation of the land they occupy. Such land may either be listed as local government property, or its private ownership may simply be too difficult to trace.

Government institutions have for the most part failed to address the needs of the poor for housing, just as they have failed to meet their other basic needs. Furthermore, whereas original settlers in informal housing areas used their limited financial resources and collective efforts to address their needs, today the situation is different. Despite the current diversity and complexity of informal housing types and subtypes, today's newcomers encounter great difficulties in obtaining housing units or land plots at reasonable cost. On the other hand, if the government were today to begin to regulate informal housing areas, the urban poor might be able to participate in the development process. This would help reduce poverty for three main reasons. First, in the case of legalization of informal housing areas, it would allow the private developers to construct or speculate on vacant available land within informal areas, which would increase the housing stock within these areas. Second, if settlers could feel secure in land tenure, additional housing units might be constructed/added, which would offer additional rental housing units for the newcomers. Third, increased investment in housing would enhance the economic situation, which would offer job opportunities for people who are most in need. Government involvement would also provide reliable information about the needs and capacities of such communities, and it might lead to development of a social delivery vehicle that would value the health of the communities themselves. Sound information and efficient delivery might also save money, both by preventing waste and by ensuring that the outcome would be appropriate to people's needs. This would also conform to the government's requirements and policies.

An urgent readjustment program should be developed to evaluate and upgrade informal housing areas. The indispensable step is land regularization. To be sure, all projects and works must obey existing legislation so that relevant government bodies may approve them. But the sale of property to beneficiary families should also proceed according to principles of social justice. Thus, monthly payments should be established with respect to the capacity of each family to pay.

The correct way to tackle informal housing areas is to urbanize them and regularize ownership of the land they occupy, thus formally integrating them into cities. Such actions should take place according to a specific national plan for each type of informal housing area. This plan should have three main goals: physical and environmental recovery, land regularization, and community participation. Such a program should further be implemented by stages, in an organized and progressive way, as resources become available. Such an approach would be national because it would include the whole establishment; and it would be integrated because it would involve physical, judicial, and social aspects. Such an approach to the problem of informal housing areas would optimize the use of public resources and avoid waste. To facilitate community participation, a group of reference should be formed at the beginning of the program. Participation would then occur at all stages of the process, mainly through periodic meetings with the group and irregular meetings with the whole community.

Community politics and the work of private developers should be linked to national politics, not simply as a reflection of national decision-making, but also as an active agent in the formulation of national policies. Every community, planner, or project organizer is strongly aware of the political system and of the potential of government to serve as a resource for people at the grassroots. But the reverse is also true; people are a resource for national politicians and the government. Their potential for the future is huge, and the challenge for the Egyptian community is to ensure the right environment within which a proper partnership can flourish.

NOTES

1. The title of this paper is based on a reference to Cervantes' *Don Quixote*. Use of the terminology "tilting at" reflects the author's view that various housing policies for the urban poor in Egypt have gone in the wrong direction. "Tilting" is another name for the medieval practice of jousting with lances. But in the sense of "tilting at windmills" established in *Don Quixote*, it means attacking the wrong targets or policies in search of simple solutions to complex realities.

Likewise, the use of the image of the sphinx highlights an important symbol in Egyptian civilization. To the ancient Egyptians, the sphinx symbolized the elevation of mind over body, mental over physical, as in man rising above his animal (i.e., baser) desires through a life of *maat* (living the principles of truth, justice, righteousness, balance, harmony, reciprocity, and order). The Sphinx is therefore inscrutable. "Tilting at sphinxes" is thus meant to express a present situation in which housing policies for the urban poor have gone wrong, and the poor are getting poorer, while informal housing is continuing to spread in urban areas in the place of correct government intervention.

Often, the people who perceive one object and describe it as something else are poets. Thus, Don Quixote might be seen as not simply crazy in his refusal to see things as they really are, but more like a person who wants to accomplish a greater good and so refuses to compromise his ideals. In this sense, he dreams an impossible dream. Not all such people are ultimately ineffectual, however, as indicated by the success of such figures a Nelson Mandela, Mahatma Gandhi, and Dr. Martin Luther King Jr.

2. In 1996 the author and David Sims produced a quick classification of informal housing areas in Alexandria and Cairo, respectively.

3. A district consists of 6–8 *shiskha*, each containing between 1,500–2,500 people, while a *qaria* (village) contains between 5,000–10,000 people.

4. The following were some of the assumptions used.

Dwelling unit size. This is the estimated average size of dwelling unit types in gross square meters, defined to include stairways and other shared built space associated with the typical unit.

Building value per square meter. The asset value of dwelling units was defined as the current replacement value of a particular dwelling unit, calculated as estimates of total construction cost per square meter. Architects, contractors, and informal builders were consulted to make these estimates.

Associated land per unit. This is the average net land area associated with each unit. This was calculated by taking the average unit size and dividing by the average plot coverage ratio, and by the number of floors in an average building. The average number of floors was kept on the low side to reflect the fact that many buildings in informal areas are unfinished.

Land value per square meter. The current market prices of vacant land in informal areas were solicited from land brokers and residents. These values in all cases referred to interior locations, i.e., those on secondary roads and side streets where there was little or no commercial potential contributing to the land value. These values are based on current year 2000 land prices, and thus reflect the general economic depression of land values in the Greater Cairo and Alexandria land markets that began in 1997–98.

5. CAPMAS, General Statistics for Population and Housing: Population Census (Cairo, 1986).

6. Informal areas are called *el manatiqe el ashwaiyya* in Arabic, and are sometimes also called *ashwaiyyat* (plural for *ashwaiyya*). This common public term literally means "half-hazard."

7. For further details of the Open Door Policy, see A. Soliman, "A Prognosis for Housing Development in New Towns in Egypt," *Netherlands Journal of Housing and Environmental Research* 7, no.3 (1992), 283–305.

8. Egyptian Popular Parliament, *A Preliminary Survey of Informal Residential Settlements in Egypt* (Cairo: 1992).

9. Ezbet El Haganah is located at the far eastern fringe of Cairo. It was set up in the second half of the 1930s by members of the frontier guards/camel corps (*el-haganah* in Arabic — thus the name Ezbet El Haganah). Officers of the camel corps allowed their soldiers to build houses for their families beside their camp. Plot sizes were rather large, ranging between 1,000 and 2,000 square meters. See A. Soliman, *A Field Survey of Informal Housing Settlements in Three Egyptian Cities* (Alexandria: Alexandria University, mimeo, 1997).

10. El Akhbar, *Egyptian Newspaper* (Cairo, October 24, 1996).

11. A. Soliman and D. Sims, "A Final Draft Report on Informal Housing Typologies in Egypt," Report submitted to the Institute of Liberty and Democracy, Cairo, 2000.

12. A. Gilbert, "Planning Invasions and Land Speculation: The Role of the State in Venezuela," *Third World Planning Review* 6, no.3 (1984), 225–38.

13. S. Leckie, "Housing as a Human Right," *Environment and Urbanization* 1, no.2 (1989), 90–108.

14. J. Abu Lughod, *Cairo: 1001 Years of the City Victorious* (Princeton, N.J.: Princeton University Press, 1971).

15. A. Soliman, "Housing the Urban Poor in Egypt: A Critique of Present Policies," *International Journal of Urban and Regional Research* 12, no.1 (1988), 65–86; and "Housing Mechanisms in Egypt: A Critique," *Netherlands Journal of Housing and Environmental Research* 4, no.1 (1989), 31–50.

16. A. El-Sayed, "Balance of Sustainable Development of New Urban Communities: The Role of Private Sector in the Financial Aspects," paper presented to "New Urban Communities: Past Experience and Failure Responses of the INTA 20 Annual World Congress," Cairo, October 13–17, 1996.

17. C. Pugh, "The Role of World Bank in Housing," in B. Aldrich and R. Sandhu, eds., *Housing the Urban Poor: Policy and Practice in Developing Countries* (London: Zed Books, 1995), 34–92.

18. W. Lewis, "Economic Development with Unlimited Supplies of Labour," *Manchester School of Economics and Social Studies* 22 (1954), 139–91.

19. K. Hart, "Informal Income Opportunities and Urban Employment in Ghana," *Journal of Modern African Studies* 11, no.1 (1973), 61–89. Hart's paper was originally presented to a conference in 1971, before the ILO mission to Kenya completed its work.

20. International Labor Office, "Employment, Income, and Equality: A Strategy for increasing Productive Employment in Kenya" (Geneva, Switzerland: ILO Press, 1972).

21. R. Bromley, "A New Path to Development? The Significance and Impact of Hernando De Soto's Ideas on Underdevelopment, Production, and Reproduction," *Economic Geography* 66, no. 4 (October 1990), 328–48.

22. R. Burgess, "Petty Commodity Housing or Dweller Control? A Critique of John Turner's view on Housing Policy," in P. Ward, ed., *Self-help Housing: A Critique* (London: Mansell Publishing Co., Alexandrine Press, 1982), 55–97.

23. A. Portes, M. Castells, and L. Benton, *The Informal Economy: Studies in Advanced and Less Developed Countries* (Baltimore, Md.: The John Hopkins University Press, 1989).

24. L. Peattie, "Urban Research in the 1990s," in M. Cohen et al., eds., *Preparing for the Future: Global Pressures and Local Forces* (Washington, D.C.: The Woodrow Wilson Center Press, 1996), 371–91.

25. H. De Soto, *The Other Path: The Invisible Revolution in the Third World* (New York: Harper & Row, 1989).

26. A. Hasan, *Housing for the Poor: Failure of Formal Sector Strategies* (Karachi: City Press, 2000).

27. H. De Soto, *The Mystery of Capital: Why Capitalism Triumphs in the West and Fails Everywhere Else* (New York: Basic Books, 2000).

28. H. De Soto, *The Mystery of Capital*.

29. Ministry of Housing, Utilities, and Urban Communities [Government of Egypt], *Housing in Egypt* (Cairo: 1989).

30. P. Ward and A. Gilbert, *Housing, the State, and the Urban Poor: Policy and Practice in Three Latin American Cities* (Cambridge, U.K.: Cambridge University Press, 1985).

31. A. Soliman, "Housing the Urban Poor in Egypt."

32. N. AlSayyad, "Culture, Identity, and Urbanism in a Changing World: A Historical Perspective on Colonialism, Nationalism, and Globalization," in Cohen et al., eds., *Preparing for the Future*, 108–22.

33. A. Soliman, "Partnerships in Three Egyptian Cities," in G. Payne, ed., *Making Common Ground: Public/Private Partnerships in Land for Housing* (London: Intermediate Technology Press, 1999), 89–112.

34. For example, R. Burgess, "Development Strategies and Urban Housing Policies in Latin America in the Post-War Period," in M. Carmona, ed., *Urban Restructuring and Deregulation in Latin America* (Delft, the Netherlands: Publikatieburo Bouwkunde, Faculty of Architecture, Delft University of Technology, 1992), 99–120; C. Rakodi, "Housing

Markets in Third World Cities: Research and Policy into the 1990s," *World Development* 20, no. 1 (January 1992), 39–55; and N. AlSayyad, "Squatting and Culture," *Habitat International* 17, no. 1 (1993), 33–44.

35. A. Soliman, "Housing the Urban Poor in Egypt"; and A. Soliman (in Arabic), *Housing and Sustainable Development in Developing Countries: Sheltering the Urban Poor in Egypt* (Beirut: Dar El Rateb El Jamiah Press, 1996).

36. A. Soliman, "Legitimizing Informal Housing: Accommodating Low-Income Groups in Alexandria," *Environment and Urbanization* 8, no.1 (April 1996), 183–94.

37. Awqaf is the traditional religious form of tenure in Islamic countries. *Waqf* land has two classifications: *waqf khayri* (charity), and *waqf ahli* (private). The former occurs in three ways: 1) the beneficiaries die, at which point the property is absorbed into the *waqf khayri*; 2) the property deteriorates to the point where the original value is totally dissipated, at which time it is returned to the open market as freehold; or 3) long-term leases on the property are granted to investors with capital.

Waqf ahli (private family) is transferred from the owner of a property to a religious foundation, but the owner continues to receive its revenues personally during his lifetime. After his death, the revenues from the property will be transferred to his descendants, merely making an arrangement for their eventual disbursement to a charitable purpose, if and when the owner dies. Often the owner himself is appointed to administrate his property, although after several generations this administration generally passes into the hands of a professional. After many generations (under the condition of the *waqf*) the *waqf ahli* could be transferred into freehold land, but this may often require a court order.

38. *Oxford English Dictionary* (London: Wm. Collins Sons & Co. Ltd., 1985).

39. J. Sen, *The Unintended City Revisited: A Transnational's Perspective*, paper presented at the Symposium "Urban Informality in an Era of Liberalization: A Transnational Perspective," University of California at Berkeley, January 26–27, 2001.

40. N. AlSayyad, "Squatting and Culture."

41. *Wada'yad* is an Arabic word for illegal occupation of land.

42. H. De Soto, *Dead Capital and the Poor in Egypt* (Cairo: The Egyptian Center for Economic Studies, 1997); and De Soto, *The Mystery of Capital*.

43. LE: Livre Egyptian. The U.S. dollar was equal to 3.4 LE at the time this survey was carried out (October 1999–June 2000).

8

Control, Resistance, and Informality: Urban Ethnocracy in Beer-Sheva, Israel

Oren Yiftachel and Haim Yakobi

Informal development — that is, spatial dynamics that are not shaped, controlled, or sanctioned by the state — has been recognized as a major component of urbanizing regions. It has been subject to groundbreaking research, mainly in the Latin American context.[1] Yet the potential of the concept to account for the dynamics of urban change has not by and large been realized in the rich scholarship on cities in other regions and under different political regimes. In this chapter we aim to take a step toward broadening the concept by exploring urban informality in what we have termed "ethnocratic cities."

We begin by briefly discussing several theoretical accounts of urbanization, planning, nationalism, and ethnocratic societies. We suggest that the phenomenon of urban informality is a surface expression of the unresolved tensions between three main "engines" of the urban order: (a) the logic of capital accumulation; (b) the evolution of modern governance; and (c) the drive for ethnic and national control.[2] The interaction between these forces, as played out within the dense webs of local and institutional settings, often produces urban informality as a central component of a conflictual urban space. Hence (and despite the emphasis in the literature on processes of globalization, poverty, and underdevelement), we contend that urban informality is a product of a multitude of forces, including but not limited to the logic of capital.

The latter part of this chapter explores the emergence and persistence of urban informality in the Beer-Sheva urban region, Israel. We show that despite the urban potential to erode ethno-spatial exclusion and domination, and despite early signs of economic and cultural liberalization, the region's ethnocratic structure has not been seriously dented. However, we also demonstrate that the uneven ethnocratic space shaped by Israeli planners and policymakers has created a conflict-riddled, and ultimately unstable, urban order. This is linked with Israel's ethnocratic policies in the region, which have spawned pervasive urban informality and growing levels of Arab resistance.

THEORETICAL ASPECTS: ETHNOCRATIC STATES AND URBAN INFORMALITY

We will first take a few preliminary steps toward a theoretical exploration of urban informality in ethnocratic cities. To this end, we begin with a brief discussion of several "building blocks" from which a more tightly formulated framework will eventually emerge.

During the last few decades rich and diverse bodies of scholarly knowledge have developed to account for the immense transformation of human society during modernity. Three scholarly fields have been conspicuous in this endeavor: urbanization, governance, and nationalism. The knowledge, ideas, and concepts developed in each of these debates are highly relevant to understanding the phenomenon studied here — urban informality. Let us touch in a nutshell on the content and connections between these bodies of knowledge.

The literature on modern urbanization has relied on seminal texts by the likes of Karl Marx, Max Weber, Lewis Mumford, and Herbert Gans, and later David Harvey, Manuel Castells, and Doreen Massey, to name but a few. Key issues here have been the restructuring of economic and political orders associated with modernity and their impact on urbanization, production, and politics.[3]

In recent years a new wave of studies has begun to dominate scholarship on cities, increasingly incorporating issues of economic and cultural globalization and the ever-quickening movement of capital and immigrants as key factors in understanding today's urban regions. This body of writing has critically examined the material and oppressive consequences of urbanization and the new avenues it has opened for exploitation and structural stratification. The recent groundbreaking works of Friedmann, Marcuse and Van Kempen, Sassen, and Taylor are but a few examples of this fast-growing field of inquiry.[4] Globalization and urbanization are omnipresent and intimately related processes, reshaping human society through the deep restructuring of urban areas. This has been well articulated by Marcuse, who summarizes the gist of a vast literature on the subject as follows:

> There is a new spatial order of cities, commencing somewhere in the 1970s, in a period often described as one of a globalizing economy. While cities have always been divided along lines of culture, function, and status, the pattern today is a new, and in many ways deeper-going, combination of these divisions. . . . Although it varies from city to city, by historical development, . . .

economic structure, . . . forces involved in development, . . . the role of "race" and ethnicity, and the place in the international economy, nevertheless there are basic features in common. . . . The market produces and reproduces these divisions, but the state is deeply involved in their creation and perpetuation.[5]

Human governance has provided another rich area for scholarly debate, both generally and as it relates to the evolution of cities. Strong links exist between urbanization and civil forms of governance, and in particular, liberalism and democracy. For leading writers in this field, the city is the heart of enlightenment, modernization and progress, and of politics itself.[6] Thus, Held traces the very idea of democracy to the setting of an urban community, stretching back to ancient Athens, through medieval Florence, and to its recent flourishing in the highly urbanized industrial cities of the West.[7]

A large group of scholars has further explored the links between the spatial changes entailed by urbanization, and the transformations these have caused in political ideology and mobilization.[8] In particular, Katznelson develops the links between urbanism and liberalism, and finds that the actual city space, with its typical density, diversity, and size, has been an essential platform for the translation of liberal ideas to actual practices and regulations. According to Katznelson:

Cities were more porous, open to flows of people, capital, communication, and ideas. Without this dynamism, liberalism's insistence on human autonomy and choice would have been merely speculative. . . . Liberalism and the city . . . have been deeply intertwined for centuries. Liberalism was inconceivable . . . without the urbanization of early modern Europe . . . which became the location for political emancipation and free citizenship.[9]

In parallel, a third and equally impressive body of scholarship has evolved over the phenomenon of nationalism. Here, too, a seminal first wave of classical works from the likes of Anderson, Smith, and Gellner formed the basis for illuminating new approaches, with recent valuable additions by Brubaker, Connor, Greenfeld, Billig, and Canovan.[10]

But despite the importance of their breathtaking attempts to propose grand accounts of nationalism, these theories have often treated "the nation" as relatively uniform. They have often collapsed nation and state, thereby "flattening" the diverse and often oppressive history, geography, and internal divisions of nation and state. This angle of social analysis has also tended to ignore the ethnoclass interests behind the national project. For, indeed, under the very rhetoric of "national goals" and "patriotic unity," the state's leading ethno-classes have quite often enhanced their material and political position, hence sharpening the disparities and tensions between the "nation and its fragments."[11]

Most nationalism literature has also overlooked the central role of cities and urban planning in facilitating nation- and state-building, and in maintaining national consciousness and identity. Such oversight of the city-nation connection has also amplified the tendency of most nationalism scholarship to downplay the impact of internal divisions on the ethno-national project. A firmer inclusion of "the urban" (and especially "the globalizing urban") in the analysis of "the national" would focus attention on the disparities and tensions between ethnic collectivities, which are often revealed in their sharpest dimension at the urban levels.

Yet the city is where ethnic communities tend to congregate and generate intellectual, political, and economic elites. The city also often plays host to key symbolic and cultural resources. Hence, conflicts between ethno-classes regularly occur on urban turf, with major consequences to the shaping of nations and states. Here, planning — that is, the public production of urban habitat — has played a key role in molding spatio-political relations between ethnic groups. This has been clear in diverse and distant cities, such as Montreal, Brussels, Jerusalem, Istanbul, Johannesburg, Kuala Lumpur, and Colombo. Sibley articulates well the contradictions between national xenophobia and the exigencies of capitalist developments. These find expression in the production of segregative urban space:

> The built environment assumes symbolic importance, reinforcing a desire for order and conformity, . . . [and thus] space is implicated in the construction of otherness and deviancy. Pure space exposes difference and facilitates the policing of boundaries. . . . This xenophobia is based . . . on a purified national identity; [it] sits uneasily with the flows and cultural fusions, which are generated by global capitalism. But the contradiction between a racist nationalism and the imperatives of capitalist economies is denied. . . . The myth of cultural homogeneity is needed to sustain the nation-state. . . . It is convenient to have an alien other hovering on the margins.[12]

In a similar vein, a recent, more critical wave of nationalism studies has emerged, with scholars such as Comaroff, Jackson and Penrose, Mann, Lustick, and Yuval-Davis unpacking the myths, histories, and spaces constructed as "naturally" national.[13] These works, which represent but a small sample, have exposed the multilayered, politically contested, and socially constructed entity called "the nation-state," with the need to treat it as contingent, and not "a given," in order to fully understand its impact on intergroup politics, economy, and geography.

Unfortunately, the new horizons thrown open by the three major areas of scholarship discussed above have remained largely detached. For example, there has been little attempt by scholars to engage seriously with the interaction of the various — often conflicting — tensions and relations emanating from the nature of ethnonational territoriality, the economic forces shaping contemporary cities, and the cities' institutions and power structures. Even the important recent work on cities within ethnonational conflicts has tended to privilege issues of national control and territory and not engage seriously enough with the urban dynamics concealed beneath the more visible national surface.[14] Similarly, recent novel work on urban diversity and difference vis-à-vis the onset of globalization and neoliberalism, has rarely incorporated issues of ethnonationalism or governance into the heart of their analyses, overlooking the ever-presence of this force in shaping contemporary urban regions.[15]

But such an engagement is sorely needed, because, as well argued by AlSayyad and Castells, no one body of knowledge is complete or credible without the others.[16] That is, no discussion of the emergence of nationalism and the management of ethnic relations in modern nation-states can ignore the pivotal role of cities, for both generating and challenging the ethnonational order. Likewise, no serious historical account of urbanization, or discussion of contemporary, globalizing cities, can overlook the central role of ethnonationalism in shaping urban living and political space, or the constant surfacing of noneconomic, ethnocratic, and often antiglobalizing logics in the political agendas of cities and urbanizing regions. As observed by Comaroff and Comaroff in their essay on changing environments in the Cape Town region:

> . . . the moral panic about strangers and immigrants becomes over-determined
> . . . the very existence of "human aliens" embodies the contradictions of borders
> and boundaries in the age of global capital. This is where universal liberal ide-
> ology runs up against a politics of exclusion whereby identity is mobilized to
> create "closed" spheres of interest within "open" neoliberal economies. . . .[17]

Our attempt here is to begin integrating these bodies of knowledge by analyzing the interaction between urbanizing, ethnicizing, and "governmentality" forces, and by examining the impact of these interactions on the emergence of urban informality. Our analytical approach is highlighted by the accompanying diagram, which portrays a "trialectical process" (to use a Lefebvrian formulation), whereby urban regions and their regimes are constantly shaped and "produced" by the interaction and tensions between various poles (see FIGURE 8.1).[18]

This approach links our discussion to a growing body of literature dealing with urban regimes which examines the link between structural forces and the nature of local politics and policies.[19] Our account further gives a central role to the logics of capital, governance, and ethnic control. Needless to say, these interactions — often in the form of "clashes" — can be found in most contemporary cities, in varying intensities and forms. However, within the limits of this chapter, we will constrain our focus to one type — the ethnocratic city — which is likely to bring into sharp relief the simultaneous workings of the two major societal forces.

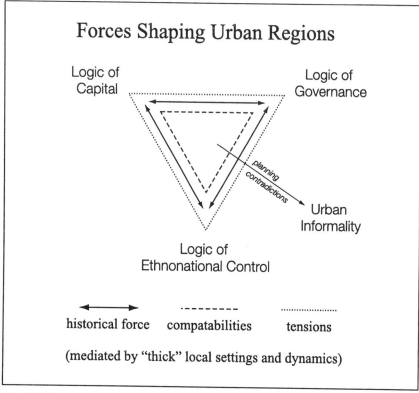

Figure 8.1. Trialectical model of the origins of informality.

Furthermore, as demonstrated below, the ethnocratic setting highlights a powerful spatial logic which often counters the forces of globalization and capital accumulation. That is, both international and local capital may "lose" in a series of "policy struggles" to what is perceived to be the higher imperative of "purifying" ethnic space, even at considerable societal cost. Hence, and despite the emphasis in the literature on a close link between informality and globalization, poverty, and underdevelopment, we contend that this phenomenon is a product of a multitude of forces, including but not limited to the logic of capital.

ETHNOCRATIC CITIES AND REGIMES

The ethnocratic city embodies the tensions and contradictions outlined above. On the one hand, it is "officially" an open and accessible space; on the other, it is segregated, controlled, and hierarchical. On the one hand, it is increasingly part of the (local outreach of) a globalizing culture and economy, international migration, development bursts, and the discourse of human rights, civil society, and democracy associated with late capitalism/modernity. Yet on the other hand, it is a product of the nationalist, expansionist logic of "purified" ethnic space. As we shall see later, urban informality becomes a common planning strategy in such settings, allowing both "orderly" and "modernist" planning to proceed, while containing the tensions and preserving the control over the "unplannable" elements in these cities. In that sense the ethnocratic city is a dynamic and uneven hybridity of what AlSayyad has termed the colonial, the national, and the global urban orders.[20]

Ethnocratic cities develop within an imposing political order — that of the ethnocratic state. This is a distinct regime type established to enhance the expansion and control of a dominant ethnonation in multiethnic territories. In such regimes, ethnicity, and not citizenship, forms the main criterion for distributing power and resources. As a result, such regimes typically display high levels of ethnic segregation, and they are dominated by a polarizing ethnic politics. Ethnocratic regimes can be found in states such as Sri Lanka, Estonia, nineteenth-century Australia, and Israel/Palestine. They combine a degree of political openness and formal democratic representation with political structures that facilitate the seizure of contested territory by a dominant ethnonation and its diasporas. As part of this process, the dominant group appropriates the state apparatus and marginalizes or excludes peripheral ethnic and national minorities.

As elaborated elsewhere, ethnocratic states emerge from the time-space fusion of three main historical-political forces.[21] One is settler-colonialism, which may be external (into another state or continent) or internal (within the state).[22] Another is ethnonationalism, which draws on the international legitimacy to national self-determination to buttress the political and territorial expansionist goals of the dominant ethnonation.[23] A third force is the conspicuous "ethnic logic" of capital, which tends to cause ethno-class stratification through uneven processes of capital mobility, immigration, and economic globalization.[24] The parallel working of these structural forces has shaped the characteristics of ethnocratic regimes.

Our conceptual approach here draws inspiration from the material-cultural paradigm in the social sciences, and especially from the neo-Gramscian school, which points to the firm linkages between hegemonic political and cultural "truths" and their underlying material foundations.[25] This is not the place to elaborate on this theoretical framing, except to note that ethnocracy in general, and urban ethnocracy in particular, are driven by deeply rooted hegemonic assumptions about space, ethnicity, and power relations. Our analysis traces in detail both the spatial and political consequences of these reigning hegemonies, and explores the contradictions and tensions which may challenge and destabilize their foundations.[26]

Returning to ethnocratic cities, we first note that their politics often reflect wider ethnonational tensions and conflicts. Local politics usually revolve around struggles for space, economic resources, and political power, most commonly along the ethnonational lines. But these cities never fully replicate the dynamics of the wider conflict, mainly because the urban arena is governed by a different combination of powers, regulations, and forces than those which prevail in nonurban regions. There are two main differences. First, in terms of sheer territory, urban areas are quite small. For this reason, national movements have generally emphasized control over the vast tracts of rural lands as a symbol of sovereignty, rather than over the streets of contested cities. Second, exclusion and segregation of minorities is far less feasible, or even desirable, in urban, as opposed to rural, areas. In the latter, the state (on behalf of the dominant ethnoclass) can "legally" and effectively marginalize and exclude members of ethnic minorities. This is commonly achieved though the allocation of large tracts of land on the basis of ethnic affiliation, the implementation of ethnically biased programs and policies, the manipulation of municipal boundaries, or the activities of special (ethnic) rural arms of the ethnocratic state. Such policies are common in most ethnocratic states, especially during the formative years when patterns of ethnic dominance over rural space are formed — as has been the case in Malaysia, Sri Lanka, Estonia, and Israel. The effect has been to prevent ethnic minorities from owning and controlling rural land.

However, given the representation and legitimacy of most ethnocratic states as democratic, the prevalence of a relatively open and increasingly liberalizing market system, and the need for cheap labor in proximity to major industrial and service centers, the urban areas in such states have been more open and accessible. Thus, the need to ensure, at least on a formal level, the free flow of commerce and population in these urban systems opens up cracks and contradictions in the grids of ethnocratic control. Here we can note the coterminous operation of the various "engines" of urbanization. Thus, the ethnocratic city is developed by both the logic of capital and the drive for reinforcing ethnonational urban control. Yet its development creates openings and spaces for minorities who draw on the democratic and liberal possibilities emanating from the new spatial-political formations of modern urban governance. The presence of mobilized minorities thereby often challenges both the hegemony of ethnonational control and the "exigencies" of capitalism.

How do ethnocratic states respond to this potential challenge? In general, they attempt to concentrate their minorities in small areas, thereby minimizing their spatial control.[27] Such a policy often creates several characteristic features: the partial urbanization of near-metropolitan minority localities; the relocation of distant minority communities to major urban regions; and the creation of urban informality. In most cases the ethnocratic state attempts to establish a clear segregation between majority and minority, even in putatively "open" urban settings, even when a more subtle urban segregation would normally occur on its own based on "cultural" or "market" features.

The dynamics of the urban ethnocratic regime thus assume the following characteristics:

1. The city is classified and represented as "mixed," but dominated by one ethnonational group; urban citizenship is unequal, with resources and services allocated on the basis of ethnicity, not residency.
2. Urban politics are ethnicized, with a gradual process of ethnopolitical polarization.
3. Housing and employment markets are officially "open," yet marked by deep patterns of ethnic segregation.
4. Planning and development strategies reflect a deep ethnocratic logic, couched in "professional," "civil," and "economic" reasoning.
5. Land and housing are allocated so as to minimize the control of minority members over urban resources.
6. Municipal boundaries are "gerrymandered" to prolong spatial and urban control by the dominant ethno-classes.
7. The above generate urban-ethnic resistance, with constant minority challenges to the prevailing order.
8. Finally, urban informality emerges as a conspicuous component of the metropolis, and becomes a central part of the region's planning strategy.

The increasing occurrence and visibility of urban informality is linked directly to the concurrent working of the intertwined and opposing urban forces noted in Figure 8.1. The first of these is the urbanizing logic of late-capitalist economies, particularly within a globalizing, and hence centralizing, urban system.[28] The second is the ongoing drive for ethnic control over space. The third force is the emergence of the city as the site of modernizing governance, with an emphasis on law and order, as well as on rights, liberalism, and democracy. But the resulting urban order is never stable, as tensions arising from the interaction of these forces generate constant challenges to ethnic control and capitalist-generated inequalities. These emerge mainly from local minorities, but increasingly they may also be caused by the presence of migrant workers and long-term undocumented ("illegal") residents.

In these unstable settings, a common planning response is allowing, condoning, and even facilitating urban informality. Whole communities are thus left out of the planning process, or overlooked by the content of urban policies. Typically, such populations are mentioned as "a problem," but their undocumented, unlawful, or even fugitive existence allows most authorities to ignore them as having full "planning rights" to the city.[29] In other words, policymakers define urban informality as a method of indirectly containing the "ungovernable." The tactic is avoidance and distant containment; but the result is the condemnation of large communities to unserviced, deprived, and stigmatized urban fringes.

Here lies a main feature of urban informality as a planning strategy: it allows the urban elites to represent urban government as open, civil, and democratic, while at the same time denying great numbers of urban residents and workers basic rights and services. The elite draw legitimacy from this partial and distorted representation, which enables them to preserve their privileged ethno-class position and maintain their ethnocratic system.

The use of planning to create, maintain, and facilitate urban informality is an example of its use as a form of social control. As discussed elsewhere, in certain conditions, planning exposes a "dark side," whereby the very agencies and tools, originally designed to promote social reforms and amenity are used to contain and oppress marginalized communities.[30] Let us turn now to the unfolding of these processes during the transformation of Israel/Palestine.

THE MAKING OF ETHNOCRACY IN ISRAEL/PALESTINE

Israel is an ethnocratic regime which enables, assists, and promotes the central Zionist project of Judaizing Israel/Palestine. The ethno-national struggle over land and state control has been the major determining factor in the evolution of Jewish-Palestinian relations, as well as the major factor in relations between ethnic groups within these two nations.[31] The Judaization project is driven by the Zionist premise that Israel is a territory and a state that "belongs" to, and only to, the Jewish people. It was hence constructed as an ideological and moral project that implements the Jewish "right" to the land, and which strives to fill it with the majority of the Jewish people, thereby offering a solution to the history of anti-Semitism and diaspora.

The ethnocratic characteristics of the Israeli regime are quite vivid. Rights and powers in Israel are largely stratified according to an ethno-class configuration.[32] Furthermore, state protection of the country's Arab minority against the tyranny of the majority is quite limited.[33] In addition, there is no distinct Israeli "demos." The occupation of the West Bank and Gaza Strip and the existence of Jewish settlements in these partially annexed territories, along with the sovereign roles accorded to diaspora Jews and their representative organizations in Israel, has resulted in a lack of clear political or territorial boundaries.[34]

The Judaization strategy is at the heart of Israel's ethnocratic regime. Its roots lie in pre-1948 Jewish settlement methods, which attempted to create contiguous "blocks" and "chains" of segregated Jewish localities, mainly along the coastal plains and northern valleys. But this project only swung into full force after 1948, when it was backed by the legal, planning, and armed force of an internationally recognized state. This Judaization and parallel de-Arabization of space employed a range of strategies after the flight and eviction of Palestinian refugees in the 1948 Naqbah (Disaster). These included the prohibition of any legal right of return, the destruction of some 400 Arab villages, and the expropriation of some 50–60 percent of the land owned by Arabs who remained in Israel. A central policy thrust was also to create Jewish settlements in areas with Arab majorities, such as the Galilee and the northeastern Negev (the Beer-Sheva region).

What made this massive Judaization project possible? Clearly, military force, violent imposition of state rule, and international political clout played their part. The toughness and resilience of Zionism was also important, resulting from the horrors of the Nazi holocaust and intensifying Arab hostilities. I have elsewhere characterized pre-1948 Jewish settlement in Palestine as "colonialism of collective survival."[35] But here we also need to account for a powerful process of cultural construction which enabled Jewish leaders to proceed with the dispossessing project, while presenting it, internally and externally, as moral, necessary, and derived from the necessities of modern planning. As noted by Israel's first national plan:

> Modern nations all over the world attempt to decentralize their population, so they do not become dependent on central congested cities. . . . In Israel this task is more urgent but also easier. . . . Urgent, because Israel holds the world record with 82 percent of the population in three main cities. . . . Easy, because unlike Britain, we do not require to move existing populations, but simply settle new immigrants in the country's empty regions. Israel can thus decentralize its population [read: Jews] to the north, Jerusalem corridor, and Negev regions, as part of the only rational way to develop this country for the age of modern, industrial future.[36]

The combined discourses of nationalism, modernity, and professional planning put in train during the late 1940s and 1950s produced an exclusive form of Jewish territoriality, which aimed to quickly "indigenize" immigrant Jews, and to conceal, trivialize, or marginalize the prior existence of Palestinian Arabs. The "frontier" and "internal frontier" became central icons, and the planning and implementation of frontier settlement became one of the highest achievements of any Zionist. In some respects the entire country (within whatever borders) became a frontier.

In this vein, David Ben-Gurion, the longtime leader of the Zionist movement and Israel's first prime minister, claimed, regarding the need for settling (Jews) in the Negev (the region to which this chapter's second part is devoted):

The people of Israel will be tested by the Negev. . . . Only by settling and developing the Negev can Israel, as a modern, independent, and freedom-seeking nation, rise to the challenge that history put before us. . . . All of us — veterans and olim [new immigrants], young and old, men and women — should see the Negev as their place and their future and turn southwards. . . .[37]

In a similar spirit, Yossef Weitz, chairman of the Jewish National Fund, the main Zionist arm of land purchase and settlement, claimed on January 19, 1948:

. . . the Hebrew state will have to embark on a wide settlement strategy in its first three years . . . [and a] big part of it in the Negev. . . . In the Negev we'll be able to implement immediately our development laws, according to which we shall expropriate land according to a well-designed plan. . . .[38]

Such sentiments, pertaining to the entire state, and specifically to the Negev region, were translated into a pervasive program of Jewish-Zionist territorial socialization, expressed in school curriculum, literature, political speeches, popular music, and other spheres of public discourse. Settlement thus continued to form a cornerstone of Zionist nation-building, well after the establishment of a sovereign Jewish state.

A central element of the spatial Judaization of Israel has been state planning — that is, land and settlement — policies. One of the Israeli government's first actions was to enact a series of land laws and establish a number of institutions that transferred most Arab lands to Jewish state control. In doing so, the state was able to exploit the transition between British and Israeli legal systems, with the latter conveniently set up so as to not recognize any previous title to land apart from individual private title (*tabu*). Given the multiple possibilities of ownership and use of land prior to 1948, this was a major tool in dispossessing Palestinian Arabs. In addition, the institutions of Israeli land policymaking and professional administration became nearly totally Jewish, empowering representatives of world Jewry in key decision-making positions, but without including or consulting local Arab citizens. The result was a massive and unidirectional transfer of land from Arab individuals to the (Jewish) state. Currently, Palestinian-Arab citizens in Israel possess only about one-third of their prestate land holdings.

Further, in Israel 93 percent of the land is registered as public, the vast majority of which is classified as state lands (the rest belongs to public Jewish bodies such as the Jewish National Fund). The state gained control of these land resources in a number of ways: by nationalizing nearly all property owned by Palestinian refugees; by classifying all *mawat* ("dead land") as state land; and by expropriating large tracts of land from its Arab citizens.

Such conditions are highly important in terms of the subject matter of this chapter, due to the direct link in the Israeli system between land ownership and "informality"/"illegality." The link is as follows: no building can receive a permit unless it is included in an approved town planning scheme (known in Israel as an "outline plan"). However, no approval may be given to such schemes without substantial resolution of local land disputes. Given the complexity of land claims in the Arab sector, this means that plans are often delayed for decades. In the meantime, the Palestinian-Arab population in Israel has expanded rapidly, but land for approved building "cannot" be released due to a lack of approved plans. Given the dire need for housing, many among Israel's Arab population have naturally begun to build without official approval, almost always on their private lands. But these houses are immediately considered "illegal" and are constantly under threat of demolition. Such a problem keeps surfacing in Israel at regular intervals, and has often seriously threatened relations between Jews and Arabs.[39] It also stands at the basis of the Bedouins' urban informality in the Beer-Sheva region, a situation we will document in the following section.

The state's planning and settlement system has been equally effective in enhancing the Judaization of the land. Among other things, it facilitated the construction of some 700 Jewish settlements, while prohibiting Arabs from building new localities (except for Bedouin sedentarization and concentration, as discussed below). The land ownership system and the settlement landscape have also been thoroughly transformed, making Israel a conspicuous case of an ethnocratic regime. This is the historical, political, and geographical context within which Beer-Sheva has developed.

Significantly, "the frontier" has also been alive in Israel's mixed Arab-Jewish cities, especially in planning discourse where it has been common to speak about "the need" to build Jewish housing on, or immediately adjacent to, Arab urban neighborhoods. Thus, in the plans of most mixed cities specific goals appear about "keeping the Jewish character," and combating the "danger" of increasing Arab population which might create a "demographic threat" to the city.[40]

This planning rationale has received stark physical expression in mixed urban areas such as Akko, Haifa, Jaffa, Ramla, and Lod, where high-density Jewish neighborhoods have been rapidly constructed around the small Arab enclaves that are all that remain of previously Arab cities. The treatment of urban Arab neighborhoods as "internal frontiers" into which Jewish presence should expand has, in fact, turned all mixed Arab-Jewish cities in Israel into urban ethnocracies. The Arab presence there has thus been delegitimized and constantly portrayed as a "danger," causing deep patterns of planning discrimination. This has spawned the emergence of various degrees of urban informality, from whole neighborhoods "unseen" by urban authorities (such as the "railway locality" in Lod), to recognized neighborhoods which nevertheless receive inferior levels of services and planning and whose residents have often been excluded from the city's communal life and policymaking. The Beer-Sheva urban region, to which we now turn, illustrates yet another kind of Israeli urban ethnocracy.

THE BEER-SHEVA URBAN REGION: ETHNOCRATIC MANAGEMENT AND URBAN INFORMALITY

Beer-Sheva was established by the Ottoman Empire at the beginning of the twentieth century as a small urban service center for the Bedouin-Arab population of the northern Negev (al-Naqab) region. It remained a small Arab town of 5,000–6,000 inhabitants, until its conquest by Israel in 1948. Since then it has turned into an icon of Israel's efforts to settle, develop, and Judaize the "internal frontier." In particular, Beer-Sheva has become a Jewish city, and has remained a focal point for planning and development strategies aimed at creating and maintaining a Jewish majority in the northern Negev.

Beer-Sheva was planned by the Israeli authorities as an arch example of a modernist, national city.[41] During the 1950s and 1960s Israel worked to realize this vision as a series of "garden cities," mainly north and west of the old Arab town. The "garden" neighborhoods were typified by high-density, low-standard, public housing blocks and large, mainly empty and underdeveloped open spaces.

The vast majority of the population settled in these new areas were Jewish immigrants from Muslim countries (Eastern Jews, or Mizrahim), who formed the social, economic, and political margins of Israeli-Jewish society. In addition, Beer-Sheva was planned as the capital of southern Israel and became the center for a series of small frontier towns and agricultural settlements, in what was termed by Gradus and Stern the "Negev Regiopolis."[42] Part of this regiopolis has been a large and sparsely settled "Siyag area," northeast of the city, into which most of the Bedouin Arabs of the Negev were forcefully moved during the 1950s.

During the 1980s and 1990s the city began to suburbanize, with the middle classes moving either to new low-density, higher-quality neighborhoods or to relatively wealthy satellite towns mainly north and east of the city. A further transformation occurred during the 1990s, with a massive influx of migrants, arriving mainly from the former Soviet Union and Ethiopia, who congregated in several newly built neighborhoods, chiefly in the city's western areas. Beer-Sheva and its regional setting have thus become dominated by binational and multicultural ethno-class divisions, many of them expressed spatially.[43]

In parallel, the Beer-Sheva region has increased in importance as an economic and administrative center, servicing a large region in the northern Negev. As a result, it has managed to attract outside private capital — initially Israeli, but more recently international. And it has undergone physical restructuring during the late 1990s, gradually developing a modern central business district, replacing the old Ottoman-Arab city center. At the beginning of the third millennium the Beer-Sheva regional economy is still mainly based on traditional sectors such as minerals, labor-intensive industries, and governmental employment. But with the onset of processes of restructuring and globalization, these sectors have been declining in relative importance, while electronics, computing, and sophisticated service industries have begun to rise.[44] Nonetheless, the Beer-Sheva region can still be regarded as a peripheral, medium-size, planned urban center, which is only now beginning to link itself to the national and global economy.[45]

Our attention here, however, will focus on the Arab parts of the Beer-Sheva region, primarily located north and east of the city (see FIGURE 8.2). These have not been included in the Beer-Sheva plans but have rather been administered by a different set of authorities and institutions. Consequently, the Arab localities

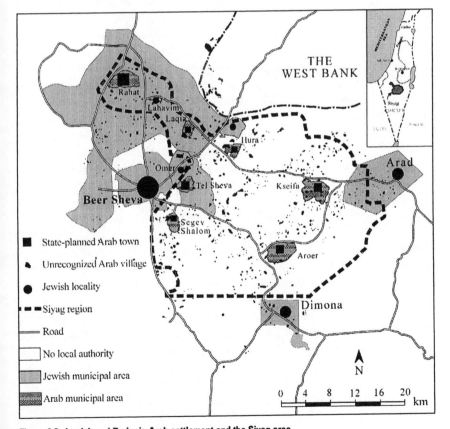

Figure 8.2. Jewish and Bedouin Arab settlement and the Siyag area.
Source: Ministry of the Interior records, aerial photograph analysis (1999).

have shared in very little of the economic or physical development of the region, while increasing their dependence on its urban functions. This has caused many settlements in Arab areas to be classified by the region's planning authorities as "illegal," "unrecognized," or "spontaneous." At the end of 1999 the "illegal" localities accommodated an estimated population of 65,000–70,000. A further population of the same size currently resides in impoverished, and only partially "planned," "Bedouin" towns.

The Beer-Sheva region has thus developed into an urban ethnocracy. Multiple sets of boundaries segregate citizens who reside in the same urban region on the basis of their ethnicity. This strategy mainly reflects the ethno-national policies of the Israeli state, aiming to facilitate the expansion and control of the dominant Jewish-Zionist group. Thus, high levels of segregation in the region are testimony to ongoing difficulties in achieving civil equality, mobility, and democracy, despite the formal openness of the city itself.

Returning for a minute to our theoretical discussion of the oft-clashing economic, civil, and ethnoterritorial "engines" shaping urban space, we can discern in Beer-Sheva a clear, though not absolute, dominance of ethnoterritorial priorities. The segregated nature of urbanization around Beer-Sheva has been caused by Israel's drive to Judaize the region (which would have been impossible without planned and institutionalized segregation). But at the same time, the Bedouin Arabs in the region did gradually urbanize, and they have become an influential, if marginalized, force in the Beer-Sheva region.[46] The prevalence of "illegality" and massive informality among Bedouin Arabs is hence, first and foremost, a result of Israel's drive to maximize Jewish land control in a predominantly Arab area. It has not necessarily been due to the dictates or exigencies of capital accumulation, be they local or global.

However, these ethnocratic forces, which have prevailed in Beer-Sheva for decades, are being gradually challenged, and the logic of capital and democracy may yet begin to exert some pressure on the shaping of the urban region. This has appeared mainly in the form of Arab resistance to the dictates of state and planners, as we shall see below.

As in most other ethnocratic societies, the expansion and development process in Beer-Sheva has also amplified and created disparities on the local level, most notably among internal Jewish and Arab ethno-classes — such as among Mizrahi and Russian Jews; or among "real Bedouins," *falahin* ("agricultural" Arabs), and *abid* (ex-slaves). While this is a central aspect of all ethnocratic societies, our scope here does not allow its proper analysis. Hence, we shall concentrate on the ethnonational level — that is, on the relations between Negev Jews and Arabs, who in turn are part of larger Jewish-Zionist and Palestinian-Arab national collectivities.

THE BEDOUIN ARABS, AND THE JUDAIZATION OF THE BEER-SHEVA REGION

Some 130,000 Arabs reside in the northern Negev, mostly within the Beer-Sheva urban region. Until the 1948 establishment of the state of Israel, this previously semi-nomad community relied for their livelihood on cattle herds, rain-fed agriculture, and commerce.[47] During and immediately following the 1948 war some 80–85 percent of the Negev Arabs either fled or were expelled by Israeli forces to Egypt, Jordan, and the West Bank. Approximately 11,000 remained in Israel and were transferred to an area named the "Siyag" (Fence), known for its low agricultural fertility, immediately northeast of Beer-Sheva. Twelve tribes were relocated into the Siyag, joining six tribes who already lived there. This area stretches over a tenth of the Negev area, and was under military rule until 1966 (refer to FIGURE 8.2). No stone or concrete building activity was allowed in the Siyag, forcing most tribes to erect settlements of shacks and tents.

The Siyag's infertile lands, the shrinking grazing and agricultural space, and the urban proximity have dramatically transformed the lifestyle of Bedouin Arabs. From controllers of the desert region, they became fringe dwellers of a growing, modernizing Beer-Sheva urban region. At the same time, the military government, which severely restricted their mobility outside the Siyag region, further hampered their (already limited) ability to compete in the Beer-Sheva labor market. During the first decade most of the Bedouins in the Siyag thus returned to a traditional self-sustaining lifestyle. But later they did begin to seek employment and commerce with the surrounding Jewish population.[48]

The confinement of the Arab population in military-controlled areas was officially justified on security considerations, but it resulted in preferential treatment for Jewish immigrants to the area, who could gain employment with little competition from local Arabs. The immigrants were mainly low-income Mizrahim (Eastern Jewish immigrants from Muslim countries) who were settled by the government (often against their will) in the peripheral Negev during the 1950s and 1960s. Their absorption into the labor market was particularly important for the authorities, which aspired to create an integrated Jewish-Zionist nation and minimize intra-Jewish political and social tensions.[49]

Following 1948 nearly all lands held by Negev Arabs were declared to be state property. In a series of legal moves the Israeli government classified this land as either "dead" (in legal terminology, *mawat* — that is, unregistered and uncultivated), or "absentee property" belonging to refugees who "left" the state during the 1948 war. Such classifications gave the state permission, under its own rules, to nationalize the land.[50] Given the self-declared nature of Israel as Jewish, and the active involvement of worldwide Jewish organizations (such as the Jewish National Fund and the Jewish Agency) in the official state apparatus of land administration, the declaration of these areas as state lands meant their exclusive use by Jews. Indeed, the lands were subsequently allocated to some fifty Jewish settlements that were established in the Beer-Sheva metropolitan region. These were mainly small "development towns" and communal villages whose farms now occupy most land previously held by Palestinian Arabs.

The classification of the vast majority of the Negev as state land blocked virtually every possibility of their registration in the name of Arabs, who had held them for generations.[51] In addition, Israel's Land Acquisition Law (1953) expropriated the land of every person who was not residing upon, or cultivating, their land on one decisive date (April 1, 1952). Because the vast majority of Negev Bedouin had been forcibly removed from their land prior to this date, this meant they lost all right to the land even when they possessed documented proof of ownership.[52] In this way the pre-1948 Arab community of the Negev — refugees and locals alike — lost more than 95 percent of their landed property. This was reflected in the bitter statements made in 1997 by Hassan abu-Quidder, a Bedouin activist, protesting against Israel's land policies:

> Only in one instance shall the Bedouin Arabs get their full and equal rights in the Jewish State: only if miraculously we'll stop occupying, needing, or using any land. Then we shall receive what we truly deserve — full air rights. . . .[53]

But not all local Arabs have accepted this legal situation. Those who have become Israeli citizens have submitted some 3,200 legal claims to their expropriated lands, based on traditional Ottoman or British records which attested to their past holdings. To date, however, not even one Arab claimant has been awarded full ownership rights. The Israeli legal system has consistently followed only its own legal precedents.[54] And it has so far refused to award ownership without documented proof of individual title.[55] On the other hand, the state has recognized partial holding rights for some Bedouin Arabs, either in accordance with land arrangements practiced before 1948, or according to regulations agreed upon by the state and the traditional Arab elites after the transfer to the Siyag area.[56] However, these rights have remained vague, thus depriving the Arabs of basic development and planning capabilities.

Five decades after these events, tension over Bedouin-Arab land ownership is still a central issue in the Beer-Sheva region. Some 95 percent of Arab claims to land have yet to be settled, regarding an area of approximately 800,000 dunams.[57] Half of these lands are in areas settled by Jews. The compromises reached so far between Negev Arabs and the state amount only to 30,000 dunams. This low figure not only reflects the slow pace of the Israeli legal system, but also steadfast Arab resistance to state policies. In particular, the state has attempted to link settlement of land disputes with forced relocation into seven planned towns within the Siyag region. The two sides have thus found themselves in a political, legal, and planning deadlock, causing widespread urban informality in the Beer-Sheva region.

It should be reiterated that the forced concentration of Arabs in the Siyag area was an integral part of a broader state policy to Judaize the entire disputed territory of Israel/Palestine. It followed the same logic as Israel's policies elsewhere of concentrating the Arabs and dispersing the Jews.[58] In the Negev, however, Israel recognized virtually no Arab land rights. In other areas, like the Galilee and the Triangle (see inset to FIGURE 8.2), Israel respected Arab private ownership, based on British documentation. But even in these regions the state often used its powerful planning capabilities to expropriate private Arab lands.

Following the population transfer, the Siyag was neglected by planning authorities for twenty years. In several key regional plans — either for the Negev or the Beer-Sheva metropolitan area (including the 1972 District Plan; the 1991 "Negev Front" (Kidmat Negev) strategy; the 1995 Beer-Sheva Metropolitan Development Plan; and the 1998 renewed District Plan) — the areas occupied by the informal settlements of Bedouin Arab were either left blank, as if they were empty, or designated for such public uses as sewerage plants, recreation forests, or industrial zones. No settlement, agricultural, or industrial plans were prepared for these regions, causing the emergence of widespread urban and rural informality. Thus, dozens of "spontaneous" Arab localities evolved, characterized by tin shacks, cabins, or tents. The vast majority of these have been denied basic infrastructure and services such as electricity, running water, and roads. Nevertheless, the number of people inhabiting them has grown to some 65,000–70,000, constituting Israel's most marginal and deprived community.

During the same period, parallel arms of the Judaization strategy continued to operate in the region. In particular, some twenty Jewish towns and rural localities have been established around the Siyag, thus creating an Arab enclave. Later, Jewish development also penetrated into the Siyag region. This first came with construction of the Nevatim airport in 1978 (resulting in the forced resettlement of some 7,000 Arabs).[59] But later it also included establishment of Jewish suburban localities, such as Meitar and Livna, and the expansion of older Jewish settlements.

CONSOLIDATING URBAN ETHNOCRACY: PLANNING FOR THE BEDOUIN ARABS

A further step in the effort to Judaize the Beer-Sheva region was the launching in the mid-1960s of a plan to urbanize the Siyag's Bedouin-Arab population. The first mention of the plan was in 1959, when Ben-Gurion announced a general five-year plan for Israel's Arab sector, in which "the government will bring down legislation to move and concentrate the Bedouins into permanent settlements."[60] Later, an intense policy debate ensued, with two main positions. Moshe Dayan, then minister of agriculture and a dominant force in shaping policy toward the Arabs, strongly advocated the urbanization of Bedouin Arabs into mixed cities, mainly Beer-Sheva, Jaffa, Lod, and Ramla. Yigal Alon, then Minister of Labor, and the central-government member with the strongest ties to Bedouin communities, pushed for a more gradual urbanization strategy, mainly in the southern Siyag area.[61]

Eventually, it was the latter strategy which won the day (although segments of the Dayan plan were also implemented with the settlement of some 4,000 Bedouins in Lod and Ramla). In the Negev, seven towns were established into which Arabs in the region were supposed to relocate: Rahat, Laqiya, Hura, Tel-Sheva, Kusseifa, Aru'er, and Segev-Shalom (refer to FIGURE 8.2). The government's aim was to further decrease Arab land control and concentrate Arabs "permanent-ly" in urban localities. Its method of implementing such a top-down Judaization and modernization program for the Bedouin Arabs was to use the allure of modern services such as housing, roads, schools, clinics, and electricity. Thus, the Arabs who agreed to relocate into the towns were to receive heavily subsidized plots of state land and connections to roads, water, and electricity. But this allocation depended on the cessation of all disputes over lands elsewhere in the Negev. The deal, there-fore, was clear: accept fully registered, planned, and (partially) serviced blocks of land in a new Bedouin-Arab town, but withdraw all claims against the state. The alter-native was to remain in an "illegal," unserviced locality, subject to constant danger of house demolition, and exposed to a wide range of legal penalties.

As might have been expected, most Arabs who actually took up the offer and relocated into the new towns were landless *falahin* (farmers) who had lived for generations under the protection of the Bedouin tribes. The new towns allowed them to pass by their social inferiority within Bedouin-Arab society, by breaking centuries-old forms of patronage and dependence, by achieving political domi-nance in several towns, and by modernizing their living standards. Therefore, the state's urbanization policy, not accidentally, deepened the tensions between vari-ous Arab ethno-classes, by allocating privileges and resources (such as cheap serv-iced lands) to the landless and weaker group, and by making life miserable for the upper echelons of Negev Bedouin-Arab society.[62]

But due to the lowly social status of most urbanizing Arabs, and despite their promise of modernization, the planned towns quickly evolved into pockets of dep-rivation, unemployment, dependency, crime, and social tension. Although one should not underestimate the power of modernization to form a foundation for social and political mobilization, relocation to the towns also set in train processes of social disintegration.[63] The towns also positioned the Arabs in spatial isolation, with little opportunity for local mobility or development.[64] The seven towns thus became, as potently described by a Bedouin activist, "suburban ghettos."

By relocating the Arabs into these towns at the periphery of the Beer-Sheva region, and by separating them municipally from the stronger Jewish areas, Israeli planners laid the long-term structure for the creation of urban ethnocracy. This was coupled with a total refusal to provide services within old Beer-Sheva, which might otherwise have attracted urbanizing Bedouin Arabs. Hence, no Arab schools, religious facilities, or community centers are available in the main Beer-Sheva city area, and only some 3,500 Arabs now reside in Beer-Sheva, spread over a number of distant neighborhoods, without notable residential, cultural, or religious centers.[65]

The uneven separation imposed by the region's planners and leaders created a near total Arab-Jewish segregation, backed by planning and institutional rationales. Needless to say, not all segregation is negative, and many Bedouin Arabs do wish to remain in homogenous localities in order to protect their culture and community. But the creation of a highly segregated human landscape also ensured total control by Jews of the economic, political, and cultural resources of this binational metropolitan region. The Beer-Sheva urban ethnocracy thus incorporated unevenly the seven planned Arab towns and a large number of unrecognized (informal) Arab localities.

Israel's strategy to remove the unrecognized villages and coerce the migration of their inhabitants into the planned towns was accompanied by a range of pressure tactics. On the institutional level, special government authorities were set up especially for this task, including the Orwellian-sounding "Authority for the Advancement of the Bedouins," the "Implementation Authority," the "Green Patrol," and "Rotem" (a police unit for law enforcement among the Arabs). All special bodies were geared, at least in part, to the task of concentrating the Bedouin Arabs in the planned towns, and controlling their informal spaces.

On a planning level, beyond pervasive neglect, the state also initiated a series of tactics to urbanize the Bedouin Arabs. These have included the following:

1. Strict nonrecognition of existing settlements located outside the planned towns, and the subsequent denial of most municipal services routinely provided to other citizens (water, electricity, telephone, health and public services, accessible educational services).
2. Intensive legal penalties against unauthorized homes.
3. Actual demolition of some 1,300 homes and structures between 1990–1998.[66]
4. The frequent issuing of eviction notices and fines in order to remove "Arab invaders" from state land.
5. Delay of land-settlement proceedings, which have often lasted more than three decades, with the intent to make Arabs give up on their hopes to win back lands.
6. Heavy environmental restrictions on grazing and the subsequent seizure and destruction of most Bedouin herds.
7. The poisoning of fields planted on disputed land.
8. Activation of the state's tax authorities against "problematic" Bedouin Arabs.

Over the years, the drive to concentrate the Bedouin Arabs has been bolstered by two other state concerns. First, geopolitically, Israel has been worried about the Siyag forming an Arab "land bridge" between the West Bank and the Gaza Strip, thereby threatening the contiguity of Jewish land control. Second, the state has been concerned about the costs involved in recognizing, planning, and servicing dispersed populations. The use of planning to control a weak minority was thus also justified on geopolitical and rational economic grounds.

POLICY ENFORCEMENT AND PERSISTING INFORMALITY

Despite the consistent, harsh, and often violent pressure exerted by all Israeli governments since the 1960s to implement the seven-towns strategy, only 55 percent of the region's Arabs have actually moved into these towns. A significant, and rapidly growing, group has remained on the land in the "illegal" or unrecognized semi-urban localities.

Let us reiterate that the "illegal" Arab settlements exist in their current locales today either due to their residence in the area before 1948 or as a result of forced government relocation — that is, not through any form of "illegal" invasion. Hence, their treatment by state authorities is a testimony to the deep discrimination associated with the ethnocratic state and its urban extensions. This has caused widespread alienation among Bedouin Arabs, and more recently it has contributed to mobilization either toward Palestinian nationalism, or (more commonly) Islamic traditionalism and fundamentalism.[67] To illustrate this process, in the 1999 elections the Arab party associated with the Islamic movement (The Arab List) received 64 percent of the Arab vote in the south, eight times higher than the vote for any other party, while the rest of the votes went mainly to parties supporting Palestinian nationalism.[68]

Currently, the legal status of the unrecognized localities is complex. Most are located in areas with no municipal jurisdiction and hence have no outline planning scheme. This has resulted in an absurd situation, where building activity is "impossible," because permits are granted only for areas with approved plans. In this way all construction — even in a settlement that has existed for centuries — is regarded "illegal." All this is part of a vicious cycle: municipal status is denied, no plans can be approved, and all buildings are deemed "illegal." Policymakers then refrain from granting recognition and municipal status because this may be seen as "folding to criminal elements who violate state laws." This, in turn, only forces Arabs to continue to build illegally.

The problem of unauthorized Arab building has caused growing tensions across the entire state of Israel. In 1987 the government adopted the recommendations of the Markowitz Report, which introduced an "interim classification" of "gray zones," in which de-facto recognition would be granted to thousands of unauthorized buildings in Arab settlements, while all permanent building activity in these zones would continue to be outlawed. Although thirteen years have passed since the adoption of these recommendations, this "temporary" policy is still in force, disallowing permanent (stone and wood) construction in unrecognized localities. The policy has been enforced with rigor, with some 1,800 home demolitions in the Arab sector since 1987.

But during this same period the Arab population has grown by about 53 percent, thus creating unbearable pressures on the typically small "temporary" homes.[69] The "gray zone" policy has thus forced the neglected villages to remain "frozen" as high-density clusters of unserviced, dilapidated dwellings — the poorest, most run-down communities in Israel.

Finally, a qualification is in order: the distress of the Arabs in the region does not only stem from Israel's planning policies. It is also part of a traumatic transition of a traditional, semi-nomad community into the modern, industrial age. This has been accompanied by geographic uprooting and monumental changes in community structure, family relations, and gender roles which have put in train a severe internal crisis.[70] This has been reflected in rising crime rates, poor economic and educational achievements, and paralyzing political divisions.[71] Still, the state's planning policies, with their emphasis on de-Arabizing the region, have played a major role in deepening this communal crisis. Let us turn now to several recent examples of such policies, and to the emergence of organized Arab resistance.

PERSISTING ETHNOCRATIC MYOPIA AND LOCAL RESISTANCE

A recent and telling example of Israel's ethnocratic dynamic was a March 2000 decision by the Israeli Minister of the Interior to expand the municipal boundaries of the Jewish suburban town of Omer, abutting Beer-Sheva to the east. The minister nearly doubled Omer's municipal area, annexing en-route several Arab "illegal" localities that accommodated some 4,000 people (refer to FIGURE 8.2). Omer's mayor defined these Arab residents as "trespassers," despite the documented history of some of these communities stretching back to the Ottoman period.

Following the annexation, Omer's mayor refused to extend the well-developed services of this wealthy town to its new Arab residents, claiming that they needed to leave the area, "according to government policy."[72] Local Arabs and some Jewish residents of Omer have since begun a political and legal campaign against the annexation, which may ultimately force the Arabs from their forefathers' land, or alternatively, lead to serious violence. This conflict, which has yet to be concluded, attests to the ongoing ethnocratic elements in the region's planning policies which still attempt to pressure the Bedouins to relocate into permanent towns.

Like Omer, most other councils whose municipal areas cover the unrecognized villages have ignored this population in their planning or service provision. These councils include Bnei Shimon, Merhavim, Har Hanegev, Arad, and Dimona, in all of which Bedouin-Arab residents have never had the right to vote. The Arab residents of these localities, many of whom inhabited the area before the Jewish councils were established, have thus become transparent. This denial of "right to the city" seriously taints the meaning of their local and Israeli citizenship.[73] It also now forms the platform for gradual "centrifugal" withdrawal from the state and its institutions.[74]

In another policy arena, various Israeli governments have periodically announced new efforts to "eliminate the Bedouin problem." In 1997 a new strategy was announced by the Netanyahu government, initiating a series of steps to increase pressure on Arabs to relocate into the seven planned towns. The strategy included measures to contain the "spread" of the scattered Arab population, prevent "further invasion into state land," and tighten the enforcement of the state's planning and construction laws.[75]

The three years following the introduction of these steps were also accompanied by the construction of new Jewish settlements in and around the Siyag region. These small suburban-like satellites were built according to a recent plan titled the "Hebron Ring," under which ten more Jewish settlements are planned for the next decade. The Hebron Ring plan expresses clearly, once more, the ethnocratic and discriminatory nature of Israeli policies in the region: Bedouin villages hosting more than 1,000 inhabitants are often asked by planners to relocate into the towns because they are "too small," while at the same time Jews are allowed to establish smaller localities.

Another discriminatory aspect of the policy is the link between land ownership and planning rights. The authorities deny planning and infrastructure for the Arabs in the region, officially due to land disputes with the states. However, land disputes also exist between Jewish localities and the states, but planning in these settlements proceeds normally, and communal facilities are duly provided.

This systematic inequality has not escaped the eyes of residents in the informal localities, who have increasingly mobilized and organized to counter the Israeli Judaization strategy. A number of "bottom-up" planning initiatives have recently been launched, aiming to influence the planning in Arab areas. In the mid-1990s locally drafted plans were prepared for a number of unrecognized villages (such as Darijjat, Al-Sayyad, and Umbattin). These were presented to the public as alternatives to state plans, and as an expression of new Arab assertiveness vis-à-vis the authorities. While none of these plans have been approved, they have managed to influence the public discourse, and they have raised consciousness in Jewish circles for the need to change the plight of the informal dwellers.

Another notable "bottom-up" initiative was the 1998 establishment of the Regional Council of Unrecognized Villages (known as al-Una), a voluntary body representing most villages. In December 1999 it submitted a plan for the recognition and long-term planning of 45 villages, as an amendment to the recently approved District Plan. Finally, an Alliance of Bedouin Organizations has been formed. It coordinates a range of self-help and NGO programs for community empowerment, education, and legal representation of the Beer-Sheva informal sector.

The Bedouin Arabs have also begun to launch "proactive" legal action. This has aimed to find cracks in the Israeli legal structure in order to oppose the one-sided policy of Judaization. Most notable here are two recent high-court challenges — one against the recent regional outline plan, on the grounds of unduly and unjustly ignoring Bedouin-Arab citizens, and the other against the decision to enlarge Omer's municipal boundaries and coercively annex rightless Bedouin communities. Both have received positive interim rulings by the Supreme Court, with a final decision expected in 2001.

The problems of implementing official plans for the area, together with the effect of grassroots pressure, recently began to have an influence on the Negev's planning authorities. These may be interpreted as the first signs of a weakening of Jewish ethnocratic rule. First, the metropolitan development plan of Beer-Sheva (adopted in 1998), in a significant symbolic move, defined the region as a "bi-national metropolis." While this definition has remained declaratory, it does grant some legitimacy of Arab residence in this urban region.

Further, in October 1999 the District Committee approved an amendment to District plans that added — for the first time in thirty years — three new Arab towns. This broke the "seven-towns-only" strategy which had strictly guided Israeli policy in the region for three decades, and had been the source of numerous conflicts and tensions. Based on initial reactions, however, the locations of these new settlements are problematic, since they still require the Bedouins to move from their existing villages. Hence, the new plan is not likely to receive wide support, except for its breaking of a formerly rigid planning concept.

The issue of informal settlement in the Beer-Sheva region has thus entered a new stage, with the old seven-town policy deeply discredited, but with no new policy in existence yet to direct near-urban settlement among the Bedouin Arabs. The ethnic map of the region is still determined by the contours laid down during the 1950s, with Jews concentrating in the region's central, northern, and western parts, while Arabs are mainly to the east. Even in the unlikely event that Israel recognizes most of the Arab "illegal" settlements, urban citizenship will continue to be unequal. The "right to the city" will continue to be hierarchical, with Jews enjoying greater access and powers. Similarly, various forms of informality, old and new, are likely to persist, albeit in a more controlled and orderly manner.

In the meantime, new forces have also began to play a role in shaping the Beer-Sheva urban area, most notably the gradual globalization and liberalization of Israel's economy and culture. In an indirect way the massive Russian immigration can be seen as part of this process, as well as the employment in the Negev of tens of thousands of immigrant laborers, mainly from Asia, Africa, and Eastern Europe. Several multinational companies have also located in the Beer-Sheva area, and some Israeli companies have been sold to international investors. But so far these structural economic and cultural changes have left little mark on the region's Arab population or geography, except by creating greater competition for the lower rungs of the labor market. Particularly, they have created no significant new openings or opportunities for the region's Arabs to break out of their structural marginalization. The liberalization and mobilization potential of the new urban order are thus yet to be realized in the ethnocratic city.

A CONCLUDING COMMENT

This chapter has attempted to initiate a discussion on urban informality in ethnocratic cities. In such settings the authorities generally use their power to classify, impose boundaries, and declare "illegality" for the purpose of marginalizing, excluding, and impeding the development of an entire ethnic sector. Ethnocratic cities, we have shown, exhibit a "clash of logics" between the forces of globalization, liberalization, and civic (nonethnic) urban order and a persisting ethnocratic drive for expansion, segregation, and control. Hence, the promise of the city as open, dynamic, and liberating is not fulfilled. An urban ethnocracy, instead, becomes just another arena where ethnonational dominance may be institutionalized and reproduced. However, urban dynamics, whether relating to capital flow or to the more open nature of urban governance, do provide some openings for minority resistance and are likely to generate challenges to the ethnocratic order.

Early signs of this process have begun to surface in the Beer-Sheva region. State policies of developing and Judaizing the Beer-Sheva region have focused their impact on the "unseen" parts of the emerging metropolis — the "unrecognized" and "informal" Bedouin-Arab localities. The persistence and growth of urban informality here thus stems from both Israel's strategy of using planning (or lack of) as an instrument of ethnic control, and from widespread Arab resistance.

Returning, finally, to the theoretical level, it is clear that to understand such complex systems as multiethnic and multinational cities, we need to broaden our analytical focus. We noted above that three of the most central debates in contemporary human sciences — urbanization, governance, and nationalism — have evolved in parallel, with little mutual engagement. We suggest that any credible conceptualization and empirical exploration of urbanizing regions in general, and ethnocratic cities in particular, urgently requires such engagement. Only by accounting for the "trialectical process" of economic, globalizing, and liberalizing urban forces, in their interactions with segregative, expansionist ethnic motives, can we begin to fathom urban change in ethnocratic societies. This includes the emergence and persistence of urban informality and its impact on the urban region. This chapter is a first, partial, effort in this direction. Far more work is obviously needed, both theoretically and empirically, to advance toward a theory of ethnocratic urban informality.

NOTES

1. For examples of this research, see N. AlSayyad, "Squatting and Culture: A Comparative Analysis of Informal Development in Latin America and the Middle East," *Habitat International* 17, no. 1 (1994), 33–44; E. Fernandes and A. Varley, "Law, the City, and Citizenship in Developing Countries: An Introduction," in D. Fernandes and A. Varley, eds., *Illegal Cities: Law and Urban Change in Developing Countries* (London: Zed Books, 1998), 3–17; A. Gilbert, *The Latin American City* (Los Angeles: The Latin America Bureau, 1998); A. Gilbert, "Financing Self-Help Housing: Evidence from Bogota, Colombia," *International Planning Studies* 5, no. 2 (June 2000), 165–90; and C. Pugh, "International Urban and Housing Policy: A Review of the 'Cambridge Studies,' 1989–1995," *Environment and Planning A* 29 (January 1997), 149–67.

2. These "engines" are presented here, for analytical purposes, as "ideal types." We fully recognize that in reality the forces that shape the urban order are more complex and intertwined.

3. P. Hall, *Cities of Tomorrow: An Intellectual History of Urban and Regional Planning* (London: Blackwell, 1988).

4. J. Friedmann, "Two Centuries of Planning Theory: An Overview," in S. Mandelbaum, L. Mazza, and R. Burchell, eds., *Explorations in Planning Theory* (New Brunswick, N.J.: Center for Urban Policy Research, 1996), 10–30; P. Marcuse and M. Van Kempen, eds., *Globalising Cities: A New Spatial Order?* (London: Blackwell, 1999); S. Sassen, *Globalization and Its Discontents* (New York: Wiley and Sons, 1998); and P. Taylor, "World Cities and Territorial States under Conditions of Contemporary Globalization," *Political Geography* 19, no. 1 (January 2000), 5–32.

5. Marcuse and Van Kempen, eds., *Globalising Cities*, 3–4.

6. R. Dahl, *Democracy and its Critics* (New Haven, Conn.: Yale University Press, 1989); and C. Lindblom, *Politics and Markets* (New York: Basic Books Publishers, 1977).

7. D. Held, *Models of Democracy* (London: Polity Press, 1990).

8. See J. Habermas, "The European Nation-State: Its Achievements and Its Limits. On the Past and Future of Sovereignty and Citizenship," in G. Balakrishnan, ed., *Mapping the Nation* (London: Verso, 1996), 281–94; and I. Katznelson, "Social Justice, Liberalism, and the City," in A. Morrifield and E. Swyngedouw, eds., *The Urbanization of Injustice* (London: Lawrence and Wishart, 1995), 45–64.

9. Katznelson, "Social Justice, Liberalism, and the City," 57.

10. B. Anderson, *Imagined Communities: Reflections on the Origin and Spread of Nationalism* (London: Verso, 1991); A. Smith, *Nations and Nationalism in a Global Era* (Cambridge, U.K.: Polity Press, 1995); E. Gellner, *Nations and Nationalism* (Oxford, U.K.: Basil Blackwell, 1983); R. Brubaker, *Nationalism Reframed: Nationhood and the National Question in the New Europe*

(London: Cambridge University Press, 1996); W. Connor, *Ethnonationalism: The Quest for Understanding* (Princeton, N.J.: Princeton University Press, 1994); L. Greenfield, *Nationalism: Five Roads to Modernity* (Cambridge, Mass.: Harvard University Press, 1992); M. Billig, *Banal Nationalism* (London: Sage, 1995); and M. Canovan, *Nationhood and Political Theory* (Cheltenham, U.K.: Edward Elgar, 1996).

11. P. Chatterjee, "Whose Imagined Community?" in Balakrishnan, ed., *Mapping the Nation*, 214–25; and J. Penrose, "The Limitation of Nationalist Democracy: The Treatment of Marginal Groups as a Measure of State Legitimacy," *Hagar: International Social Science Review* 1, no. 2 (2000), 33–62.

12. D. Sibley, *Geographies of Exclusion* (London: Routledge, 1996), 86, 107–8.

13. J. Comaroff, "Reflections on the Colonial State in South Africa and Elsewhere: Factions, Fragments, and Fictions," *Social Identities* 4, no. 3 (October 1998), 321–61; and J. Comaroff and J. Comaroff, "Naturing the Nation: Aliens, Apocalypse, and the Postcolonial State," *Hagar: International Social Science Review* 1, no. 1 (2000), 8–40; P. Jackson and J. Penrose, eds., *Constructions of Race, Place, and Nation* (London: UCL Press, 1993); M. Mann, "Democracy and Ethnic War," *Hagar: International Social Science Review* 1, no. 2 (2000), 115–34; I. Lustick, *Unsettled States, Disputed Lands* (Ithaca, N.Y.: Cornell University Press, 1993); and N. Yuval-Davis, *Gender and Nation* (London: Sage, 1996).

14. S. Bollen, *Urban Peace-Building in Divided Societies* (Boulder, Colo.: Westview Press, 1999); M. Benvenisti, *City of Stone: The Hidden History of Jerusalem* (Berkeley, Calif.: University of California Press, 1996); and M. Dumper, *The Politics of Jerusalem since 1967* (New York: University of Columbia Press, 1996).

15. R. Fincher and J. Jacobs, eds., *Cities of Difference* (New York: Guilford Press, 1998); L. Sandercock, *Toward Cosmopolis: Planning for Multicultural Cities and Regions* (London: Wiley and Sons, 1998).

16. N. AlSayyad, "Culture, Identity, and Urbanism in a Changing World: A Historical Perpsective on Colonialism, Nationalism, and Globalization," in M. Cohen, B. Ruble, J. Tulchin, and A. Garland, eds., *Preparing for the Urban Future: Global Pressures and Local Forces* (Baltimore, Md.: The Woodrow Wilson Center Press, 1996); and M. Castells, *The Power of Identity: Economy, Society, and Culture* (Oxford, U.K.: Blackwell, 1997).

17. Comaroff and Comaroff, "Naturing the Nation," 34–35.

18. The "trialectical" model presented in Figure 8.1 is a conceptual representation, denoting a departure from the classical binary Marxist logic of capital-labor antagonism. At the same time, our approach preserves the logic of structural analysis, which attempts to account for major loci of power and mobilization, be they three, four, or more. Hence, we recognize that the forces shaping the city may be conceptualized by any number of poles. The "trialectical process" is thus driven by dialectical tensions between opposing loci of power as a major force behind urban transformation. These tensions may simultaneously operate along the various axes created between poles. The trialectical representation hence represents a move beyond binarism, with a continued search for more complex, yet omnipresent, structures of power and meaning which determine the activity and mobilization of groups and individuals.

19. K. Dowding, D. Desmond, et al., "Regime Politics in London Local Government," *Urban Affairs Review* 34, no. 4 (March 1999), 515–45; G. Stoker and K. Mossberger, "Urban Regime Theory in Comparative Perspective," *Planning and Environment* C 12, no. 2 (May 1994), 185–212; and M. Lauria, *Restructuring Urban Regime Theory* (London: Sage, 1997).

20. AlSayyad, "Squatting and Culture."

21. O. Yiftachel, "Planning and Social Control: Exploring the Dark Side," *Journal of Planning Literature* 12, no. 4 (1998), 395–406.

22. Lustick, *Unsettled States, Disputed States*; and J. McGarry, "Demographic Engineering: The State-Directed Movement of Ethnic Groups as a Technique of Conflict Regulation," *Ethnic and Racial Studies* 21, no. 4 (July 1998), 613–38.

23. Connor, *Ethnonationalism*; and M. Mann, "The Dark Side of Democracy: The Modern Tradition of Ethnic and Political Cleansing," *New Left Review* 253 (June 1999), 18–45.

24. Sassen, *Globalization and Its Discontents*; and Y. Soysal, "Citizenship and Identity: Living in Diasporas in Post-War Europe?" *Ethnic and Racial Studies* 23, no. 1 (January 2000), 1–15.

25. For elaboration, see S. Hall, "Introduction: Who Needs Identity?" in S. Hall and P. du Gay, eds., *Questions of Cultural Identity* (London: Sage, 1997), 1–18; Castells, *The Power of Identity*; H. Lefebvre, *The Production of Space* (Oxford, U.K.: Blackwell, 1991); and D. Massey, *Space, Place, and Gender* (Oxford, U.K.: Blackwell, 1994).

26. For theoretical elaboration, see O. Yiftachel, "Social Control, Urban Planning, and Ethno-Class Relations: Mizrahi Jews in Israel's 'Development Towns,'" *International Journal of Urban and Regional Research* 24, no. 2 (June 2000), 417–34.

27. McGarry, "Demographic Engineering," 613–38.

28. Sassen, *Globalization and Its Discontents*; and Marcuse and Van Kempen, eds., *Globalising Cities*.

29. H. Lefebvre, "Philosophy of the City and Planning Ideology," in H. Lefebvre, ed., *Writings on Cities* (London: Blackwell, 1996), 97–101.

30. B. Flyvbjerg, "The Dark Side of Planning: Rationality and Realrationalitat," in S. Mandelbaum, L. Mazza, and R. Burchell, eds., *Explorations in Planning Theory* (New Brunswick, N.J.: Center for Urban Policy Research, 1996), 383–96; and O. Yiftachel, "The Dark Side of Modernism: Planning as Control of an Ethnic Minority," in S. Watson and K. Gibson, eds., *Postmodern Cities and Spaces* (Oxford, U.K.: Basil Blackwell, 1994), 216–42.

31. O. Yiftachel, "'Ethnocracy': The Politics of Judaizing Israel/Palestine," *Constellations* 6, no. 3 (September 1999), 364–90.

32. G. Shafir and Y. Peled, "Citizenship and Stratification in an Ethnic Democracy," *Ethnic and Racial Studies* 21, no. 3 (May 1998), 408–27.

33. A. Ghanem, "State and Minority in Israel: The Case of Ethnic State and the Predicament of Its Minority," *Ethnic and Racial Studies* 21, no. 3 (May 1998), 428–47; D. Kretzmer, *The Legal Status of the Arabs in Israel* (Boulder, Colo.: Westview Press, 1990); and R. Gavison, "Jewish and Democratic? A Rejoinder to the 'Ethnic Democracy' Debate," *Israel Studies* 4, no. 1 (Spring 1999), 44–72.

34. Yiftachel, "Ethnocracy"; and A. Kemp, *Talking Boundaries: The Making of Political Territory*

in Israel 1949–1957 (Tel Aviv: Tel Aviv University, 1997). The ethnocratic regime also has far-reaching repercussions in other areas (for example, gender relations and the environment), whose analysis will have to await another article. See O. Yiftachel and S. Kedar, "Landed Power: The Emergence of an Ethnocratic Land Regime in Israel," *Teorya Uvikkoret (Theory and Critique)* 19, no. 1 (Hebrew, 2000), 67–100.

35. O. Yiftachel, "Planning and Social Control."

36. Israel's First National Plan (1952), 3–7.

37. Y. Gradus, "The Emergence of Regionalism in a Centralized System: The Case of Israel," *Environment and Planning D: Society and Space* 2, no. 1 (1984), 87–100.

38. Mapai conference, quoted in Y. Weitz, *The Struggle for the Land* (Tel Aviv: Tabersky (Hebrew), 1950), 367.

39. R. Khamaisi, *Planning and Housing among the Arabs in Israel* (Tel Aviv: International Center for Middle East Peace, 1990).

40. See, for example, the plan for Akko (1988); Lod (1999); or the Greater Jerusalem strategy (1997).

41. AlSayyad, "Culture, Identity, and Urbanism in a Changing World"; and Gradus, "The Emergence of Regionalism in a Centralized System."

42. Y. Gradus and E. Stern, "Changing Strategies of Development: Toward a Regiopolis in the Negev Desert," *Journal of the American Planning Association* 46, no. 4 (October 1980), 410–23.

43. Y. Gradus, "Beer-Sheva — Capital of the Negev Desert," in Y. Golani, S. Eldor, and M. Garon, eds., *Planning and Housing in Israel in the Wake of Rapid Changes* (Jerusalem: The Ministry of the Interior, 1993), 251–65.

44. Y. Gradus and R. Livnon, *Industry in the Negev: Processes, Structure, and Location* (Beer Sheva, Israel: Negev Development Authority, 1998).

45. Gradus and Livnon, *Industry in the Negev*; and I. Abu-Saad and H. Lithwick, *An Urban Development Strategy for the Negev's Bedouin Community* (Beer Sheva, Israel: Negev Center for Regional Development and the Center for Bedouin Culture, 2000).

46. Abu-Saad and Lithwick, *An Urban Development Strategy for the Negev's Bedouin Community.*

47. I. Ben-David, *Feud in the Negev: The Land-Conflict Between the Bedouin and the State* (Beit Berel, Israel: Center for the Research of Arab Society, 1995).

48. G. Falah, "The Development of Planned Bedouin Resettlement in Israel, 1964–82: Evaluation and Characteristics," *Geoforum* 14 (1983), 311–23.

49. Gradus, "The Emergence of Regionalism in a Centralized System," 87–100; A. Meir, *When Nomadism Ends: The Israeli Bedouin of the Negev* (Boulder, Colo.: Westview, 1997); and Yiftachel, "Planning and Social Control," 395–406.

50. For details, see Ben David, *Feud in the Negev*; S. Kedar, "Minority Time, Majority Time: Land, Nation, and the Law of Adverse Possession in Israel," *Iyyunei Mishpat* 21, no. 3 (1998), 665–746; and I. Lustick, *Arabs in the Jewish State: Israel's Control over a National Minority* (Austin, Texas: University of Texas Press, 1980).

51. S. Kedar, "Minority Time, Majority Time."

52. A. Babai, "The State of the Bedouin in Israel," *Karka* 23 (1997), 83–74.

53. Minutes of meeting with A. Burg, Chairman of Israeli Knesset, December 6, 1997.

54. Such as *Al Hawashla vs. State of Israel* (1983) and *Al Qaleb vs. Ben-Gurion University* (1984).

55. R. Shamir, "Suspended in Space: Bedouins under the Law of Israel," in D. Guttwein and M. Mautner, eds., *Law and History* (Jerusalem: Shazar Center for Israeli History, 1997), 473–96.

56. Babai, "The State of the Bedouin in Israel"; Ben-David, *Feud in the Negev*; and Shamir, "Suspended in Space."

57. Mana Commission, 1997.

58. O. Yiftachel, "The Internal Frontier: The Territorial Control of Ethnic Minorities," *Regional Studies* 30, no. 5 (August 1996), 493–508.

59. T. Fenster, "Gender and Space: Aspects of Planning and Development in the Significance in Planning and Development," *Research of the Geography of Eretz Yisrael* 16 (1998), 77–97.

60. Knesset speech on August 5, 1959.

61. Y. Boymel, "Israel's Policy towards the Arab Minority, 1958–1968," Ph.D. dissertation, Haifa University, Department of Middle East History, 2000; and Falah, "The Development of Planned Beduin Resettlement in Israel."

62. A. Meir, "Nomads and the State: The Spatial Dynamics of Centrifugal and Centripetal Forces among the Israeli Negev Bedouin," *Political Geography Quarterly* 6 (1988), 251–70.

63. Meir, *When Nomadism Ends.*

64. T. Fenster, "Settlement Planning and Participation Under Principles of Pluralism," *Progress in Planning* 39, no. 3 (1993), 169–242; and Abu-Saad and Lithwick, *An Urban Development Strategy for the Negev's Bedouin Community.*

65. Negev Center, *Statistical Yearbook of the Negev* (Beer Sheva, Israel: Negev Center for Regional Development, 1999).

66. Negev Center, *Statistical Yearbook of the Negev.*

67. I. Abu-Saad and H. Lithwick, *A Way Ahead: A Development Plan for the Bedouin Towns in the Negev* (Beer-Sheva, Israel: The Center for Bedouin Studies, 2000).

68. Negev Center, *Statistical Yearbook of the Negev.*

69. Ibid.

70. Fenster, "Gender and Space"; and Meir, *When Nomadism Ends.*

71. I. Abu-Saad, "Minority Higher Education in an Ethnic Periphery: The Bedouin Arabs," in O. Yiftachel and A. Meir, eds., *Ethnic Frontiers and Peripheries* (Boulder, Colo.: Westview Press, 1998), 269–86; Falah, "The Development of Planned Bedouin Resettlement in Israel"; and Abu-Saad and Lithwick, *An Urban Development Strategy for the Negev's Bedouin Community.*

72. *Kol Hanegev* (July 11, 2000).

73. Lefebvre, "Philosophy of the City and Planning Ideology," 97–101.

74. Meir, *When Nomadism Ends.*

75. *Haaretz* (September 2, 1997).

PART III

TRANSNATIONAL INTERROGATION

9

Informality of Housing Production at the Urban-Rural Interface: The "Not So Strange Case" of the Texas *Colonias*

Peter M. Ward

Originally I had planned to subtitle this paper "The Strange Case of the Texas *Colonias*," after a generic Sherlock Holmes story. However, the more I thought about it, and the more my work has examined informally produced housing in the United States at large, the less strange the phenomenon has appeared. In fact, what I am now coming to call "quasi-formal homestead subdivisions" (a.k.a. *colonias*) are not an exotic species of housing production found exclusively in the U.S.-Mexico border region; they are a much more widely distributed and segregated feature of the peri-urban landscape.[1] Moreover, *colonia*-type housing production in the United States — as elsewhere in the world — is invariably highly rational given prevailing socioeconomic constraints that prevent people from homesteading normally. In short, there is little about *colonias* that is "strange," or even surprising. The only strange thing, perhaps, is that the phenomenon has not been more widely recognized. Extending the level of public understanding of such housing trends in the United States is a drum I have been beating for the past year or two — hence, my contribution to this anthology.

I will return to the ability to generalize about the *colonia* phenomenon shortly, but first I would like to underscore two points relating to the issues discussed at the originating symposium and throughout this volume. One is how we can learn from less developed contexts about informality in our own backyards. The other is how informality in certain transnational contexts may reproduce inequality and social stratification patterns.

URBAN INFORMALITY: LEARNING FROM ELSEWHERE

In highly developed nations there are many socioeconomic activities that replicate processes usually associated with underdevelopment. This has been particularly true since deregulation has rolled back state control and provoked or revealed practices that were previously provided formally—or if they were formerly illegal, were obscured or underground. Moreover, much of the understanding and awareness of those processes has come from researchers such as those represented in this volume, whose primary interests have been in the so-called Third World, but whose work has now begun to inform awareness about these new or previously hidden practices in the First and (former) Second Worlds.

For example, much of what is now known about sweatshop activities, outworking, and formal-informal contracting within flexible production regimes in U.S. metropolitan areas has come directly from analysts who have worked in less developed countries and have now brought their experience back home. Sometimes, too, it has come from local researchers picking up on ideas from their development-specialist colleagues.[2] The same applies in our understanding of social mobilization. In the 1970s research in this area eschewed class-based organization and rationality in favor of social movements forged around struggles for the means of collective consumption. Then in the following decade it embraced more generalized struggles for urban services, the defense of community, and the assertion of popular and other cultures or citizen rights.[3] Today, however, the huge volume of literature on urban social movements and new social movements around the world is directly informing our understanding of local politics, community and grassroots organization, and coalition building in the United States.[4] A third example involves self-help housing. A traditional form of rural housing production worldwide, it emerged periodically during crises of capitalism in Germany, the United Kingdom, and the United States during the nineteenth and twentieth centuries.[5] But until research intensified about the nature and rationality of self-help in less developed contexts, few were able to recognize its importance in practices back home. I propose to develop this point below.

In part, of course, this relative blindness to the importance of self-help reflects the particular social construction of informality and urban settlement in the United States. Housing practices here are heavily vested in a legal system that privileges full property titles and compliance with codes and standards as prerequisites to both successful market functioning and state intervention through planning, taxation, etc. But legal systems vary throughout the world in the extent to which they privilege private property or common property, individual rights versus collective rights, etc.[6] Here is not the place to engage in a review of law, urbanization, and planning in less developed countries and how these factors are changing today.[7] Suffice it to say that over the past thirty years or so there has been an important shift away from heavily centralized and doctrinal traditions of legal scholarship in urban development, toward a more pragmatic "law and development" approach, in which social-science considerations have begun to play a role in establishing legal practices and precedents.[8] Although British-colonial common-law traditions have proven highly resistant and ill equipped to make this transition, even these bastions are today beginning to break down.[9] Whether conditions in the United States will also become more flexible is an important question that goes to the heart of how public policy will respond to informality in the future. As one author argues cogently, the U.S. legal system is not yet ready to address the concept of informality sensibly; instead, it sees informality as a fundamental abuse of the law.[10] Clearly, the idea of informal and formal markets coexisting alongside each other, with flows and interactions between them, is not one that sits comfortably in the United States. Nor, therefore, does the idea of upgrading and progressive convergence toward code compliance — what Larson refers to as "progressive realization" of compliance obligations.[11]

TRANSNATIONAL AND TRANSBORDER INFORMALITY: REPRODUCING INEQUALITY?

Personally, I am not particularly impressed by contemporary globalization theory, especially when it repeats the gross generalizations of dependency theorists from thirty years ago. Nevertheless, there is no doubt that both the speed and extent of global communications and the greater physical mobility of people have enhanced the potential for transfer of informal practices to other contexts. Transnational migration is especially important today in generating cultural and economic exchanges and flows. Certain notorious cases spring to mind: for example, the transfer of gangland practices from Hispanics in New York and Los Angeles to low-income neighborhoods in Mexico or Central America, as young men are "repatriated" (in the case of undocumented immigrants or convicted noncitizen felons), or when their parents simply send them "home" in the often vain hope that their grandparents will sort them out.[12]

Yet, while these are highly publicized cases, they are also relatively superficial. More profound are the new forms of informality that are emerging between social groups, or within labor market niches within society, thereby intensifying the segmentation of people in the same socioeconomic class. Most common are the cases of particular labor groups who are exploited and paid below-statutory wages and/or are forced to live in unacceptably poor conditions by virtue of their informality (illegal status). This is not new, of course; but what is new in an emerging transnational family context is that *within* families one may find different levels of informality that seriously erode the life chances of particular individuals, exposing them to higher levels of risk than their siblings or partners. For example, Mexican transnational families — even nuclear ones — in the United States may combine citizens, legal residents, and undocumented household members under the same roof. This can intensify problems resulting from differential power relations within the family — where, say, a male head of household may possess the absolute security of citizenship, while his wife, who is undocumented, may be powerless and vulnerable.[13] Thus, inequalities may be intensified where gender and immigration status intersect, invariably exposing women and girls to greater vulnerability. Structurally, too, laws such as the Illegal Immigration Reform and Immigrant Responsibility Act (IIRRA) and Welfare Reform (both of which came into effect in 1996) now demand proof of full citizenship. Thus, access to work and social benefits are also stratified by citizenship and residency status.

Similarly, in border regions, where a certain socioeconomic and cultural osmosis is typical, inequalities may be intensified by a tightening of restrictions on mobility. The U.S.-Mexico border region, with its long tradition of labor mobility back and forth, is a case in point. Here tighter control on border crossing has polarized relations within labor groups — sometimes within a single family. For example, some residents of Mexican border cities have visas or citizenship status that allow them free movement and full working rights in the United States. Meanwhile, others with the *mica* (a kind of local cross-border pass) have mobility, but no right to work. Thus, when *mica* holders use their mobility status to work illegally in the United States, they must take care to vary their crossing routes and times to reduce the chances of being discovered by observant INS officials.[14] Finally, of course, illegal workers must run a gauntlet of border patrols, whose greater numbers now make crossing increasingly difficult, expensive, and dangerous.[15] The point here is that within cross-border and transnational contexts, vulnerability is often tied to different levels of informality. Moreover, it seems likely that vulnerability increases with greater transhumance and when receiving countries tighten benefits tied to citizenship.

MISCONSTRUING URBAN INFORMALITY: THE TEXAS CASE

The idea of learning from informal practices in the Third World in the areas of employment, housing, community organization, and housing production, to name just a few, has become an important feature of my recent work in Texas.[16] Arriving at the University of Texas in 1991, I was surprised to find that unserviced *colonias* were legion in the state, especially in the border region. Estimates at the time put their number at around 1,300 settlements, housing 350,000 people. My arrival coincided both with a legislative and public-policy "wake-up call" about such housing areas and the first serious attempts at public intervention. But

Texas policymakers appeared at the time to be caught in a time warp, regarding these settlements as rural, or as pathological aberrations visited upon urban areas. The settlements were seen as foci of vice, crime, indigence, and illegal-immigrant residence that above all presented a major public-health problem. Furthermore, the very name used to describe them, *colonia* (Spanish for "neighborhood"), underscored the view that they were Mexican in origin and local to the border (something that has greatly retarded the capacity of policymakers to "see" *colonia*-type development elsewhere in the state).

Described thus, many readers may experience the same sense of *déjà vu* I did, recalling, for example, the erroneous 1960s constructions of urban marginality debunked by Perlman and others.[17] Equally troubling, however, was the familiar orientation of the policy solutions proposed: outlaw and criminalize the continuation of such development practices; prevent the growth of new settlements; generate funding for basic infrastructure to reduce health risks; and introduce social services. That the state should seek to provide infrastructure is not troubling, of course — both social and physical infrastructure are urgently needed and solicited by residents. But the authorities' attitude toward providing it was often paternalistic and patronizing. Thus, instead of recognizing the latent social capital of such communities, they saw them instead as highly welfare dependent, and as an aberration to be fixed with top-down action and resources and through one-off "task forces" and "strike forces." What they did not see was that such developments were a rational response to the statewide lack of housing for the working poor in a regional economy predicated on low wages. In short, state policymakers were treating the symptoms and not the causes.

Invited to join one such task force, I sought to persuade my colleagues that we might learn from Mexico's twenty years of public-policy development toward similar areas, rather than seek to reinvent the wheel. However, my proposal fell upon deaf ears, in part because of Texas chauvinism (Texas claims to be a "whole other country," after all), but also because of the entrenched engineering mentality among public-policy officials and within the construction industry — i.e., among those who would benefit most from providing traditional infrastructure. Above all, *colonias* were not seen as a housing problem in structural terms, but as a public-health issue, itself the product of dysfunctional urbanization among Mexican Americans. The policy solution was therefore to promote regulations to prevent the proliferation of *colonias* in the future, and to engage in "strike-force" interventions to bring existing unserviced settlements up to code.

A number of studies during the 1990s offered a more accurate understanding of the true nature of *colonia* populations, however. For example, they showed that while *colonia* populations were Spanish speaking and often Mexican born, they invariably comprised legal residents and citizens. Furthermore, they showed that while *colonias* did house many low-income people with relatively high levels of unemployment, these were the working poor, and their aspirations as home-steaders were legitimate. Nevertheless, there remained an apparent resistance to looking south to Mexico and Latin America for possible insights about the nature of the housing production process in such settlements. Likewise, there was a resistance to consider the successful models for public-policy intervention developed there: regularization of land title, servicing priorities, self-help building supports, community-development programs and mutual aid, and appropriate institutional arrangements and programs.

Knowing that sister cities along the Texas-Mexico border enjoy close working relations with each other, I set about constructing a comparative research project that would analyze housing production, infrastructure, and public policy across some twenty settlements in three paired cities: Ciudad Juárez–El Paso, the two Laredos, and Matamoros-Brownsville. I hoped that these case studies might create a demonstration effect, and that by analyzing *colonia* housing production in a comparative perspective, I might help officials gain insight about the process — and possible policy solutions. The resulting study, Colonias *and Public Policy in Texas and Mexico: Urbanization by Stealth*, was targeted at the biennial 1999 and 2001 legislative sessions. It identified several areas of policy reform, some of which are gradually being implemented.[18] A later study focused on the low densities and poor land-market performance of fifteen additional *colonias* statewide.[19] That second study was targeted specifically at shaping policy in the 2001 and 2003 legislative sessions.[20] These two studies are now in the public domain, and it is not my intention to dwell further on their methodology and findings. Instead, the analysis that follows seeks to identify how informality is alive and well in contemporary urbanization in Texas, and to suggest that we should start looking for quasi-formal homestead subdivisions (a.k.a. *colonias*) beyond the border, and probably far beyond Texas.

COLONIAS: A NOT SO STRANGE CASE

Colonias subdivisions first began to gain notice in Texas in the poorest counties along the border with Mexico. Located in the peri-urban fringe — either within the extra-territorial jurisdiction (ETJ) of a city or, more usually, just beyond it[21] — they are "hidden" within the weakly empowered and poorly resourced jurisdiction of counties.[22] They comprise unserviced or poorly serviced settlements in which low-income homesteaders may buy lots on which to place either trailer-type dwellings or more upmarket and less portable forms usually called "manufactured homes." In some cases, too, families build homes on site, either through self-help or by working with kinsmen and local contractors to construct permanent dwellings on concrete-slab foundations. But even in such cases of "consolidated" homes, the homesteading process may begin with life in a shack, camper, or second-hand trailer until resources allow investment in a more permanent form of housing. This mirrors, if it does not exactly resemble, the "upgrading" process in irregular settlements in less developed countries.

In Texas, as I have already observed, *colonias* are not a small-scale phenomenon. According to the Texas Water Development Board, the principal agency mandated to provide them with water and wastewater service, there are today approximately 1,500–1,600 such settlements housing more than 400,000 people (see FIGURE 9.1). In fact, the board's and my own data indicate that many similar homestead subdivisions that have yet to be counted exist elsewhere in Texas. Thus, estimates of the phenomenon are likely to grow, as *colonias* are more systematically identified. Indeed, counties throughout Texas are beginning to realize that they confront a common set of problems presented by what they see as unregulated substandard subdivisions. To date, however, such developments have gone almost entirely unstudied — a condition I am urging that we seek to rectify.[23]

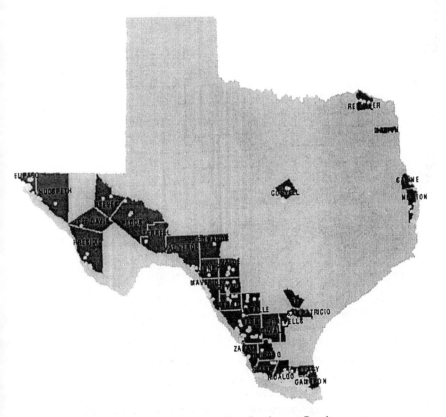

Figure 9.1. Map of *colonias* identified by the Texas Water Development Board.
Source: Texas Water Development Board Website: http://www.twdb.state.tx.us/colonias/tx_col.gif.

In most cases the developments are springing up because they offer the only affordable homestead for low-income households. In this context, low-income refers to households earning generally between $12,000–$25,000 a year — although many households actually earn considerably less, often only half that amount. Certainly, very few earn much more (see FIGURE 9.2). Thus, such settlements are most likely to be found in low-income labor-market areas, and in those regions experiencing wage and labor polarization between highly paid professional or industrial workers and low-paid service-sector employees. Living in cities with higher housing costs, these families cannot aspire to home ownership and

DIMENSIONS OF ANALYSIS AND COMPARISON	COLONIA RESIDENTS	
Total cases (N)		(261)
Characteristics		
Ethnicity		
Anglo	5%	(13)
Mexican born	67%	(166)
Mexican American	27%	(66)
Years in U.S. (Mexicans)	18.3 years	
Average household size	4.531	
Total household income		
<$600 per month	14%	(36)
$600–$1,000	32%	(79)
$1,001–$1,600	29%	(73)
$1,601–$2,500	14%	(34)
>$2,500	11%[1]	(26)
Lot purchase: year, lot size, & real prices at 1999 values		
When bought?		
Pre-1980	20%	(51)
1981–1990	33%	(857)
1991–1999	47%	(120)
Average cost of lot[2]	$13,281	
Size of lot[3]	15,482 sq.ft.	
Cost per sq.ft.[4]	$1.09	
Principal reason for original lot purchase?[5]		
As a home in long term	49%	(169)
To own property	4.9%	(17)
As an investment	4.9%	(17)
An inheritance for kids	9%	(31)
Good deal/opportunity	8%	(26)
Other reasons[6]	19%	(64)

Figure 9.2. Absentee lot owners and *colonia* residents in Texas compared. (Continued on next page.)

Source: P. Ward in collaboration with R. Stevenson and A. Stuesse, "Residential Land Market Dynamics, Absentee Lot Owners, and Densification Policies for Texas Colonias," policy report, LBJ School of Public Affairs, University of Texas, Austin, 2000.

DIMENSIONS OF ANALYSIS AND COMPARISON	COLONIA RESIDENTS	
Housing conditions		
Current tenure		
Own	ALL[7]	
Renter		
Previous tenure		
Own	25%	(58)
Renter	60%	(138)
Sharer (kin)	13%	(29)
Number of bedrooms now	2.816	

1. Of whom 18 percent had a total income of over $50,000.
2. Trimmed mean value.
3. Trimmed mean value. Median is 13,250 sq.ft. Lots in many *colonias* vary between 1/8, 1/4 and 1/2 acre in size (5,445, 10,890 and 21,780 sq.ft.).
4. Trimmed mean value.
5. These numbers are greater than the sample size since they are cumulative responses for first and second responses, etc.
6. Other reasons were wide ranging. "To be close to family" was especially important.
7. The survey was targeted only at owners. Renting is prohibited, but there is a modest level of sharing lots/homes with kin. Fourteen percent of lot owners interviewed had kin sharing on their lot, 41 percent of whom had some co-ownership rights to the lot.

Note: Dollars and cents were converted to constant (1984) values and have been raised to 1999 equivalents in the table.
NA = Not Applicable

must live at the lower end of the rental-housing market, whether in apartments or trailer parks. Yet many wish to become homesteaders, because they recognize the advantages of moving out of trailer-park accommodations in which they have no equity, and into subdivisions (albeit poorly serviced) where they can own property and — they hope — improve its value through mutual aid and self-help efforts.

Colonias are not homogeneous, but vary markedly in a number of key respects. Among these are size, layout, mode of development, housing type and mix, lot dimensions, soil and vegetation, lot occupancy rates, level of servicing, development prospects, land-market turnover, ethnic composition, income level, and relative poverty. Thus, in Texas there is no "typical" *colonia*, only a range of modalities that vary significantly between counties (see FIGURES 9.3, 9.4). For example, in some border counties, such as Hidalgo, Starr, and Zavala, the norm is for a large number of small and very small *colonias* (comprising less than 80 and 40 lots, respectively), often with relatively small individual lot sizes. Meanwhile, in other counties, such as El Paso, Valverde, and San Patricio, *colonias* tend to house many more families and have larger average lot sizes. In the overall database used in my 2000 study, although the two smaller settlement sizes comprised 70 percent of all 1,381 *colonias* analyzed, they housed less than 30 percent of the total population. In contrast, very large settlements (i.e., those with more than 300 lots) housed 35 percent of all *colonia* residents.[24]

Although the size of these settlements is generally much smaller than those found in less developed countries (which often run from several hundred to several thousand lots), they are akin to "irregular" settlements in many other respects and have similar reasons for being: a low-wage economy; a rising demand for housing; a lack of state housing-supply systems capable of meeting demand; and a private sector uninterested in or unable to produce housing at levels people can afford. However, unlike their irregular settlement cousins elsewhere, *colonias* rarely illegally occupy land. Nevertheless, many aspects of their production might be regarded as "quasi-formal."

INFORMALITY IN THE PROCESS OF LAND PRODUCTION AND OCCUPATION

In order to enter the housing market, prospective homesteaders must seek low-cost alternatives and use their "sweat equity" to self-build and self-finance their homes.[25] In less developed countries it is the illegality of the land-development process and the lack of services that reduce the market price to affordable levels.[26] In Texas, however, the method of land acquisition is almost always legal, and it is the unserviced nature and poor location of *colonias* that lowers the cost.

A second element of affordability involves informal financing outside of regular mortgage and credit markets. In the case of Texas *colonias* this is articulated by developers who sell off land without services and infrastructure under a process called Contract for Deed.[27] Contract for Deed is quite commonplace throughout the United States. Often known as a "poor man's mortgage," it is a way to finance a

COLONIA SIZE	TOTAL NUMBER OF *COLONIAS*	PERCENT OF TOTAL *COLONIAS*	NUMBER AND PERCENT OF ALL *COLONIA* RESIDENTS	
Very small (< 40 lots)*	629	45.6	49,768	(12.9)
Small/medium (41–80 lots)	356	25.8	60,965	(15.8)
Medium (81–150 lots)	193	14.0	67,399	(17.4)
Large (151–300 lots)	112	8.1	68,261	(17.6)
Very large (> 300 lots)	91	6.6	136,360	(35.2)
Total	1381	100.1	386,982	(98.9)

* Includes some 144 cases, most of which fall into the "small" category, comprising *colonias* registered as having less than 10 lots.

Figure 9.3. Distribution of *colonias* by size.

Source: P. Ward in collaboration with R. Stevenson and A. Stuesse, Residential Land Market Dynamics, Absentee Lot Owners, and Densification Policies for Texas Colonias, policy report, LBJ School of Public Affairs, University of Texas, Austin, 2000, 8. Calculated from data contained in LBJ School of Public Affairs, Colonia Housing and Infrastructure, Volume 2, Water and Wastewater (1997), and also based on the Texas Water Development Board database.

real estate purchase if one cannot afford a down payment, or if one's income does not qualify for more conventional methods.[28] As such, it is a legal, yet highly flexible mechanism for the conveyance of real estate, or any other commodity, in which full

COUNTY	PERCENT AND NUMBER OF VERY SMALL COLONIAS (<40 LOTS)	PERCENT AND NUMBER OF SMALL/ MEDIUM COLONIAS (41–80 LOTS)	PERCENT AND NUMBER OF MEDIUM COLONIAS (81–150 LOTS)	PERCENT AND NUMBER OF LARGE COLONIAS (151–300 LOTS)	PERCENT AND NUMBER OF VERY LARGE COLONIAS (>300 LOTS)	TOTAL PERCENT AND NUMBER OF ALL TEXAS COLONIAS [PERCENT TOTAL COLONIA POPULATION REPRESENTED]
Cameron	33.3 (35)	32.4 (34)	16.2 (17)	8.6 (9)	9.5 (10)	105 7.6 [9.9]
Coryell	38.5 (5)	38.5 (5)	15.4 (2)	7.7 (1)	—	13 0.9 [0.1]
El Paso	24.8 (36)	26.2 (38)	22.1 (32)	15.9 (23)	11.0 (16)	145 10.5 [18.8]
Hidalgo	57.5 (438)	24.5 (187)	10.9 (83)	5.2 (40)	1.8 (14)	762 55.2 [35.6]
Jim Wells	25.0 (4)	37.5 (6)	25.0 (4)	6.3 (1)	6.3 (1)	16 1.2 [0.1]
Maverick	28.6 (12)	23.8 (10)	14.3 (6)	14.3 (6)	19.5 (8)	42 3.0 [3.6]
San Patricio	11.1 (2)	22.2 (4)	22.2 (4)	16.7 (3)	27.8 (5)	18 1.3 [2.8]
Starr	37.1 (46)	37.9 (47)	16.1 (20)	4.0 (5)	4.4 (6)	124 9.0 [8.9]
Val Verde	27.3 (3)	9.1 (1)	9.1 (1)	36.4 (4)	18.2 (2)	11 0.8 [0.1]
Webb	32.6 (14)	14.0 (6)	27.9 (12)	11.6 (5)	14.0 (6)	43 3.1 [5.3]
Zavala	50.0 (6)	16.7 (2)	—	8.3 (1)	25.0 (3)	12 0.9 [1.0]
Total	601	340	181	98	71	1291 93.5 [86.2]

Figure 9.4. Distribution of *colonias* by county, size, and population.

Source: P. Ward in collaboration with R. Stevenson and A. Stuesse, Residential Land Market Dynamics, Absentee Lot Owners, and Densification Policies for Texas Colonias, *policy report, LBJ School of Public Affairs, University of Texas, Austin, 2000, 9. Based upon Texas Water Development Board Database.*

ownership (title) is not transferred until the price has been paid in full. In the realm of real estate transactions it is a particularly profitable form of seller financing.

Most *colonia* lots in Texas sold in the early 1980s for between $7,000–$8,000 (around $11,000–$12,500 at 1998 prices). According to the Contract for Deed for Sale process, upon signing the contract the buyer pays the seller a down payment which may vary from "whatever the buyer has in his pocket at that moment" — say, $25 — to as much as 10–20 percent of the total price.[29] Thereafter, the purchaser makes a low, fixed, monthly payment, usually in the range of $80–$120, until he has retired the debt. In this way the total cost of a land purchase may be spread over a period of between five and ten years, with the possibility at any time to make a "balloon" payment to clear the debt. As an all-inclusive legal document for property development, financing, and transfer of title, Contract for Deed has much to commend it, since transaction and closing costs are minimal or nonexistent. However, the practice has been widely abused in Texas, partly because such contracts have been written in English and are poorly understood by purchasers, and because they offer no consumer protection. Most importantly, the buyer can lose his entire stake if he fails to meet a single payment. Legislation in 1995 largely remedied this, but only in the border region.

Developers quite deliberately create new *colonias* beyond the urban fringe in areas of county jurisdiction where there is little or no land-use and planning regulation. City authorities, who are normally better endowed, will resist such unregulated and unserviced development. But historically, there has been a lack of regulation in areas just beyond the city's urban limit or its extra-territorial jurisdiction (ETJ). Lots there may be sold off in a piecemeal fashion, often spreading households across the whole of a *colonia*, as developers seek to give the impression of development over a wider area. The broadcast approach (rather than block-by-block), large lots, lack of services, and relative security of a legal land-development process combine to create a pattern of development with large vacant areas and very low densities.

Such a form of development is also not without conflicts over title, making "regularization" a nascent policy-development issue in Texas — although not one of anywhere near the scale present in Latin American countries, where almost all land capture is illegal in one form or another.[30] Land disputes in Texas *colonias* are especially common where a developer may allocate lots by "metes and bounds," so that actual lot boundaries are imprecise. As a result, purchasers may unwittingly occupy each other's lots, making subsequent regularization necessary (usually through informal dispute resolution and lot "swaps"). Similarly, multiple lot sales under Contract for Deed, where the original purchaser has defaulted, sometimes lead to counterclaims and conflict (even if such claims are not likely to be upheld under Contract for Deed). Furthermore, unscrupulous land developers may sometimes sell the same lot several times over, and because people do not occupy their lot from outset, there is little to prevent them from doing so. It may only be much later that the fraud is discovered.

The relative legality embodied in creating quasi-formal homestead subdivisions means that it is not imperative to occupy one's lot from the outset. Some people wait until they have paid for a lot in full and have a deed in hand before daring to settle there. Others may want basic services to be installed. And most will want to save up enough money to place a trailer or manufactured home on site. Since new trailers start around $18,000 (although second-hand ones come much cheaper), it is therefore usual for a considerable time to elapse between lot purchase and occupancy.

These two processes — spotty land development and slow take-up of occupancy — have led to high levels of "absentee" lot ownership, so much so that in some settlements more than half of all lots are vacant. These absentee lot owners were the focus of a recent study that revealed that on average between one-quarter and one-sixth of all lots in many mid-sized and large Texas settlements may be unoccupied. Thus, *colonias* are sold through, but not built through. Together with the large average lot sizes (usually between one-eighth [minimum] and one-half an acre or more) and the legal requirement that these be occupied by only a single family, such absentee conditions make for very low housing densities. Ten to twelve persons per acre is not an uncommon level — several times lower than the norm for Mexican settlements.

JURSIDICTIONAL "SOFTNESS" AND INFORMALITY

Counties have little jurisdictional power in Texas, and their relative weakness makes them ripe for quasi-formal residential development. In addition to this virtual lack of regulation, development of *colonias* on county land may benefit from the fact that developers are in cahoots with county commissioners and judges. Indeed, in at least one case we studied the developer was a judge! This latter case, at least, offers direct parallels with the all-too-familiar "softness" and corruption among local officials in less developed countries.[31] I raise this issue here only to make the point that informality and softness occur in local government in the United States as well as overseas, and it needs to be factored into any analysis of urban informality in a transnational perspective.

But unlike Mexico, where local municipalities are akin to cities in the powers with which they are charged and the responsibilities for servicing that they have (whether they fulfill them or not), county governments and their equivalents in the United States are often weak. That weakness and lack of effective and fiscal empowerment contributes to informality, not just in the land-development process, but also in the failure to provide essential services. This, in turn, makes for informality in procuring those services.

INFORMALITY OF PHYSICAL INFRASTRUCTURE AND SERVICES

As is the case in informal self-help more generally, in Texas it is the lack of services that cheapens the land-acquisition process, even though those services have to be obtained somehow and doing so informally may end up being considerably more expensive.[32] Most basic services in the United States are provided privately, with state and local regulation occurring through planning ordinances and ensuring minimum code compliance. In Texas counties, this regulation is less strict, and the fiscal resources for local-government provision (road improvements, etc.) are minimal. Given that there is no need to occupy one's lot from the outset, one does not see the sort of "pirate" electricity hookups and informal provision common in less developed countries.

Power and Cabling. Most services are provided under contract — electricity being the first to be installed, along with TV cable, phone lines, etc. Indeed, private companies are often quite willing to lay in the power and service lines above or below ground to large *colonias* especially, sometimes before generalized occupancy has occurred, but certainly before roads are paved and other major infrastructure is in place. This has two benefits: first, it reduces the eventual costs of installation by obviating later digging and repaving costs; second, and more importantly, it "locks in" that particular service provider to that particular community, extending its market and reducing the likelihood of competition from other utility companies.

Gas and Garbage Removal. Where households use gas, it is provided by individual propane tanks or by a private provider who fills a common tank on-site periodically. Solid waste (garbage) may be dealt with informally (by dumping and/or burning), but more usually it is removed under private contract, with families placing it in above-ground receptacles (dumpsters) to reduce dog and rodent access. In certain large *colonias*, which may have incorporated themselves as cities, local taxes usually cover the cost of formalized, city-contracted, garbage-collection service.

Sewer and Water Service. Given their costly nature, sewer and water services are a problem in many *colonias*. Yet these are key services from the point of view of both the residents and the state, given the state's concern with environmental and health risks. Thus, as early as 1991 major bonds were approved to empower the Texas Water Development Board to extend water and wastewater service to *colonias*.[33] After a slow start, the TWDB has had considerable success in extending water to many *colonias*, often working in conjunction with private municipal utility districts (MUDs), which thereafter are responsible for maintenance and operation. However, by the TWDB's own estimates, the resources available are scarcely enough to do the job, and they barely touch the surface of what will be needed to establish a fully integrated sewage and drainage system.

Therefore, most residents must fend for themselves. In the early phase of the development of a *colonia*, water may be purchased from water trucks and stored in

500–1,000 gallon tanks. Ingenious solutions are also found, such as the use of small water-collection rigs on pickups. Drinking water must be purchased, of course, either in large jars or from dispensers. Ultimately, *colonia* residents may collaborate to create their own service district to provide water. These initiatives are usually promoted by the TWDB, but they may also emerge spontaneously if a settlement is of sufficient size.

Sewage removal is almost entirely the responsibility of the resident. In the past, developers either promised this essential service at some unspecified future date, or explicitly stated that each purchaser was responsible for building an on-site septic system, usually costing $1,200–$2,000. Today, however, legislation in the border region requires developers to either "build it" (the septic system) or "bond it" (set aside $2,000) before they are allowed to sell lots in approved, platted subdivisions. While most households have a septic system of some sort, there are inevitable problems of undercapacity and poor maintenance that create significant health hazards. Thus, while few people resort to illegal or informal systems of sewage, occasional seepage of effluent remains a problem.

It is primarily because of state and local concern with the potential health hazards of inadequate sewerage that there has been virtually no experimentation to date with low-technology or less orthodox systems of removal. Instead, the emphasis has been on setting the bar of code compliance sufficiently high to make septic systems functional.[34] This generally means that lots must be large enough to support a drain field; that they can support only a single household; and that they may not be subdivided or used for multi-occupancy (rental). Such factors have intensified the official resistance to findings and arguments such as my own that seek to lower the bar on standards and codes; and which propose raising densities, allowing for shared septic systems complemented by periodic vacuum removal, and piloting and developing innovative "low-tech" approaches.

Street Paving and Street Lighting. One area where low-tech approaches have been adopted is street paving, but even here codes continue to require that regular fire hydrants be installed and that roads be improved. Fortunately, homesteaders are willing to make do with slow-circulation, caliche (unpaved hard-core) roads, at least where these are not main access routes. Alternatively, roads may be paved, but it is usually to an "austere" level without curbs or stormwater culverts. Washouts and potholes are common, but correcting this problem is not usually perceived as a high priority by residents. Construction and maintenance are usually the county's responsibility — hence, the austerity.

Street lighting is rare, but neither is it generally needed, except to offer improved security to pedestrians at night. Here, some residents have copied the practice of Mexican municipal authorities, which is to install street lamps on every second or third post in order to provide a modest (but usually adequate) level of street lighting. Indeed, in Mexico this is called an *"austero"* level of supply. In

Texas, however, it is done privately, as residents will sometimes place a street lamp on the pole outside their lot running off their own metered supply. More usually, however, such installations are self-serving, with the light placed on a subsidiary pole above the house, to illuminate the yard.

SELF-HELP OR SELF-MANAGED HOUSING?

In our recent survey of fifteen *colonias* (two of which are outside the border area) 64 percent of *colonia* residents interviewed said they were living in a "consolidated" home. This could be a self-built dwelling, but more usually it was a pre-fabricated or moveable housing structure shipped to the site. These could either be less portable "manufactured homes," or actual trailer homes (sometimes it was difficult to tell the difference). An additional 16 percent of households in the fifteen *colonias* lived in what were unequivocally trailers, while 3 percent lived in campers or shacks. The remaining 20 percent (41 cases) lived in housing arrangements that represented a combination of these options. In these cases, a consolidated dwelling formed the principal structure in 39 percent of "mentions," sometimes in combination with trailers (29 percent of "mentions"), or with shack-like structures (24 percent). It is likely that our survey overestimated the consolidated homes category, however. Had we performed a lot-by-lot count and description of the housing as part of an initial "windshield" survey, we would probably have arrived at a more accurate breakdown. But these data confirm the reality that most homes in *colonias* are not dilapidated, but are relatively new and well-kept structures. Furthermore, they offer a mix of housing types to meet a variety of needs and budgets. Such heterogeneity is also a commonly noted feature of consolidated irregular settlements in Latin American cities.

It appears that while processes similar to the "upgrading" (self-improvement) of housing that one sees in Mexico also occur in Texas, they are substantially different in nature. In Texas, most people "self-manage" rather than self-build their dwellings. As already mentioned, owners frequently delay occupying a lot until they have been able to acquire a dwelling to place on it. Until then, they are reluctant to live in cramped conditions, without services, far from the city. Another option is to live in a temporary dwelling and to upgrade later — for example, swapping a dilapidated trailer for a new one, or for a manufactured home which may be extended later. Others will live in trailers while they self-build or oversee the construction of a consolidated home. Indeed, one important advantage of *colonias* is that there is ample space in which to develop such multiple housing arrangements. Thus, in the 20 percent of combination cases we found in our study, it was common to see several "stages" of dwelling development on a single lot, with older trailer-type lodgings, or even campers, being used as spillover bedrooms or "dens."

The upshot is that most *colonia* residents live in larger homes than they did prior to moving to their current lots. In our survey, the average number of bedrooms in the current *colonia* residence was 2.8 (median 3), which compares with 2.4 (median 2) at previous residences. Yet even though current homes may be larger than previous homes, this may not indicate a lower level of overcrowding since overall household size is also likely to have increased.

Costs Associated with Mobile Homes and Manufactured Homes. To better understand two prevalent sources of *colonia* housing — mobile homes and manufactured homes — research was conducted at three different manufacturer/vendors outside Austin during February 2000. Prices for new trailers/mobile homes there began at $19,000 for a single-wide (14 x 68 ft.) unit. This price usually included transport to the owner's site (within 100 miles), and it occasionally included bonuses such as full hookup to a sewer/septic tank and vinyl skirting. Some dealers even offered to roll these and other site improvements into a mortgage, if desired. Thus, monthly payments would run around $300, with at least a 5 percent down payment depending on the purchaser's credit history. However, one mobile home manufacturer/vendor claimed that a client would never be turned down for bad credit, and might even be offered a free entertainment center, complete with a 25-inch television and VCR, with the purchase of a new unit.

The best annual percentage rate (APR) we found was 8.5 percent, again dependent on credit worthiness and the amount of money originally put down (the larger the down payment, the better the rate). Costs for double-wide mobile homes and manufactured homes ranged from nearly $40,000 to $100,000. And similar financing and expanded site-improvement packages (including deck, landscaping, and sidewalks) were available for these larger homes. Mortgages usually ranged from seven to thirty years, with a lien generally only on the house, so it could be repossessed like a car in case of default.

Lot Sharing and Lot Densities. Unlike self-build housing arrangements in less developed countries, it appears that, on the surface at least, there is little or no lot sharing in Texas *colonias*. Some 86 percent of respondents stated that there was only one home on a lot, and of the few who said there was more than one home, the majority (60 percent) shared only with kin. Most of these other family members did not have ownership of their section (59 percent), although a significant minority did have part ownership. Not all extra dwellings were shared with kin, however, and 19 percent of those who admitted to having more than one dwelling on their lot said the other dwelling was empty or currently not in use. We had no way of knowing whether this was true, but it should be borne in mind that subletting or sharing with families who are not close kin is illegal under current *colonia* subdivision codes, which stipulate single-family residence, with sharing only permitted between close kin. Nevertheless, some 8 percent did freely admit to renting the other dwelling on their lot. An additional 13 percent gave other explanations for the use of these additional dwellings: on loan to family, used as a store/shop, etc. Overall, there appeared to be no significant difference in sharing between border and nonborder *colonias*, with 86 and 79 percent of participants claiming single-family residence, respectively.

To recap, 86 percent of respondents indicated that there was only one home on their property, while 12 percent had two homes, and 3 percent had three homes on the same lot. Thus, our study of *colonia* residents revealed a total of 275 households on 235 lots (a sharing ratio of 1.17 families per lot). Taking the trimmed mean for lot size as 15,482 sq.ft. (a third of an acre, approximately) and an average household size of 4.53 members, this sharing ratio gives an average lot density of 5.3 persons. This is equivalent to 2,920.03 sq.ft. of lot space per person, or 14.9 persons per occupied acre. By Mexican standards this represents a very low population density, since *colonia* densities of around 100 people per acre are the norm there.[35]

Texas Colonias: Freedom to Build?[36] One of the important issues relating to quasi-formal residential homesteading in the United States is the extent to which stronger legislative and regulatory frameworks (local ordinances and codes) and local institutional practices here may inhibit upgrading and improvement. Therefore, in our survey we sought to ascertain people's awareness of legal restrictions. Despite increasing legislative restrictions on the development and proliferation of *colonias* statewide and rising publicity about their plight, most individuals (72 percent) stated that they were not aware of any legal restrictions upon their self-help housing activities. Perhaps this was a case of ignorance being a good excuse. However, the 28 percent who were aware offered a multiplex list of legal and other constraints. For example, 17 percent of respondents knew it was prohibited to subdivide one's lot, while a similar percentage knew that special codes applied to dwelling construction.

Some respondents were also aware that it was prohibited to have more than one home on a lot (12 percent); that special codes applied to septic systems (6 percent); that certain types of animals were not permitted (5 percent); and that setback requirements established the minimum distance of a home from the street (5 percent).[37] An additional 11 percent of individuals were aware of the existence of legal restrictions, but were not able to identify them specifically. Just more than one-quarter (26 percent) of respondents mentioned a number of "other" restrictions.[38]

THE RELATIVE ABSENCE OF FORMAL SOCIAL SERVICES

Provision of formal services such as police, fire, and ambulance is limited, partly because of the relative isolation of *colonia*-type subdivisions, but also because of limited county resources. Policing is clearly the responsibility of the county sheriff, but often counties contract with nearby cities for EMS and fire service on a pay-as-you-go basis. Other social services are largely absent, and residents must seek them in nearby cities. A number of community centers have been constructed in the larger *colonias*, and these act as important conduits for NGOs and a range of other social-service providers.[39] However, the involvement of these providers tends to be top-down and helps little in strengthening local leadership and organizational capacity.

Another distinctive feature of quasi-formal residential subdivisions, especially when compared with their Mexican counterparts, is the almost total absence of small commercial establishments and workshops. This is partly due to the prohibition on nonresidential uses, but it also reflects low absolute population densities, which fail to provide the critical mass needed to support petty commerce. Low population density also makes public transport nonviable, although some large settlements may have minimal service in the early morning and late afternoon. Private transportation is therefore essential, and most residents own pickup trucks, cars, etc. School buses pick up and drop off children daily as part of the ISD service.

Informal Social Infrastructure: Settlements or Communities? Self-help communities are normally associated with high levels of local informal social organization — residents associations, church groups, soccer teams, and the like. In less developed countries the process of illegal land acquisition and the defense of fledgling settlements, combined with the need to hustle and petition for services, all make community organization essential if the settlement is to survive, let alone thrive.[40] Indeed, community-development programs often require some level of community participation. And, in general, communities are also tight-knit social entities, with relatively high levels of social interaction between neighbors and kin, especially among women.

In Texas, however, one does not see anything like the same level of informal social organization, and social capital is often almost nonexistent. What this means is there is minimal horizontal social interaction among neighbors, and little or no organizational linkage into supralocal authorities and organizations (see FIGURE 9.5). This is why I have characterized *colonias* as "settlements" rather than "communities."[41] In short, whereas in Mexico the sense of community develops spontaneously (albeit instrumentally) out of a settlement's initial precariousness, in Texas the challenge is to forge the sense of community out of a settlement.

This failure to develop a sense of community is partly a function of low population density. But it also stems from the relative security of the process of land acquisition and the highly individualized nature of homesteading in Texas. Thus, there is little or no incentive for collective mobilization. Instead, people keep to themselves, deals are struck individually with land developers, the timing of land occupation is each family's choice, there is little need to cooperate with other homesteaders (in terms of self-build and mutual aid), and services are contracted individually. Little wonder, therefore, that officials in Texas see these populations as highly dependent on the state, with little internal capacity for local organization and development.

THE DIRECTION OF PUBLIC POLICY

A little more than a decade ago Texas was faced with the withholding of federal grant support unless it prevented further *colonia* expansion. As a result, several of the biennial legislative sessions since have taken action both to stop *colonia* growth and stimulate *colonia* upgrading. *Inter alia*, these actions have included the following.

1991: Model Subdivision Rules requiring minimum service levels for new *colonias* (later also applied to "grandfathered" developments).
1991: Appropriation of funds (but less than half the amount needed) to provide water and wastewater service.
1995: Application of consumer protections to Contract for Deed titling.
1995: Moratorium on further lot sales in unapproved (unserviced) *colonias*, and "build-it" or "bond-it" mandates to developers.
1999: More effective coordination between government agencies in tackling the *colonia* "problem," and increasing the responsibilities of counties.

In addition to not providing sufficient resources to tackle the problem of lack of services, an underlying weakness with all these initiatives is that they have

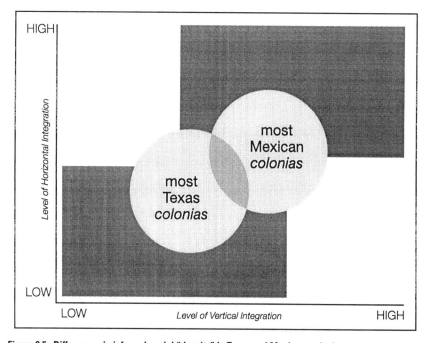

Figure 9.5. Differences in informal social "density" in Texas and Mexican *colonias*.
Source: P. Ward, Colonias and Public Policy in Texas and Mexico: Urbanization by Stealth (Austin: University of Texas Press, 1999), 167.

applied only in the border region and/or in specially designated economically distressed (EDAP) counties.[42] Everywhere else the process continues pretty much unabated. Furthermore, the development of legal (serviced and approved) *colonias* has now become common — although this pushes the total cost of a lot, with a trailer or manufactured home on it, toward the lower end of the formal housing market (i.e., into the low to mid-$40,000s).

The alternative is to develop subdivisions formally and to code. But this reduces lot size significantly. And although the overall cost of formal development is not that much more (running between $14,000–16,000 per lot), together with higher transaction costs, the additional increment effectively shifts acquisition beyond the reach of a significant proportion of the target market.[43]

POLICY IMPERATIVES FOR TEXAS *COLONIAS*

In summary, one must ask what can be learned either directly or indirectly for Texas from informal practices and policy approaches in less-developed countries. Elsewhere, I have developed five broad policy imperatives that I have urged legislators and policymakers in Texas to consider.[44]

First, it is desirable to think about *colonias* differently, and see them not as rural settlements of unemployed Hispanic populations bedeviled by social pathologies and unhealthy living conditions. Instead, they should be seen for what they are: settlements of the working poor, tied primarily to urban economies, representing a rational response to low wages and a lack of viable housing alternatives offered by either the public or private sector. While they require public intervention and assistance, principally in terms of services, these are "bootstrap" communities capable of developing self-help and mutual-aid solutions to their problems; they are not waiting for windfall handouts from government. If Texans were able to shift the way they view *colonias* as social constructions, they might better appreciate their potential for development and formulate more imaginative and appropriate policies.

This leads me to a second imperative — that of new institutional practices and intergovernmental relations. In Texas, the largely negative and top-down view of *colonias* has been compounded by poor local-government structures and intergovernmental coordination. In particular, the responsibility for *colonias* has fallen between the cracks of county and city authority. To remedy this situation, institutional and policy development will be required to reduce the (very real) liability that jurisdictions perceive in taking responsibility for *colonias*. This might take a number of forms: greater planning empowerment for counties; fiscal incentives for cities to extend infrastructure to *colonias* close to existing service areas; relaxation of liability laws associated with minimum standards; and greater collaboration in sharing social services on a pay-as-you-go basis. In short, it is necessary for government to step up to the plate and respond positively and collaboratively to the needs of *colonia* populations.

The third policy imperative I have urged is an examination of ways to promote *colonia* densification. The simple reality that *colonias* are likely to increase in population by one-third to one-half through infill in the coming decade should concentrate the mind of policymakers. But such inevitable *colonia* densification can also provide solutions: as a housing policy to meet low-income demand; as a means of reducing the unit cost of services by sharing and recovering costs among a larger population; and as a way to attain greater social density and local capacity for community self-help. To achieve these results, however, policies need to address blockages in the land market that currently prevent or act as a disincentive to lot sales and occupancy (including current legislative prohibitions on new sales, lot subdivisions, etc.). In Mexico, fiscal measures (land taxes) are used to penalize nonoccupancy of lots and land speculation, and they are used to reward social use of property (housing and low-cost rental). Something along these lines could be made to work in Texas. However, only recently have state agencies begun to track absentee lot owners and identify what might bring their lots into occupancy or into the land market for sale.[45]

My fourth, and in some ways most controversial, proposal has been to call for greater responsiveness to "low-tech" infrastructure approaches. This would include lowering infrastructure and house-building standards, at least on a temporary basis while settlements get up to code. I have already mentioned as an example how Mexico provides "austere" levels of servicing (for example, modest street lighting and nonpaved side-road infrastructure).[46] But while such minimum (rather than maximum) standards legislation is common enough in less developed countries, it is anathema in Texas for reasons of politics and local liability. Yet it makes little sense to criminalize self-builders or to place them in "Catch 22" situations where they can't apply for service hookups or financial support if a *colonia* is unserviced. Nor, I believe, should low-tech septic systems and/or lot-shared septic systems be considered an inappropriate solution, particularly on large lots. Indeed, provided they are monitored and complemented by vacuum removal when needed, such combination septic fields could additionally provide valuable open space. The point is that formal waterborne sewage systems make little sense in desert regions like El Paso, and the alternative — separate individual septic systems — is overly expensive.[47] Of course, the controversy surrounding such arguments concerns the establishment of a double standard. But this could be circumvented by deeming the designation temporary, with the expectation that a *colonia* would converge with code requirements over, say, a ten- to fifteen-year period — what Larson refers to as "progressive realization." After all, "enterprise zone" designation is common enough. Why not establish "social interest/housing zones"? These have been shown to work well enough in several Brazilian cities.[48]

My last proposal concerns the need to improve social infrastructure and community participation. As I have already mentioned, this emerges spontaneously in Mexico, and is often tied to the land-settlement process. But in Texas it has to be cultivated, turning settlements into communities. Raising densities in the manner described above will help. But much more needs to be done to recast the top-down mentality of social-service providers and create greater public (local) participation in community-development programs. Tying community participation to decisions about relative standards, liability waivers, and so on might help ensure the full involvement of *colonia* residents in local planning decisions.

INFORMAL HOUSING PRODUCTION IN THE UNITED STATES: THE BIG PICTURE

In this chapter I have argued that our understanding of urban informality — specifically in the arenas of land use and self-help housing — in less developed contexts can inform thinking about housing processes here in the United States. By comparing Texas *colonias* to their Mexican counterparts I have sought to demonstrate how we can better appreciate the nature, rationale, logic, and dynamics of low-income homesteading here. Moreover, while Texas *colonias* may be different in many important respects from their Mexican counterparts, the policy approaches and practices adopted by Mexican authorities often have much to commend them. Innovative thinking about regularization, appropriate codes and standards, land-market fine tuning, densification, community strengthening, turning urban land to productive use that will allow for rental opportunities, and so on: these are all worth considering in Texas and in the United States at large.

By way of a conclusion, I want to point to where this current research potential leads. I have already suggested that *colonias* are not just a border phenomenon; indeed, similar subdivisions exist across Texas and, almost certainly, across much of the United States. As long as low incomes and inequality remain a structural feature of the urban and economic landscape in the United States, and as long as the public sector continues to be unable or unwilling to help low-income households obtain housing of their own, there will continue to be a demand for low-cost shelter options. Where those options embrace the desire for urban homesteading, informally produced housing options are likely to fill the gap, and the phenomenon so far described largely with reference to the border states will be increasingly recognized elsewhere. That being the case, we should probably not call such developments *colonias* at, all since they are as likely to be populated by Anglos or African Americans as by Mexican Americans or other Hispanics. The more appropriate (if less elegant) term I have proposed is "quasi-formal homestead subdivisions," or homestead subdivisions for short.

The widespread distribution of such developments throughout Texas is just beginning to be acknowledged. Even now, counties far from the border are beginning to recognize the existence of similar unregulated "rural" subdivisions that in fact house an urban labor force. For example, the Texas Water Development Board's database has identified *colonias* in several nonborder counties, and in the densification study reported on earlier, I deliberately selected several nonborder *colonias* to underscore how this is not just a feature of border landscapes. Indeed, I chose three neighborhoods in the peri-urban area of Austin — the high-tech, relatively affluent capital of the state.

My proposition is that it is perfectly logical for quasi-formal homestead subdivisions to exist widely elsewhere in the United States, even if, as yet, they are largely undocumented.[49] In what ways is this logical? The answer lies in the fact that such homestead subdivisions offer the only accessible means to home ownership for urban households earning less than $20,000 a year. And while there are significant private transport costs associated with living in poorly serviced communities several miles beyond the urban fringe, families of all ethnicities have been quick to recognize the advantages of self-managed home ownership on relatively large lots over renting in more urban trailer parks and apartment complexes.

In the big picture, homestead subdivisions are affordable to these low-income working populations. They offer greater flexibility and are less onerous in terms of payments. They provide homesteaders with a foothold in the property-owning market. And while my own data suggest that the windfall and valorization gains associated with *colonia* upgrading and consolidation fall well below the average for other (higher-income) sectors of the residential market, *colonias* nevertheless offer the possibility for appreciating equity. In some cases, too, in South Texas and Florida these subdivisions cater to "snowbird" or recreational communities. Used only several months of the year, this is a relatively cheap real estate option for retirees wanting to get away from the Midwest winter, or for less well-off families who wish to take extended low-cost summer vacations with their children. There are also multiple and largely unexplored social advantages that accrue from homestead subdivisions. The opportunity to live close to kin (in adjacent lots), or to subdivide and share lots, provides the potential for independence yet support in terms of social interaction, childcare, etc. They also provide a relatively cheap housing option for families who wish to take care of elderly or infirm parents.

Prima facie evidence for the existence and expansion of homestead communities near a town is the proliferation of trailer and manufactured-home sale companies along nearby highways. These may be catering to buyers who are placing their purchases on lots in low-serviced subdivisions. Alternatively, if one looks out an airplane window some five to ten minutes before landing or after takeoff (at about 7,000–10,000 feet), one may readily identify such subdivisions below. Once one knows what to look for, the evidence for their existence becomes even more compelling. Indeed, in a recent research symposium participants began to explore mechanisms for developing a national inventory using remote sensing protocols interleaved with Geographical Information Systems.[50]

Truly, what we see here is urban informality in an era of liberalization. The aim of my discussion has been to demonstrate that in both the case of Texas and the United States at large we should not neglect our own transnational backyard.

NOTES

1. P. Ward, "Self-Help and Self-Managed Housing — á la Americana," in *Irregular Settlement and Self-Help Housing in the United States* (Seminar proceedings, Cambridge, Mass.: Lincoln Institute of Land Policy, September 2001) (available at http://www.lincolninst.edu/main.html); and P. Ward, *Residential Land Market Dynamics, Absentee Lot Owners, and Densification Policies for Texas Colonias*, working paper, Lincoln Institute of Land Policy, Cambridge, Mass., 2000, 144.

2. K. Hart, "Small-Scale Entrepreneurs in Ghana and Development Planning," *The Journal of Development Studies* 6 (April 1970), 104–20; R. Bromley, "Globalization and the Inner-periphery: A Mid-Bronx View," *Annals of the American Academy of Political and Social Science* 555 (May 1997), 191–207; V. Lawson and T. Klak, "An Argument for Critical and Comparative Research on the Urban Economic Geography of the Americas," *Environment and Planning A* 25, no. 8 (August 1993), 1071–84; and V. Lawson, "Tailoring is a Profession; Seamstressing is just Work!" *Environment and Planning A* 31, no. 2 (February 1999), 209–27.

3. M. Castells, *The Urban Question* (London: Edward Arnold, 1977); and *The City and the Grassroots: A Cross-Cultural Theory of Urban Social Movements* (Berkeley, Calif.: University of California Press, 1983).

4. D. Harvey, *The Condition of Postmodernity* (Oxford, U.K.: Basil Blackwell, 1989); and *Justice, Nature, and the Geography of Difference* (Oxford, U.K.: Blackwell, 1996).

5. H. Harms, "Historical Perspectives on the Practice and Purpose of Self-Help Housing," in P. Ward, ed., *Self-Help Housing: A Critique* (London: Mansell, 1982).

6. P. Ward, "Regularization in Latin America: Lessons in the Social Construction of Public Policy," in G. Jones, ed., *Urban Land Markets in Transition* (Cambridge, Mass.: Lincoln Institute of Land Policy, 2002).

7. See A. Durand Lasserve, "Law and Urban Change in Developing Countries: Trends and Issues," in E. Fernandes Edésio and A. Varley, eds., *Illegal Cities: Law and Urban Change in Developing Countries* (London: Zed Books, 1998), 233–57; and C. Farvaque and P. McAuslan, *Reforming Urban Land Policies and Institutions in Developing Countries* (Washington, D.C.: Urban Management Program, The World Bank, 1992).

8. P. McAuslan, "Urbanization, Law, and Development: A Record of Research," in Fernandes Edésio and Varley, eds., *Illegal Cities*, 18–52.

9. McAuslan, "Urbanization, Law, and Development"; and J. Matthews Glenn and J. Wolfe, "The Growth of Informal Sector and Regularization of Spontaneous Settlement: Lessons from the Caribbean for Planning Law Reform," *Third World Planing Review* 18, no. 1 (February 1996), 59–77.

10. J. Larson, "Informality, Illegality, and Inequality," *Yale Law and Policy Review* 20 (2002), 137–82.

11. Larson, "Informality, Illegality, and Inequality."

12. R. Smith, "Transnational and Local Communities, Problems, and Transnational Solutions," in P. Ward, comp. and ed., *Reducing Vulnerability among Families in the Mexico and U.S. Border Region* (prepared on behalf of the University of Texas system and the Integrated Family Development agency, Mexico, June 1999).

13. L. Stephens, "The Mexican Immigrant Family Encounters the American Medical System: Quality Care or Collision Course?" in Ward, *Reducing Vulnerability*; and P. Ward, "The Role of Housing and Community as Social Capital in the Dynamics of Family and Household (Hogar) in the Texas-Mexico Border Region," in Ward, *Reducing Vulnerability*.

14. R. Hernández de León, "Impacts of U.S. Immigration Controls on Mexican and Binational Border Families: Observations from the Nuevo Laredo and Reynosa Cases," in Ward, *Reducing Vulnerability*.

15. W. Cornelius, "Death at the Border: Efficacy and Unintended Consequences of U.S. Immigration and Control Policy," *Population and Development Review* 27, no. 4 (December 2001), 661–85.

16. P. Ward, Colonias *and Public Policy in Texas and Mexico: Urbanization by Stealth* (Austin: University of Texas Press, 1999).

17. W. Mangin, "Latin American Squatter Settlements: A Problem and a Solution," *Latin American Research Review* 2, no. 3 (Summer 1967); J. Perlman, *The Myth of Marginality: Urban Poverty and Politics in Rio de Janeiro* (Berkeley, Calif.: University of California Press, 1976); A. Portes, "Rationality in the Slums: An Essay in Interpretative Sociology," *Comparative Studies in Society and History* 14, no. 3 (June 1972), 260–86; P. Ward, "The Squatter Settlement as Slum or Housing Solution: Some Evidence from Mexico City," Land Economics 52, no. 3 (August 1976); and A. Gilbert and P. Ward, *Housing, the State, and the Poor: Policy and Practice in Latin American Cities* (Cambridge, U.K.: Cambridge University Press, 1985).

18. P. Ward, Colonias *and Public Policy in Texas and Mexico*.

19. P. Ward in collaboration with R. Stevenson and A. Stuesse, *Residential Land Market Dynamics, Absentee Lot Owners, and Densification Policies for Texas* Colonias, policy report, LBJ School of Public Affairs, University of Texas, Austin, 2000, 251.

20. Ibid., 145. See also P. Ward and J. Carew, "Absentee Lot Owners in Texas *Colonias*: Who Are They, and What Do They Want?" *Habitat International* 24, no. 3 (September 1999), 327–45.

21. The ETJ is a fringe area beyond the city limits over which the city may, at its discretion, exercise jurisdiction and extend services. The actual size of a city's fringe area varies according to total city population. Cities with populations of less than 5,000 have an ETJ of one half a mile, while those with populations of more than 100,000 may extend as far as five miles.

22. P. Ward, "Squaring the Circle: Whither or Wither Segregation in Latin American Cities," unpublished manuscript, 2001.

23. P. Ward, "Dysfunctional Residential Land Markets: *Colonias* in Texas," *Landlines* 13, no. 1 (January 2001).

24. See Ward with Stevenson and Stuesse, *Residential Land Market Dynamics, Absentee Lot Owners, and Densification Policies for Texas* Colonias, 8–9.

25. C. Davies and R. Holz, "Settlement Evolution of 'Colonias' along the U.S.-Mexico Border: The Case of the Lower Rio Grande Valley of Texas," *Habitat International* 16, no. 4 (1992), 119–42.

26. Gilbert and Ward, *Housing, the State, and the Poor.*

27. J. Larson, "Free Markets in the Heart of Texas," *Georgetown Law Journal* 84, no. 2 (December 1995), 179–260; and Ward, Colonias *and Public Policy in Texas and Mexico.*

28. J. Jensen, "Regulation of Residential Contracts for Deed in Texas: Senate Bill 336 and Beyond," M.A. professional report, LBJ School of Public Affairs, University of Texas, Austin, 1996; and S. Mettling, *The Contract for Deed* (Chicago: Real Estate Education Company, 1982).

29. Developer Cecil McDonald, as cited in Ward, Colonias *and Public Policy in Texas and Mexico,* vii.

30. In 2002 I was engaged in a study that analyzes a major land-regularization program undertaken by the Community Resources Group at the behest of the state government in several large *colonias* in Starr County. One of the aims of that study is to assess how residents view full title, and the linkage (if any) between being given clean property titles and housing improvements and leveraging of credit using property as collateral. This is an important argument in the work of De Soto, although it is one that is also challenged — see A. Gilbert, "On the Mystery of Capital and the Myths of Hernando De Soto: What Difference does Legal Title Make?" paper presented at the ESF/N-AERUS International Seminar "Coping with Informality and Illegality in Human Settlements in Developing Cities," Leuven and Brussels, Belgium, May 23–26, 2001; and Ward, "Squaring the Circle."

31. "Softness" was a term coined by Gunnar Myrdal (*Asian Drama*) to cover informal practices which were not considered as "hard" as outright corruption. This would include bending the rules or turning a blind eye in return for relatively small bribes.

32. P. Ward, *Welfare Politics in Mexico* (London: Allen and Unwin, 1986). For example, in Texas *colonias* residents will pay $22 per 1,000 gallons of water delivered by tanker truck, whereas a resident hooked up to a city network would pay $1.5 for the same amount.

33. R. Wilson and P. Menzies, "The *Colonias* Water Bill: Communities Demanding Change," in R. Wilson, ed., *Public Policy and Community: Activism and Governance in Texas* (Austin: University of Texas Press, 1997), 229–74.

34. J. Carew, "The Viability of Low-Cost Infrastructure Technology for Affordable Housing Subdivisions in the Texas Border Region," Masters thesis, School of Architecture, University of Texas, Austin, 2000; and J. Carew, "Minimum Standard Residential Subdivisions: Can They Increase Affordability?" in *Irregular Settlement and Self-Help Housing in the United States* (Seminar proceedings, Cambridge, Mass.: Lincoln Institute of Land Policy, September 2001); and R. Stevenson, "Alternatives to Convention," in *Irregular Settlement and Self-Help Housing in the United States.*

35. In Mexico, the modal lot size in *colonias* is 200 sq.m. or 1,800 sq.ft. Assuming a similar average household size (of 4.5) and no lot sharing (both are conservative assumptions), this would amount to 108.9 persons per acre. In short, densities in Mexico are six times as high as for one-quarter-acre lots.

36. This is the title of a major self-help advocacy text by John Turner and Bob Fichter, published in 1972.

37. Although they may not be fully cognizant of the legal codes on setbacks, in fact everyone follows the normal practice in Texas, which is to place dwellings well back from the road and from boundary lines.

38. Ward with Stevenson and Stuesse, *Residential Land Market Dynamics, Absentee Lot Owners, and Densification Policies for Texas* Colonias, 78.

39. Ward, Colonias *and Public Policy in Texas and Mexico*, 224–41.

40. Gilbert and Ward, *Housing, the State, and the Poor*.

41. Ward, Colonias *and Public Policy in Texas and Mexico*.

42. EDAP stands for Economically Distressed Areas Program.

43. Carew, "The Viability of Low-Cost Infrastructure Technology for Affordable Housing Subdivisions in the Texas Border Region."

44. Ward, Colonias *and Public Policy in Texas and Mexico*.

45. P. Ward and J. Carew, "Tracking Land Ownership in Self-Help Homestead Subdivisions in the United States: The Case of Texas 'Colonias,'" *Journal of Land Policy* 18, no. 2 (2001), 165–78; and Ward with Stevenson and Stuesse, *Residential Land Market Dynamics, Absentee Lot Owners, and Densification Policies for Texas* Colonias.

46. See also Larson, "Informality, Illegality, and Inequality."

47. Stevenson, "Alternatives to Convention."

48. W. Assies, "Restructuring the Meaning of Urban Land in Brazil," in G. Jones and P. Ward, eds., *Methodology for Land and Housing Market Analysis* (London: University College London Press, 1994), 102–17.

49. In Arizona, similar types of informal settlements are being identified both as "*colonias*" and as "wildcat" settlements. See E. Holgium and A. Donelson, "Social Infrastructure in Colonias in Arizona and New Mexico," in *Irregular Settlement and Self-Help Housing in the United States*.

50. K. Crewes-Meyer, "Detection of QFHSs via Remote Sensing/Geographic Information Systems Analysis," in *Irregular Settlement and Self-Help Housing in the United States* (also available at http://www.lincolninst.edu/main.html); and M. Ratcliffe, "Identification of *Colonia*-Type Settlements in Census 2000," in *Irregular Settlement and Self-Help Housing in the United States* (also available at http://www.lincolninst.edu/main.html).

10

Power, Property, and Poverty: Why De Soto's "Mystery of Capital" Cannot Be Solved

Ray Bromley

Hernando De Soto's *The Mystery of Capital* was triumphantly released in the year 2000 at the height of a global economic and stock market boom.[1] At the time, the United States economy seemed very strong, Europe was doing well, and Japan was prosperous but concerned about recession and its aging and declining population. The fanfare of publicity for the book was reminiscent of the English-language launch of his earlier book, *The Other Path*, in 1989.[2] It seemed De Soto had created another instant bestseller which claimed to be full of penetrating and original insights.

The immense self-confidence of *The Mystery of Capital* begins at first touch. The jacket carries a picture of the World Trade Center and tributes from Margaret Thatcher, Jeanne Kirkpatrick, David Owen, Javier Perez de Cuellar, William F. Buckley Jr., Walter Wriston (Chairman Emeritus of Citigroup), and Ronald Coase and Milton Friedman, both Nobel prizewinners in economics. The summary begins as follows:

> The hour of capitalism's greatest triumph is, in the eyes of five-sixths of humanity, its hour of crisis. Beginning with these words, this book revolutionizes our understanding of what capital is — and why, since the collapse of communism, capitalism has continued to fail the majority of mankind.

Born of the heady 1990s, *The Mystery of Capital* assumes that all the developed capitalist countries (the West) are triumphantly prosperous, locked into a self-sustaining system of economic growth based on their citizens' creative use of private property to build wealth. These countries are never listed out, but they clearly include the United States, Canada, Japan, Australia, New Zealand, and the nations of Western Europe. Meanwhile, the remaining five-sixths of the world (the developing or Third World nations, and the former communist nations) are locked in a crisis of poverty and economic stagnation. The summary goes on to say:

> Five years ago, Hernando De Soto and his research team closed their books and opened their eyes. They went into the streets of developing and former communist nations to learn what real people are achieving inside and outside the underground economy. Their findings are dramatic. The data they have collected demonstrate that the world's poor have accumulated all the assets needed for successful capitalism. The value of their savings is immense: many times all the foreign aid and investment received since 1945. In Egypt alone the assets of the poor are fifty-five times greater than all foreign investment ever recorded, including the funding of the Suez Canal and the Aswan Dam.

The Mystery of Capital is presented here as tremendously innovative — rejecting all previous research and scholarship, and for the very first time directly and personally observing what the poor five-sixths of humanity actually do and learning that they have great assets. Turning to the obvious question, the summary concludes as follows:

> Why then are these countries so underdeveloped? Why can't they turn these assets into liquid capital — the kind of capital that generates new wealth? For Hernando De Soto, this is "the mystery of capital." With elegance and clarity he produces an answer of dazzling originality. De Soto reminds us that the present global crisis is the same kind of crisis that the advanced nations suffered during the Industrial Revolution, when they themselves were Third World countries teeming with black markets, pervasive mafias, widespread poverty and flagrant disregard of the law. The Western nations, he argues, created the key conversion process 150 years ago, and their economies began to soar into wealth without their ever realizing what they had done. De Soto explains how this unwitting process, hidden deep in thousands of pieces of property law throughout the West, came to be, how it works, and how today it can be deliberately set up in developing and former communist nations.

Thus, *The Mystery of Capital* is a message of enormous hope, written in a period of global optimism, providing a way for all the poor developing and former communist nations of the world "to soar into wealth." All that is needed is for their governments and elites to focus on one key policy — providing legal title to real estate currently held under a wide range of "extra-legal" forms, including squatting, illegal subdivision, indigenous and communal laws, and many forms of commons and cooperatives. If this "dead" extra-legal property could be made legal, according to De Soto, the real property involved would become "liquid capital," and this new capital could power a broad-ranging economic development process that might enable the world's poor to achieve prosperity.

De Soto uses the term "extra-legal" synonymously with "informal," and the sum of extra-legal activities and properties is the "informal sector" of the economy. His approach to informality is thus "legalist" rather than "structuralist."[3] He does not discuss the modern/traditional dual-economy models or the neo-Marxist theories of domination and dependency which underlay informal-sector debates in the 1970s and 1980s. Instead, he focuses on the ways that the state creates legal and bureaucratic obstacles to legitimate enterprise and the ownership of property. His conceptual framework leads directly to calls for deregulation, debureaucratization and privatization (DDP), reducing the role of government and focusing the state's energies on law and order, defense, money supply, infrastructure, and protecting private property so as to unleash the power of market forces to accelerate economic development.[4]

De Soto's analysis is based on a three-way split of activity and property: legal, extra-legal, and illegal; synonymous with formal, informal, and criminal. The key to this approach is a separation of means and ends. If means and ends are legal, the activity or property is legal (formal). If ends are legal but means are blocked by unnecessary bureaucratic procedures or unjust charges, or prohibited by an unjust law or arbitrary administrative decision, the activity or property is extra-legal (informal). If both means and ends are illegal, the activity or property is illegal (criminal). Most importantly, the "extra-legal" category requires a moral judgment as to whether the bureaucratic procedures are unreasonable, charges are onerous, laws are unjust, or decisions are arbitrary. The key here is whether the benefit of an activity or property which accrues to some is greater than the harm it may do others. A squatter home, for example, is informal (extra-legal) because the objective (end) is socially desirable (to provide housing and a potential place of business for people who need it); only the means (squatting) is illegal because it involves occupation of real property. To this way of thinking, if the squatter home is on unused, low-value land for which no immediate use is proposed, then the benefits to the household that lives in the home — and to the owner of the home if the occupants are tenants — can be considered to justify squatting. Similarly, a street seller of food is informal if s/he has no license to sell, but s/he is exercising a right to do business as a means to generate income and is simultaneously providing a service by making food available to the public. In such cases the condition of informality may be produced by a municipality which refuses to issue new licenses; which imposes high charges or tedious bureaucratic procedures on those who seek licenses; or which allows police and inspectors to harass vendors in search of bribes. De Soto's underlying argument is that unnecessary and unjust laws, cumbersome bureaucratic procedures, and corrupt law enforcement exclude many people and enterprises from legality, forcing them to live, own property, and do business extra-legally.

This chapter analyzes the broader arguments and significance of *The Mystery of Capital*. It adds to the stock of reviews of this book.[5] And it complements the discussions of the limitations of real property titling prepared by Ediseo Fernandes and Alan Gilbert.[6]

THREE KEY METAPHORS

The Mystery of Capital makes a powerful case for legalizing extra-legal real estate in all developing and former communist countries. De Soto shows that this must be done country by country, with national governments taking the lead, and with the active participation of regional and municipal authorities. Legal systems, institutions and traditions vary enormously from country to country, and De Soto wisely recognizes that legalizing the extra-legal will require careful local research and documentation, as well as the incorporation of indigenous and traditional legal systems into the prevailing Western law.

Though the case for accelerated and thorough legalization and titling of real property is made repeatedly in *The Mystery of Capital*, there are no detailed contemporary case studies of such legalizations or discussions of their cost. It is not a "how to do it book," but rather a "why to do it book." Further, it is based on three metaphors: "the mushrooming extra-legal sector"; "lifting the bell jar"; and "going out into the streets to listen to the barking dogs." These metaphors are used repeatedly, and they reflect the three primary assumptions which underlie the book.

The "mushrooming extra-legal sector" is De Soto's way of asserting that informality in general, and extra-legal property in particular, are rapidly growing in significance as former feudal, colonial, rural, tribal, aristocratic or communist orders break down, and as population grows and becomes increasingly urbanized. No evidence is presented to prove this proportionate growth in the significance of informality, but it is depicted as an accepted truth. Building on the arguments of *The Other Path*, the Third World and former communist poor are presented as hardworking, entrepreneurial, and ingenious. But they have been economically disenfranchised by a power elite (the "mercantilists"), who use the legal and regulatory apparatus of the state to dominate the economy and enrich themselves. The poor have thus been forced to live and work extra-legally, and the value of their properties and enterprises has been dramatically reduced by exclusion from the legal (formal) system of titles, credits, government support programs, and international aid. The answer, as suggested in *The Other Path*, is a broad-ranging program of deregulation, debureaucratization, and privatization, designed to emancipate the excluded, unleash entrepreneurial energies, and downsize the state apparatus.

The second metaphor, "lifting the bell jar" (a term borrowed from Fernand Braudel[7]), embodies the idea of breaking down the distinctions between the haves and the much larger number of have-nots, and removing the legal barriers which exclude the poor from effective participation in the economy. In De Soto's terms, this means formalizing the informal sector so that the whole population can participate fully in the national economy.

Finally, "listening to the barking dogs" is a metaphor for learning to understand traditional real property systems based on local knowledge, documents, and consensual agreements. Traditional property lines are not necessarily designed to be spotted by satellites or marked by surveyors. And there is no substitute for detailed local surveys involving intensive interviewing, negotiation, and documentary research. Thus, De Soto argues that courts must be persuaded to be more open, and to incorporate indigenous and traditional practice into mainstream law, so that all properties can be legally recognized, titled, and protected. Computer, remote-sensing, and geographic-information-systems (GIS) technologies can be useful in recording and mapping properties once the careful local research and documentation has been done, but there is no way that land and buildings can be justly and equitably titled from a remote location. De Soto rightly asserts that investment alone will not create adequate property systems. But, characteristically, he then overstates his case when he writes, without referencing a source, that "developing and former communist countries are forever spending hundreds of millions of dollars on mapping and computerized record-keeping technology to modernize their property systems" (p. 201).

The rationale for legalization is based on two main assertions: that market prices and demand for the properties which are currently extra-legal will rise when those properties have legal title; and that property owners will be able to borrow more easily and cheaply once their properties are accepted as security for commercial bank loans. It is assumed that legality increases both tenurial security and business confidence, and that "money presupposes property" (p. 64). In this regard, an old and important argument is repeated: that ownership of real property provides a stake in both the society and the economy, and that "people with nothing to lose are trapped in the grubby basement of the precapitalist world" (p. 56). Though no source is cited, De Soto claims that "the single most important source of funds for new businesses in the United States is a mortgage on the entrepreneur's house" (p. 6). This same mechanism is then presented as the principal way for poor people to grow richer in developing and former communist countries; after obtaining title to their real property, they can then take out a mortgage to capitalize a business.

THE MAGIC OF FINANCE CAPITAL

At times De Soto takes on a more mystical tone, extolling a potential which enables "the great practitioners of capitalism, from the creators of integrated title systems and corporate stock to Michael Milken . . . to reveal and extract capital where others saw only junk" (p. 7). Unfortunately, there is no recognition here that, unlike most financial wizards, Michael Milken was jailed for engaging in illegal trading practices.[8] Instead, only the good is presented, and the future prosperity of the world's poor is based on "devising new ways to represent the invisible potential that is locked up in the assets we accumulate" (p. 7).

As I write this chapter in mid-2002, De Soto's optimism about financial wizardry for the benefit of the poor seems incredibly naïve. The world is in a period of financial crisis, seemingly triggered by the terrorist attacks on the World Trade Center and the Pentagon on September 11, 2001, but more profoundly associated with the ongoing financial chicanery, greed, and fraud of hundreds (and perhaps thousands) of corporate executives and board members associated with such firms as Enron, Global Crossing, WorldCom, RiteAid, and Arthur Andersen. The current crisis has robbed millions of shareholders, workers, and former workers of a large part of their savings, insurance, and retirement plans. Many have lost their jobs, their homes, or savings they had gradually accumulated to send their children or grandchildren to college. Meanwhile, most of the corporate executives and board members who masterminded the inflation of share values, insider trading on the stock market, export of capital to offshore tax havens, price manipulation in newly deregulated energy markets, and fraudulent accounting to hide illegal financial practices are free to enjoy their ill-gotten gains. Some of these contemporary "Robber Barons" even lobby for further corporate and accounting deregulation, and for the abolition of capital-gains and inheritance taxes — crude ploys to further widen the social and economic gaps between rich and poor in the United States.[9] Their capacity to succeed is based not only on the ways they manage corporate finances, but also on corporate manipulation of the mass media to divert attention elsewhere; on predatory lawsuits to silence opposition; and on using large sums of corporate and personal money to purchase the support of key politicians in both the Republican and Democratic parties.[10]

Just as the United States has a financial crisis associated with deficiencies in its regulatory system and a grave lack of corporate ethics, Argentina in mid-2002 is in a state of financial collapse. Argentina's crisis resulted from a failed economic-development and financial-management strategy adopted in 1991 and abandoned in 2001, which was based on pegging the value of the peso to the U.S. dollar. For much of the 1990s Argentina was praised by the International Monetary Fund (IMF) and leading international finance experts as a country which had taken decisive steps to ensure financial stability and economic growth. Over the last year, however, widespread praise has been replaced by universal criticism, the peso-dollar parity has been abandoned, and the economy is in ruins. According to one prominent journal, Argentina has made a transition "from poster child to basket case."[11] Particularly when major policy innovations with long-term implications are under discussion, hindsight is so much easier than foresight!

Meanwhile, mid-2002 in Haiti has brought crises of a different kind:

> Intoxicated by the promise of easy money, thousands of Haitians ... sold their cars, mortgaged their homes and emptied their savings accounts in recent months to invest in cooperatives that promised astonishing monthly returns of 10 percent. Economists and bankers long warned government officials that the unregulated cooperatives were little more than a pyramid scheme and possible money-laundering operation. But when President Jean-Bertrand Aristide hailed cooperatives as "the people's capitalism" that would drive economic development, many investors said their skepticism vanished. Soon, too, did their money. More than $200 million has been lost in unsound or illegal cooperatives that took their investors' money and bought luxurious properties, fleets of buses or just spirited it abroad.[12]

Sadly, Haiti's demise is far from unusual. In the search for a good return on their investments, poor investors can easily be fooled into backing pyramid schemes and other fraudulent financial devices, borrowing to invest in a volatile stock market, or saving with banks and finance companies which collapse and refuse to pay their investors.

THE INADEQUACY OF DUALISM

The conclusions of mid-2002 are remarkably obvious, and yet they are ignored or dismissed in *The Mystery of Capital*. Consider how our categories of "the West," "the developing nations," "the Third World," "informality," and "the informal sector" are socially constructed. How, then, could problems and solutions be miraculously confined to one part of the world, or one type of country? It would be far more logical to expect them to different degrees in all countries. Indeed, though we often use dichotomous (dualistic) models — dividing the world into Western countries and developing countries, or dividing businesses into legal and extra-legal — there are at least as many complex, mixed and intermediate cases as there are simple cases which fit clearly into one or other category. In response, many authors have inserted intermediate and mixed categories.[13] Others have tried to emphasize the existence of a continuum.[14] But the old polarized categories still persist in many minds, including De Soto's.

Using De Soto's definition of informality as "extra-legal behavior," it is easy to argue that the rich and powerful are much better at informality than the poor. In the United States, the creative financing and accounting techniques pioneered by such companies as Enron, WorldCom, and Arthur Andersen generated billions of dollars of wealth, enriched prosperous insiders, and defrauded millions of ordinary workers and investors. In De Soto's home country of Peru, Vladimiro Montesinos, a "national security advisor" to the government of President Alberto Fujimori from 1990 to 2001, ran a network of bribery, extortion, narcotics, and arms trafficking, enriching himself, humiliating political opponents, controlling most of the news media, and manipulating the president, his cabinet, and military leaders.[15] Montesinos' power came from his contacts as a former military officer and associate of the CIA and KGB, and from his creative double accounting of government funds derived from the privatization of former state corporations in accordance with the recommendations of the IMF — and subsequent use of these illusory funds to purchase arms on the world market. Offshore banks, secret accounts, and personal links with the Soviet intelligence community further facilitated his "insider trading" in Russian-manufactured weaponry. Meanwhile, he was able to use Peru's "war on terrorism" (trying to control the Shining Path and MRTA insurgencies), its border conflicts with Ecuador, and collaboration with the U.S. in the "war on drugs" to preserve both the secrecy of his operations and international networks of support for the Fujimori administration.

In *The Other Path*, informality is described as property or economic activity whose ends are legal but whose means are currently proscribed by inefficient bureaucracy, exorbitant charges, unjust laws, or arbitrary administrative decisions. In reality, however, cases of formality and informality may be remarkably complex, often mixing legal and illegal, and the interests and concerns of rich and poor. Legality depends on a whole series of procedures and permits, some of which may be followed and others ignored, and tacit assumptions that activities can proceed while paperwork is being obtained. The pace of real estate development and technological change, combined with the slowness of traditional bureaucracies, constantly creates new opportunities and pressures for improvisation. The story of two nightclub tragedies helps to illustrate how formality and informality can be interwoven, and how neither is clearly the domain of the rich or the poor.

On its surface, the first tragedy would seem to reinforce the stereotype of Third World informality. At 3:30 AM on Saturday, July 20, 2002, a fire erupted in Utopia, a discotheque at Jockey Plaza Center, Lima's largest and most elegant shopping mall, located in the opulent Surco neighborhood.[16] Of at least 600 persons inside when the fire began (most of them members of middle- and upper-class families), thirty were killed, and more than one hundred were injured. Located in a basement, the discotheque was barely two months old. Although it had adequate emergency exits, it was full of flammable materials, its ventilation was deficient, its fire extinguishers were locked away, and the water supply to the bathrooms had been cut off by the management.

However, when one looks more closely at this case, a far more complex situation becomes apparent. Jockey Plaza Center had been carefully planned by its developers and licensed by the Municipality of Surco. And Inversiones Garcia

North S.A.C., the legally registered company which operated the discotheque, had formally leased the premises from Jockey Plaza. Yet despite this overall level of formality, certain informal arrangements also existed. Most importantly, the Municipality of Surco had never licensed the discotheque, either before or during its two months of operation. Indeed, it had inspected it and several other establishments in Jockey Plaza, and indicated that the club was not in compliance with some of the many municipal fire and safety regulations. Nevertheless, the municipality had not ordered that the discotheque be closed. Furthermore, initial reports on the tragedy revealed numerous irregularities in the finances of Inversiones Garcia North, and in the relationship between Jockey Plaza and its tenants and lessees.

Seemingly a world away in the developed, capitalist United States, a similar tragedy had already taken place. At 2:40 AM on Sunday, March 25, 1990, an arson fire had been set in the doorway of the Happy Land Social Club, a much smaller discotheque located on Southern Boulevard in the Borough of the Bronx in New York City.[17] Of the ninety-three people inside at the time, only six escaped alive, because the building had no windows or rear exits, and because some of the furnishings emitted toxic fumes when burned. The victims were mainly low-income Hispanic immigrants, and almost half were undocumented. However, just as in the case of Utopia in Lima, Happy Land revealed a complex chain of ownership and authorization, mixing legality and extra-legality. At the top of a pyramid of ownership was Alexander DiLorenzo III, heir to one of New York's real estate empires. He had leased the building to Peachtree Properties, a legal company partly owned by Jay Weiss, husband to actress Kathleen Turner. In turn, Peachtree had leased the property to Elias Colon, who had obtained permits to operate a social club, but who was in violation of numerous building and fire code regulations. Under these conditions the club had operated intermittently for two years before the tragedy, with notices of violation being sent by the City of New York to its owners — but without decisive official action to close it.

The complexity of cases like Enron, Montesinos, Utopia, and Happy Land illustrates how enormously challenging it is to classify all the properties or enterprises in a city or country into "formal" and "informal" categories. The closer the scrutiny of economic activity and property, the more evident complexities and inconsistencies seem to become. In fact, part of the creativity of a Michael Milken or Vladimiro Montesinos is to take advantage of ambiguities to enhance their own power, property, and privilege. For some this is financial wizardry; for others it is crude gangsterism. But in most cases it is only in retrospect that one can understand and reflect on the curious ways that laws and improvisation are blended.

THE MISSING RULE OF LAW

The chain of examples, from Enron to Montesinos, and from Utopia to Happy Land, serves to illustrate how tightly interwoven our globalized world is becoming. De Soto's assumption that it can be easily divided into two parts, "the West" and "the developing and former communist countries," is becoming increasingly questionable. And even if such a division is made, it is doubly difficult to link that division with assumptions of legality and extra-legality. In Enron's case, many lawyers and accountants were employed to find and exploit loopholes — including overseas tax havens — rather than comply with the laws of the United States. One result was that no U.S. taxes were paid on the company's declared profits in four of the five years preceding corporate collapse (1996–2000).[18] To crown it all, an elaborate corporate code of ethics was published on the World Wide Web as a way of fooling gullible shareholders, workers, and members of the general public into believing that Enron was a company with the highest ethical standards and a profound respect for both the environment and human rights.[19]

Friedrich Hayek, one of the leading economists and political philosophers of the twentieth century, and a major inspiration to De Soto, wrote not only of the importance of free markets, deregulation, debureaucratization and privatization, but also of "the rule of law" — the vital role of national government and international institutions in creating and maintaining a system of law, order, and economic stability which may facilitate fair competition, free markets, and economic growth. According to Hayek, the rule of law has several vital principles, including the following: "government can infringe a person's protected private sphere only as punishment for breaking an announced general rule"; "the importance which the certainty of the law has for the smooth and efficient running of a free society can hardly be exaggerated"; "any law should apply equally to all"; "the separation of powers . . . requires independent judges who are not concerned with any temporary ends of government"; "the private citizen and his property are not an object of administration by the government"; "the safeguards of individual liberty which constitutionalism provides;" "no expropriation without just compensation"; and "procedural safeguards such as habeas corpus, trial by jury, and so on."[20]

Simply legalizing extra-legal real estate does not institute a rule of law, and it does not guarantee economic stability. In Peru in the 1990s, Dr. Montesinos and his assistants reported people who questioned the government to SUNAT, the government taxation authority, so that they would be audited, declared in violation of tax laws, and come to owe large sums of money to the government. Since complex tax laws and strict documentation requirements made it easy for a malicious auditor to find faults in anyone's tax return, such audits on demand were really a selective form of victimization.

Alternatively, in Argentina in mid-2002 many people who took out dollar loans when real estate prices were high and the peso was pegged to the dollar now face, or are in danger of facing, foreclosure. With the value of their property far below the value of their debts, they find themselves unable to make interest payments as their real incomes have dropped precipitously. All this shows how the owners of real property cannot escape the significance of changes in exchange rates, interest rates, real estate markets and stock markets for their investments. And many of the world's poorer countries frequently experience dramatic fluctuations in these financial indices. Some countries even experience hyper-inflation, a situation which is devastating for most poor and middle-income groups, but which offers great opportunities for profiteering to select insiders. Even in Japan, a "Western" country in De Soto's model, mortgages granted on real estate during "bubble" periods of price inflation have turned to widespread negative equity and repayment defaults, endangering the whole banking system.[21] Similar problems contributed to the 1997 East Asian financial crisis, affecting both "Western" and Third World nations, from Japan to Indonesia.[22]

In countries where "the rule of law" is weak or nonexistent, holding real property extra-legally offers some degree of anonymity and reduced likelihood of taxation. Until a well-functioning legal, constitutional, and electoral system is established, which guarantees democracy, civil liberties, private property, and the right to legal representation and justice, property holders are often unwilling to take full advantage of their equity. In many countries with a history of instability or authoritarian rule, it may take property holders decades to accept that a new legal, constitutional, and electoral system is really functioning and secure.

Finally, even with "the rule of law," it is important to recognize that some companies, investments, and loans will fail, and hence there is a need for bankruptcy laws, government guarantees on mortgages, and an elaborate system of identification and records. Banks normally seek much more than a property title when reviewing a loan application, including personal data on the loan-recipient's background, employment, health, family, and credit record. These legitimate provisions are easily abused, especially when a national security apparatus claims to be fighting drugs, crime, terrorism, or revolutionary movements. With someone like Dr. Montesinos controlling the state apparatus, credit records may be secretly inspected and altered; loans to political opponents may be denied or cancelled; and real property may be confiscated in lieu of supposedly missing taxes or payments.

SPURIOUS PRECISION

The detailed content of *The Mystery of Capital* bears little relation to the assertions made on its dust jacket, and it raises very serious methodological questions. The book is reportedly based on ten years of research in five cities — Lima, Manila, Port-au-Prince, Cairo, and Mexico City — involving researchers from De Soto's

Lima-based Liberty and Democracy Institute (ILD), "assisted by knowledgeable local professionals" (p. 31). Little information is provided on funding or participants, but the team "spent many thousands of days counting buildings block by block" (p. 31). The claim is thus made that it is reasonable to assume good estimates of real property markets were produced in those five cities. However, most of the statistics are then presented as typical of Peru, the Philippines, Haiti, Egypt, and Mexico, even when there is no indication how estimates were made for parts of these countries outside their capital cities. More remarkably still, the data on the five cities are apparently extrapolated to cover five-sixths of the world. De Soto writes that "by our calculations, the total value of the real estate held but not legally owned by the poor of the Third World and former communist nations is at least $9.3 trillion" (p. 35). These data are disaggregated by major world regions in Table 2.1 (p. 36), providing estimates of the number of informal dwellings by region (Africa, for example), and a total value for those dwellings — presumably derived from an estimated average value of dwellings multiplied by the estimated total number of dwellings. There is no further discussion of sources or methodology, and there is no discussion anywhere of exchange rates, compounding and discounting rates, or the precise list of countries which fall into each category. The reader is left to wonder, for example, how such countries as Singapore, South Korea, Taiwan, Israel, the Czech Republic, and Slovenia were classified; and how estimates were produced for "China, NIS and Eastern Europe" when none of the five case study cities were located in those areas of the world.

The effort to estimate the quantity of any variable or phenomenon at the world level is fraught with difficulty because of gaps and inconsistencies in the available data, and because weather, economic, and exchange-rate fluctuations, or wars and disasters, can produce dramatic changes from one year to another. De Soto and his colleagues deserve congratulations for their effort to produce a global figure but criticism for their lack of methodological explanation. Their global figure is approximate, and it might well vary by at least plus or minus 50 percent. Similar comments apply to their even more ambitious and precise national estimates. The Philippines, for example, is reported to have US$132.9 billion of informal capital, an amount representing fourteen times the value of total direct foreign investment in the Philippines between 1973 and September 1998 (p. 251). For Egypt, the comparable figure, as stated on the book jacket, is fifty-five times the value of direct foreign investment up to 1996, extending at least as far back as the building of the Suez Canal, which began in 1859. Again, without a meticulous nationwide survey, careful adjustment of all prices to a single date, and rigorous comparison of national data sources, any claim of accuracy for these figures must be regarded as spurious, and as conveying a false sense of precision.

EYES OPEN, READING HISTORY

One of the enigmas of *The Mystery of Capital* is that despite its emphasis on the importance of setting books and established knowledge aside, and despite the effort to go out into the streets and listen to the barking dogs, some of the most interesting and thorough sections of the book are based on historical scholarship and breadth of reading in philosophy, politics, and economics. Chapter 5 on "The Missing Lessons of U.S. History" is a carefully documented interpretation of the history of the United States since English colonial times, focusing on how U.S. real property systems emerged during a complex process which involved European settlement, nation-building, widespread squatting, and gradual legalization. The message is compelling, explaining how over the last two hundred years the United States has gradually moved from Third World status, with a predominance of extra-legal land tenure and a very "wild" west, to a society governed by the rule of law where real property is a fundamental pillar of democracy and prosperity. Nevertheless, two major questions arise in the reader's mind. First, why does De Soto's narrative say so little about the more negative aspects of U.S. history — manifest destiny and territorial conquest; the displacement and exclusion of people of color; a heritage of slavery; the widespread incidence of land speculation; massive government subsidies to railroad, mining and timber companies through land grants and concessions; and the 1980s Savings and Loan crisis?[23] Second, does the settlement of a large and sparsely populated country in the horse-and-buggy era, initially under British colonial rule and then as an independent federal republic with an increasingly elaborate system of constitutional checks and balances, have much to tell us about the contemporary real property markets of Lima, Cairo, Manila, Port-au-Prince, and Mexico City, or about appropriate land titling policies for such countries as China, Turkmenistan, and Togo?

In Chapter 7, "By Way of Conclusion," De Soto reflects on globalization, anti-globalization, and Marxism. Here he shows himself as a populist, advocating the interests of poor people and countries, condemning Soviet bureaucracies and authoritarianism, and advocating the continued relevance of Marxism as a means to analyze the dynamics of class and inequality. The fundamental message of *The Other Path* is reiterated: the problem of poor countries is the lack of internal reform — deregulation, debureaucratization, and privatization — reforms which are resisted by local elites because they have a vested interest in the continuation of current systems. In De Soto's view, the world system is not one of domination and dependency, whereby rich nations exploit poor ones; rather it is one where stubborn vested interest groups prevent the great mass of poor people from pulling themselves up by their own bootstraps. Thus, the trigger to rapid global change will be private property — giving the poor a stake in the system, so that they can advance economically. If real property is not legalized rapidly throughout the developing and former communist world, the danger is that the forces of anti-globalization will gather momentum, and many contemporary nation-states will collapse into civil war, banditry, and destitution. De Soto's message is seductive, but like all simple solutions to complex global situations, it relies on a very questionable set of assumptions. It is much easier to imagine a set of global luminaries endorsing De Soto's recommendations, as indeed they do on the jacket, than tens of thousands of opinion leaders and government officials in poor countries committing their bureaucracies to years of painstaking work "going out into the streets to listen to the barking dogs."

By emphasizing U.S. history and casting it in such a favorable light, De Soto establishes the United States as the leading model for Third World nations. Of all the Western nations, the United States most strongly advocates the values of capitalism, individualism, and the importance of private property. As the sole military superpower and the largest national economy in the world, it is the hub of a rapidly globalizing system. Indeed, *The Mystery of Capital* argues that by replicating the historical experience of the United States in land settlement and the legalization of real property, Third World nations can achieve economic parity with "the West." The message is appealing, both to U.S. interests and to the elites of poor countries. The United States is not to blame for global poverty, but provides the principal example of how such poverty can be overcome. It is hardly surprising that ever since his emergence on the global scene in the mid-1980s, most of De Soto's support and funding has come from the United States, most notably the Heritage Foundation, the Cato Institute, and USAID.

EPILOGUE: A CREDIBLE FUTURE

Hernando De Soto is a highly effective transnational policy entrepreneur. He is able to use his European education, his U.S. support base, and his Peruvian nationality to work internationally and develop a global message. Fluently trilingual in French, English, and Spanish, with the name of a famous Spanish *conquistador*, and with close personal friendships in high-level Washington and United Nations circles, he is a celebrity who can market his ideas with unusual ease. His reputation is frequently enhanced by effusive praise from other celebrities and by feature articles in major magazines and newspapers. Because he primarily preaches to the converted — groups which abhor theories of imperialism and exploitation; which reject cooperatives, state enterprises, and government regulation; and which laud individualism, private property, and entrepreneurship — De Soto can spread his ideas widely without having to rigorously document the surveys and calculations that underlie them.

Though property titles are enormously important, and significant advances can be made in many countries through the development of a more inclusive property system, it is difficult to imagine that many countries will follow De

Soto's advice and move swiftly to legalize all their extra-legal real property. Many vested interests are happy with the status quo, and most poor countries face a succession of other concerns and priorities: new economic opportunities through resource extraction or assembly industries, mushrooming foreign debt, increasing outmigration to richer countries, possible wars, disasters, terrorist and secession movements, the need to keep military leaders happy, the spread of AIDS and other health problems, and the global trades in narcotics and armaments. More broadly, the pace of globalization may overtake all other development issues, as arguments rage in different parts of the world about the pros and cons of social and religious pluralism, the merits of trade liberalization, the continuing protectionism of many of the world's richest countries, growing limits on international migration, the refusal of the United States to support many multilateral institutions and authorities, the policy dictates of the International Monetary Fund (IMF), the weight of foreign debt on the world's poor, and the possibility of restraining offshore tax havens and instituting a Tobin Tax.

The Mystery of Capital is reminiscent of one of the bestsellers of the nineteenth century, Henry George's Progress and Poverty.[24] Like De Soto, George saw real property as the path to economic development. But in his writing, the key was "the single tax" — the idea of land value taxation. He argued that poverty resulted from the growing social inequalities associated with land speculation and inheritance. The rich owned most land, made fortunes through speculation, and transferred those fortunes to their children. Meanwhile, the poor lived in cramped dwellings and could not produce or earn very much because they had little access to all the productive opportunities that the land offered. Most owners of buildings invested little in their structures because they feared having to pay increased property taxes. The incentive for workers to increase their productivity and consumption was reduced by income and sales taxes. With dramatic simplicity, George proposed that all taxes be levied on the intrinsic value of land, encouraging its more intensive utilization, and the sale of underused parcels to those who would use it with greater efficiency. Worker productivity and consumer purchases would rise because there would no longer be taxes on incomes, production, and consumption, and land speculation would disappear because speculators would divert their capital to productive uses rather than pay so much in land value taxes. Through time, many of the landless would become farmers, old buildings would be maintained and expanded, new buildings would be constructed, full employment would be attained, poverty would disappear, and inequalities in income and wealth would gradually disappear.

Henry George was sometimes viewed as America's answer to Karl Marx. His ideas are still advocated by a wide range of Georgist societies, journals, and books around the world, and a significant number of towns and cities in different countries have experimented with land value taxation.[25] Nevertheless, no national government has ever adopted George's single tax, and Georgists have achieved nothing more than fringe-movement status in economics, government, and city and regional planning.

The Mystery of Capital is very similar to *Progress and Poverty* in that it produces a simple global explanation for poverty and a simple policy prescription for economic development. It will remain an important book in the background, and it will be cited to justify investment in property systems and micro-credit programs. However, it will not achieve the grand transformation of "dead" to "live" capital that it promises, because the real world is much more complex than De Soto indicates, and because other issues and priorities will take precedence in most places. Even if somehow, magically, De Soto's ideas were universally accepted and US$9.3. trillion of dead capital were brought to life, the current global economic system would concentrate the newfound wealth, rather than allow it to create universal prosperity. Further limitations result from current technologies and the great pressures which the global economy is placing on the environment. Private property may well be considered as a human right, but it is no guarantee of universal prosperity.

Solving "the mystery of capital" requires a much broader understanding of the global economy and financial system, and major policy and technological changes are needed to create a new world system which is more equitable and sustainable. De Soto has not solved the mystery, but he has highlighted one small part of the solution.

NOTES

1. H. De Soto, *The Mystery of Capital* (New York: Basic Books, 2000).

2. H. De Soto, *The Other Path: The Invisible Revolution in the Third World* (New York: Harper and Row, 1989).

3. C.A. Rakowski, "The Informal Sector Debate, Part 2: 1984–1993," in C.A. Rakowski, ed., *Contrapunto: The Informal Sector Debate in Latin America* (Albany: SUNY Press, 1994), 31–50.

4. R. Bromley, "A New Path to Development? The Significance and Impact of Hernando De Soto's Ideas on Underdevelopment, Production, and Reproduction," *Economic Geography* 66, no. 1 (October 1990), 328–48; and R. Bromley, "Informality, De Soto Style: From Concept to Policy," in Rakowski, ed., *Contrapunto*, 131–51.

5. E.g., R. Skidelsky in *New York Times Book Review*, December 24, 2000; J. Madrick in *New York Review of Books*, May 31, 2001; G. Payne in *Habitat Debate* 7, no. 3 (September 2001), 23; and C. Woodrull in *Journal of Economic Literature* 39, no. 4 (December 2001), 1215–23.

6. E. Fernandes, "The Influence of De Soto's The Mystery of Capital," *Land Lines* 14, no. 1 (January 2002), 5–8; A. Gilbert, "On the Mystery of Capital and the Myths of Hernando De Soto: What Differences Does Legal Title Make?" *International Development Planning Review* 24, no. 1 (February 2002), 1–19.

7. F. Braudel, *The Wheels of Commerce: Civilization and Capitalism 15th–18th Century, Volume 2* (New York: Harper and Row, 1982), 248.

8. B. Stein, *A License to Steal: The Untold Story of Michael Milken and the Conspiracy to Bilk the Nation* (New York: Simon and Schuster, 1992); and R. Sobel, *Dangerous Dreamers: The Financial Innovators from Charles Merrill to Michael Milken* (Washington, D.C.: Beard Books, 1993).

9. M. Josephson, *The Robber Barons: The Great American Capitalists 1861–1901* (New York: Harcourt Brace and Co., 1934).

10. G. Palast, *The Best Democracy Money Can Buy* (London: Pluto Press, 2002); M. Kelly, *The Divine Right of Capital: Dethroning the Corporate Aristocracy* (San Francisco: Berrett-Koehler, 2001); E. Lubbers, *Battling Big Business: Countering Greenwash, Front Groups and Other Forms of Corporate Deception* (Monroe, Maine: Common Courage Press, 2002); P.C. Fusaro and R.M. Miller, *What Went Wrong at Enron* (New York: John Wiley, 2002); and C.W. Mulford and E.E. Comiskey, *The Financial Numbers Game: Detecting Creative Accounting Practices* (New York: John Wiley, 2002).

11. M. Pastor and C. Wise, "From Poster Child to Basket Case," *Foreign Affairs* 80, no. 6 (November/December 2001), 60–72.

12. D. Gonzalez, "A Get-Rich Scheme Collapses, Leaving Haiti Even Poorer," *New York Times*, July 26, 2002, A6.

13. W.F. Steel, "Empirical Measurement of the Relative Size and Productivity of Intermediate Sector Employment: Some Estimates from Ghana," *Manpower and Unemployment Research* 9, no. 1 (April 1976), 23–31; G. Arrighi and J. Drangel, "The Stratification of the World-Economy: An Exploration of the Semiperipheral Zone," *Review* 10, no. 1 (Summer 1986), 9–74; and A.M. Soliman, "Typology of Informal Housing in Egyptian Cities: Taking Account of Diversity," *International Development Planning Review* 24, no. 2 (May 2002), 177–201.

14. R. Bromley, ed., *Planning for Small Enterprises in Third World Cities* (Oxford: Pergamon Press, 1985).

15. See C.M. Conaghan, *Making and Unmaking Authoritarian Peru: Re-election, Resistance, and Regime Transition* (Coral Gables, Fla.: University of Miami, North South Agenda Papers no. 47, 2001); National Security Archive, *Fujimori's Rasputin: The Declassified Files on Peru's Former Intelligence Chief, Vladimiro Montesinos*, Electronic Briefing Book no. 37 http://www.gwu.edu/~nsarchiv/NSAEBB/NSAEBB37/; and G. Gorriti, "The Betrayal of Peruvian Democracy: Montesinos as Fujimori's Svengali," *Covert Action Quarterly*, Summer 1994, 4–12 and 54–59.

16. E. Guerrero and D. Flores, "28 Muertos tras Infierno en Jockey Plaza," *La República*, July 21, 2002; and Anon., "Utopía Calcinada," *Caretas* 1731, July 25, 2002.

17. A. Logan, "Around City Hall: Happy Land," *The New Yorker*, April 23, 1990, 102–9; and Anon., "New York's Happy Land Fire Drew Attention to Code Enforcement Efforts in Social Clubs," *Building Official and Code Administrator*, May/June 1990, 28–33.

18. V. Fleischer, "Enron's Dirty Little Secret: Waiting for the Other Shoe to Drop," *Tax Notes* 94, no. 8 (February 2002) (New York: Columbia University); D.C. Johnston,

"Enron Collapse: The Havens, Enron Avoided Income Taxes in 4 of 5 Years," *New York Times*, January 17, 2002, A1; and Glenn R. Simpson, "As Tax Haven Enron Found a Dutch Treat," *Wall Street Journal*, February 7, 2002, A2.

19. www.enron.com/corp/pressroom/responsibility/human_rights_statement.html (September 1, 2002).

20. Quotes drawn from F.A. Hayek, *The Constitution of Liberty* (Chicago: University of Chicago Press), 205–19 (Chapter 14, "The Safeguards of Individual Liberty"). See also A. Gamble, *Hayek: The Iron Cage of Liberty* (Oxford: Polity Press, 1996), 94–99, 135–40.

21. D. Kerr, "The 'Place' of Land in Japan's Postwar Development, and the Dynamic of the 1980s Real-Estate 'Bubble' and 1990s Banking Crisis," *Environment and Planning D: Society and Space* 20, no. 3 (June 2002), 345–74; and B. Bremner, "It's Koizumi vs. Japan's Broken Banks," *Business Week*, August 8, 2001.

22. K. Mera and B. Renaud, eds., *Asia's Financial Crisis and the Role of Real Estate* (Armonk, NY: M.E. Sharpe, 2000).

23. See, for example, A.M Sakolski, *Land Tenure and Land Taxation in America* (New York: Robert Schalkenbach Foundation, 1957); D.M. Friedenberg, *Life, Liberty, and the Pursuit of Land: The Plunder of Early America* (Buffalo: Prometheus Books, 1992); C.A. Beard, *An Economic Interpretation of the Constitution of the United States* (New York: Macmillan, 1913); B. DeVoto, *The Course of Empire* (New York: Houghton Mifflin, 1952); P. Jacobs and S. Landau with E. Pell, *To Serve the Devil: A Documentary Analysis of America's Racial History and Why It Has been Kept Hidden* (New York: Vintage Books, 1971, 2 vols.); and M. Waldman, *Who Robbed America? A Citizen's Guide to the Savings and Loan Scandal* (New York: Random House, 1990).

24. H. George, *Progress and Poverty* (New York: D. Appleton & Co., 1880).

25. R.V. Andelson, *Land Value Taxation around the World* (Oxford: Blackwell, 2000, 3rd ed.); and F.K. Peddle, *Cities and Greed: Taxes, Inflation and Land Speculation* (Ottawa: Canadian Research Committee on Taxation, 1994).

11

Transnational Trespassings:
The Geopolitics of Urban Informality

Ananya Roy

To teach about cities and development, about urban informality, is to engage in the act of representation. That act, as Spivak reminds us in her seminal work on the "subaltern," can be understood in two ways: "representation as 'speaking for,' as in politics, and representation as 're-presentation,' as in art or philosophy," "a proxy and a portrait."[1] It is an act that claims an object — to be represented — and through that claim, asserts what Spivak calls a "sovereign subject" — that which can represent.[2] The political economy of urban informality is thus also the politics of representation; the poetics of representation is thus also the geopolitics of late capitalism.

GENEALOGIES OF REPRESENTATION

In the urban studies courses that I teach at the University of California, Berkeley, I often start my discussion of housing struggles and policies with two contrasting images, asking students to situate them in time and place (see FIGURES 11.1, 11.2). While the responses cover a wide range of territory and history, perhaps because the discussion is located within courses dealing with developing countries, students most often identify the two images as "Third World."[3] This designation of a horribly dismal, but ineluctably foreign, "Other" is strangely comforting, particularly for a "First World" generation that bumps and weaves its way through panhandlers, bag ladies, and street bums on a daily basis.

Of course the two images belong to quite different moments, and embody strikingly varied genealogies of social documentation and commentary. The first comes from late-nineteenth-century New York, as captured by Jacob Riis.[4] The

Figures 11.1. and 11.2.

second is a snapshot from a Cali squatter settlement that Edward Popko pho-
tographed in the 1970s.[5] While they both belong to a rich tradition of photographic journalism, Riis's work comes laced with fear:

> The sea of a mighty population, held in galling fetters, heaves uneasily in the
> tenements. Once already our city, to which have come the duties and respon-
> sibilities of metropolitan greatness before it was able to fairly measure its task,
> has felt the swell of its relentless flood. If it rises once more, no human power
> may avail to check it.[6]

The above passage is quite aptly quoted by Hall in his analysis of "The City of
Dreadful Night" — the persistent theme of tumorous tenements and a sick urban
body politic that emerged on both sides of the Atlantic in the late nineteenth century.[7] Riis's words present a distilled and timeless poverty, characterized by what
seem to be immutable traits of mob rowdiness, base instincts, and social immoral-
ities. In other words, Riis's touching photojournalism turns out to be an unfortunate, though perhaps unintended, forebearer of "culture of poverty" discourses.
    In contrast, Popko's work firmly situates Cali's squatter settlements in the
political economy of urbanization:

> Urban growth is the result of a hunger-dictated "push" from the country
> rather than an economic "pull" from the city. The city has created the illusion
> of providing jobs and opportunities for all. Although many migrants do find
> work and remain, the benefits often tend to be more social than economic,
> and thus the only initial change for the migrant is an urbanization of his
> poverty.... Faced with these realities, many urban poor resort to illegal means
> of finding housing for themselves and their families. They become squatters.[8]

Popko's lively photographic documentary is appropriately entitled *Transitions*, focusing as it does on the ways in which rural-urban migrants negotiate and create access to shelter, services, and community.

These two images comprise a constellation of moving similarities but crucially important analytical differences. First, as I have already briefly mentioned, Popko's *Transitions* is ultimately concerned with the political economy of housing and urban change. The central culprit of this narrative, unlike Riis's work, is neither poverty nor deplorable slums and tenements. Instead, it is the very socioeconomic structure of Latin American development and urbanization.

Second, Popko's words — and images — vest agency in the urban poor. Thus, his pithily dramatic note: "They become squatters." Migrants, squatters — these are all terms evocative of movement and action. They are markers of subjectivity, of personhood, of specific notions of citizenship. In contrast, Riis writes of "the other half," a heaving mass capable perhaps of revolutionary action, but subject for the most part to the organized violence of state power, as well as to the more genteel violence of poverty, redevelopment, and social reform. His urban poor, while foremost in the minds of reformers, are the "grounds" rather than the subjects of debate — they have been spoken for in the act of re-presentation. I borrow this terminology of subjectivation, or the lack thereof, from revisionist interpretations of British colonialism.[9] It is ironic, but perhaps only mildly so, that the suitable analogy for American urban planning is with colonial liberalism and its inevitably truncated concept of citizenship and selfhood.

This in turn takes me to my third point. If Popko's migrants and squatters are positioned as social and political agents, then they are so because their agency is linked to a wide gamut of shelter practices. Unlike Riis's emphasis on the city's heart of darkness, and the implicit fuel that this provides to middle-class fears and flight, Popko presents squatter settlements as an integral and indispensable part of the urban fabric. His squatters produce the city; they even demand what Harvey has recently called the "right to the production of the city."[10]

I do not mean to suggest that there is some immutable difference between Riis and Popko, between First World and Third World housing and poverty debates. However, I am arguing that there are specific genres of Third World housing and urbanization research that constitute a significant break with the language of urban pathologies and crises. For example, this book has taken as its starting point the well-established tradition of research on urban informality, much of it initially conducted in Latin America in the 1970s, and then continued through the 1980s and 1990s in various settings. The comparison between Riis and Popko highlights differences in such regional productions of knowledge, between the Anglo-American imaginary and the Latin American tradition, albeit in broad brushstrokes. Such differences are not merely at the level of discourse. Regional genres of housing knowledge are in turn rooted in varying pathways of shelter struggles and housing practices. Holding the two genealogies of representation in tension with one another thus initiates important conversations about housing policy and housing politics, an issue to which I will return.

The photojournalism of Riis is haunted by the specter of poverty as social disease. Riis, writing with great sympathy, recognizes the "grinding poverty" that leads to homelessness, but then labels "young vagabonds" as the deviant "street Arabs."[11] In their naming, he demonstrates his unshakeable sense of the poor as essentially different, and of this difference as comprising lawlessness. Today, the American poverty debates continue to coalesce around a few keywords of difference, such as "underclass" and "ghetto." They reveal a cumbersome historical legacy of defining poverty in terms of behavioral pathologies and individualist moralities.[12] In contrast, the Third World research on urban informality, particularly its Latin American variant, has shattered the "myth of marginality."[13] If the American debates contemplate difference as the "culture of poverty," then the Third World debates map the differential geography of capitalism.[14] If the American debates anguish over the dependencies of the poor — on controlled substances or the state — then the Latin American perspective has made evident the fragile dependence of entire economies in the context of global capitalism. Here, dependency is inscribed as participation in capitalist production, and underdevelopment is seen as constantly produced through development.[15] Within this historico-geographical setting, struggles over urban resources such as housing are carefully noted but rarely celebrated.[16] The brilliance of the Latin American research is to show how the urban poor are able to stake claims to land, shelter, and services, but how such popular mobilizations spin webs of dependency, co-opting the poor through intricate relations of territorialized patronage.[17]

But holding the photo-narratives of Riis and Popko in tension with one another is useful beyond the comparison of differences and similarities. This transnational enterprise allows an examination of the norms and standards of urban discourse. Cast in the crucible of development, First World urban theory and urban planning has imagined an underdeveloped Other, the problem-ridden Third World city that must be reformed and managed. On the one hand, underdevelopment is narrated in an idiom of grim and stark crisis. On the other, the First World city is constructed as an ideal type, the normative model to be replicated through developmentalist practice, its history aestheticized and naturalized. The simultaneous discussion of Riis and Popko unsettles both the anomaly and the ideal. As New York comes to light as the site of a gruesome capitalism, so Cali emerges as the site of innovative shelter practices.

I believe that such transnational strategies constitute an important part of a pedagogy that challenges the normalized hierarchy of development and underdevelopment. For example, over the years, a steady stream of freshmen students have visited my concrete, minimalist office in UC Berkeley's Wurster Hall seeking advice on how to write papers on homelessness in the Third World. They are frustrated by the rarity of the terminology of homelessness as they journey beyond U.S. borders. And while never fully admitted, there is quite a bit of surprise and even profound unease at the idea that "home" rather than "elsewhere" might be the underdeveloped Other, a site of the lack, or failure, so often reserved for the Third World. As they begin their research projects, they find themselves surrounded by a rich array of housing terms that are used in Third World settings — from "slums" and "squatter settlements" to "pavement dwellers" and "informal subdivisions" — a vocabulary that indicates a spectrum of housing practices. In many ways, the dominance of the term "homelessness" in the American context bears testimony to the poverty of housing responses here. In the transnational space between First and Third Worlds, my students are forced to interrogate their ideas of self and Other, development and underdevelopment.

It is important to take this a step further. As I have detailed elsewhere, transnational strategies can not only highlight different political economies of representation or deconstruct the normalized standards against which we have judged the Third World, but they can also do something more radical — i.e., pose Third World questions of First World processes.[18] Unlike comparative methodologies that search for similarities and differences between two mutually exclusive contexts, transnational examinations can use one site to interrogate another. For example, in studying informal housing settlements in Texas, Ward looks across the border and asks why similar settlements in Mexico enable higher standards of living. His view of Texas via Mexico allows for an innovative discussion of American housing struggles and policies.[19] Or, in the constellation of poverty representations, the Third World research on squatting raises the question of how and why the American urban poor have been unable to similarly stake claims to shelter and services.[20] Such transnational epistemologies have great potential, as in Fraser and Gordon's exploration of internationalist meanings of "dependency" in their discussion of welfare reform, Wacquant's analysis of ghetto studies in the postcolonial sense of a "new urban Orientalism," and Davis's use of the provocative apartheid metaphor of "bantustans" to map socio-spatial segregation in contemporary Los Angeles.[21] In each case, the mapping of the marginal, the marginalized, makes apparent the margins present within the normal, in the normalization:

> I would argue that we can learn from other regions by realizing that it is always the marginal or peripheral case which reveals that which does not appear immediately visible in what seem to be more "normal" cases.[22]

THE GEOPOLITICS OF DESIRE

Transnational epistemologies can enable new policy and political possibilities. Thus, in recent decades Third World solutions are being brought to bear on First World problems.[23] For example, there has been a great deal of interest in replicating the success of the Grameen Bank microcredit program. From the Good Faith Fund of Arkansas to microcredit programs in inner cities, such transnational borrowings seem to promise hope for the thorny dilemma of persistent American poverty.[24] In the broadest sense, such border crossings are welcome, for transnational policy-making disrupts the teleology of development, which sees Anglo-America as the idealized yardstick against which all else is to be judged. But they require some critical analysis.

If I have earlier advanced the cause of transnational pedagogy, I now call for caution in how the transnational imagination is deployed and used. The attempt to simply mimic success elsewhere is not only pragmatically naïve but also methodologically problematic, for it maintains the universalist logic of development. While in First World borrowings of Third World policies the hierarchy of development and underdevelopment may be reversed, the erasure of geopolitical difference continues through the mechanics of imitation and replication. Against this universalist transnationalism, I argue for a *critical* transnationalism, one given to learning the paradoxes and contradictions of place-based policy rather than copying a litany of best practices or development miracles. To this end, I analyze two forms of transnational appropriation: a growing First World interest in Third World urban informality, and an enduring Third World interest in American urban reforms. Advancing a critical transnationalism, I show how each First World/Third World axis can provide important lessons. These lessons are not the blueprints of success, awaiting construction. Rather, they are historicized lessons about the peculiar vulnerabilities and exclusions that accompany each genre of representation and each model of political economy. It is in this way that the deconstructive critique embedded in critical transnationalism can lead to reconstruction.

THE SEDUCTION OF SQUATTING

The previous fin-de-siècle was marked by rabid discourses about the chaos of the First World metropolis. Likewise, at the turn of this century the Third World metropolis has emerged as the trope of social disorganization and unfathomable crisis. Urban planning emerged as a nineteenth-century drive to rationalize the city. Now, the ideology of "civil society" — a celebration of grassroots movements and self-management by the urban poor — bears the new millennial promise of taming the Third World. From the idiom of crisis, the pendulum has swung to a utopian recovery of Third World urban communities. Academic and policy discourses are rife with tales of self-sufficient squatter settlements, self-help housing, and thriving women's cooperatives. Particularly important is how this culture of entrepreneurship is being directed against a culture of poverty, a transaction that has taken on the form of Third World solutions for First World problems.

The popularity of such "Third World" models requires a closer look. How is the Third World and its informality represented in the transnational space of knowledge transaction? How, within the geopolitical space of the First World academy, are the practices of the Third World poor depicted and appropriated? Let me take the liberty of drawing upon two pedagogical examples from my academic home. In Spring 2002 two graduate studios dealing with Mexico City were offered in the College of Environmental Design at UC Berkeley. In each case I was invited by the students to provide critical review and advice. The first, a design studio aimed primarily at Master's students in Architecture, chose as its site a squatter settlement. Rather than a design program, the studio pursued a "found objects" philosophy, encouraging students to collect materials from the squatter settlement as inspiration for their designs. During their brief site visit students recorded the sounds of poverty, collected the dirt of poverty, acquired discarded objects of poverty, and returned to Berkeley to make a montage of their excavations. The squatter settlement figured in their imagination as an aesthetic experience, unshakably exotic, undeniably distant. For one student the experience of the squatter settlement was embodied by a battered drum she came across in her wanderings there. Returning to Berkeley, she placed gravel collected from the settlement on the drum, and played it to create contours and shapes that would then determine the topography of her design.

It would be easy to dismiss this exercise as the manifestation of an architectural discipline and profession prone to self-centered ignorance, one where design as an egotistical enterprise can only proceed by being hostile to the knowledge of material realities. Or it could be read as the inevitable epistemic violence of the act of design — and indeed also of the act of planning. But there is something particular about *how* this studio offends that bears consideration beyond the usual diatribe about professional hegemonies.

It is the second studio that reveals the issues at hand. This one was a sophisticated environmental planning studio, co-organized with universities in Mexico City, with students making frequent trips to the site, where they became deeply engaged with its natural and built landscapes. The mandate of the studio was to devise a master plan for Tlahuac, a site on the southwestern perimeter of Mexico City with an unusual ecology of "*chinampas*," artificial agricultural islands developed in pre-Hispanic times now facing extinction through the pressures of urbanization. The studio was an admirable effort, and the first round of design work yielded intricate models, gorgeous drawings, and very real enthusiasm. But in those first models, students were obsessively concerned with the need to create "defensive strategies" for the protection of the *chinampas*. As a reviewer, I asked: "Who are you defending against?" Their answer was telling: they were defending against thousands of squatters who occupy the land around the *chinampas*. In the multilay-ered models that had represented every gradient of the topography, every flow and ebb of the watershed, the land that had been represented as blank and empty, as frontier, was in fact the living fabric of the site, inhabited by squatters. "Defending for whom?" I asked. Defending, intentionally in this case, for "intentional urban-ization," came the answer — for the bourgeois city, for neatness and order.

Despite their differences, the aesthetic imperialism of the first studio and the well-meaning interventions of the second converge around two issues. The first is the portrayal of the informal city as tabula rasa, as clean slate, awaiting the sov-ereign hand of the architect-planner to write upon it. In the context of environ-mental planning, squatting was seen as a destructive process, while "intentional urbanization" was seen as environmentally safe. This allowed the history of the natural landscape to be carefully considered, while the history of the lived land-scape was ignored. "If you had started not with slope gradients and water tables but with maps of land ownership or cartographies of livelihood, what would your master plan have then looked like?" I asked the students. "What would your design look like if you defined environmental sustainability not simply as the restoration of the *chinampas* but as the survival of the people who occupy this land?" In subsequent rounds of design, these environmental planning students met these challenges admirably, taking into account both informal housing and informal work, and situating them within the context of global change.

The second issue brought to light by the studio is less easily mitigated, how-ever. It is the aestheticization of poverty.[25] By this I mean the gaze that looks toward a squatter settlement and sees in the original lines of beauty, the primitive organicism of the vernacular. Take, for example, the accompanying sketch, done in 1983 by a group of architecture students as they studied a squatter settlement in Colombia (see FIGURE 11.3). The student sketch contrasts provocatively with Popko's 1978 black-and-white photo-documentary of squatting. The contrast does not simply express a distinction between representation and reality. What is at stake are varying genealogies of representation. In particular, the aesthetic imagination sees the squatter settlement as organic beauty, a museum-like space that is pure and clean. Elsewhere, I have linked this representational genre to the museumification practices of colonial elites who sought to recover spaces of native tradition amidst the modernization of colonial planning.[26]

One element of this aesthetic argument is the emphasis on the architecture of squatting, on the physical expression of informality. Thus, Serageldin talks about "an architecture of empowerment — that is, a built environment which responds to the needs of the poor and destitute, while respecting their humanity and putting them in charge of their own destinies."[27] This is indeed a noble sen-timent, but the question that needs to be asked is whether or not a design imagi-

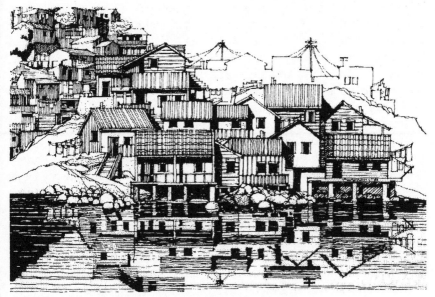

Figure 11.3. Artist rendering of squatter settlement, Colombia, 1983.
Courtesy of UC Berkeley Slide Library.

nation can foster empowerment. Is the architecture of squatter settlements their most significant component? Seeing squatter settlements as primarily a built environment has crucial implications. For example, it would imply that the "upgrading" of such settlements should primarily entail a package of environmental reforms. And it would further imply that the form of such upgrading should be determined by aesthetic considerations — specifically, by the aesthetic desires of professionals as they interpret informality and poverty. Such of course has been the common route of interventions in the urban informal sector, and often with unfortunate consequences.

For example, in a recent critique of such aesthetic interventions, Verma incisively analyzes how the award-winning Indore Slum Networking Project (Aga Khan Award for Architecture, Global Best Practices at Habitat II) was a miserable failure on the ground.[28] Citing extensive surveys, interviews, and local newspaper accounts, Verma tells a compelling story of how slum upgrading came to be defined primarily as the provision of physical infrastructure and landscaping. But such environmental reforms failed to take account of the socioeconomic structure of the slums. Thus, the Aga Khan Award citation claimed that by paying for and building individual toilets and connections to the water and sewerage systems, the project allowed slum dwellers to "enhance their quality of life and hence their pride in home ownership."[29] But Verma shows how households were unable or unwilling to make such an investment. The reasons varied: some were tenants with no incentives to engage in these physical improvements; others lacked the space; others were without access to water mains, and thus could not waste their precious water on toilets. Without total hook-up, the sewage lines choked, and other slum residents became even less willing to connect to this infrastructure. Even the community-development projects lost legitimacy because the people's most urgent problem, choked drainage, was not being solved. Other components of the upgrading never materialized so that slum residents, when asked about "soft landscaping," said that if they did not have enough water to drink, how could they possibly maintain plants? And yet, as Verma provocatively argues, all through this period, the project received international accolades and transnational attention. When the British Prime Minister, John Major, arrived to pay a visit, the slums were once again aesthetically presented for viewing. A cartoonist in a local paper captured the spirit of the situation in his drawing of two IDA engineers in conversation saying: "If only we had the information of his arrival a little earlier we could have changed the huts into bungalows!"[30]

This is not to say that the provision of physical infrastructure or the aesthetic upgrading of slums is necessarily unimportant or unwelcome. Indeed, as Jacobs perceptively notes, aestheticization can be much more than simply the "legitimizing skin of capital accumulation." As she argues, this "staging of difference" can "activate political struggles that are fundamentally about how different interests should be registered (aesthetically and materially) in the space of the city."[31] The issue then is not aestheticization per se, but rather what Peattie calls "aesthetic politics."[32] In the context of slum redevelopment, my concern is with how such environmental reforms are seen as the sole component of urban policy agendas, and how in turn these aesthetics represent the sensibilities of urban professionals. The Aga Khan Award citation for the Indore project claims definitively that "landscaped riverbanks now overlook a clean river that was formerly a sewage-filled, low-water river lined with decrepit slums."[33] However, such an aesthetic evaluation (the upgrading of the built and natural environment) is clearly different from other social criteria that could have been used to gauge the project's success: the upgrading of livelihoods, the upgrading of housing rights, the upgrading of political participation. Such, I will argue later, is the ideology of space — that what is redeveloped is space and buildings rather than people's socioeconomic experience. The parallels with gentrification are obvious.[34] And it is thus not surprising that slum redevelopment projects have often triggered processes of gentrification.

The Indore Slum Networking program stands in sharp contrast to the model of infrastructure provision developed in the Orangi Pilot Project, Karachi, Pakistan. Here, urban professionals provided expertise, but squatters determined the hierarchy and sequence of priorities, opting in this case for a sewage system that served their particular needs.[35] Similarly, Appadurai describes the "toilet festivals" organized by an alliance of NGOs in Mumbai. At each celebration, "functioning public toilets designed by and for the poor, incorporating complex systems of collective payment and maintenance with optimal conditions of safety and cleanliness" are unveiled.

> When a World Bank official has to examine the virtues of a public toilet and discuss the merits of this form of faeces management with the defecators themselves, the condition of poverty moves from abjection to subjectivation.[36]

While we run the risk of romanticizing these self-help efforts, of instituting a model where the poor dig their own sewers and design their own toilets, there is nonetheless a difference between aesthetic purity and what Appadurai calls the "politics of shit."[37] The shift from one to the other is the move away from the professional hierarchy of needs to a public discourse about the politics of needs.[38] Here, the aesthetic agenda is transformed into what Jacobs terms the "activated spheres of practice."[39]

Another element in the aestheticization of poverty is the interpretation of squatter settlements as vernacular, authentic, or traditional. Peattie asks: What do we see when we see a Third World shantytown?[40] She notes how Perlman, in her effort to undermine "the myth of marginality," presented as frontispiece of her book of the same name a photograph of a Rio *favela* spilling down a hillside. In the place of older representations of disorderly and chaotic slums, Perlman saw in this image a neighborhood in progress, careful planning, and innovative construction techniques. But at what point does this urban reality shade into pastoral nostalgia? In her article, Peattie reflexively notes how she too, in Venezuela, fell in love with a squatter settlement:

> It took an American anthropologist struggling for a sense of balance in the modern technology utopia of a new city-planning project to look up the beach, see fragile beauty at the human scale, and fall in love with exactly that.... Both the building technique and the style of the house we bought evoked small-settlement roots, but to the builders the solution was dictated by poverty.[41]

In the context of teaching a transnational housing course, Peattie's writings returned me to my own field notes and field photographs. How had I gazed upon the squatter shack and the peasant hut? How had subsequent audiences interpreted my images? What were the spaces that had become icons? I reflected upon Amirjan's simple shack in a Calcutta squatter settlement (see FIGURE 11.4); and Noyon's peasant hut in a Bengali village (see FIGURE 11.5). How was it that various viewers had seen in them the pure elements of indigenous building, the simplicity of simple people? Had I not too? In the act of selection? In the act of representation?

The aestheticization of poverty has numerous implications. Most importantly, it mutes the social, political, and economic narratives that also underlie

Figure 11.4. Amirjan's shack,
Patuli squatter settlement.
Photo by author, 1997.

Figure 11.5. Noyon's family hut, Tetultola village.
Photo by author, 1997.

poverty. Amirjan, a desperate migrant from the West Bengal countryside, had built this shack over the course of many months, only to see it demolished a few weeks later. Noyon's family owned no land other than this tiny homestead plot. Unable to feed their children, they sent all three daughters to work in the city as domestic servants at the age of six or seven. To present these stories as embodied in aesthetic structures is to imagine poverty or the informal sector as a precapitalist domain, free of material corruptions. Primitive organicism, as it turns out, can be directly related to a brutal primitive accumulation.

These aesthetic impulses also contain a particular ambivalence toward the commercialized aspects of poverty or informality. If the poor peasant's mud hut or the desperate migrant's flimsy shack become icons of vernacular beauty, how should we interpret the forms that coexist in the differentiated spaces of the rural-urban interface? For example, in Noyon's village, a well-to-do peasant wife proudly poses with her few possessions — a poster of the *hajj*, tinsel lanterns left over from Ramadan, clothes on a clothesline, her daughter in her fanciest dress, a newly painted house (see FIGURE 11.6). In Amirjan's squatter settlement a grandmother and child are similarly proud of their acquisitions: a refrigerator, solid furniture, electricity (see FIGURE 11.7). Taking note of this upgrading means challenging our aesthetic politics, that which leads us to turn away from the forms of capitalization that the upwardly mobile urban and rural poor engage in, and aspire to, in the spaces of informality.

The aesthetic unwillingness to see urban informality as a commercialized domain has served urban policy poorly. For example, Doshi's famous and award-winning Aranya Low-Cost Housing Scheme in Indore has been presented and re-presented as "creating a community character by establishing harmony

Figure 11.6. Peasant home, Tetultola village.
Photo by author, 1997.

Figure 11.7. Squatter home, Patuli squatter settlement.
Photo by author, 1997.

between people and the built environment, imitating the scale and security of a village community."[42] Steele has even credited Doshi's research institute, the Vastu-Shilpa Foundation, with having discovered the "hidden order" of slums, including the determination that the "monthly incomes of the economically weaker sector are underestimated in the national statistics as they do not take into account the income from the informal economy."[43] Here, the informals are seen at once as entrepreneurs and as precapitalist or authentic villagers. But notice the surprise with this turn of events:

> In a local report prepared for the Aga Khan Award for Architecture, which the Aranya Low-Cost Housing Scheme won in 1996, one observer expressed alarm at the prevalence of brokering on the project site, outside a 1-block area defined by 80 demonstration houses designed and supervised by the architect.... This suggests a lack of community spirit in the project.[44]

The mythicized community is, of course, constantly undermined by the processes of capitalist differentiation within informal settlements. In the case of Aranya, Steele goes on to note that this particular "observer" found that only 15 to 20 percent of the original plot owners still held the plots originally allotted to them, with the resale price of plots averaging approximately ten times the original purchase price.[45] Perhaps the poor had been entrepreneurial; perhaps they had been displaced through gentrification. Regardless, the dynamics of the Aranya project makes evident the broader processes of urban development at work in the informal sector. And often government policies of slum upgrading, resettlement, or redevelopment accelerate, rather than negate, such housing and land markets.[46]

Are there other ways then of seeing a slum or squatter settlement? Can we search for its essence not in the simple, poverty-induced form, but in what the processes of capitalization seek to mimic, in what Appadurai has called "houseless domesticity"?[47] What are the hegemonic forms and meanings that are thus invoked? How is this domestic desire a part of the circuits of capitalism through which housing is produced and lived in? If we understand a squatter settlement not as a static form of traditional dwelling, but as a dynamic process of capitalism, how may we formulate policy toward it (see FIGURE 11.8)? How can we move from what Spivak calls the "desiring subject" to a "theory of interests"?[48]

Such issues, of course, can only be discussed in the context of our geopolitical desires. The aestheticization of poverty is the establishment of an aesthetic and aestheticized (rather than political) relationship between viewer and viewed, between professional and city, between First and Third Worlds. It is an ideology of space. Such a relationship is expressed primarily in the form of nostalgia. This

Figure 11.8. Upgrading.
Photo by author, 1997.

is a pastoral nostalgia that craves the rurality of a magical countryside in a rapidly urbanizing world, a nostalgia that, as Williams notes, imagines a landscape without labor.[49] In an unpublished paper about slum upgrading in India, Renu Desai, a key contributor to the production of this book, shows how high-profile slum upgrading in India has been primarily a series of aesthetic interventions. The aesthetics, she argues, imagine the informal inhabitant as the embodiment of "an idealized traditional lifestyle that is derived in some manner from the physical elements tied to an 'Indian identity in architecture.'" Such, for example, is the logic of the "vernacular-based" housing projects of Correa and Doshi. Desai notes that the most commonly circulated photograph of Correa's Belapur housing project is a romanticized image of two women carrying water, as though from a well:

> The question that jumps out at me is: Does the Belapur housing project not provide running water to each house? Why portray a cumbersome daily activity in this idyllic manner in relation to a housing project?[50]

As she points out, the reason is that Correa, as the aesthetic professional engaged in a "monologue," has determined that the village well is a space of social interaction, an open-to-sky space, in his schema of space hierarchies.[51]

Such forms of representation also contain an "imperialist nostalgia," an impulse that Rosaldo has interpreted as a "mourning for what one has destroyed."[52] In the case of Aranya, the mysterious "observer" is quoted as having concluded the report thus:

> The Aranya project is based on good intentions in which the innocence of the professional designers is symbolized in the 80 demonstration houses. If only slum resettlement projects were simply architectural problems capable of being overcome with good design.[53]

How should we understand that operative term, "innocence"? It seems imperialist nostalgia simultaneously establishes innocence and allows the excavation of an "authentic" and "exotic culture" through paradigms of salvage. What is thus salvaged is seen as timeless and unchanging, standing in opposition to the modernizing forces of history.[54] Thus, Pugh, in a recent piece on the "sustainability, architectural contributions, and socio-economic roles" of squatter settlements contrasts self-help as a "human" impulse with the "modern" as "20th century technology."[55] While the aestheticization of poverty can be seen as an attempt to return dignity to the urban poor, it must also be seen as a geopolitical enterprise that ignores the terribly difficult conditions under which the poor survive and struggle and aspire.

But there is one more question that must be asked about the seduction of squatting: Why is it so prevalent at this particular historical moment? Why is there so much policy interest in Third World informality? A straightforward answer is that such celebrations of poverty serve and reinforce the agenda of neoliberalism, shifting the burden of coping from the privatizing state to the shoulders of the poor.[56] But what are the rhetorical mechanisms of this displacement? Of the popularity of this displacement?

The popularity of such a view is amply evident in the latest work of Hernando De Soto.[57] In another chapter in this book, Ray Bromley skillfully tackles De Soto's key ideas. I want to pose a somewhat different question here: Why are De Soto's ideas so seductive? I would venture to say that the basis of this seduction are the two elements of the transnational transaction that I earlier outlined: the tabula rasa imagination, and the aestheticization of poverty. In *The Mystery of Capital*, De Soto imagines many different spaces as tabula rasa. The American frontier, for example, is represented as empty land, an unoccupied wilderness settled and improved by pioneering homesteaders. The Third World too is presented as tabula rasa, without colonial or imperial histories. And, as such, it is separated from the First World through the mechanical metaphor of a bell jar, rather than bound to it through dependency theory's geopolitical metaphor of an uneven geography of core and periphery.

Particularly provocative is De Soto's conceptualization of poverty as heroic entrepreneurship, a continuation of his earlier idea of informality as revolution.[58] In De Soto's words, the informal economy is "an epic struggle waged by the informals, . . . a long march toward private property, subjugating the state and formal society as they go."[59] As the culture of poverty allowed blame to be placed on the poor, so the culture of entrepreneurship allows the Third World poor to bear responsibility for their destinies. Furthermore, the idea that informality is simply a response to the cumbersome regulations of the state, a way of reducing transaction costs, demonstrates De Soto's concern with social capital rather than social power. For example, his interpretation of the market as revolutionary indicates his neoliberal interpretation of rights — granting informals the right to property rights, but not property rights themselves. That the market does not honor any rights, not even the right to participate, is of negligible concern. De Soto's narration of informality is thus an aestheticization of poverty. It presents capitalism as a benign trade in assets, and thereby presents informality and poverty as neither exploited nor exploitative.[60] The popularity of his work must be understood in relation to other such "nostalgic narrations," ones that seek to aestheticize the anxieties of global inequality.[61]

THE PROMISE OF "THE RATIONAL CITY"[62]

There is a particular transnational geography to De Soto's argument, one that enables a First World appropriation of Third World informality, of the culture of entrepreneurship. But such a geopolitical transaction is fundamentally based on a

Third World desire for First World truths, for the history of developmental, even imperialist, success. Articulating the teleology of capitalism as the formalization of the informal sector, De Soto looks toward the American reforms of the nineteenth century, to the frontier and its institutionalization through the Homesteading Act. As I have argued elsewhere, this is a mythicized history, cleansed of its genocidal and feudal elements and packaged as a policy commodity to be consumed within the circuits of transnational consultancies.[63] Against De Soto, it could be argued that the wealth of the American landscape required the wholesale displacement of indigenous people, that propertied citizenship for the select was made possible through the impossibility of shelter and property for all. A critical transnationalism makes evident such gory histories, thereby laying bare the objects of desire. These objects include the rationalized Anglo-American city; the suburban home, luxurious in its free-standing spaciousness; the profession of urban planning as bolstered by the technologies of zoning, counting, and mapping. Such objects are, of course, myths concealing both their inherent disorder and their order of exclusion. While transnational transactions thus borrow the myths, critical transnationalism seeks to trace the troubled genealogy of both the objects and the desire.

As an example, let me return briefly to Riis and his crystallization of an anxious urban moment. That moment, the late nineteenth century, was particularly important in the formation of the Anglo-American city. Here emerges a series of urban reforms, the portfolio of planning, the shape of the city-region. The moment casts a long shadow on the twentieth century and beyond, bequeathing a legacy of urban diagnosis and cure that continues to set urban agendas. I do not mean to imply that the history of the Anglo-American city can be traced with definitive linearity, but I do think that the late nineteenth century, the moment of Riis and his "other half," can be interpreted as a prefiguration of contemporary anxieties and responses.

One such enduring legacy is the understanding of the Anglo-American city as chaotic, lawless, unnatural, and unholy. As Wilson notes, in the 1890s, "the medical metaphors of disease, degeneration, and filth coalesced into the rhetorical creation of 'cesspool city.'"[64] There are key elements to this rhetoric of disorder. It is a medicalized vocabulary that refuses to acknowledge the structural processes of poverty. In disassociating urban poverty from industrial capitalism, in rendering poverty ugly for the bourgeois gaze, it is an aestheticization. Indeed, it can be seen as a mirror image of today's aesthetic interest in Third World informality. Each embodies a pastoral nostalgia. The neo-urban representation of the dark city imagines a pastoral realm of refuge, such as the suburban home, to which to escape.[65] The entrepreneurial representation of the informal city imagines it as the pastoral refuge, the village in the city, as evident in the examples I have discussed earlier.

The implications of such forms of aestheticization are far reaching. In the contemporary American context, poverty continues to be defined as an aesthetic problem — as in the ongoing debates about the presence of the homeless in public spaces. In the late nineteenth century the color line was often maintained through the rhetoric of disease and the practice of quarantine.[66] Today the urban poor are similarly managed and controlled through acts of spatial cleansing. The technology of disease begets the technology of containment.

It is interesting to make note of the various practices of nineteenth-century urban reform that constitute the myth of the rational Anglo-American city. Riis excavated the "other half" of the city, bringing into view tumorous tenements, the drunken masses, and lawless street Arabs. But he began on an important note: by recognizing the tenement as a type of speculative property holding, and by arguing that neither legislation nor charity could solve this problem.

> The greed of capital that wrought the evil must itself undo it as far as it can now be undone. Homes must be built for the working masses by those who employ their labor; but tenements must cease to be "good property" in the old, heartless sense.[67]

This fleeting moment — of locating the housing problem in cycles of property speculation, of linking the question of housing to the issue of decent wages — was radical. It conceived of the dark city as the heart of commercialization and capitalization, rather than separate from it. It thus linked production and social reproduction, making evident the structural basis of urban form and space. But it was just that — a fleeting moment. Merely ten years later, recounting the "battle with the slum in New York," Riis lost track of the nuances of structural causes in the imperative to reform and rationalize. And he identified two main professional themes: the need to "cure the blight of the tenements," and the need to appeal to the community's conscience.[68] Such themes, I would argue, are enduring elements of the rational Anglo-American city, that object of transnational desire.

In the U.S. a language of conscience and charity has dominated the discourse of poverty. In late-nineteenth-century American cities, social reformers sought to avoid providing direct aid, and instead attempted to act as "friendly visitors" for the tenement classes.[69] Today, "compassionate conservatism" places a similar emphasis on the evils of public aid and the need for personal kindness. Thus, a recent *New York Times* editorial celebrating Jacob Riis sounds the theme of neighborly service: "What Riis knew was that the greatest giving is an act of personal charity."[70] But such ideas require close scrutiny at a time of great structural inequality. Riis had insisted that "reform by humane touch" would not be about the delivery of "coal and groceries," but rather would create "bridges upon which men go over, not down, from the mansion to the tenement."[71] The implicit promise, of course, was that those in the tenements might just, with the right social behavior, make it into the mansion. Here are the seeds of that culture of entrepreneurship which is constantly transacted in transnational discourses and desires. Today the American poor are given neither coal nor groceries; they are instead asked to have faith in faith-based charities. It is through the invisible hand of free-market economics that the moralism of a compassionate nation is made possible. And it is through the promise of private charity that crony capitalism is legitimated.

"We shall solve it by the world-old formula of human sympathy, of human touch," wrote Riis in 1900 of the "battle with the slums":

> Somewhere in these pages I have told of the woman in Chicago who account-ed herself the happiest woman alive because she had at last obtained a play-ground for her poor neighbors' children.[72]

In U.S. cities the conscience of the community, it turns out, took shape in a series of environmental reforms meant to cure the slums of "blight." In New York, housing reformers created the improved tenement, nicknamed the dumb-bell tenement, which promised to solve the problems of the slum through slivers of air and light. In Chicago, Burnham envisioned the classical White City, its daz-zling civic grandeur obliterating the dark city. All across the country, urban pro-fessionals created parks and playgrounds to ensure the moral-behavioral improvement of the poor. What was at stake in such reforms was not only the rationalization of the city but also the preservation of the family. As the city was seen as the site of prostitution and sin, of an unmaking of the natural order, so these environmental reforms sought to return the family to its rural settings.[73] Thus, Veiller declared of his tenement reforms that by according the "proper share of space, natural light, and air," they would "restore the family, the most conservative unit in civilization," and thus redeem the tenement classes.[74] The "corporeal vocab-ulary of the city" thus gave way to the "imagination of the city as a space of govern-ment, authority, and the conduct of conduct." Indeed, by the end of the nine-teenth century, the city was seen as "a space of transparency and perfect adminis-tration," "a spatial projection of social happiness."[75] In this "spatialization of virtue,"[76] the city as diseased body was cured through the regulation and contain-ment of social bodies — of the family as a gendered body, of the racialized body of Chinese laborer or black migrant, of the out-of-place body of the vagrant and the street Arab. And in this, environmental determinism was a technique par excellence.

The persistence of environmental determinism is today evident in the crim-inalization of America's homeless. As Mitchell notes, these techniques serve to "spatialize a problem that is not at root geographical, thereby deflecting attention from roots and causes of homelessness into questions about 'order' and 'civility' in public spaces."[77] They are evident in how housing reforms such as Hope VI rehearse the tired rhetoric of environmental change as socioeconomic change — that a shift from high-rise public housing projects to mixed-income, low-density housing will negate poverty. It is also evident in the seductive lure of Third World informality, in the interpretation of squatting as spatial entrepreneurship, and in the efforts to respond environmentally to informal settlements. For all its lauda-tory work in bestowing honor on a slum-upgrading project such as the Indore Slum Networking scheme, in seeking to develop a "conscience for architecture," the Aga Khan Award citation ultimately makes the untenable claim that "major design innovations helped alleviate the poverty of the slums."[78]

THE IDEOLOGY OF SPACE

The practice of environmental determinism is rooted in the ideology of space: of there always being space, of there not being any struggles over space, of spatial freedoms and mobility, of the ability of reformers and professionals to design and create space and spatial meanings, of tenements giving way to parks and playgrounds and eventually mansions. The seduction of squatting lies in a similar ideology of space: of informality as the urban frontier, unchecked and unfettered. The material reality of squatting is, of course, that it is very much about territorial exclusions, about the lack of space, about the spatial ties of liveli-hood that bind squatters to the most competitive terrains of the city.

I also mean the ideology of space in a specific sense. It is a borrowing of Castells's concept of an "urban ideology," one that "sees the modes and forms of social organization as characteristic of a phase of the evolution of society, closely linked to the technico-natural conditions of human existence, and ultimately, to its environment." The consequence of such an ideology, as Castells notes, is the belief that one may analyze a specific form of social organization, urban society, and explain it on the basis of the effects it produces.[79] This naturalization of the urban, this ide-ology of seeing it as a unique ecology, is surely a key aspect of the aestheticization of poverty — one that leads urban reformers to practice environmental determinism.

In other words, the rational city is an object of desire precisely because it per-petuates the ideology of space. It is this desire that is apparent in De Soto's invo-cation of the American frontier of homesteading as a model of property rights and land markets. It is this desire that is apparent in the long haul of urban devel-opment that has sought to reform the Third World's unruly cities in keeping with First World experiences. Against such transactions, I am arguing for a critical transnationalism that borrows not the ideology of space but rather the bitter les-sons of geopolitical reality. Here it is worth returning once again to the late nine-teenth century, and specifically to a quintessential American text: Mark Twain's *Adventures of Huckleberry Finn*. This iconic novel makes evident the social rights and exclusions associated with the American paradigm of propertied citizenship. *Huck Finn* is perhaps a surprising choice for a discussion about the city and its spaces. It is, after all, about boyish adventures, the pleasures of drifting on a raft:

It was kind of solemn, drifting down the big still river, laying on our backs looking up at the stars, and we didn't ever feel like talking loud. . . . Sometimes we'd have that whole river all to ourselves for the longest time. . . . We had the sky up there, all speckled with stars, and we used to lay on our backs and look up at them, and discuss about whether they was made, or only just happened.[80]

And yet it is precisely this notion of dwelling in space, the freedom of drifting, of imagining an endless frontier of land and water and sky, which for me so quintessentially represents the rational city. Huck's life on the raft can be interpreted as an American longing for the harmonious natural order, one that sees city life as a tearing asunder of such natural laws. In the closing words of the book, Huck rebels against the idea of civilization, of being forced to "sivilize":

But I reckon I got to light out for the Territory ahead of the rest, because Aunt Sally she's going to adopt me and sivilize me, and I can't stand it. I been there before.[81]

For him, dwelling in the journey is an act of freedom. But this is a freedom that coexists with great unfreedoms. On the raft is Jim, the unfreed slave, and Huck believes that he is committing a great crime by not turning him in. He legitimates his action by inscribing the raft as a separate moral world, parallel to the norms and regulations of the adult world.

The freedom of Huck's boyish adventure, albeit a flight from an abusive father, can only be understood in the context of enduring slavery. Nowhere is this more apparent than in the controversial ending of the book.[82] By the end of the novel, Jim, the slave, is imprisoned in a tiny hut at the edge of Aunt Sally's property. But Huck's long-term friend, Tom Sawyer, sets about an elaborate scheme to free him. Here is the catch: Tom already knows that Jim is a free man. His white owner had set him free in her will. Not only does Tom not inform Jim of this, but he proceeds to spin a game to free him, thereby inscribing slavery in the idiom of boyish adventures and pranks. This ending has been seen as "a unique cruelty," the long, drawn-out humiliation of Jim.[83] Tom even jokes that he could drag the prank out for eighty years because he is having so much fun — that he could leave it to his children to get Jim out. And besides, Jim would come to like it as he got used to it.

The ending can, of course, be read as the failure of post–Civil War Reconstruction, with the persistence of social, economic, and political slavery long after the formal trappings of slavery were dismantled. And ironically, the eighty-year mark after 1884, the date of publication of the novel, was 1964, the high point of the Civil Rights movement, when Jim Crow laws in the South were finally abolished.[84]

Toni Morrison has titled an essay on *Huck Finn* "This Amazing, Troubling Book." In this territory that is "so falsely imagined as open," she writes, "the nation, as well as Tom Sawyer, was deferring Jim's freedom in agonizing play."[85] Urban policies have played a crucial role in this racialized time-space deferral, in this agonizing postponement of social justice. Riis himself mapped the color line in New York:

> If, when the account is made up between the races, it shall be claimed that he falls short of the result to be expected from twenty-five years of freedom, it may be well to turn to the other side of the ledger and see how much of the blame is borne by the prejudice and greed that have kept him from rising under a burden of responsibility to which he could hardly be equal.[86]

But such concerns were overwhelmed by the "battle in the slums," in the calculus of disease and cure through which the rational city was to be created. In this rational city, the ideology of space is the promise of freedom in a land of great unfreedom, of environmental democracy in a structure of capitalist authoritarianism. Critical transnationalism reminds us that as desire for the Third World model of self-help must be tempered with a series of cautionary notes, so the desire for the American dream must be located within a historical understanding of the brutality of this context.

THE TRANSNATIONAL TRANSACTION

The transnational is a transaction. As a transaction of imitation and replication, it is an odd combination of universalist outcomes achieved through geographical difference. It is what Spivak has termed "the itinerary of recognition through assimilation of the Other."[87] The Other is acknowledged as essentially different, and in that appropriation of difference is assimilated into the hegemonic logic of the Self. This congruence of difference and similarity is very much at the heart of how Third World models are gaining transnational popularity, and how First World histories remain objects of transnational desire. Thus, the Third World informal city perpetuates the aestheticization of poverty and the techniques of environmental determinism in the First World. And the First World rational city maintains the promise of tabula rasa, of land waiting to be improved and developed, in the Third World.

There are other ways of doing the transnational, of borrowing across borders. Ward, for example, in his work on *colonias*, crosses the U.S.-Mexico border for policy lessons that are at once fruitful and sobering, taking careful note of the specific vulnerabilities of each country's system of housing production.[88] And Gupta indicates that rather than simply erasing geopolitical difference, development analysis can in fact make possible a critique of home:

Faced with the violence of its effects in the Third World, development discourse forces the West to confront a version of its own "childhood" in which colonial violence, ecological destruction, the genocide of native peoples, and the repression and displacement of its poor otherwise find no place.[89]

A critical transnationalism, then, makes evident the *"mechanics* of the constitution of the Other,"* rather than invokes the *"authenticity* of the Other" — yet another phrase from Spivak.[90] It does not seek to borrow successes and best practices or claim assimilation; rather, it examines the processes through which geopolitical realities are constructed and depicted.

One more point. The transnational transaction is inevitably spatial, transacting across geographical difference and distance. This is yet another dimension of its ideology of space. Here it is worth turning to Jameson's spatialized interpretation of ideology. If Althusser conceptualized ideology as the "representation of the subject's Imaginary relationship to his or her Real conditions of existence," then Jameson argues that such a transaction occurs through the experiences of space. And it is in this sense that the aestheticization of squatter settlements and slums spins an ideology of space. It is in this sense that the narrative of Huck Finn embodies an ideology of space. But Jameson goes a step further. Drawing upon the ideas of Lynch, he calls for an "aesthetic of cognitive mapping," defining it as a crucial part of a radical socialist project. In his view, the cognitive map, the mapping of space, "enables a situational representation on the part of the individual subject to that vaster and properly unrepresentable totality which is the ensemble of society's structures as a whole."[91] In the context of my discussion of urban informality, the aesthetic of cognitive mapping can be seen as a process of subjectivation, allowing the occupiers of the spaces of informality to articulate spatial meaning. Surely, such is the power of a statement such as this, the statement of a resident of a Rio *favela*:

> One has to be an artist to survive as a poor person — you have to imagine
> space where there is none.[92]

Transnational techniques of analysis can also be seen as a type of cognitive mapping, enabling what Jameson sees as the "coordination of existential data (the empirical position of the subject) with unlived, abstract conceptions of the geographic totality."[93]

And yet such imaginations beg caution. Jameson's call for cognitive mapping can too easily turn into an ideology of space that imagines a transparent and navigable truth-economy, a global realm of circulation and dissemination that is unconstrained. It can resemble what I have earlier called a universal transnationalism. In contrast, a critical transnationalism is concerned with the frictions of place and power, with how "the suppression of distance" is often the old space of the capitalist world-system rather than a "new space."[94] Note, for example, the provocative contrast between Jameson's politico-aesthetic project and the cognitive maps assembled by Hayden in her discussion of power and segregation in Los Angeles. While she is sympathetic to Jameson, she adds in a footnote that she is not sure how cognitive mapping would operate in terms of global capitalism.[95] More importantly, her examples demonstrate that for many social groups—in this case, poor African Americans and Latinos—cognitive mapping simply narrates a claustrophobic urban space. Thus, the geopolitics of place is not overcome by the poetics of representation. Similarly, our use of the term "liberalization" throughout this book indicates precisely such uneven geographies and unequal transactions. And my use of the term "trespassings" indicates an unease of spatial movement and a similar opacity of spatial knowledge. If critical transnationalism is not about assimilating geographical difference, then it is also not about bridging geographical distance. Rather, it is in the spirit of what Probyn has called "working in and against the local."[96] Such is the writing of Adrienne Rich: "I choke on the taste of bread in North America / But the taste of hunger in North America / is poisoning me."[97] Here, the transnational transaction becomes an effort to unmake the ideology of space.

   If I have taken as my starting point the idea that the political economy of urban informality is also a politics of representation, I now want to end by observing how the politics of representation must engage with the political economy of urban informality. It is in this geopolitical transaction that the ideology of space can be unmade. Jameson remains fascinated by "city space," and particularly by the "precartographic operations . . . the itineraries" of cognitive mapping.[98] I have argued for caution in such projects of mapping and itineraries. His fascination resurrects a nostalgia — about a cognition that precedes lived cartographies of power; about an itinerary that winds its way through penetrable city space. It is a nostalgia that bears resemblance to the pastoral and imperialist nostalgias I have already discussed. It is a nostalgia that is dismantled by the vast and continually growing body of research on urban informality, the stuff of which this book is made. Against the "urban ideology," this genealogy of representation views the city not as a unique ecology but as a mundane articulation of production and social reproduction; not as a magical precartographic realm of vernacular authenticity but as a mapping and unmapping of interests and power; not as a separation of First and Third Worlds but as the constant interpenetration of these geopolitical axes.

NOTES AND ACKNOWLEDGEMENT

I would like to thank Renu Desai for research assistance and intellectual collegiality, and especially for sharing with me her unpublished writings on slum redevelopment in India.

1. G.C. Spivak, "Can the Subaltern Speak?" in C. Nelson and L. Grossberg, eds., *Marxism and the Interpretation of Culture* (Chicago: University of Illinois Press, 1988), 275–76.

2. Ibid., 271.

3. My use of the terms "First World" and "Third World" is not meant to gloss over the geopolitical diversity that exists within and across these categories. Rather, it is meant to refer to these concepts as inventions, whose coinage signifies an international project of development launched at a specific historical moment, i.e., during the Cold War.

4. J. Riis, *How the Other Half Lives: Studies Among the Tenements of New York* (New York: Hill & Wang, 1975 edition, original 1890).

5. E. Popko, *Transitions: A Photographic Documentary of Squatter Settlements* (Stroudsburg: Dowden, Hutchinson & Ross, 1978).

6. Riis, *How the Other Half Lives*, 296.

7. P. Hall, *Cities of Tomorrow* (Oxford: Blackwell, 1996), 35.

8. Popko, *Transitions*, 2.

9. L. Mani, "Contentious Traditions: The Debate on Sati in Colonial India," in K. Sangari and S. Vaid, eds., *Recasting Women: Essays in Indian Colonial History* (New Brunswick: Rutgers University Press, 1990).

10. D. Harvey, *Spaces of Hope* (Berkeley: University of California Press, 2000), 251.

11. Riis, *How the Other Half Lives*, 65, 71.

12. M. Katz, *The Undeserving Poor* (New York: Pantheon, 1989); L. Wacquant, "Three Pernicious Premises in the Study of the American Ghetto," *International Journal of Urban and Regional Research* 21, no. 2 (1997), 341–53.

13. J. Perlman, *The Myth of Marginality: Urban Poverty and Politics in Rio de Janeiro* (Berkeley: University of California Press, 1976).

14. A. Portes and J. Walton, *Labor, Class, and the International System* (New York: Academic Press, 1981).

15. A.G. Frank, *Dependent Accumulation and Underdevelopment* (New York: Monthly Review Press, 1979).

16. M. Castells, *The City and the Grassroots* (Berkeley: University of California Press, 1983).

17. See, for example, S. Eckstein, *The Poverty of Revolution: The State and the Urban Poor in Mexico* (Princeton: Princeton University Press, 1977); and A. Gilbert and P. Ward, *Housing, the State, and the Poor* (Cambridge: Cambridge University Press, 1985).

18. A. Roy, "Paradigms of Propertied Citizenship: Transnational Techniques of Analysis," *Urban Affairs Review* (forthcoming, March 2003). In this paper, I demonstrate the various possible uses of transnational techniques, specifically in relation to housing struggles and policies.

19. P. Ward, *Colonias and Public Policy in Texas and Mexico: Urbanization by Stealth* (Austin:

University of Texas Press, 1999).

20. Roy, "Paradigms of Propertied Citizenship."

21. N. Fraser and L. Gordon, "A Genealogy of Dependency: Tracing a Keyword of the U.S. Welfare State," *Signs* 19 (1994), 309–36; Wacquant, "Three Pernicious Premises"; and M. Davis, *City of Quartz: Excavating the Future in Los Angeles* (London: Verso, 1990).

22. D. Slater, "On the Borders of Social Theory: Learning from Other Regions," *Environment and Planning D: Society and Space* 10 (1992), 324.

23. B. Sanyal, "Knowledge Transfer from Poor to Rich Cities: A New Turn of Events," *Cities* (1990), 31–36.

24. L. Servon, *Bootstrap Capital: Microenterprises and the American Poor* (Washington, D.C.: Brookings Institution Press, 1999).

25. This, of course, resonates with Walter Benjamin's concept of aestheticization, which is discussed in S. Buck-Morss, *The Dialectics of Seeing: Walter Benjamin and the Arcades Project* (Cambridge: MIT Press, 1991).

26. A. Roy, "Traditions of the Modern: A Corrupt View," *Traditional Dwellings and Settlements Review* 12, no. 2 (2001), 7–21.

27. I. Serageldin, ed., *The Architecture of Empowerment: People, Shelter, and Livable Cities* (Lanham: Academy Editions, 1997), 8.

28. G.D. Verma, "Indore's Habitat Improvement Project: Success or Failure?" *Habitat International* 24 (2000), 91–117.

29. C. Davidson, ed., *Legacies for the Future: Contemporary Architecture in Islamic Societies* (London: Thames and Hudson, 1998), 59.

30. Verma, "Indore's Habitat Improvement Project," 96–107.

31. J.M. Jacobs, "Staging Difference: Aestheticization and the Politics of Difference in Contemporary Cities," in R. Fincher and J.M. Jacobs, eds., *Cities of Difference* (New York: The Guilford Press, 1998), 274–75.

32. L. Peattie, "Aesthetic Politics," *Traditional Dwellings and Settlements Review* 3, no. 2 (1992), 23–32.

33. Davidson, *Legacies for the Future*, 54.

34. For a theory of gentrification, see N. Smith, "Gentrification, the Frontier, and the Restructuring of Urban Space," in N. Smith and P. Williams, eds., *Gentrification and the City* (Boston: Allen and Unwin, 1986).

35. A. Hasan, "The Urban Scene in Pakistan," in Serageldin, ed., *The Architecture of Empowerment.*

36. A. Appadurai, "Deep Democracy: Urban Governmentality and the Horizon of Politics," *Environment and Urbanization* 13, no. 2 (2001), 37.

37. Ibid.

38. N. Fraser, *Unruly Practices: Power, Discourse, and Gender in Contemporary Social Theory* (Minneapolis: University of Minnesota Press, 1989).

39. Jacobs, "Staging Difference," 275.

40. Peattie, "Aesthetic Politics," 23–32.

41. Ibid., 26, 28.

42. J. Steele, *Rethinking Modernism for the Developing World: The Complete Architecture of Balkrishna Doshi* (London: Thames and Hudson, 1998), 115.

43. Ibid., 115–21.

44. Ibid., 121.

45. Ibid., 121.

46. See V. Mukhija, "Enabling Slum Redevelopment in Mumbai: Policy Paradox in Practice," *Housing Studies* 16, no. 6 (2001), 791–806, for a discussion of how slum redevelopment in Mumbai takes place through highly marketized strategies, such as the key role of private developers or the elaboration of cross-subsidy schemes.

47. A. Appadurai, "Spectral Housing and Urban Cleansing: Notes on Millennial Mumbai," *Public Culture* 12, no. 3 (2000), 627–51.

48. Spivak, "Can the Subaltern Speak?" 273.

49. R. Williams, *The Country and the City* (New York: Oxford University Press, 1973).

50. R. Desai, "From Monologues to Dialogue: The Architecture Profession and 'Housing for the Poor' in India," unpublished paper. Desai wrote this paper for a City Planning/Architecture graduate seminar co-taught by Roy and AlSayyad as part of the Ford Foundation "Crossing Borders" project.

51. C. Correa, *The New Landscape* (Bombay: The Book Society of India, 1985).

52. R. Rosaldo, "Imperialist Nostalgia," *Representations* 26 (1989), 107. A note of thanks to Rami Farouk Daher for bringing this piece to my attention.

53. Steele, *Rethinking Modernism*, 128.

54. Rosaldo, "Imperialist Nostalgia," 108; J. Clifford, "The Others: Beyond the Salvage Paradigm," in R. Araeen, S. Cubitt, and Z. Sardar, eds., *The Third Text Reader: On Art, Culture and Theory* (New York: Continuum, 2002), 162.

55. C. Pugh, "Squatter Settlements: Their Sustainability, Architectural Contributions, and Socio-Economic Roles," *Cities* 17, no. 5 (2000), 325–37.

56. A. Roy, "Marketized? Feminized? Medieval? Urban Governance in an Era of Liberalization," in J. Tulchin, ed., *Perspectives on Urban Governance*, (Washington, D.C.: Woodrow Wilson Center, 2002).

57. H. De Soto, *The Mystery of Capital: Why Capitalism Triumphs in the West and Fails Everywhere Else* (New York: Basic Books, 2000).

58. R. Bromley, "Informality, De Soto Style: From Concept to Policy," in C. Rakowski, ed., *The Informal Sector Debate in Latin America* (Albany: SUNY Press, 1994), 135.

59. H. De Soto, *The Other Path* (New York: Harper & Row, 1989), 14, 57.

60. A hallmark of De Soto's writing is the conflation of informality and poverty.

61. See D. Chakrabarty, "Adda, Calcutta: Dwelling in Modernity," *Public Culture* 11, no. 1 (1999), 109–45. I am borrowing the phrase "nostalgic narration" from his discussion of "adda" as simultaneously a modernist practice and nostalgic narration "that occupies the place of another — and unarticulated — anxiety."

62. The term is taken from C. Boyer, *Dreaming the Rational City: The Myth of American City*

Planning (Cambridge: MIT Press, 1987).

63. Roy, "Paradigms of Propertied Citizenship."

64. E. Wilson, *The Sphinx in the City: Urban Life, Control of Disorder and Women* (Berkeley: University of California Press, 1991), 37.

65. Williams, *The Country and the City*.

66. S. Craddock, *City of Plagues: Disease, Poverty, and Deviance in San Francisco* (Minneapolis: University of Minnesota Press, 2000).

67. Riis, *How the Other Half Lives*, 6.

68. J. Riis, "A Ten Years' War: An Account of the Battle with the Slum in New York," in F. Cordasco, ed., *Jacob Riis Revisited: Poverty and the Slum in Another Era* (Clifton N.J.: Augustus M. Kelley Publishers, 1973, original 1900), 339, 400.

69. Wilson, *The Sphinx in the City*.

70. *New York Times*, February 25, 2001.

71. Riis, "A Ten Years' War," 413.

72. Ibid., 415.

73. Wilson, *The Sphinx in the City*; Boyer, *Dreaming the Rational City*.

74. Hall, *Cities of Tomorrow*, 37.

75. T. Osborne and N. Rose, "Governing Cities: Notes on the Spatialisation of Virtue," *Environment and Planning D: Society and Space* 17 (1999), 742, 747.

76. Ibid.

77. D. Mitchell, "Anti-Homeless Laws and Public Space: Further Constitutional Issues," *Urban Geography* 19, no. 2 (1998), 103.

78. R. Khosla, "A Conscience for Architecture," in C. Davidson, ed., *Legacies for the Future: Contemporary Architecture in Islamic Societies* (London: Thames and Hudson, 1998); Davidson, *Legacies for the Future*, 64.

79. M. Castells, "The Urban Ideology," in I. Susser, ed., *The Castells Reader* (Oxford: Blackwell Publishers, 2002, original 1972), 34–35.

80. M. Twain, *Adventures of Huckleberry Finn* (Oxford: Oxford University Press, 1999, original 1884), 109.

81. Ibid., 262.

82. Despite Twain's warnings against attempts to find a motive or plot in the novel, the ending has been subject to unceasing literary and social scrutiny. For a discussion, see G. Graff and J. Phelan, eds., *Adventures of Huckleberry Finn: A Case Study in Critical Controversy* (New York: St. Martin's Press, 1995).

83. J. Cox, "The Controversy over the Ending," in Graff and Phelan, eds., *Adventures of Huckleberry Finn*.

84. E. Elliott, ed., *Adventures of Huckleberry Finn* (Oxford: Oxford University Press, 1999), xxxiv.

85. T. Morrison, "This Amazing, Troubling Book," in T. Cooley, ed., *Adventures of Huckleberry Finn: A Norton Critical Edition* (New York: Norton, 1999), 389, 392.

86. Riis, *How the Other Half Lives*, 59.

87. Spivak, "Can the Subaltern Speak?" 294.

88. Ward, *Urbanization by Stealth*.

89. A. Gupta, *Postcolonial Developments: Agriculture in the Making of Modern India* (Durham: Duke University Press, 1998), 42.

90. Spivak, "Can the Subaltern Speak?" 294.

91. F. Jameson, *Postmodernism, or the Cultural Logic of Late Capitalism* (London: Verso, 1991), 51.

92. B. Opalach, "Political Space: The Architecture of Squatter Settlements in Sao Paulo, Brazil," *Traditional Dwellings and Settlements Review* 9, no.1 (1997), 35–50.

93. Jameson, *Postmodernism*, 52.

94. Ibid., 351.

95. D. Hayden, *The Power of Place: Urban Landscapes as Public History* (New Haven: Yale University Press, 1995), 254.

96. E. Probyn, "Travels in the Postmodern: Making Sense of the Local," in L. Nicholson, ed., *Feminism/Postmodernism* (New York: Routledge, 1990).

97. A. Rich, "Hunger," in *The Fact of a Doorframe: Poems Selected and New, 1950–1984* (New York: W.W. Norton & Company, 1984, poem written in 1974–75), 231.

98. Jameson, *Postmodernism*, 51.

SELECTED BIBLIOGRAPHY

Abrams, C., *Man's Struggle for Shelter in an Urbanizing World* (Cambridge, Mass.: MIT Press, 1964).

Basu, S., *Politics of Violence: A Case Study of West Bengal* (Calcutta: Minerva, 1982).

Bayat, A., *Street Politics: Poor People's Movements in Iran* (New York: Columbia University Press, 1997).

Bromley, R., ed., *The Urban Informal Sector: Critical Perspectives in Employment and Housing Policies* (New York: Pergamon Press, 1979).

Bromley, R., and C. Gerry, eds., *Casual Work and Poverty in Third World Cities* (New York: John Wiley & Sons, 1979).

Brown, K., et al., eds., *Urban Crisis and Social Movements in the Middle East* (Paris: Editions L'Harmattan, 1989).

Brown, N., *Peasant Politics in Modern Egypt: The Struggles vs. The State* (New Haven, Conn.: Yale University Press, 1990).

Cammack, P., *Capitalism and Democracy in the Third World: The Doctrine for Political Development* (London: Leicester University Press, 1997).

Carmona, M., ed., *Urban Restructuring and Deregulation in Latin America* (Delft, the Netherlands: Publikatieburo Bouwkunde, Faculty of Architecture, Delft University of Technology, 1992).

Castells, M., *The Urban Question: A Marxist Approach* (Cambridge, Mass.: MIT Press, 1977).

———, *The City and the Grassroots: A Cross-Cultural Theory of Urban Social Movements* (Berkeley: University of California Press, 1983).

———, *The Power of Identity: Economy, Society, and Culture* (Oxford, U.K.: Blackwell, 1997).

Chant, S., *Women and Survival in Mexican Cities: Perspectives on Gender, Labor Markets, and Low-income Households* (Manchester, U.K.: Manchester University Press, 1991).

Cohen, M., et al., eds., *Preparing for the Future: Global Pressures and Local Forces* (Washington D.C.: The Woodrow Wilson Center Press, 1996).

Dasgupta, N., *Petty Trading in the Third World: The Case of Calcutta* (Avebury: Brookfield, 1992).

Davis, M., *City of Quartz: Excavating the Future in Los Angeles* (London: Verso, 1990).

de Soto, H., *The Other Path: The Invisible Revolution in the Third World* (London: I.B. Taurus, 1989).

————, *The Mystery of Capital: Why Capitalism Triumphs in the West and Fails Everywhere Else* (New York: Basic Books, 2000).

Eckstein, S., *The Poverty of Revolution: The State and the Urban Poor in Mexico* (Princeton, N.J.: Princeton University Press, 1977).

Escobar, E., *Encountering Development* (Princeton, N.J.: Princeton University Press, 1995).

Fernandes, E. and A. Varley, eds., *Illegal Cities: Law and Urban Change in Developing Countries* (London: Zed Books, 1998).

Fincher, R. and J. M. Jacobs, eds., *Cities of Difference* (New York: The Guilford Press, 1998).

Frank, A. G., *Capitalism and Underdevelopment in Latin America* (New York: Monthly Review Press, 1967).

————, *Dependent Accumulation and Underdevelopment* (New York: Monthly Review Press, 1979).

George, H., *Progress and Poverty* (New York: D. Appleton & Co., 1880).

Gilbert, A., ed., *The Mega-city in Latin America* (New York: United Nations University Press, 1996).

————, *The Latin American City* (London: Latin America Bureau, 1998).

————, *Postcolonial Developments: Agriculture in the Making of Modern India* (Durham: Duke University Press, 1998).

Gwynne, R. and C. Kay, eds., *Latin America Transformed: Globalization and Modernity* (London: Arnold, 1999).

Harvey, D., *Spaces of Hope* (Berkeley: University of California Press, 2000).

Hasan, A., *Housing for the Poor: Failure of Formal Sector Strategies* (Karachi: City Press, 2000).

Hoodfar, H., *Between Marriage and the Market: Intimate Politics and Survival in Cairo* (Berkeley, Calif.: University of California Press, 1997).

Hoogvelt, A., *Globalization and the Postcolonial World* (Baltimore, Md.: The Johns Hopkins University Press, 1997).

Huntington, S. and J. Nelson, *No Easy Choice: Political Participation in Developing Countries* (Cambridge, Mass.: Harvard University Press, 1976).

Hurrell, A. and N. Woods, eds., *Inequality, Globalization, and World Politics* (Oxford, U.K.: Oxford University Press, 1999).

Katz, M., *The Undeserving Poor* (New York: Pantheon, 1989).

Lewis, O., *Five Families: Mexican Case Studies in the Culture of Poverty* (New York: Basic Books, 1959).

————, *The Children of Sanchez: Autobiography of a Mexican Family* (New York: Random House, 1961).

————, *La Vida: A Puerto Rican Family in the Culture of Poverty* (New York: Random House, 1966).

Lustick, I., *Unsettled States, Disputed Lands* (Ithaca, N.Y.: Cornell University Press, 1993).

Marcuse P. and M. Van Kempen, eds., *Globalising Cities: A New Spatial Order?* (London: Blackwell, 1999).

Morrifield, A. and E. Swyngedouw, eds., *The Urbanization of Injustice* (London: Lawrence and Wishart, 1995).

Payne, G., *Informal Housing and Land Subdivisions in Third World Cities: A Review of the Literature* (Headington, Oxford, U.K.: Centre for Development and Environmental Planning, 1989).

————, ed., *Land, Rights and Innovation: Improving Tenure Security for the Urban Poor* (London: ITDG Publishing, 2002).

————, ed., *Making Common Ground: Public/Private Partnerships in Land for Housing* (London: International Technology Press, 1999).

Perlman, J., *The Myth of Marginality: Urban Poverty and Politics in Rio de Janeiro* (Berkeley: University of California Press, 1976).

Piven, F. and R. Cloward, *Poor People's Movements: Why They Succeed, How They Fail* (New York: Vintage, 1979).

Portes, A. and J. Walton, *Labor, Class, and the International System* (New York: Academic Press, 1981).

Portes, A., M. Castells, and L. Benton, eds., *The Informal Economy: Studies in Advanced and Less Developed Countries* (Baltimore: The Johns Hopkins University Press, 1989).

Rakowski, C., ed., *Contrapunto: The Informal Sector Debate in Latin America* (Albany: State University of New York Press, 1994).

Richards, A. and J. Waterbury, *A Political Economy of the Middle East: State, Class, and Economic Development* (Boulder: Westview Press, 1990).

Roy, A., *City Requiem, Calcutta: Gender and the Politics of Poverty* (Minneapolis: University of Minnesota Press, 2003).

Schuurman, F. and T. Van Naerssen, *Urban Social Movements in the Third World* (London: Croom Helm, 1989).

Scott, J., *Weapons of the Weak: Everyday Forms of Peasant Resistance* (New Haven, Conn.: Yale University Press, 1985).

Singerman, D., *Avenues of Participation: Family, Politics, and Networks in Urban Quarters of Cairo* (Princeton, N.J.: Princeton University Press, 1995).

Sklair, L., *Assembling for Development* (Boston, Mass.: Unwin Hyman, 1989).

Tulchin, T., ed., *Perspectives on Urban Governance* (Washington, D.C.: Woodrow Wilson Center, 2002).

Valentine, C., *Culture and Poverty: Critique and Counter Proposals* (Chicago: University of Chicago Press, 1968).

Wacquant, L., *The Ghetto Underclass: Social Science Perspectives* (Newbury Park, Calif.: Sage Publications, 1993).

Walton, J. and L. Magotti, eds., *The City in Comparative Perspective* (London/New York: John Willey, 1976).

Ward, P., ed., *Self-help Housing: A Critique* (London: Mansell Publishing Co., Alexandrine Press, 1982).

———, *Colonias and Public Policy in Texas and Mexico: Urbanization by Stealth* (Austin: The University of Texas Press, 1999).

Ward, P., and A. Gilbert, *Housing, the State, and the Urban Poor: Policy and Practice in Three Latin American Cities* (Cambridge, U.K.: Cambridge University Press, 1985).

Worsley, P., *The Three Worlds: Culture and World Development* (London: Weidenfeld and Nicholson, 1984).

INDEX

CONTRIBUTORS

NEZAR ALSAYYAD is Professor of Architecture and Planning and Chair of the Center for Middle Eastern Studies at the University of California at Berkeley. He is also the Director of the International Association for the Study of Traditional Environments.

ASEF BAYAT is Professor of Sociology and Middle East Studies at the American University in Cairo, Egypt.

RAY BROMLEY is Professor and Chair of Geography and Planning at the University of Albany, the State University of New York.

ALAN GILBERT is Professor of Geography at University College, London.

ARIF HASAN is an architect and planner based in Karachi, Pakistan, and is currently teaching the postgraduate urban design course at Dawood College, Karachi.

JANICE PERLMAN is Founder and President of the Mega-Cities Project, Inc., a transnational nonprofit network with headquarters at Trinity College in Hartford, Connecticut.

ANANYA ROY is Assistant Professor of Urban Studies in the Department of City and Regional Planning at the University of California at Berkeley.

AHMED M. SOLIMAN is Professor and Dean of Architectural Engineering at the Beirut Arab University, Lebanon and Professor of Planning at the University of Alexandria, Egypt.

PETER M. WARD is Professor in the LBJ School of Public Affairs and the Department of Sociology at the University of Texas at Austin. He is also the C.B. Smith Sr. Centennial Chair in U.S.-Mexico Relations.

HAIM YAKOBI is a Research Fellow in the Department of Politics and Government at the Ben-Gurion University of the Negev, Beer-Sheva, Israel.

OREN YIFTACHEL is Associate Professor and Chair of Geography and Environmental Development at the Ben Gurion University of the Negev, Beer-Sheva, Israel.